HYPNOSIS & SUGGESTION
IN PSYCHOTHERAPY

HYPNOSIS & SUGGESTION
IN PSYCHOTHERAPY

A Treatise on the
Nature and Uses of Hypnotism

BY **H. BERNHEIM**, M.D.

PROFESSOR ON THE FACULTY OF MEDICINE AT NANCY

TRANSLATED FROM THE SECOND REVISED EDITION
BY CHRISTIAN A. HERTER, M.D.

UNIVERSITY BOOKS   *New Hyde Park, New York*

COPYRIGHT© 1964 BY UNIVERSITY BOOKS, INC.
Library of Congress Catalogue Card Number: 63-22664
Manufactured in the United States of America

The original title of this book was **Suggestive Theraputics,**
the sub-title remains as in the original. The present title is more
nearly appropriate to the contents of the book and the present terminology.

Thanks are due Columbia University Libraries and Peabody Institute Library
for providing copies of this work for reproduction purposes.

CONTENTS

INTRODUCTION BY ERNEST R. HILGARD　　　　　　　　　　　　ix

CHAPTER I

Manner of hypnotizing.—Sleep and hypnotic influence.—Variable sensitiveness of subjects.—Classification of the various degrees of sleep according to M. Liébault :—1st. Drowsiness ;—2d. Suggestive catalepsy ;—3d. Rotary automatism ;—4th. Auditory relation of subject with the operator only ;—5th. Light somnambulism ;—6th. Deep somnambulism. Author's classification : A. Memory preserved on waking : 1st. Suggestibility to certain acts only ; —2d. Inability to open eyes ;—3d. Suggestive catalepsy liable to be broken ; —4th. Irresistible catalepsy ;—5th. Suggestive contraction ;—6th. Automatic obedience ;—B. Memory lost on waking, or Somnambulism :—7th. Without susceptibility to hallucinations ;—8th. Susceptibility to hallucinations during sleep ;—9th. Susceptibility to hypnotic and post-hypnotic hallucinations.— Varieties :—Suggestion without sleep.—Definition of hypnotism.—Of fascination.—Of waking.—Proportion of subjects susceptible to hypnotism　　1–20

CHAPTER II.

Phenomena noticed in hypnotic sleep.—Sensibility.—Spontaneous or suggested anæsthesia.—Hypnotism cannot replace chloroform.—Alterations in motility.—Suggestive catalepsy.—Automatic movements.—Movements by imitation.—Suggestive paralysis.—Somnambulism with forgetfulness upon waking. —Automatic obedience.—Sensorial suggestions.—Suggested hallucinations. —Acts, sensorial illusions, and hallucinations suggested for the time which follows waking.—Negative hallucinations.—Psychical amaurosis and deafness.—Hallucinations to be realized after a long interval (à longue échéance)　　21–53

CHAPTER III

Observations on different types of somnambulism.—Double personality in certain somnambulists.—Spontaneous dreams with or without preservation of the sense of reality　　54–72

CHAPTER IV

Circulation and respiration in hypnotism.—Changes observed by authors are due to the emotion of the subjects.—Influence of the hypnotic suggestion on the functions of organic life : retardation and acceleration of the pulse ; influence upon the vaso-motor circulation ; inflammation, blisters, hemorrhages produced by suggestion　　73–77

v

CONTENTS

CHAPTER V

Suggestion in the waking condition.—Production of the same phenomena by simple affirmation in subjects who can be hypnotized and in those who cannot be hypnotized.—Transfer of hemianæsthesia in a case of hysteria.—Sensorial suggestions.—Hallucinations.—Suggestive modifications of the visual field.—Auto-suggestion in ecstacy.—A question of priority   78-86

CHAPTER VI

Reply to critics.—The three phases of hypnotism according to the school of the Salpêtrière.—Experiments of transfer.—Experimental illusions.—The real image and the hallucinatory image   87-104

CHAPTER VII

Historical sketch,—Mesmer and mesmerism.—His condemnation by the learned societies.—Husson's report.—Abbot Faria and sleep by suggestion.—Alexandre Bertrand's doctrine.—Gen. Noizet's experiments and the fluidic doctrine.—Second Period: Braid and Braidism.—Analysis of the doctrine.—Grimes and Electro-biology in America and in England.—Durand de Gros' experiments and doctrine.—Dr. Charpignon's moral medicine: his fluidic doctrine.—Braidism in France: Prof. Azam's communication.—Application to surgical anæsthesia.—Experiments and doctrine of Dr. Liébault of Nancy: hypnotic sleep compared with ordinary sleep.—Hypnotism in animals: Kircher, Czermak, Preyer, Wilson, Beard.—Induced somnambulism in France: Chas. Richet's experiments.—Induced sleep in cases of Hysteria: Charcot's and Dumontpallier's experiments.—Hypnotism in man in Germany: experiments of the Danish magnetizer, Hansen; Rumpf's physiological theories; Preyer's chemical theories; Schneider's, Berger's, and Heidenhain's psycho-physiological theories.—Prosper Despine's theory.—Recent publications,   105-124

CHAPTER VIII

The author's theoretical conception of the interpretation of the phenomena of suggestion.—Automatism in daily life.—reflex acts; automatic instinctive acts.—Automatism in the new-born child, and in the adult.—Moderating influence of the mind.—Sensorial illusions rectified by the mind.—A. Maury's experiments.—Hypnagogic hallucinations.—Credulity. — Sensorial suggestions by imitation.—Automatic obedience.—Influence of the idea upon the act.—Despine's doctrine: Abolition of the state of consciousnoss.—Continuity of the state of consciousness.—Exaltation of reflex ideo-motor, ideo-sensitive, and ideo-sensorial excitability.—Negative suggestion.—Inhibition.—Sleep by suggestion, from fatigue of the eyelids, from occlusion of the eyes, from monotonous, feeble, continuous impressions.—Suggestion without sleep.—Chambard's classification of the various periods of hypnotic sleep.—Objections.—Attempted interpretation of latent memories, and of suggestions *à longue échéance*.—Answer to M. Beaunis's objections   125-158

CHAPTER IX

General applications of the doctrine of suggestion.—Moral and psychological standpoint.—Education.—Legal standpoint.—Criminal suggestions.—Ob-

CONTENTS

servation.—Retroactive hallucinations.—The Tiza-Eslar affair.—Instinctive imbecility.—Reply to M. Paul Janet   159–191

PART II

THE APPLICATION OF SUGGESTION TO THERAPEUTICS

CHAPTER I

Imagination as a therapeutic agent.—Talismans and amulets.—The therapeutic effect of magnets.—Report of the Royal Society of Medicine upon the magnetotherapy of Abbot Lenoble.—Medicinal magnetism falls into discredit, and is again revived.—Various practices, ancient and modern ; the healers.—Observations upon cures effected through the influence of the imagination.—Observations upon the miraculous cures at Lourdes —Therapeutic suggestion.—The hypnotic condition exalts susceptibility to suggestion.—Cures obtained by the ancient magnetizers.—Braid's doctrine ; his theoretical ideas upon the mechanism of the cures.—M. Liébault's method ; suggestion by speech.—A general picture of the results obtained ; the various methods of suggestion.—Failure inherent in the disease or in the subject.—Auto-suggestionists   192–217

OBSERVATIONS

I.—Organic Affection of the Nervous System	217
II.—Hysterical Affections	260
III.—Neuropathic Affections	300
IV.—Neuroses	324
V.—Dynamic Pareses and Paralyses	353
VI.—Gastro-intestinal Affections	356
VII.—Various Painful Affections	361
VIII.—Rheumatic Troubles	370
IX.—Neuralgias	392
X.—Menstrual Troubles	399

CHAPTER II

Suggestive therapeutics acts upon function.—Rôle of functional dynamism in disease.—Dangers of Hypnotism.—Spontaneous sleep.—Exaggerated hypnotic suggestibility.—Suggestion corrects these inconveniences.—Can hypnotism injure the cerebral faculties ?—Abuse of induced hallucinations.—Susceptibility to hallucination in the waking condition.—Medical advice   408–416

AUTHOR'S INTRODUCTION TO THE REVISED EDITION	417
PREFACE TO THE REVISED EDITION	423
INDEX	425

INTRODUCTION

THIS BOOK IS A CLASSIC in the history of hypnotism and of psychotherapy. The first part of the book, consisting of nine chapters on the nature of hypnosis, was first published in French in 1884; the second, consisting of two chapters and 105 case studies, was first added in 1886, with a new preface in 1887; the English translation appeared the following year, in 1888. In order to date this in time, it is well to recall that it appeared before William James' *Principles of Psychology* (1890), Pierre Janet's *The Mental State of Hysterics* (1892), and Josef Breuer and Sigmund Freud's *Studies in Hysteria* (1895).

The two great names in hypnosis in France at the time were those of Jean Martin Charcot (1825-1893), whose point of view toward hypnosis took the name of his hospital, the Salpêtrière; the other was Hippolyte Bernheim (1837-1919), the author of this book, who was the spokesman of the Nancy school, named for the place in which he and his predecessor, A. A. Liébault (1823-1904), both practiced. Pierre Janet (1859-1947) had not yet come to prominence, although he was presently to become Charcot's successor.

Sigmund Freud (1856-1939) and Janet both came under the influence of Charcot, and when Freud returned to Germany after his year in Paris he translated Charcot into German. At the same time he noted that those opposed to Charcot also had a good deal to offer that was overlooked by Charcot, and he proceeded at about the same time to translate two books of Bernheim into German. Freud's German translation of this book, with an introduction by him, appeared at the same time as the English edition. The following year (1889) Freud went to visit Bernheim and Liébault, taking along a patient for Bernheim to treat. From there he went to Paris to attend the first International Congress of Hypnotism.

We thus find this book appearing at one of those moments in history in which hypnosis was accepted as a significant field of scientific inquiry, and as a useful tool for psychotherapy. Such recurrent moments have not tended to endure, so that the history of hypnosis is a peculiarly cyclical one. The heightened interest under Franz Anton Mesmer (1734-1815) was demolished by the attack on his erroneous theory of animal magnetism, which sidetracked attention from the very real phenomena he produced; the rising interest in hypnosis as an anaesthetic, particularly through James Esdaile (1808-1859), was cut short by the introduction of ether and chloroform as anaesthetics. Although James Braid (ca. 1795-1860) gave hypnotism its name and succeeded in making it acceptable in England, therapeutic interest in hypnosis died out, and it is to the period of this book that we owe the renewed interest. Fortunately Charcot was beyond reproach as a neurologist, and Bernheim was fully respected in medical circles. The controversy between them was over the interpretation of hypnotic phenomena, not over the reality of hypnosis, or over its legitimate place in medicine. The fact that Freud, interested in establishing himself as a practicing neurologist, should find both men worth translating, shows that the issues were of the kind subject to open discussion. This was indeed the heyday of hypnosis; according to Bramwell, Bernheim attempted to hypnotize 10,000 of his hospital patients and succeeded with over 80 per cent of them.

What happened later? In part, owing to his initial enthusiasm for hypnosis and his later rejection of it, Freud must bear some of the responsibility for the reduced interest in hypnosis. Those psychiatrists who early in this century were most interested in the psychogenesis and psychotherapy of mental illness tended to be most influenced by Freud; hence those who might otherwise have been attracted to hypnosis were deflected away from it when Freud turned away. This does not mean that there were not those who used hypnosis in psychotherapy through these years; rather, it did not become a standard tool of psychiatry, and was seldom taught to medical students or to psychiatric residents.

The experimental studies by Clark L. Hull (1884-1952), begun at the University of Wisconsin and completed at Yale, led to his book entitled *Hypnosis and Suggestibility* (1933), and again made hypnosis a promising field for scientific inquiry. However, his own abandonment of the field after his book appeared, and the failure of his students to carry on after he left the field, may in fact have produced a delay in further research.

It was the Second World War that reintroduced hypnosis as a useful adjunct to psychotherapy, and widespread contemporary interest dates from that time. With favorable action by the British Medical Society and the American Medical Association, courses in hypnosis are appearing in medical school curricula and in training programs for psychiatric residents. Numerous psychologists interested in physiological functioning and in personality are turning to hypnosis as a fertile source of problems and possibilities. It is fitting that, with this revival of interest, there should be made more widely available the careful observations of the classical writers of the nineteenth century.

In introducing the work of Bernheim to a contemporary public, it is profitable to summarize Freud's introduction to the German edition, for the light it throws upon the intellectual climate at the time this book appeared. Freud's introduction appears in translalation as the first paper in the fifth volume of his *Collected Papers;* its translator notes that it may perhaps claim to be Freud's earliest published writing in the field of psychology.

To begin with, Freud sets the warm commendation of Professor Forel of Zurich against the unjustified criticisms of hypnosis by Professor Meynert of Vienna, with whom Freud had been carrying on a running debate. Freud pleads against those who object to hypnosis out of ignorance, with the statement "It remains true that in scientific matters it is always experience, and never authority without experience, that gives the final verdict, whether in favor or against." He argues also against the interpretation that hypnosis is dangerous because it results in "an experimentally produced psychosis." He points to the cases in Bernheim's book to show how harmless hypnosis is in fact.

Freud then takes up the debate between Bernheim and Charcot, with Bernheim insisting that all the phenomena of hypnotism arise from suggestion (or auto-suggestion), while Charcot believes that some, at least, of the phenomena of hypnosis are based upon physiological processes independent of that part of the brain that produces consciousness, thus with displacements of excitability that are *not* the products of suggestion. Freud attempts to mediate the controversy by showing that they are both right: Charcot is right for "major hypnotism" (grande hypnotisme), which is the hypnotism of true hysterics, and Bernheim is right in normal, minor hypnotism (with non-hysterics), which cases Freud, in agreement with Bernheim, believed to be the more important for the understanding of the phenomena of hypnosis. The verdict of history is against Charcot and Freud, and in favor of Bernheim, but this keeping by Freud of a respectable tie to physiology may indeed have favored the acceptance of hypnosis at the time. Freud's argument is that the lawfulness of hysterical phenomena would be destroyed by accepting Bernheim's position against that of Charcot; this merely shows how ingrained was the notion that lawfulness had to be guaranteed by physiology, with the concept of lawfulness among psychological events (independent of physiological explanations) not yet well established.

While Bernheim's book speaks for itself, there are a few comments that should be made to place it in context with things going on at the present time; because of his careful observations and essential empiricism there is a timeless quality about ais writing, but even so no writer can escape the limitations of his time.

Consider the relationship between hypnosis and sleep. While this has been a matter of controversy for some time, modern studies, using the electroencephalograph, show that the brain waves of hypnosis are not those of sleep. Bernheim insists at many places that there is no difference between hypnosis and sleep. Thus:

> ...suggested sleep differs in no respect from natural sleep. The same phenomena of suggestion can be obtained in natural sleep, if one succeeds in putting one's self into relationship with the sleeping person without waking him (pages 15-16).

Actually, however, he does not *identify* hypnosis with sleep, for it is suggestion that to him is all-important:

> To define hypnotism as induced sleep is to give too narrow a meaning to the word—to overlook the many phenomena which suggestion can bring about independently of sleep. I define hypnotism as the induction of a peculiar psychical condition which increases the susceptibility to suggestion. Often, it is true, the sleep that may be induced facilitates suggestion, but it is not the necessary preliminary. It is suggestion that rules hypnotism (page 15).

He thus leaves the problem approximately where it is today, with some controversy still going on about the enhancement of suggestibility during natural sleep.

A number of attempts have been made in recent years to arrange measuring scales by which to estimate the degree of sensitivity to hypnotic suggestions. It is instructive to find how much these devices have been anticipated by Bernheim with this scheme of nine stages— a variety of personality test that is indeed an early one in the history of psychological measurement. Many of the items are very similar to those in use today. Emphasis is placed especially upon the achievement of "somnambulism" which is defined by amnesia for the events within hypnosis when the subject is aroused from the hypnotic state; the term is still used today to refer to the subjects who go deeply into hypnosis. It is sometimes thought that Bernheim insisted on *spontaneous* amnesia as the criterion of somnambulism. This is clearly not the case, for he includes under somnambulism those cases who are amnesic only when he tells the subject while hypnotized, "When you wake you will remember absolutely nothing" (page 54). He notes: "Everyone has his special individuality in the somnambulistic as in the waking condition" (page 71).

Again, one has the tendency to assign enthusiastic overstatement to those of an earlier day, reserving caution to the more objective scientists of the present. It is refreshing, therefore, to find Bernheim's cautions, his careful reports of his failures, or his uncertainties. Against a common belief that hypnosis can produce supernormal ability he says bluntly:

> ...up to the present time, I have never observed an intellectual phenomenon exceeding the normal in degree. I have not been able to make lawyers or preachers out of subjects not naturally endowed with the gift of eloquence (page 60).

In the case studies listed, while there are many successes, there are also failures; Bernheim did not try to "oversell" hypnosis.

Another issue that continues to trouble contemporary writers on hypnosis is the extent to which the phenomena of hypnosis can be produced by waking suggestion, that is, without going through a prior trance induction. Because Bernheim defined hypnosis as a state of *heightened* suggestibilty, he would appear to have been on the side of those who believed a prior induction to be necessary for the manifestation of hypnotic phenomena. While perhaps a little illogical at this point, Bernheim's empiricism always takes precedence over his theories, and in his chapter on waking suggestion he comes to the conclusion that

> ...*paralysis, contracture, sensitve and sensorial anesthesia, sensorial illusions, and complex hallucinations* may be obtained by *suggestion* in a great number of subjects susceptible to hypnotism, *without hypnosis,* just as absolutely as with it... (page 86).

If one took him strictly at his word, these subjects, unchanged by hypnosis, would not qualify as hypnotized; this is a puristic conception, however, for if they are *easily* hypnotized by direct suggesttion, and act the same as some others who *require* an initial induction, there is no reason for denying the equivalence of the states. This is, however, a point of dispute among writers today.

The hypnotic phenomena described by Bernheim cover nearly all that we know today, and it is hard to recapture the excitement that must have accompanied the discovery of some of them. We often use the concept of *negative* hallucination today, to refer to the case in which something present to the sense is *not* perceived (by contrast with *positive* hallucination, in which something not present *is* perceived). This we owe to Bernheim, and he defends himself against the attack on the notion by Binet and Féré. Another is the *retroactive* hallucination, which is essentially a falsified memory. Had Freud read this account (page 164ff) with a little more careful attention when he translated it, he might have been saved the pain that came to him much later when he discovered the falsified memories brought to him by his patients.

Although a rich mine of information on hypnosis, the book's main purpose is to present a method of therapy. The summary of 105 cases (pages 404-407) indicates the care with which Bernheim tried to show what he found. Allowing for some differences in diagnosis then and now, there is no doubt that the people who came to him were suffering and had symptoms, and they commonly left without them; of the 105 cases summarized only 2 were downright failures of cure, 22 improved or were cured with qualifications (partial, gradual, or temporary), while 81 were considered to be cured of the symptoms with which they came, and there is no evidence that substitute symptoms developed. The assertion, attributed to Bernheim by Freud, that he was successful only with hospital patients, and not with private ones, was made by Freud many years after the Bernheim visit, in a statement with other errors of memory in it; even if it were true, there is no point in thereby discrediting the hospital cures. Bernheim himself says that he believes Liébault to have had somewhat greater success than he because of dealing with common people who show "greater cerebral docility than more intelligent people" (page 19). At the same place he indicates his success, however, in his office practice.

Is there any psychotherapeutic theory implied, other than symptom removal through suggestion? The answer is clearly in the affirmative, although it is true that one reads some of this theory back into the observations, with the perspective of things we have learned since then. Take, for example, the role of what is now called transference, that is, the special relationship between the patient and the therapist. Bernheim saw that this was more than the ability to produce the hypnotic trance; he saw it as a "special relationship." For example, he gives the case of a young woman, readily hypnotized, who could not be cured of her hysterical symptoms because this "special relationship" never developed (page 69). While granting the essential similarity between spontaneous and induced sleep, in spontanous sleep the sleeper is in relationship to himself alone, although he proceeds to hallucinate (i.e., to dream). In induced sleep, however, the subject retains the memory of the person who has put him to sleep, and hence the hypnotizer's special power over him (page 141). In order to make suggestions effective during sleep, it is necessary to put the subject into relationship with the hypnotist by instructing him to continue to sleep while listening to the hypnotist (page 152). Thus "rapport" in hypnosis has some of the earmarks of transference, but the role of transference in therapy is, of course, not developed by Bernheim.

Bernheim gives a good deal of attention to what he calls "functional" and "dynamic" processes, clearly a forerunner of later interpretations of psychodynamics.

> ...*The functional trouble in disease of the nervous centers often exceeds the field of the anatomical lesion; this latter is*

is reflected by the shock or dynamic irritation upon the functions of neighboring zones. *And it is against this modified dynamic state, independently of a direct material alteration, that psychotherapeutics may be all-powerful* (page 229).

Or again:

> ...A consideration which should never be lost sight of in therapeutics is this: a functional trouble may survive the cause or organic lesions which gave it birth; this trouble is no longer kept up by the lesion, but is retained, if I may so express it, by the nervous system (page 410).

Thus he argues that psychotherapy is valued beyond hysteria, neuroses, and purely functional nervous maladies (these are his categories); such a claim for psychotherapy does no violence to the notion that psychotherapy is helpless in direct attack upon material organic damage.

His theorizing about hypnosis is always modest but cogent. He himself calls his attempts at explanation of hypnosis "only a formula ...I do not pretend to advance a theory" (page 139). His formula is that suggestion increases reflex *ideo-motor, ideo-sensitive,* and *ideo-sensorial* excitability. The distinction between ideo-sensitive and ideo-sensorial is in a terminology no longer current; ideo-sensitive refers to modification of sense organ function through ideas, as in changing thresholds for detecting stimuli impinging on the sense organs, while ideo-sensorial refers to the whole sensory system in perception, including central processes, hence illusions, hallucinations, revived memories, and so on.

Bernheim's book is rich in observations and in ideas. In introducing his book to the reader I have tried to place it in context, and to highlight just enough of his ideas to urge the reader to go on and explore for himself. It was Bernheim, largely through this book, who gave currency to the near synonymity between hypnosis and suggestion, so that these words have appeared paired in many book titles since his. In this classical volume he not only gives powerful arguments for this identification of hypnosis with suggestion but makes an earnest and well-documented plea for the wise use of suggestion in dealing with illness.

ERNEST R. HILGARD

Stanford University, Stanford, California

HYPNOSIS & SUGGESTION
IN PSYCHOTHERAPY

CHAPTER I

Manner of hypnotizing.—Sleep and hypnotic influence.—Variable sensitiveness of subjects.—Classification of the various degrees of sleep according to M. Liébault : —1st. Drowsiness ;—2d Suggestive catalepsy ;—3d. Rotatory automatism ;—4th Auditory relation of subject with the operator only ; 5th. Light somnambulism ; 6th. Deep somnambulism. Author's classification : A.—Memory preserved on waking : 1st. Suggestibility to certain acts only. 2d. Inability to open eyes. 3d. Suggestive catalepsy liable to be broken. 4th. Irresistible catalepsy. 5th. Suggestive contraction. 6th. Automatic obedience. B.—Memory lost on waking, or Somnambulism. 7th. Without susceptibility to hallucinations. 8th. Susceptibility to hallucinations during sleep. 9th. Susceptibility to hypnotic and post-hypnotic hallucinations. Varieties :—Suggestion without sleep. Definition of hypnotism—Of fascination :—Of waking—Proportion of subjects susceptible to hypnotism.

I PROCEED to hypnotize in the following manner.

I begin by saying to the patient that I believe benefit is to be derived from the use of suggestive therapeutics, that it is possible to cure or to relieve him by hypnotism ; that there is nothing either hurtful or strange about it ; that it is an *ordinary sleep* or torpor which can be induced in everyone, and that this quiet, beneficial condition restores the equilibrium of the nervous system, etc. If necessary, I hypnotize one or two subjects in his presence, in order to show him that there is nothing painful in this condition and that it is not accompanied with any unusual sensation. When I have thus banished from his mind the idea of magnetism and the somewhat mysterious fear that attaches to that unknown condition, above all when he has seen patients cured or benefited by the means in question, he is no longer suspicious, but gives himself up, then I say, " Look at me and think of nothing but sleep. Your eyelids begin to feel heavy, your eyes tired. They begin to wink, they are getting moist, you cannot see distinctly. They are closed.'' Some patients close their eyes and are asleep immediately. With others, I have to repeat, lay more stress on what I say, and even make gestures. It makes little difference what sort of gesture is made. I hold two fingers of my right hand before the patient's eyes and ask him to look at them, or pass both hands several times before his eyes, or persuade him to fix his eyes upon mine, endeavoring, at the same time, to concentrate his attention upon the idea of sleep. I say, "Your lids are closing, you cannot open them again. Your arms feel heavy, so do your legs. You cannot feel anything. Your hands are motionless. You see nothing, you are going to sleep." And I add in a commanding tone, "Sleep." This word often turns the balance. The eyes close and the patient sleeps or is at least influenced.

I use the word sleep, in order to obtain as far as possible over the patients, a suggestive influence which shall bring about sleep or a state closely approaching it; for sleep properly, so called, does not always occur. If the patients have no inclination to sleep and show no drowsiness, I take care to say that sleep is not essential; that the hypnotic influence, whence comes the benefit, may exist without sleep; that many patients are hypnotized although they do not sleep. (See farther on.)

If the patient does not shut his eyes or keep them shut, I do not require them to be fixed on mine, or on my fingers, for any length of time, for it sometimes happens that they remain wide open indefinitely, and instead of the idea of sleep being conceived, only a rigid fixation of the eyes results. In this case, closure of the eyes by the operator succeeds better. After keeping them fixed one or two minutes, I push the eye-lids down, or, stretch them slowly over the eyes, gradually closing them more and more and so imitating the process of natural sleep. Finally I keep them closed, repeating the suggestion, "Your lids are stuck together; you cannot open them. The need of sleep becomes greater and greater, you can no longer resist." I lower my voice gradually, repeating the command, "Sleep," and it is very seldom that more than three minutes pass before sleep or some degree of hypnotic influence is obtained. It is sleep by suggestion,—a type of sleep which I insinuate into the brain.

Passes or gazing at the eyes or fingers of the operator, are only useful in concentrating the attention. They are not absolutely essential.

As soon as they are able to pay attention and understand, children are as a rule very quickly and very easily hypnotized.

It often suffices to close their eyes, to hold them shut a few moments, to tell them to sleep, and then to state that they are asleep.

Some adults go to sleep just as readily by simple closure of the eyes. I often proceed immediately without making use of passes or fixation, by shutting the eye-lids, gently holding them closed, asking the patient to keep them together, and suggesting at the same time, the phenomena of sleep. Some of them fall rapidly into a more or less deep sleep.

Others offer more resistance. I sometimes succeed by keeping the eyes closed for some time, commanding silence and quiet, talking continuously, and repeating the same formulas; "You feel a sort of drowsiness, a torpor; your arms and legs are motionless. Your eyelids are warm. Your nervous system is quiet; you have no will. Your eyes remain closed. Sleep is coming, etc." After keeping up this auditory suggestion for several minutes, I remove my fingers. The eyes remain closed. I raise the patient's arms; they remain uplifted. We have induced cataleptic sleep.

Others are more rebellious, preoccupied, unable to give themselves up: they analyze their own feelings, are anxious, and say they cannot sleep. I command them to be calm. I speak only of drowsiness, of sleepiness. "That is sufficient," I say, "to gain a result. The suggestion alone may be beneficial even without sleep. Keep perfectly quiet and do not worry." When a patient is in this frame of mind, I do not try to get cataleptiform effects, because, being only drowsy yet always awake, always apt to regain full consciousness, he is easily roused out of this state. Sometimes then, satisfied with a doubtful state of somnolence, and without wishing to prove if the patient is really influenced, I leave him to himself, asking him to remain in this condition for some time. Some remain under this influence for a long period without being able to say whether they have done so voluntarily or involuntarily. Generally during the second or third séance I succeed by means of this suggestive education which the patient has had, in inducing a more advanced stage of hypnotic influence which is no longer doubtful but accompanied with suggestive catalepsy or even with somnambulism.

Whilst with some patients success is more readily obtained by acting quietly, with others quiet suggestion has no effect. With these, it is better to be abrupt, to restrain with an authoritative voice the inclination to laugh, or the weak and involuntary resistance which this manœuvre may provoke.

Many persons, as above stated, are influenced at the very first séance, others not until the second or third. After being hypnotized once or twice, they are speedily influenced. It is often enough to look at such patients, to spread the fingers before the eyes, to say, "Sleep," and in a second or two, sometimes instantly, the eyes close and all the phenomena of sleep are present. It is only after a certain number of séances, generally a small number, that the patients acquire the aptitude for going to sleep quickly.

It occasionally happens that I influence seven or eight persons successively, and almost instantly. Then there are others who are refractory or more difficult to influence. I only try for a few minutes. A second or third séance often brings the hypnosis which is not obtained at first.

Patients in whom hypnotic suggestibility is very well developed, fall asleep, however slight may be the idea of sleep that is given them. They can be hypnotized by correspondence,—for example, by assuring them that as soon as they have read a letter they will fall asleep. They can be hypnotized by means of the telephone, as M. Liégeois has shown. No matter what voice conveys the suggestion it produces its effect.

Some people can be hypnotized with chloroform before they are really under its influence. All surgeons have seen patients go to sleep suddenly without any period of excitement, after a few breaths of the anæsthetic and before it certainly has done its work. I have noticed this fact in some of my own patients whom I have chloroformed in the presence of the dentist in order that a tooth might be extracted. Profiting by this observation, each time I use chloroform I take care to suggest to the patient before he has taken the first inspiration that he will fall asleep quietly and quickly. In some cases the hypnotic sleep thus comes before the anæsthesia. If it is deep enough to cause complete anæsthesia, as I have seen it, the operation can be performed without delay; if not, I keep on giving chloroform until the anæsthesia is complete, which takes place more rapidly, because aided by suggestion. By acting in this manner, I also prevent the period of excitement in these cases.

It is wrong to believe that the subjects influenced are all weak-nerved, weak-brained, hysterical, or women. Most of my observations relate to men, whom I have chosen on purpose to controvert this belief. Without doubt, impressionability varies. Common people, those of gentle disposition, old soldiers, artisans, people accustomed to passive obedience, have seemed to me, as well as to M. Liébault, more ready to receive the suggestion than preoccupied people, and those who often unconsciously oppose a certain mental resistance. Cases of insanity, melancholia, and hyponchondria are often difficult or impossible to influence. The idea of being hypnotized must be present; the patient must submit entirely to the hypnotizer, using no cerebral resistance; then, I repeat, experience shows that a very large majority of people are easily influenced.

I have hypnotized very intelligent people belonging to the higher grades of society, who were not in the least nervous, at any rate in the sense in which that word is commonly used. Doubtless, it is often impossible to influence people who make it a point of honor to show that they cannot be hypnotized, that they have minds better balanced than others, and that they are not susceptible to suggestion, because such persons do not know how to put themseves into the psychical state necessary to realize the suggestion. They refuse to accept it, consciously or unconsciously; in fact they oppose a kind of counter-suggestion.

The degree of influence produced varies according to the subject. The following is the classification of the various degrees proposed by M. Liébault.

Some subjects experience only a more or less pronounced dulness, a heaviness in the lids, and sleepiness. This occurs in the smallest number of cases; it is the first degree of M. Liébault. This sleepiness may vanish as soon as the operator's influence is withdrawn. In some cases it lasts for several minutes, in others longer, an hour, for instance. Some subjects remain motionless. Others move a little, and change their position, but still remain sleepy. At the following séances, this condition may pass to a more advanced degree, though often one cannot go beyond that first attained. For example, in the case of a woman, I induced more than a hundred times a sleepiness lasting from half an hour to an hour, but only this somnolence of the first degree.

In some cases, somnolence, properly so-called, cannot be

induced, but the eyelids remain closed and the patients cannot open them. They speak, answer questions, and assert that they are not asleep, but I say, "You cannot open your eyes." They make fruitless efforts to do so. The lids are as if cataleptic. It has seemed to me, though I cannot state it as a fact, that this form of hypnotism is more frequent in women than in men. One woman made strange efforts to open her eyelids. She laughed and spoke fluently. I repeated, "Try to open them." She used all her force of will without succeeding, until I brought the charm to an end by saying, "You may open them."

I consider this also a variety of the first degree.

In the second degree, the patients keep their eyes closed. Their limbs are relaxed, they hear everything that is said to them as well as what is said around them, but they remain subject to the inclination to sleep. Their brain is in the condition called by magnetizers, hypotaxic, or charmed.

This degree is characterized by suggestive catalepsy.

By this word the following phenomenon is meant. If, as soon as the patient falls asleep, the limbs being relaxed, I lift his arm, it stays up; if I lift his leg, it remains uplifted. The limbs passively retain the positions in which they are placed. We call this suggestive catalepsy, because it is easy to recognize that it is purely psychical, bound up in the passive condition of the patient, who automatically keeps the attitude given just as he keeps the idea received. In fact, in the same or in different patients, one sees the phenomenon more or less marked according to the depth of the hypnotic influence and the psychical receptivity. At first, this cataleptiform condition is hardly apparent. The lifted limb remains up a few seconds, but falls down afterward with a certain hesitancy; or the fore-arm only remains lifted. If one wishes to lift up the whole arm, it falls down again. The individual fingers do not keep positions into which they are put, but the entire hand and the forearm remain fixed.

With some patients, for example, if one arm be quickly raised and let alone, it falls back again, but if it is held up for a few seconds to fix the idea of the attitude in the brain, so to speak, then it remains up.

Finally, with others, catalepsy is only obtained through a formulated verbal suggestion. The person hypnotized has to be told, "Your arms remain up. Your legs are up." Then only do they remain so. Some keep the new position passively, if nothing is said to them, but if they are dared to change it they regain consciousness, so to speak, call upon their dull will power, and drop the limb. Then they often wake up. These cases constitute the intermediate phases between the first and second degrees. Most cases, on the contrary, in spite of every effort cannot alter the attitude impressed upon them.

The progressive development of suggestibility can thus be traced by the special phase of the cataleptiform condition. In a vast number of cases this condition is very pronounced from the first. After a patient has been hypnotized for the first time, the limbs keep the position imposed without the necessity of formulated suggestion. They remain fixed, sometimes as long as the hypnotic condition lasts, sometimes falling down again slowly, gradually, at the end of a few minutes, a quarter of an hour, half an hour, or a still longer period.

On waking again, some patients who have not gone beyond the second degree, imagine that they have not been asleep because they remember everything they have heard. They believe that they have been influenced from a wish to be obliging, but if the experiment is repeated, suggestive catalepsy again appears. If this is not sleep, it is at least a peculiar psychical condition which diminishes the force of cerebral resistance, and which renders the mind receptive to suggestion.

In the third degree the drowsiness is more pronounced. Tactile sensibility is diminished or destroyed. Aside from suggestive catalepsy, the patient is capable of making automatic movements. I move both arms, one about the other. I say, "You cannot stop." The arms keep up the rotation for a longer or shorter time or indefinitely. The patient hears everything that is said around him.

In some cases this automatic rotation follows the impulse given to the arms. The verbal suggestion is not necessary. In cases of this degree, suggestive contracture can also be brought about.

The fourth degree is characterized, in addition to the preceding phenomena, by the loss of relationship with the outer world. The patient hears what the operator says, but not what the others around him say. His senses are only in communication with the operator. They are, however, susceptible of being put into relationship with any one.

The fifth and sixth degrees—characterized according to M. Liébault, by forgetfulness, upon waking, of all that has happened during sleep—constitute somnambulism. The fifth degree is light somnambulism. The patients still remember in a vague sort of way. They have heard some things confusedly; certain memories awake spontaneously. Destruction of sensibility, suggestive catalepsy, automatic movements, hallucinations caused by suggestion,—all these phenomena of which we shall speak later in greater detail, reach their greatest expression.

In deep somnambulism, or the sixth degree, the remembrance of all that has happened during the sleep is absolutely destroyed and cannot revive spontaneously.

We shall see later that these memories can always be revived artificially.

The patient remains asleep according to the operator's will, becoming a perfect automaton, obedient to all his commands.

This division of hypnotic sleep into several degrees, is purely theoretical. It permits us to classify each patient influenced, without making a long description necessary. There are variations and cases intermediary between the several degrees. All possible transitions may be noticed from simple drowsiness and doubtful sleep to the deepest somnambulism.

I add that docility to suggestion and the ease with which diverse phenomena are provoked, are not always in proportion to the depth of the hypnotic sleep. Certain patients sleep lightly, answer questions, remember everything upon waking. Nevertheless, contracture, insensibility, automatic movements, ordered or communicated, therapeutical suggestions, succeed well with them. This will be easy to understand when I have spoken of suggestion in the waking condition.

Others, on the contrary, fall into a deep, heavy sleep and remember absolutely nothing upon waking. While they are asleep they can be questioned in vain,—tormented with questions, yet they remain inert. Suggestive catalepsy is very difficult to induce in these cases. The arms are held up only for a short time. Suggestions, actions, illusions, hallucinations, commands to be carried out upon waking, are not realized; we might suppose they are not in relation with the operator; however, it is enough to pronounce the word, "awake," for them to wake spontaneously;—an evident proof that this relationship does exist. In several cases where sleep was such as I have just described, I have obtained immediate therapeutic effects through auditory suggestion. Return of sensibility, disappearance of melancholy, increase in muscular strength measured by the dynamometer, prove that in spite of their apparent inertia, they have been in relationship with me during the sleep.

Others, finally, answer all questions, speak fluently, and appear wide awake, except that the eyes are closed. They are not cataleptic or only slightly so. Neither hallucinations nor illusions can be provoked in them, but nevertheless on waking, amnesia is complete.

Each sleeper has, so to speak, his own individuality, his own special personality. I only wish to emphasize that the aptitude for realizing suggestive phenomena is not always proportional to the depth of the sleep.

Such is the classification of the various degrees of induced sleep as pointed out to me by Dr. Liébault and published in the first edition of this book. I have, indeed, been able to confirm the truth of the facts so well observed by my colleague.

I believe, however, that it is interesting to consider these facts from a wider point of view, and to give to the word hypnotism a more extended meaning than that of induced sleep.

The observations I am about to make, far from striking a blow at M. Liébault's idea, really go to confirm it, by showing that suggestion is the key-stone of the arch of all hypnotic manifestations.

In the first place, investigation reveals the following:

Some patients influenced by hypnotism, have no recollection of what has passed as soon as they return to their normal condition. Everything is a dead letter. This is the first category.

Others retain a vague or incomplete memory. Certain facts remain, others are obliterated. Some have heard talking, but do not remember what has been said; or, they have heard the remarks of the operator, but not those of others. This is the second category.

Finally, others remember everything that has occurred. Among these, some are conscious of being stupid, drowsy, or sleepy, and yet they may have heard everything, but were not able to make any movements, and could not throw off their drowsiness. Others have no consciousness of drowsiness. They say that they have been aware of all that was going on, and that their minds are alive to all that has been said and done. They say they have not slept and in fact, the particular condition in which they have been, could not be called sleep; at least, nothing proves that there has been a real sleep. These different conditions constitute the third category.

It is with patients of the first category, with those who have lost all memory, or nearly all, upon waking, that the induced hypnotic phenomena are the most numerous and the most pronounced; that is to say, with these cases suggestibility is most marked. In them catalepsy, automatic movements, analgesia, sensorial illusions, hypnotic hallucinations, and occasionally even post-hypnotic hallucinations can often be determined. Nevertheless, this is not constant.

I have seen patients (I record an example later) sleep quite deeply, or at least be so profoundly influenced as to have all memory destroyed upon waking; nevertheless, neither catalepsy, anæsthesia, nor hallucinations could be induced. Amnesia upon waking was the only symptom which appeared to indicate this sleep, although some of these subjects could speak fluently while in the hypnotic condition.

On the other hand, I have seen patients in whom catalepsy, anæsthesia, and hallucinations could be induced while they were in the hypnotic condition and who, upon returning to their normal state, retained the recollection of everything. But such cases constitute a minority. As a rule, suggestibility is more decided if there is amnesia upon waking.

All patients who are hypnotized do not sleep. In some cases the sleep is only partial, or doubtful. I also believe that it is better, in order to get a true conception of the phenomenon, to use the words, hypnotic influence, instead of hypnotic sleep, and to say that this influence manifests itself in different patients by symptoms varying according to the degree and individual way in which they are influenced by suggestion. From this point of view each patient represents a special individuality with regard to suggestion, and the number of divisions or degrees corresponding to the diverse hypnotic influences can be multiplied indefinitely.

In order to fix the ideas by a slightly schematic classification but embracing the majority of the facts, I shall adopt the following division of the different degrees of the hypnotic condition.

First Degree.—The patient does not exhibit catalepsy, anæsthesia, hallucinations, nor sleep, properly so-called. He says he has not slept, or that he has been only more or less drowsy. If sleep is suggested to him, he is content to remain with his eyes closed. He must not be dared to open his eyes, however, because then he opens them. The influence obtained may appear as naught or as doubtful, yet it exists; because if neither sleep, catalepsy, nor any other manifestations, may be provoked, suggestibility can nevertheless assert itself through other influences. For example, a suggestion of heat on a determined part of the body may be induced, certain pains may be destroyed, and evident therapeutic effects may be obtained.

I have succeeded in some cases, to all appearance refractory, in inducing all the regular manifestations of hypnotism, by suggestion, causing pains of a muscular or inveterate nervous character to disappear,—evident proof that suggestibility exists for certain organic activities.

Second Degree.—The patient has the same appearance as in the preceding degree and presents the same negative symptoms. If sleep is suggested, he remains with his eyes closed without really sleeping, or is only drowsy; but he differs from the subjects of the preceding degree in that he cannot open his eyes spontaneously if he is dared to do so. Here the influence is evident.

Third Degree.—The patient is susceptible to suggestive catalepsy whether the eyes are open or shut and whether he is drowsy or wakeful. As we have already stated, this catalepsy varies in intensity. In the degree of which we are speaking, the patient retains the position induced or suggested, unless challenged to alter it. If he is challenged, he regains consciousness, so to speak, and succeeds in changing his position by an effort of the will. To a superficial observer the influence may appear doubtful, but this is no longer the case, if, upon repeating the experiment, it is shown that the patient keeps his passive position from inertia, so long as his dormant will is not roused.

Fourth Degree.—In this degree, the suggestive catalepsy is more pronounced and resists all efforts on the part of the subject to break it. The influence is evident. The subject may be convinced that he is influenced by showing him that he cannot alter the position induced.

Besides this, suggestive catalepsy and automatic rotatory

movement in the upper extremities may sometimes be induced, which may continue for a long time. In some cases this motion is obtained by simply communicating the impulse. In others, verbal suggestion is necessary to continue the movement. As in catalepsy, some patients succeed in checking the motion by an effort of the will if they are dared to do so; others do not succeed in spite of all effort.

Fifth Degree.—In addition to the cataleptiform condition, accompanied or unaccompanied by automatic movements, contractures varying in degree may be induced by suggestion. The patient is dared to bend his arm, to open his hand, to open or shut his mouth, and he cannot do it.

Sixth Degree.—The patient exhibits moreover a more or less marked docility, or automatic obedience. Though inert and passive if left to himself, he rises at a suggestion, walks, stands still if ordered, and remains fixed to a spot when told that he cannot advance.

As in the preceding degrees, he is susceptible neither to sensorial illusions nor to hallucinations.

The subjects in these different categories remember everything upon waking. Some, however, are conscious of having slept. They remain inert, passive, without spontaneity and without initiative. This is the case to such a degree, that they cannot be roused from their torpid state until the intellectual initiative regains the upper hand, and they come out of the condition spontaneously. Some do not know whether they have really slept, and others positively state that they have not been asleep. But in cases included under the last three degrees, the patients can be convinced that, if they have not slept, they have been at least influenced.

Between a perfectly conscious condition and deep sleep all transitions exist. It is certain that in many subjects belonging to these different categories, intelligence and sensibility remain active during the hypnosis. Others have only certain symptoms of the sleep: the lack of initiative, inertia, sensation of drowsiness and the closed eyelids, or their minds reacting to the operator whom they answer and obey, seem uninfluenced by other people whom they do not appear to hear, and to whose questions they give no answers.

It is often difficult to penetrate the psychical condition of the subjects hypnotized. Observation requires nicety, and analysis is subtle. Some cases are doubtful, simulation is possible and easy, and it is still easier to believe in simulation where it does not exist. Certain subjects, for example, keep their eyes closed while the operator is hypnotizing them. When he ceases to look at them, their eyes open, and close quickly when he again fixes his gaze upon them. There is every appearance of deceit. The assistants believe it is a fraud. They pity the operator's naïve credulity and think the subject is deceitful, or that he is acting to oblige the operator.

This occurs daily in the presence of my pupils. I show them, however, that the subject is not deceiving me, and that I am not imposed upon, by hypnotizing him again and inducing catalepsy or contracture out of which I challenge him to come, requesting him at the same time, not to think of obliging anyone.

This tendency which certain subjects have to open their eyes again, and come out of their inertia as soon as the operator ceases to influence and watch them, this apparent pretending which is especially frequent in children, exists even in certain somnambulists, and one would swear that deception had been practised in these cases. Nevertheless the subjects remember nothing upon waking.

The majority of patients, however, remain with eyes closed for some time, apparently or actually asleep. They only open their eyes after the influence has worn off or when they are told to awake.

Considering these facts, I cannot repeat too often that the hypnotized subject is not a lifeless corpse or a body in a state of lethargy, for even though he is inert he hears, is conscious, and often shows signs of life. We may see him laugh or try to smother a laugh. He may remark upon his condition. He sometimes pretends that he is cheating or that he is trying to be obliging. Behind the doctor's back he boasts in good faith that he has not slept but has only pretended to sleep. He is not always aware that he is unable to pretend and that his disposition to oblige is forced upon him, and is due to a weakening of his will or of his power of resistance. The majority, however, finally become aware of this want of power. They feel that they are influenced. They are conscious of having slept even when memory is preserved upon waking.

In the degrees of which I shall now speak there is no longer any uncertainty as to the hypnotic influence, for there is amnesia upon waking which is sometimes complete, sometimes partial.

The subject remembers imperfectly. He knows that he has heard voices but does not know what has been said. He recalls some things. Other incidents of his hypnotic life are obliterated. These degrees of hypnotism in which memory is destroyed upon waking, we call somnambulism. In certain cases, somnambulism lasts only during particular moments of the hypnosis. Here there is sleep ; if by sleep we mean that condition of the mind which leaves behind it forgetfulness of all that has occurred during its existence. It is in this somnambulistic condition that we find subjects susceptible to hallucinations, analgesia, and suggestions of acts. Suggestibility here reaches its highest development. There are many variations however in this condition.

Seventh Degree.—Cases in which there is amnesia upon waking, but in which hallucinations cannot be induced, I consider as belonging to this degree. Almost all somnambulistic subjects in this degree are susceptible to catalepsy, contractions, automatic movements and automatic obedience. One or the other of these phenomena, however, may be wanting. Sometimes all are absent, but this is exceptional, as we have said. Amnesia upon waking is the only symptom characteristic of somnambulism. The eyes may be open or shut in this as in the following condition.

Eighth Degree.—There is amnesia upon waking as well as a great number of the phenomena observed in the preceding degrees. Susceptibility to hallucination during sleep is increased, but post-hypnotic hallucinations cannot be induced.

Ninth Degree.—Amnesia upon waking with the possibility of inducing hypnotic and post-hypnotic hallucinations.

These hallucinations are more or less complete and distinct. They may succeed with certain senses; for example, the olfactory and auditory, but not with others, as the visual. In many cases all the most complex hallucinations are perfectly carried out. Many more phases could be mentioned, according to the power of mental representation, which in each subject calls forth images with greater or less clearness and vividness.

More or less complete suggestive anæsthesia or analgesia may be met with in all degrees of hypnotism. It is generally more frequent and more pronounced in instances of the degrees last mentioned; those in which there is deep somnambulism and where there is great aptitude for hallucinations.

By stating the facts in this way I believe I come nearer the truth. Hypnotism manifests itself in different subjects in different ways. There may be simply drowsiness, or other induced sensations, as heat, pricking etc. This is the lightest influence. We have more marked effects when suggestion affects motility; develops the cataleptic condition, the inability to move, contraction and automatic movements. It is still more decided when it affects the will and causes automatic obedience. All these manifestations of motion, will, and even sensibility can be affected by suggestion with or without sleep, and even when it is powerless to induce sleep. In a more intense degree, suggestion produces sleep or an illusion of sleep. The subject convinced that he is sleeping, does not remember anything upon waking. In general, the more advanced degrees of suggestion affect the sensorial and sensory spheres—memory and imagination. Illusions may be created and destroyed, and the imagination may call forth the most varied memory pictures.

I insist upon the fact that all or some of these suggestions may be realized with or without sleep. Other suggestions may succeed where that of sleep itself remains useless, for the sleep is also nothing but a suggestion. It is not possible in all cases, and it is not necessary in cases of good somnambulism in order to obtain the most diverse phenomena. They can be dissociated, so to speak, from sleep. Catalepsy, paralysis, anæsthesia, and the most complex hallucinations may be realized in many cases without the necessity of preceding these phenomena by sleep. Susceptibility to suggestion occurs in the waking estate.

To define hypnotism as induced sleep, is to give a too narrow meaning to the word,—to overlook the many phenomena which suggestion can bring about independently of sleep. I define hypnotism as the induction of a peculiar psychical condition which increases the susceptibility to suggestion. Often, it is true, the sleep that may be induced facilitates suggestion, but it is not the necessary preliminary. It is suggestion that rules hypnotism.

I have tried to show that suggested sleep differs in no respect from natural sleep. The same phenomena of suggestion can be obtained in natural sleep, if one succeeds in putting one's self into relationship with the sleeping person without waking him.

This new idea which I propose concerning the hypnotic influence, this wider definition given to the word hypnotism, permits us to include in the same class of phenomena all the various methods which, acting upon imagination, induce the psychical condition of exalted susceptibility to suggestion with or without sleep.

Such is the case, for example, with fascination induced by a brilliant object, or by the gaze. The latter form of fascination, used for the first time by Donato, has since been described by Brémaud. I have also seen it applied by Hansen. Donato, who operates especially upon young people, proceeds in the following manner. He asks the subject to lay the palms of his hands upon his own, stretched out horizontally, and to press downward with all his might. The subject's whole attention and all his physical force is absorbed in this manœuvre. All his inervation, so to speak, is concentrated in this muscular effort, and so the distraction of his thoughts is prevented. "The magnetizer" says Brémaud, according to Donato, "looks at him sharply, quickly, and closely, directing him by gesture (and by word, if need be) to look at him as fixedly as he is able. Then the operator recedes or walks around the patient, keeping his eyes fixed upon him and attracting his gaze, while the subject follows him as if fascinated, with his eyes wide open, and unable to take them from the operator's face. If once carried away by the first experiment, the simple fixation of the gaze suffices to make the subject follow. It is no longer necessary to make him first place his hand on the operator's.

Here we have to do with simple suggestion by gesture. When the magnetizer fixes his eyes upon the subject's, the latter understands that he must keep his eyes fixed and must follow the operator everywhere. He believes that he is drawn toward him. It is a suggestive psychical fascination and not physical in the least. I have seen the experiment unsuccessful with the best somnambulists when they did not understand the meaning of the operator's gesture. In such cases, the experiment may be made to succeed by imitation, if the subject has seen it performed successfully in his presence upon someone else. This then is suggestion by imitation.

Among subjects thus fascinated, some submit to the influence without sleep, just as those do who are hypnotized by another method. They are susceptible to suggestions in the waking condition. They remember afterward what they have done; they do not know why they were unable to keep from following and gazing at the operator. Others remember nothing at all after they are waked by blowing upon the eyes or by a simple word. They do not know what has happened, they have been in a somnambulistic condition with their eyes open. In this somnambulistic fascination, catalepsy and hallucinations may be induced. In these same subjects, catalepsy or hallucination may often be induced by a simple word, a gesture, or a position communicated to them without any previous fascination.

Fascination, then, does not exist as a special condition. It is always hypnosis, that is to say, an exalted susceptibility to suggestion induced by an influence exercised over the subject's imagination. Whether this influence reaches the sensorium through eye, speech, or touch, etc., the psychical condition obtained is always the same. It is always a susceptibility to suggestion which varies in degree in different individuals, and this degree depends less upon the method employed than upon the special impressionability of the subject.

The awaking may be spontaneous. Subjects who sleep lightly at the first séance, sometimes have a tendency to awake quickly. It is necessary to hold their eyelids closed, or to say from time to time, "sleep," in order to keep them under the charm. The habit of sleep is very soon acquired by the organism. The subject no longer wakes while the operator remains at his side; he may awake as soon as the operator's influence is withdrawn. The majority of subjects left to themselves sleep on for several minutes, for half an hour, or even for one or more hours. I allowed one of my subjects to sleep fifteen hours, another eighteen.

In order to awake the subject immediately, I use verbal suggestion, in the same manner as when sleep is to be induced. I say, "It is over; wake up," and this suffices, even when uttered in a low voice, to awake subjects who have already been hypnotized several times, immediately.

In some cases it is necessary to add, "Your eyes are opening; you are awake." If that is not enough, blowing once or twice on the eyes causes the subject to wake. I have never had to resort to other methods, such as sprinkling cold water on the subjects. The awaking has always been easy.

At times there is nothing so strange as this awaking. The subject is in deep sleep. I question him and he answers. If he is naturally a good talker, he will speak fluently. In the midst of his conversation I suddenly say, "Wake up." He opens his eyes, and has absolutely no remembrance of what has happened. He does not remember having spoken to me, though he was speaking, perhaps, but one tenth of a second, before waking. In order to make the phenomenon more striking, I sometimes wake a patient in the following way. "Count up to ten. When you say ten aloud, you will be awake." The moment he says ten, his eyes open; but he does not remember having counted. Again I say, "You are going to count up to ten. When you get to six you will wake up, but you will keep on counting aloud up to ten. When he utters the word six, he opens his eyes but keeps on counting. When he has finished I say, "Why are you counting?" He no longer remembers that he has been counting. I have repeated this experiment many times with very intelligent people.

It is necessary to proceed cautiously with certain hysterical subjects, avoiding touching painful points, and exciting the hysterogenic zones, lest an hysterical crisis be produced. The hypnotic sleep may in this way give place to hysterical sleep, and the operator is then no longer in relationship with the subject. Suggestion has then no effect.

Some subjects remain sleepy when they wake up. If the operator waves his hand once or twice before the eyes, he may dispel this drowsiness. Others complain of heaviness in the head, and of a dull headache or of dizziness. In order to prevent these various sensations I say to the subject before waking him, "You are going to wake up, and you will be perfectly comfortable; your head is not heavy, you feel perfectly well," and he awakes without any disagreeable sensation.

Some subjects can be awakened by suggestion after a specified time. It is enough to say, "You will awake in five minutes." They wake precisely at the moment suggested. They have a correct idea of time. Some subjects have no accurate idea of time and awake before the moment suggested. Some too, forget to awake. They remain in the passive condition and appear unable to come out of it spontaneously. It is necessary to say, "Wake up" in order to have them do so.

Many subjects upon waking rub their eyes, look wildly about, and are conscious of having slept deeply. Others open their eyes suddenly, not remembering what has passed, and do not know that they have been asleep. They are like epileptic patients who have been unconscious and ignore the void which has come into their state of normal consciousness. "Have you slept?"—"I do not know, I ought to believe it if you say so." Or, they are convinced that nothing abnormal has happened to them, and deny that they have been influenced.

The following table, made from a considerable number of cases and presented to M. Dumont by M. Liébault, gives an idea of the proportion of patients of all ages, of both sexes, and of all temperaments subdivided into the different categories of sleep.

YEAR 1880 1012 PERSONS HYPNOTIZED.

Refractory	27	Very deep sleep	230
Somnolence, heaviness	33	Light somnambulism,	31
Light sleep	100	Deep somnambulism,	131
Deep sleep	460		

It is doubtless necessary to take account of the fact that M. Liébault operates chiefly upon the common people who come to him to be hypnotized and who, convinced of his magnetic power show greater cerebral docility than more intelligent people. Perhaps the number of cases influenced would be less without these favorable and predisposing conditions. I have been able to prove, however, that refractory subjects constitute a large minority, and I succeed in hypnotizing subjects at the first séance daily who come to my office with no idea what the hypnotic sleep is.

According to this statistical table and another, also covering a year's time, prepared by M. Liébault and mentioned by M. Beaunis, the number of somnambulists in one hundred subjects chosen at random may be considered as from fifteen to eighteen.

Persons who can be hypnotized, and who, when they wake, have no recollection of what has happened during their sleep, we call somnambulists. It seems to me that this proportion may be considerably increased if the sleeping subject is told, " When you wake, you will remember nothing." In a certain number of cases, amnesia is thus produced by suggestion.

From this same table of M. Beaunis, it appears that the proportions of subjects that can be hypnotized are about the same in men as in women, and particularly that the proportion is nearly the same as regards somnambulism, contrary to current opinion.

18, 8 per cent. in men ; 19, 4 per cent. in women.

The following table, prepared by M. Beaunis from the above mentioned statistics, shows the percentage of subjects exhibiting the different degrees of sleep at different periods of life.

AGE.	Somnambulism.	Very Deep Sleep.	Deep Sleep.	Light Sleep.	Somnolence.	No Influence.
Up to 7 years.......	26,5	4,3	13	52,1	4,3	
From 7 to 14 years ..	55,3	7,6	23	13,8		
From 14 to 21 years.	25,2	5,7	44,8	5,7	8	10,3
From 21 to 28 years.	13,2	5,1	36,7	18,3	17,3	9,1
From 28 to 35 years.	22,6	5,9	34,5	17,8	13	5,9
From 35 to 42 years.	10,5	11,7	35,2	28,2	5,8	8,2
From 42 to 49 years.	21,6	4,7	29,2	22,6	9,4	12,2
From 49 to 56 years.	7,3	14,7	35,2	27-9	10,2	4,4
From 56 to 63 years.	7,3	8,6	37,6	18,8	13	14,4
From 63 and onward	11,8	8,4	38,9	20,3	6,7	13,5

M. Beaunis shows that the striking point in this table is, the great proportion of somnambulists in childhood and youth. (26, 5 per cent., from 1 to 7 years, and 55, 3 per cent., from 8 to 14 years.)

It is noticeable also that during these two periods of life, all the subjects, without exception, have been more or less influenced. In old age, on the contrary, the number of somnambulists is observed to decrease, but always remains at a relatively high figure (7 to 11 per cent.).

CHAPTER II

Phenomena noticed in hypnotic sleep.—Sensibility.—Spontaneous or suggested anæsthesia.—Hypnotism cannot replace chloroform.—Alterations in motility.—Suggestive catalepsy.—Automatic movements.—Movements by imitation.—Suggestive paralysis.—Somnambulism with forgetfulness upon waking.—Automatic obedience.—Sensorial suggestions.—Suggested hallucinations.—Acts, sensorial illusions, and hallucinations suggested for the time which follows waking.—Negative hallucinations.—Psychical amaurosis and deafness.—Hallucinations to be realized after a long interval (*a longue échéance*).

I NOW approach a rapid study of the phenomena which are manifested or which may be induced in hypnosis. Sometimes the eyes close suddenly before anything has been said and the subject falls like a lifeless mass. Sometimes the sleep comes gradually. The eyelids grow heavy, the sight becomes confused, the eyes get watery, open and shut alternately and finally close. In some cases the eyelids remain motionless when closed. In others they quiver as long as the hypnosis lasts. In light sleep, the eye-balls retain their normal position. When the sleep is deep, they are often rolled up and the pupils are hidden under the upper eyelid.

Sometimes nervous subjects have muscular twitching of the limbs and fibrillary contractions of the face while asleep. The majority, however, are inert, or become so after suggestion. Some subjects make reflex movements, scratch themselves, for example, rub their hands together and change their position. Others, on the contrary, remain perfectly quiet.

Sensibility in its different forms, is more or less modified. It is preserved in light sleep. Tickling, the prick of a pin, or the touching of a painful spot cause reflex movements and the subject wakes.

In deep sleep, sensibility is diminished or totally destroyed. According to M. Liébault, it first disappears in the extremities, and the periphery of the body is always the most anæsthetic part. " Further examination of the organs of sensation show that the senses of sight and taste are the first to become dull. The sense of smell comes next, while hearing and touch are the last to be lost. The visual sense loses its function last when the methods of the hypnotizers are employed,—(fixation on some object as, for instance, the operator's fingers or eyes),—because the forced attention of the eyes compels them to remain active the latest."

If the anæsthesia is complete, a pin may be stuck into the skin, electricity may be applied, objects may be pushed up into the nostrils, ammonia may be held under the nose and the subject will not even wince. This complete anæsthesia may be spontaneously developed by simple hypnotization.

In other subjects it is not spontaneous, but may be induced more or less perfectly by suggestion. I prick a hypnotized subject with a pin: he reacts quickly. I uncork a bottle of ammonia under his nose: he contracts his nostrils and shows that he feels it. Then I say to him, "You do not feel anything more. Your whole body is insensible. I prick you and you do not feel it. I hold ammonia under your nose and you perceive absolutely nothing." In many cases, anæsthesia thus occurs through suggestion. Sometimes only a certain degree of anæsthesia of the skin is induced while the mucous membranes of the nose and eyes cannot be affected by suggestion.

In a certain number of cases, then, the hypnotic insensibility is complete enough to enable the most difficult surgical operations to be performed. But this is not true of the majority of cases. Hypnotism cannot be generally used as an anæsthetic in surgery; it cannot take the place of chloroform. Moreover, the psychical concentration necessary to the development of the hypnotic condition is often hindered by the subject's anxiety at the time of an operation.

Changes in motility are more usually and more easily induced than changes in sensibility. All hypnotic subjects, excepting those of the first degree, are susceptible to suggestive catalepsy.

We have seen that this phenomenon is manifested in different ways, according to the manner and degree of the susceptibility to suggestion. The mind executes the suggestion with more or less contraction or contracture. Sometimes the catelepsy is flabby, if I may so express it, and the upraised limb falls at the least pressure. Sometimes the catalepsy is firmer without being rigid; —wax-like rigidity. The limbs yield to any motion communicated to them. They may be stretched or bent like soft wax (*flexibilitas cerea*), certain fingers may be stretched, others bent, one thigh may be bent, the other extended. The patient may be seated with the head inclined toward one shoulder, the different parts of the body may be put into the most curious positions. They remain fixed like the limbs of a jointed mannikin in the positions given. They take the posture communicated exactly. Catalepsy is sometimes rigid, and accompanied by a real contracture which only disappears by suggestion. For example, if an arm is lifted vertically, it remains fixed, contractured. If we wish to lower it, it offers a strong resistance; if this resistance is overcome and the limb then released, it recoils like a spring into its first position. It is a true, rigid catalepsy which I shall call tetanic catalepsy. As soon as the subject is asleep, I lift his arms and legs without speaking. They remain fixed as if tetanized, in the attitude communicated. This rigidity is generally much greater in the upper than in the lower limbs. In some cases, the whole body may be thus made immovable, and tetanized to such an extent that the head can be put on one chair, and the feet on the other, and the body pressed against without the contracture being overcome.

Suggestion alone always succeeds in destroying this tetanic condition. I say, "I can lower your arm and move it as I wish." The rigidity then vanishes and the catalepsy persists, wax-like or flabby, as in the degrees just mentioned.

In a word, all the forms which occur in pathological conditions may be observed in the hypnotic state, and if the many observations published on spontaneous catalepsy were to be re-read, it would be quickly seen, that many of them in reality are related to cases of hypnotism or spontaneous somnambulism. When Lasègue induced artificial cataleptic seizures showing the special characteristics of spontaneous catalepsy in hysterical patients by closing the eyes, he was not aware that these patients were in reality hypnotized. He had induced suggestive catalepsy.

I repeat that in the majority of subjects hypnotized, it is not necessary to formulate the suggestion in order to induce catalepsy in the limbs. The psychical condition is such that all ideas received by the brain are imprinted there, and any attitude communicated to a limb is maintained. The position given to the limb by the operator is accepted by the patient's brain like an imagined suggestion. There is not enough cerebral initiative to modify the induced muscular condition spontaneously.

Many pathological conditions may be accompanied with catalepsy because the cerebral spontaneity is suppressed, or a psychical condition is produced analogous to that which hypnotism creates artificially. I have observed this a number of times in typhoid fever, only one must look for the phenomenon in order to find it.

I will mention two cases. The first was that of a man thirty-five years old, who was attacked with a mild form of typhoid fever, complicated, during defervescence, from the fifteenth to the thirty-fifth day, with anxious melancholia. The patient was motionless and insensible to all that was going on around him. He answered questions in monosyllables, remaining silent the rest of the time. His eyes were closed, his pupils hidden under the upper eyelids. The reflexes were preserved. Sensibility was markedly diminished. The patient seemed to hear questions but did not answer them. If roused a moment by vigorous and repeated commands, he opened his eyes only to sink again immediately into his former motionless condition. His arms remained indefinitely in any position into which they were put, as in suggestive catalepsy, but there was no rigidity. He sat up for an indefinite time if so placed. This condition lasted six days, then it gave way to active delirium, stiffness and trembling of the limbs. The patient refused food, and the œsophageal sound had to be used. Recovery took place.

The second case was that of an Italian mason twenty-one years old, who had a fatal attack of typhoid fever, of a dynamic character. He died on the eleventh day. From the eighth day on, the patient was prostrated and spoke little. He answered questions, however, clearly but slowly. There was retention of urine unrelieved by the use of the catheter. Sensibility was preserved.

His eyes remained open. He did everything he was told to do, often without speaking. If he was asked for his name he would sometimes give it in a low voice. If his arm was lifted, he would keep it up a long time as in catalepsy, his face remaining expressionless like the faces of hypnotized subjects. Whatever the attitude in which the limbs were put, the patient had not enough intellectual initiative to change it. In time, however, they dropped from fatigue. This cataleptiform condition lasted three days, when death took place from cardiac failure.

The cataleptic condition never occurs in typhoid fever, nor in any other morbid states without being accompanied by this special psychical inertia which directs it. Artificial and spontaneous catalepsy seem to me to be essentially of a psychical nature.

The following phenomena are of the same order.

For example, I put the hypnotized subject's thumb up to his nose. Then I put the thumb of the other hand up to the little finger, so as to make him have his fingers up to his nose. He keeps them so, and the expression of his face does not change. If I say to him, "Your thumb is stuck fast, you cannot pull it down from your nose, your little finger is stuck to the thumb of the other hand, you may try your best to pull them apart, you cannot succeed," if I tell him that he is exhausting himself in vain attempts, his thumb remains stuck to his nose. His nose follows the thumb everywhere, and cannot be detached. This experiment succeeds with the majority of patients who have reached the second or third degree of hypnotic sleep.

I shut one of his hands and say to him, "You cannot open it again." It remains contractured sometimes to such a degree that it cannot be reopened. The more insistence, the more stress laid on the demand, "Your hand is shut, no one can open it again," the more force the patient uses in contracting it and resists the endeavors made to open it.

If, on the contrary, I open it and hold it open for several instants, and if the patient understands that this action implies that his hand should remain open, he stiffens it out spontaneously and resists any efforts made to shut it. The muscles of the jaws can be tetanized, trismus can be produced and the jaws can be kept open. Torticollis, opisthotonus, and pleurosthotonus may be also induced. The phenomenon is simply the result of suggestion, whether the eyes are open or shut, whether friction is used to contract the muscles or not.

In cases of hypnotism induced in this manner, I have never succeeded in inducing, by pressure exerted upon the nerve, the contraction of muscles enervated by this nerve,—for example, the ulnar or radial attitude, the contortion of the face, etc.,—without saying something to the patient or in his presence.

A deeper degree of hypnosis seems to be required for the production of automatic movements than for simple catalepsy. In many cases, however, these movements are induced either at the first or at one of the following séances. Both arms are lifted horizontally and rotated one about the other. The patient keeps on moving them spontaneously or in obedience to a command. Some subjects move them in a hesitating way, betraying a useless endeavor to stop them. Others who sleep more deeply, turn their arms quickly, regularly, and automatically. I say, "Do all you can to stop them." Some can make no effort, others try, uselessly bringing their hands together, hitting them one against the other, but unable to stop this perpetual and irresistible movement, which dominates what remains of their will or power of resistance. If I stop one hand, the other may keep on turning alone. If I then let the hand go again it may remain still, the subject believing that I wish to stop it, or it may spring back to its companion's side and turn around again, faster than ever. An automatic movement of the legs may also be induced, but this is much less frequent.

In some cases of deep sleep these automatic movements occur through imitation. I stand in front of the patient and turn my arms one about the other. The subject imitates me. I make the movement in the opposite direction; he does the same. I put my fingers to my nose; he imitates me. I stand on one leg; he stands on one leg also. I stamp on the floor; he does likewise. The movement I make suggests to his mind the idea of the same movement.

I am convinced that this phenomenon which magnetizers are so ready to call an effect of mesmerism, that is to say, of a fluid emanating from my body under the influence of my will and acting directly upon the subject magnetized, is nothing else than a phenomenon of suggestion. The subject sees through his half closed eyelids or hears the movement I make, and therefore imitates me. It I take care that his eyes are hermetically closed he does not imitate my movements. One of my somnambulistic cases, however, whom I hypnotized in the presence of my colleague, M. Charpentier, imitated my movements without seeing them, for I had stood behind him. I turned my arms; after a time, he did the same. I moved my foot in a certain way; in a few moments he moved his foot too, but not imitating me exactly. "Was there any fluid influence there?" I asked myself. But we may be sure that our somnambulist heard the movement made by my arms and my feet, and that the idea of the movement to be imitated was transmitted to the mind by his auditory sense; because if I moved noiselessly without even letting my clothes rustle, he remained motionless, not imitating me.

We must add that a subject who has been hypnotized and subjected to these experiments several times, executes them more promptly and more perfectly. Sometimes it is sufficient to lift both arms horizontally. He suspects what is wanted, and turns them one about the other. It is enough to close his hand lightly and he contracts it with irresistible force. He holds his arm up, rigid. In some cases, the contracture is so great that the hand can hardly be opened again when the order is given to open it.

Suggestion induces paralysis as well as contracture. I tell a patient that his arm is paralyzed. If I lift it, it falls motionless while the other arm, which I have not paralyzed by suggestion, remains up in a cataleptic condition. In some cases, this suggestion disappears quickly, the subjects forget it in a few minutes; in others it lasts a long time. In one case, I suggested paralysis of one arm and catalepsy of the other. I let the patient sleep forty minutes, then, coming quietly up, I suddenly lifted both arms. The one remained up, the other fell back. The idea suggested still continued in the mind.

The paralyses thus induced by suggestion, and capable of being developed in the waking condition as well, as I shall prove later, have been called by Charcot, "Experimental psychical paralyses," and resemble the paralyses called by Russel-Reynolds, "Paralyses by imagination, depending on idea." According to P. Richer and Gilles de la Tourette (*Progrés medical*, 1884), these suggestive paralyses have special characters, by which they can be distinguished from other paralyses, of organic nature. These characters are, complete laxity of the limbs, considerable exaggeration of the tendon reflexes, spinal trepidation, loss of muscular sense, exaggeration and modification of the muscular contraction provoked by the galvanic current, and vasomotor troubles.

I have not been able to prove the existence of these special characters. The exaggeration of the tendon reflexes, and the spinal trepidation have been wanting in many cases of suggestive paralysis, while the muscular sense was present. It seems evident to me that these suggested psychical paralyses vary in character according to individual conception and the manner of suggestion. Each subject carries out a suggestion as he conceives it, as he interprets it.

These facts and those which I shall mention later, show that the phenomena of so-called animal-magnetism are simply the phenomena of suggestion. In hypnotism, the subject's condition is such that the idea suggested imposes itself with greater or less force upon the mind, and induces the corresponding action by means of a kind of cerebral automatism. In my hypnotic cases, I have not observed a single act which cannot be thus interpreted, without calling for the intervention of any fluid analogous to the force of the magnet, or electricity escaping from certain organisms to react upon others. It is the doctrine of Braid or Braidism, the doctrine of suggestion which is deduced from observation, contrary to the doctrine of Mesmer or Mesmerism; the doctrine of a mesmeric or magnetic fluid.

The mesmerists, for example, give the following facts in support of their fluid theory. They say, if a pass is made over a limb and the parts lightly touched, the muscles contract and the limb may be raised. This is a mesmerizing pass. If the pass is then made over the limb without touching it, just moving the air, it will fall back again. This is a demesmerizing pass. If the air is agitated at one side of the head, the head turns, following the operator's hand. If the pass is made on the opposite side of the head, the head turns back to that side. Pass the hand quickly over the subject's hand and draw it away suddenly. If this is repeated several times the hand is lifted up of itself and remains in a cataleptic condition; an evident proof, the mesmerists say that the operator's hand draws the magnetized patient's hand after it as the magnet attracts iron!

Braid has proved that this is in reality only the action of suggestion,'that no fluid and magnetic influence comes into play. "The phenomena arise apart from the operator's will, if by gesture or by touch, interpreted by the subject's mind, he manifests a desire which the subject cannot resist. The same passes, accompanied or unaccompanied with touching of the limb, mesmerizing or demesmerizing in the language of the magnetizers may induce the same phenomenon, the raising or dropping of the hand. The subject's movements, induced by a certain sensorial impression, are instinctive and automatic. The patient's brain directs the movement naturally indicated by this attitude.

A muscle in repose contracts; a contracted muscle relaxes under the influence of the same manœuvre. If an impression is communicated to the hand or the arm resting on the knee, this arm cannot fall; it is raised of itself and becomes stiff. If the same impression act upon the lifted arm, it causes a most natural movement, the dropping of the limb. If the lifting or dropping of the limb is prevented, impressions will produce lateral movements."

We must add that a subject with whom the same experiment has been repeated several times, or who has seen it performed on others has kept in his memory the movements or muscular acts corresponding to each impression. He is instructed, so to speak, and repeats automatically, by cerebro-spinal reflex only, the same acts which he has seen executed or which he has executed himself in the preceding séances.

The subjects more deeply influenced by hypnotism, pass into a condition known as somnambulism. Then new phenomena appear. The automatism is complete. The human organism has become almost a machine, obedient to the operator's will. I say "Rise," and he rises. One subject gets up very quickly, another obeys slowly, the machine is lazy, the command must be repeated in an authoritative voice. I say "Walk," and he walks; "Sit down," and he sits down.

I say, "You cannot walk forwards any more, you can only walk backwards." His efforts are fruitless. He walks backwards.

"You can neither go forward nor backward." He remains fixed to the spot in spite of all the physical efforts he makes to move.

"Your legs can support you no longer." He falls as if paralyzed.

"Your right leg only, is paralyzed." He drags the right leg.

I touch him with both my hands stretched out, and making gestures as if to draw him towards me, I walk backwards. He follows me passively, wherever I go.

I order him to dance. He dances, and stops as if rooted to the spot, at my command.

General sensibility and the special senses may be modified, increased, diminished, or perverted at will. I put salt into the subject's mouth, telling him that it is sugar. Some subjects do not accept this suggestion perfectly. They still perceive the salt taste, more or less clearly. Many, however, suck the salt with pleasure, finding it very sweet. I make a subject drink water or vinegar for wine. I make him smell ammonia for cologne.

I induce deafness. The subject says that he hears nothing. He answers nothing and does not react to the most deafening noises. I make him mute and I make him stutter. The most curious illusions may be suggested. A pencil put into his mouth takes the place of a cigar, the aroma of which he draws in with pleasure, blowing puffs of imaginary smoke into the air.

In the advanced degrees of hypnosis all illusions and hallucinations are successfully carried out with surprising precision.

Moreover all actions which the operator commands are carried out. The hypnotized subject walks and dances at the word of command, shows his fist to persons pointed out, searches their pockets more or less adroitly, steals, and carries out any violent acts which are ordered. One subject acts with a certain hesitation; another resolutely.

Somnambulists can write, work, play the piano, and converse among themselves. Seeing them act thus, their eyes shut, or open as in the waking condition, one would swear they were not asleep. When left to themselves, they are generally passive and inert, but they become active and move about under the influence of suggestion.

For example, there is a woman fifty-five years old in my service, who was a housekeeper. She is troubled with rheumatism but is not at all hysterical. I induce the somnambulistic condition easily. If I say nothing, the somnambulism is passive. She sleeps quietly and her muscles are relaxed. I can induce anæsthesia, catalepsy, contracture, and hallucinations and make her come out of her passive state by affirmation. I say, " Now that you are cured, get up, do your work." She gets up, dresses, looks around for a chair, climbs upon the window-sill, opens the window, dips her hands into a pitcher containing some medicine, which she thinks is water intended for domestic use, and begins to wash the panes of glass, conscientiously, on both sides. Then she makes her bed or sweeps the floor of the room with a broom which is handed to her. When she awakes, she remembers nothing, and thinks she has been sleeping quietly in a chair.

These are not exceptional facts. If one wishes to consider this side of the question carefully, it is astonishing to find in any hospital ward where a great variety of subjects are assembled, in how many the phenomena of active somnambulism can be induced. In a room of twenty, I sometimes have three or four women at work. One crochets, the other sews, the third with her eyes shut looks for old linen and irons with which to iron it. Some, susceptible to hallucinations, perform their work with imaginary utensils. For example, one of them takes a sheet, turns the edge, threads an imaginary needle and sits down to do imaginary sewing, making all motions of hemming precisely, stitch by stitch, without mistake. All this is accomplished by means of suggestion. The eyes may be open or shut, and all memory is lost when the subject wakes.

In order to further ascertain the condition of somnambulistic subjects and the complex manifestations to which they are susceptible, I shall relate some observations later which are more eloquent than any description I could give.

But first, I wish to call attention to one of the most interesting phenomena of somnambulism. I wish to speak of the possibility of inducing in somnambulists by means of suggestion, acts, illusions of the senses, and hallucinations which shall not be manifested during the sleeping condition, but upon waking. The patient hears what I tell him in his sleep but no memory of what I said remains. He no longer knows that I spoke to him. The idea suggested arises in his mind when he wakes, but he has forgotten its origin, and believes it is spontaneous. Facts of this kind have been observed by A. Bertrand, Gen. Noiset, Dr. Liébault and Chas. Richet. I have repeated these observations successfully many times in a large number of hypnotic cases and am convinced of their accuracy.

The following are instances of suggestive acts. I have selected curious cases on purpose, in order to make the experiments more conclusive.

I suggested to D—— during sleep that upon waking he should rub his sore thigh and leg, that he should then get out of bed, walk to the window and return to bed. He performed all these acts without suspecting that a command had been given to him while he was sleeping.

I suggested to S—— on one occasion, that on waking he should put on his hat, bring it to me in the next room and put it on my head. This he did without knowing why.

On another occasion when my colleague, M. Charpentier, was present, I suggested to him when he first fell asleep that as soon as he waked, he should take my colleague's umbrella, which was lying on the bed, open it, and walk twice up and down the piazza on which the room opened. It was some time afterward when I waked him. Before his eyes were open, we went quickly out of the room so that the suggestion might not be recalled by our presence. We soon saw him coming with the umbrella in his hand, but not open (in spite of the suggestion). He walked twice up and down the corridor. I said to him, " What are you doing?" He answered, " I am taking the air."—" Why, are you warm ? "—" No, it is only my idea; I occasionally walk up and down out here."—" What is the umbrella for? It belongs to M. Charpentier."—" What! I thought it was mine, it looks something like mine. I shall take it back to the place I took it from."

Sometimes the subject tires himself out in trying to find a reason for the ideas in his brain. One day I suggested to the same subject that as soon as he waked, he should go to a certain patient in the same room and ask how he was. He did so as soon as he awoke, and when I asked him why he did it, and whether he was especially interested in that patient, he replied, " No, it was just an idea." Then after thinking a moment, added " He would not let us sleep last night." Thus he tried to explain the idea to himself by the wish to know, whether the sick patient would allow them to sleep that night or not.

On another occasion I suggested that as soon as he waked he should put both thumbs into his mouth, which he did. He connected this necessary act with a painful sensation in his tongue, owing to his having bitten it the day before in an epileptic attack.

One morning at eleven o'clock I suggested to C—— that an hour after mid-day he would be seized by an idea he could not resist, namely, to walk along Stanislas Street, and return, twice. At one o'clock I saw him go out into the street, walk along from one end to the other, return, and stop, like a lounger, under the windows. But he did not do it twice, perhaps because he did not understand the second part of the suggested command, perhaps because he resisted it. On another occasion I suggested that at the same hour he should take a direction I traced out for him, pass by the academy to a stand where he should buy a paper, and return another way. At the hour appointed, he went to the paper stand by the way pointed out, bought his paper and then returned, but by another way.

In the case of a poor boy with aortic insufficiency, I suggested that five minutes after waking up, he should take the book lying at the head of his bed and read the 100th page. A quarter of an hour after the suggestion, I waked him, and went a little way off. Three minutes afterward (he lacked an exact idea of time), I saw him take up his book and read. I approached; he was reading the 100th page. "Why are you reading on that page?" I asked.—"I do not know," he said, "I often open the book and read here and there."

I have repeated analogous suggestions in a large number of cases. For example, the following are two experiments of this kind which, I think, offer special interest from a psychological point of view.

X—— is a sailor, 51 years old, formerly an employee on a railroad. He is troubled with chronic articular rheumatism of the knees, with retraction of the limbs in flexion. He is an intelligent, well-balanced man of considerable culture and not at all nervous or credulous. When I proposed to hypnotize him he assured me that I would never succeed. I tried, and obtained closure of the eyes in the first séance. He pretended not to have slept at all.

In the second séance, I obtained suggestive catalepsy. He pretended, however, not to have slept and to have held his arms up because he wanted to, out of pure complaisance. I had to put him to sleep again and dare him to alter the different attitudes impressed upon his limbs before he would confess, when he waked, that he had been really influenced. Several days later, finding him sleeping naturally, I came up quietly and said to him, "Continue to sleep—do not wake up." I laid my hand on his forehead for two minutes, then I lifted his arm, and it remained in a condition of suggestive catalepsy. The natural sleep had gone over into hypnotic sleep. In other words, I had been able to enter into relationship with him during his sleep, by means of the organ of hearing. Upon waking, he did not remember that I had spoken to, or touched him.

Since then, that is, since the fifth or sixth séance, I have put him into a profound sleep with loss of memory on waking.

In the waking state, I induce catalepsy and automatic movements. He is susceptible to complex, post-hypnotic hallucinations. Acts or ideas can be suggested to him during sleep which he executes or formulates upon waking in the belief that they are due to his own intellectual initiative. I will mention only the following suggestion which is interesting from a psychological point of view. Having hypnotized him, I saw a manual of chemistry at the head of his bed. "There is a chemistry," I said; "when you wake the idea will occur to you to read the chapter on gold. You will look for it in the table of contents. You will read this chapter, then you will say to me, 'Gold! if I had any I would give you a great deal to thank you for your pains! Unfortunately, I have none at all. We do not make money in the merchant marine, nor in the railroad service'; this idea will come to you while you are reading."

Half an hour afterward I waked him, went away and watched from a distance. I saw him look for his spectacle case, take out his glasses, put them on, take up the book, turn over the pages for at least five minutes and finally find a place and begin to read. I came up; it was the chapter on gold. "Why do you read this article," I asked.—"It is an idea," he answered, and kept on reading: After a few minutes he looked at me and said, "Gold! If I had any I would repay you well, but I have none." He turned to his reading again and after a while added, "Railroad Companies do not enrich their employees." Then he went on with his reading in a natural way. He would have been greatly astonished to learn that the idea he expressed had been introduced into his mind by me.

X—— is an accountant, forty-seven years old, intelligent and well-balanced. He is troubled with writer's cramp, but is naturally vigorous. The therapeutic observations on the case will be given later. The first time I hypnotized him, he went into a sleep of the third degree, that is, suggestive catalepsy and automatic movements were induced, and he retained memory upon waking. There was doubt in his mind as is the case with all subjects who remember upon waking. He did not know whether he had actually slept, and asked me if he had been obliged to hold his arm up. He believed he had done so in order to please me. He had undoubtedly been influenced, however, because at the séance following, I put him into a deep sleep with loss of memory on waking. Then, only, was he conscious of having slept.

On one occasion during his sleep, I suggested the following act. "When you wake you will go to my office, and you will write on a sheet of paper, 'I have slept very well,' and you will place a cross after your name."

I waked him in a quarter of an hour. He went to the office, wrote the phrase I had put into his mind, signed it and made a cross after his name. "What does this cross mean," I asked;— "Why!" he replied, "upon my word, I do not know; I made it without thinking." The next day I made him write another sentence with two crosses after his name, the day after, his name with a star after it. On the following day, I suggested to him while he was asleep, "When you wake up, you will write, 'I will go to M. Liébault while you are away,' and you will sign it, but you will make a mistake. Instead of signing your name H—— you will sign mine, Bernheim, then you will see you have made a mistake, and you will rub out mine and put yours instead." This he did when he woke up, and seemed very much puzzled by his error. He made excuses to me but did not suspect that the responsibility of the mistake did not rest with him, and that I had suggested it.

I repeat that he is an intelligent man and is neither hysterical nor nervous. His imagination is calm and his mind is well balanced. I insist upon this, because certain people who are not sufficiently enlightened upon this subject, persist in stating that only those of a neurotic temperament are susceptible of being put into the somnambulistic condition.

"The manner in which suggestions manifest themselves in the subjects," says M. Beaunis, "gives valuable information as to the state of the will in somnambulism." From a psychological stand-point, there is nothing more curious than to trace the dawning and development of the suggested idea in the faces of the subjects. For example, we are in the midst of a light conversation which has nothing to do with the suggestion. All at once the hypnotizer, who is alert, and watching his subject without appearing to do so, seizes upon a given indication, a sort of thought-interruption, an interior shock, which manifests itself by an almost imperceptible sign, a look, a gesture, a wrinkle in the face; then the conversation goes on, but the idea again comes to the front, though still weak and indecisive. There is a little surprise in the look. We feel that something unexpected comes across the mind, now and then, like a flash. The idea soon increases in strength, little by little. It takes more and more hold upon the intelligence, the struggle has begun; the eyes, the gestures, all speak, all reveal, the internal combat. The subject still listens to the conversation but in a vague sort of way, mechanically; his mind is elsewhere. All his being is a prey to a fixed idea which forces itself more and more strongly into his mind. The time has come; all hesitation vanishes, the face wears a remarkable expression of resolution and the subject gets up and performs the act suggested.

"This internal struggle is more or less lasting, more or less energetic, according to the nature of the act suggested, and above all according to the condition of the somnambulist. When the subject has been hypnotized often, and especially by the same person, this person obtains such an influence over him that the most eccentric, the most grievous and even the most dangerous acts are performed without any appreciable endeavor to resist." I cannot but agree with these observations of my colleague.

The effect of the suggestion of post-hypnotic acts is not absolutely inevitable. Some patients resist them. The desire to carry out the act no doubt is more or less imperative, but they resist it to a certain extent.

I give some examples of more or less complete resistance.

In the following cases the struggle and hesitation before obeying the idea were manifested in the patient until the suggestion finally got the upper hand.

A young hysterical girl was brought to the Medical Society at Nancy by M. Dumont. She was hypnotized and was ordered, when she woke, to take the glass cylinder off the gas burner over the table, and put it in her pocket and take it away when she went. After she was waked, she turned timidly toward the table, and seemed confused to find everyone looking at her. Then after some hesitation, she climbed upon her knees on the table. She kneeled there about two minutes, apparently ashamed of her position, looked alternately at the people around her and at the object which she had to carry away, put out her hand, and then drew it back. Then, suddenly taking off the cylinder, she put it in her pocket and hurried away. She would not consent to give it up until she had left the room.

In the case of A—— I suggested that after waking he should walk around the room three times; he only did it once.

HYPNOSIS AND SUGGESTION

I suggested to young G—— that upon waking, he should stand upon the table. When he woke up he looked hard at the table but did not get upon it. He doubtless wished to do so, but regard for the people around gave him strength to resist the desire.

Upon one occasion, I suggested to A—— that when he woke he would see a silver spoon on a chair behind him, and that he would put it in his pocket. He did not turn around after being waked and did not see the spoon, but there was a watch on a table in front of him. I had besides suggested to him the negative hallucination that he would see no one in the room and would find himself all alone, and this came true. The idea of the suggested theft of the spoon came into his mind in relation to the watch. He looked at it, touched it, then said, "No, that would be stealing," and left it alone. If the suggestion of stealing the spoon had been repeated forcibly and imperatively I have no doubt that he would have executed it.

Since this was written I have had occasion to hypnotize S—— again. I suggested the same thing more imperatively. "You will put the spoon in your pocket, you cannot do otherwise." Upon waking he saw the spoon, hesitated an instant, then said, " Heavens, this is worse yet!" and put it in his pocket.

A young hysterical girl in my service is susceptible to post-hypnotic suggestions, illusions, and hallucinations during the hypnotic sleep. For example, I say, "When you wake up, you will walk around the room twice, or you will read prayers out of this book." She wakes up and sometimes obeys, but often pays no attention to the suggestion. The idea of doing so and so is probably in her head but she resists it, either from a spirit of opposition, or from false modesty. I say to her, "I know what you are thinking about; you want to read a prayer or walk around the room." She seems perfectly astonished that I can guess her secret thoughts and believes that I can read her mind.

It is strange that suggested actions may be carried out not only during the time immediately following the sleep but after a greater or less interval. If a somnambulist is made to promise during his sleep that he will come back on such and such a day, at such and such an hour, he will almost surely return on the day and at the hour, although he has no remembrance of his promise when he wakes up. I made A—— say that he would come back to me in thirteen days at ten o'clock in the morning.

He remembered nothing when he waked. On the thirteenth day at ten o'clock in the morning he appeared, having come three kilometres from his house to the hospital. He had been working in the foundries all night, went to bed at six in the morning and woke up at nine, with the idea that he had to come to the hospital to see me. He told me that he had had no such idea on the preceding days and did not know that he had to come to see me. It came into his head just at the time when he ought to carry it out.

Thus, a suggestion given during sleep may lie dormant in the brain, and not come to consciousness until the time previously fixed upon for its appearance. Further research is necessary to explain this curious psychological fact, and to determine how long a hypnotic suggestion may thus remain latent. It goes without saying that all somnambulists are not susceptible to suggestions which take effect after a long interval of time.

I have spoken of suggestions which give rise to acts. I proceed to consider sensitivo-sensorial suggestions. Illusions of the senses and of sensation may be suggested in the majority of somnambulistic cases. I say, "When you wake, you will experience a numbness in your foot or a cramp in the calf of your leg, a sharp pain in a tooth, or an itching of the scalp." These different sensations appear in all or almost all cases of deep sleep. A patient with aortic insufficiency to whom I had suggested itching of the head, scratched himself violently, not knowing how he had got all this vermin during his sleep. A consumptive in whom I induced the same sensation took a comb and drew it quickly through his hair from behind forwards to get rid of the imaginary louse.

The most diverse sensations may be vividly realized after waking; for example, thirst, so great that several glasses of water are taken, one after the other; hunger, with the necessity of eating something immediately; the need of micturition or of defecation. Without knowing why, one subject feels a tickling in his nose and sneezes five or six times in succession. Another yawns several times simply through hypnotic suggestion. Another will see everything as though colored green for several minutes, etc. In a word all sensorial illusions commanded during sleep are realized upon waking by many persons who sleep profoundly.

The following experiment, which I have several times repeated, shows that the suggestion is active during sleep and creates the sensorial image suggested. It is not the spoken word, but the idea conveyed by this word which is retained in the mind. In the case of a very intelligent quiet man of high social position, I gave the following suggestion after hypnotization. " When you wake, you will be conscious of a very strong odor of cologne ; I upset a bottle of it on your clothes." When I had waked him, he sniffed several times and said to me, " There is an odor about you."

"What odor?" I asked. "I do not smell anything, I have a cold in my head."

"It is like vinegar," he said; "did you not upset a bottle of vinegar in the fire?"

I replied, "No, there is no odor; it is a suggestion I gave you during your sleep, but it was not of vinegar. Try to think what it was."

"I am at a loss to say what it is; it is like vinegar."

"It is cologne."

"It is really something like that, but I should not have recognized cologne."

"Now, that you know it is a suggestion and not a reality, do you still smell it?"

He put his hand to his nose, and replied, "It is strange, I still smell it distinctly."

Thus the word cologne had not been retained. The olfactory image suggested was not very accurate in the patient's mind, as he was not accustomed to using cologne frequently. It was a similar odor, reminding him vaguely of vinegar, that the olfactory centre had evoked.

In support of this idea we cite the following fact. During the artificial sleep I said to a patient in my service, who had a cardiac affection, " Upon waking you will take the book which is lying on the table near your bed, open it at page 56 and you will find your portrait there, very well executed."

When he woke I saw him take the book. "What are you looking for?" I asked.

"A story I began; I think I left off at page 56."

"Are you looking for some particular thing on this page?"

" No, only a continuation of the story."

He looked for the page and when he found it seemed astonished. "Why, what is that? It is a portrait." He looked at it for several moments and only then recognized himself. "It is I!" He did not know when he was looking for the page that he would find his portrait, and he did not recognize the portrait as his own, immediately.

The hallucination thus provoked may be as vivid as reality. The patient cannot rid himself of it even though he may know that it is an hallucination. This may be observed in experimenting on very intelligent people. I recently hypnotized a remarkably intelligent young girl, with a positive mind, who was not in the least flighty and whose good faith I can guarantee. I made her see an imaginary rose when she waked up. She saw it, touched it, and smelt it. She described it to me. Then, knowing that I might have given a suggestion, she asked me if the rose was real or imaginary. "It is perfectly impossible for me to tell the difference," she said. I told her that it was imaginary. She was convinced of this, and in spite of it was certain that by no effort of the will could she make it disappear.

"I still see it," she said, "and touch it as distinctly as if it were real, and if you should put a true rose in its place, or by it, I should not know how to distinguish them."

I made her see it for ten minutes. She moved it, changed its place, etc. She was wide-awake, and talked coolly about the phenomenon. Then I said to her, "Look at it for the last time, it is going to vanish." Then she saw it grow less distinct, fade, and vanish insensibly.

Other subjects do not realize these sensorial images so well, for they are less vivid, less distinct. The hallucination is incomplete and sometimes obscure; in following séances, it is better marked. Others, who are less sensitive to suggestion, remember when they wake what they were expected to see, feel, and hear; what had been suggested to them,—music, for example,—but the hallucination is not evoked; they do not perceive it. I shall give examples of this farther on.

A few words more on this suggestion of simple or complex hallucinations. Deep somnambulism is often characterized by the possibility of inducing hallucinations upon waking, in which one or several of the senses take part. The following are examples.

I suggested to C——, during sleep, that upon waking, he would see M. S——, a colleague present, with only one side of his face shaved and with a big silver nose. After waking, his eyes fell by chance on my colleague and he burst out laughing. "So you have been betting," said he, "that you would allow only one side of your face to be shaved; and your nose! You have been to 'Les Invalides' have you?"

At another time, in a ward full of sick patients, I suggested that he would see a big dog in each bed, instead of a patient, and he was perfectly astonished upon waking to find himself in a hospital for dogs.

On one occasion, when he had been telling me that his proprietor's wife had abused him, I suggested that when he waked, he should see the husband come into the room and would remonstrate with him upon his wife's behavior, and that after spending five minutes in this way, he would go to sleep again spontaneously. As soon as he waked, he actually saw the proprietor, and going up to him he said, "Ah, good-day, M. H——, I am glad to meet you for I must tell you what is in my mind. Your wife is a bad woman, she struck me. Such things cannot continue; I will speak to the police, etc." After scolding vigorously in this way for a few minutes, he sat down again and went off to sleep.

I suggested to S——, in the presence of Dr. Christian, Physician-in-chief at the Charenton asylum, "When you wake you will go to your bed. You will meet a woman there who will hand you a basket of strawberries. You will thank her, shake hands, and then eat the strawberries." He was waked half an hour later, went to his bed and said, "Good day, madam, thank you very much." Then he shook hands. I came up and he showed me the imaginary basket of strawberries. "Where is the woman?" I asked. He replied, "She is gone. There she is, in the corridor." He pointed her out to me through the window which opens on the corridor." Then he ate the strawberries, one after the other, putting them daintily into his mouth, sucking them with pleasure, throwing away the stems and wiping his hands now and then, with an appearance of reality which it would have been difficult to counterfeit.

I have also made the same subject eat cherries or peaches or imaginary grapes, or when he has been constipated I have made him take an imaginary bottle of Seidlitz water. He takes the fictitious bottle, pours the water into an imaginary glass, drinks three or four glasses full, one after the other, making all the movements of swallowing. He finds it bitter, puts back the glass and several times during the day, four or five times sometimes, has a movement induced by this imaginary purgative. If the constipation is very great, however, the imagination is not sufficient to provoke the desired effect.

In Mme. G——, whose case I shall mention later, an intelligent, impressionable, but not at all hysterical woman, I induced the most complex post-hypnotic hallucinations, in which all the senses took part. I made her hear military music in the court-yard of the hospital. The soldiers came up-stairs and into the room. She saw a drum-major making *pirouettes* before her bed. A musician came up and spoke to her. He was intoxicated, and made unbecoming proposals to her. He wished to embrace her. She slapped him in the face twice, and called the sister and nurse, who ran up and put the drunken man out. This entire scene, suggested during sleep, developed itself before her, both spectator and actress, as vividly as reality. She had not been able to experience similar hallucinations before. She could not get rid of this one. She looked around and asked the other patients if they had not seen and heard what was going on. She could not distinguish between the illusion and reality, When it was all over I said to her, "It was only a vision I gave to you." She understood perfectly that it was a vision, but insisted that it was more than a dream and that it was as vivid as reality.

Another case was that of a young girl. I made her see a ring on her finger or a bracelet on her arm upon awaking, or I gave her a handsome fan, ornamented with the portraits of people she knew. She was very happy over the gift, but after three or four minutes the object disappeared from her mind, and since the experiment taught her the evanescent character of these presents, she has begged me each time to leave them with her, and not take them away.

With others, these hallucinations last much longer. I made Mme. L—— see the portrait of her husband upon waking. She saw it even the next day, knowing very well that the portrait did not exist. On another occasion I said to her, "Upon waking you will see Mme. E—— sitting in that chair." (Mme. R—— was sitting in the chair.) When she awoke, she saw Mme. E—— and spoke to the person supposed to be she.

After a conversation of ten minutes, I said, "But you are mistaken, it is not Mme. E—— but Mme. R—— who is before you." She was convinced, then, that it was Mme. R——. She knew that it was a sensorial illusion and nevertheless could not throw it off. As the illusion lasted, it was disagreeable to her. According to her request, I again hypnotized her at the end of half an hour in order to restore Mme. R—— her own features.

These suggestions of hallucinations, examples of which I could give ad infinitum, cannot be induced in all cases of somnambulism.

I assured A—— that when he woke he would see a dog in his bed and would pet it. After waking, he looked under the down spread without finding anything, saying that he thought he had dreamed that a dog was in his bed.

In another case I said, "Upon waking you will see that I have a bad nose-bleed." After waking, he looked at me and said, "you ought to be having a bad nose-bleed." He did not see any blood, the idea of a nose-bleed—remained (alone) in his mind.

Thus, among somnambulists, some obey the suggestions of acts, others are at the same time susceptible to more or less perfect sensitivo-sensorial illusions. These subjects may be affected by itching, or by pain, that is by illusions of tactile sensibility, but not by sensorial illusions. The experiment, for example, of making such patients eat salt in place of sugar during their sleep, and making them keep the taste of sugar in their mouths, does not succeed at all. Upon waking, they perceive the taste of salt and not that of sugar. They cannot be made to see objects red or yellow. The sensorial illusion does not succeed any better than the hallucination.

In others, suggestions of acts, of sensitivo-sensorial illusions, and hallucinations, all succeed. Moreover, the same subject, who, in the first séances rebels against sensorial illusions and hallucinations, may perfect himself by practice so that at the end of many séances, he can realize all the hallucinatory conceptions which are suggested to his mind.

In certain cases, a negative hallucination may be suggested during sleep. This succeeds only in cases of deep somnambulism. One day when I was with Dr. Liébault, he suggested to a hypnotized woman (not a hysterical case), that when she woke, she would no longer see me, that I would have gone, and forgotten my hat. Before going away, she would take my hat, put it on her head and take it to me at my house.

When she woke, I stood in front of her. She was asked, "Where is Dr. Bernheim?" and she replied, "He has gone. Here is his hat." I said, "Here I am, madam, I have not gone, you recognize me perfectly." She did not answer. In five minutes, having allowed the first impression to vanish, I sat down by her side and asked her, "Have you been coming to M. Liébault for a long time?" She remained silent, as if she neither saw nor heard me. Some one else asked her the same question. She replied immediately, "For fifteen days." Then I continued, "And you feel better, madam, don't you, after this treatment?" The same silence, but again a reply to the next person. I held my hands before her eyes for two minutes. She did not wink or frown. I did not exist as far as she was concerned. Finally, when about to go, she took my hat, put it on, and departed. M. Liébault went out after her into the street and asked for the hat, saying that he would take it to me himself.

I have repeated this experiment relative to negative hallucination, successfully, upon many of my somnambulistic cases.

I will mention an instance. In the case of a lady, G——, in my service, I suggested, in the presence of two ladies who had come from the town to visit the hospital, that when she waked up she would no longer see nor hear me. I would be no longer there. When she waked, she looked for me. I showed myself in vain. I whispered in her ear that I was there, and pinched her hand, which she drew back suddenly without discovering the origin of the sensation. The ladies present told her that I was there and that I had spoken to her. She did not see me and thought the ladies wanted to make fun of her. This negative illusion, which I had induced in her in other séances, but which had lasted from five to ten minutes only, continued this time all the while I remained with her,—more than twenty minutes.

One of the two ladies present was hysterical. I treated her for hysterical aphonia by hypnotism. She was susceptible both to hypnotic and post-hypnotic hallucinations. The day after the scene at which she had been present, at my request, I put her into a somnambulistic condition and said to her, "You know that when you wake you will see me no longer." She began to smile. "You laugh," I said, "because you remember the woman here yesterday, who did not see me when she woke. Well, it will be the same with you, only you will not see me, for I shall have really gone. As soon as I wake you, I shall go away and remain absent ten minutes. You will see me come in again at the opposite door." When I had waked her, she looked for me in vain, and seemed much put out at not finding me. "I am here," I said, "you see me perfectly well; I am touching you, I am tickling your forehead." She did not move. "You are making fun of me," I added : "you are playing a game, you cannot help laughing, you are going to burst out laughing." She did not frown. As she showed displeasure, I told the people present to assure her that I had been called away hastily to a patient in the neighborhood. She continued to be in a bad humor and went to sleep again spontaneously. Exactly at the end of ten minutes, she reopened her eyes, looked towards the door as if she saw me enter, bowed to me, appeared glad to see me again, and attributed her discontent to the fear she had had of a nervous crisis produced by the waking up without my influence. I then confessed to her that I had been present, but that I had given her a negative suggestion, like the one she had witnessed the day before in another case. She assured me that she had neither seen nor heard me. The disguise of my presence had been perfect.

The expression, negative hallucination, which we use at Nancy for this phenomenon, has been criticised by MM. Binet and Féré. "This name is singularly badly chosen," say these authors, "because it has nothing to do with hallucinations. The nature of this sensory trouble can be well understood only by comparing it to systematic paralysis of movement. For the eye as well as for the arm it is a question of a phenomenon of inhibition, which produces systematic paralysis." (*Revue Philosophique*, Jan. 1885.)

It seems to me that my esteemed opponents deserve the reproach which they have cast upon me, of having imperfectly grasped the nature and the signification of the phenomenon.

When I make a hypnotized subject see a person or a thing which is not before his eyes, by means of a suggestion given in the hypnotic or in the waking condition, I have created an image called forth by his mind; I have caused a visual hallucination.

If in the same subject and by the same method I have made invisible a person or a thing which is before his eyes, I have not produced a paralysis of the eye. The patient sees all the objects excepting only the one which has been suggested to him as invisible. I have obliterated a sensorial image from his mind. I have neutralized or rendered negative, the perception of this image. I call such a phenomenon, a negative hallucination.

In both cases, the psychical or psycho-sensorial phenomenon is of the same order. In both cases, I have called forth a hallucination.

Besides, in all the complex hallucinations, such as are artificially realized and spontaneously developed, the two phenomena co-exist: a lunatic believes himself in prison, sees his cell, the jailer, the chain which binds him. These are sensorial perceptions created in his brain. On the other hand, he does not see the real objects before him. He neither sees nor hears the people about him. These are real sensorial perceptions effaced.

Will anyone say, that of these two orders of phenomena, the first alone constitutes hallucination, and not the second? For an illegitimate but authorized use of a word which exists in our language (examples: negative pressure, negative value, negative quantity, etc.), the expression, negative hallucination, seems to me perfectly well chosen to express the psychical mechanism of the phenomenon connected with that which causes positive hallucination.

I have shown elsewhere, that suggestive amaurosis as well as hysterical amaurosis is not a systematic paralysis but a purely psychical amaurosis; a neutralization of the object perceived by the imagination. It is a negative hallucination. This amaurosis has no organic substratum, no anatomical localization. The subject sees by means of his retina and by means of his brain. The first receives the impression; the second, by means of the cortical visual centre, perceives it. But the subjects who are amaurotic by suggestion, or who are hysterical, unconsciously neutralize this visual image by their imagination. *Oculos habent et non vident.* They see with their material eyes, they do not see with their minds' eyes. The amaurosis is only a negative illusion.

I have remarked that of the subjects to whom I had suggested during sleep an inability to see me upon waking, some appeared not to see me at all, but others began by looking at me, as if the memory of the suggested idea no longer existed; then the memory being revived, their expression changed suddenly and they become inert as far as I was concerned. I had disappeared; they no longer saw me, and, later on, when the effect of the suggestion had worn off, they believed and assured me that they had not seen me even immediately after waking.

My *chef de clinique*, M. Ganzinotty, wished to experiment in order to determine whether this suggested unilateral amaurosis was real or feigned. He made use of Stoeber's apparatus (of which I shall speak later), which is intended to baffle any attempt at deception. He stated that the indications given by the patient were false. He was inclined to believe there was simulation. I explained to him, that as the amaurosis was purely psychical, that is, imaginary, it could not obey optical laws.

Later on, I was able to demonstrate the matter experimentally, in regard to the unilateral amaurosis of hysteria, which acts exactly like suggested amaurosis. The following is an observation which I have made upon a large number of hysterical cases in my service. The patients had complete sensitivo-sensorial hemi-anæsthesia of one side, let us say the left side, including a complete amaurosis on this side.

Now, the right eye being closed, after having proved that the patients see nothing with the left, and are totally blind, it is easy to assure one's self that this blindness is purely psychical. For this purpose, I use Dr. Stoeber's apparatus, a modification of Snellen's, which thwarts any simulation of amaurosis. A pair of spectacles in which one glass is red and the other green, is put on the patient's nose, and he is made to read six letters on a black frame, alternately covered by squares of red and green glass. Looking at them with both eyes open, all six letters can be read. Looking at them with one eye only, the other being closed, only three can be read: those covered by the glass corresponding in color to the spectacle glass through which the eye is looking; the letters covered by red glass if the eye is looking through the red glass in the spectacle, and green letters if the eye is on the side of the green glass. This occurs because green and red mixed make black. If we look at green through red, we see black.

This granted, our hysterical patients looking at the six letters through the spectacles, read them all without hesitating a moment. They read those which they were supposed not to see, therefore they must have seen with the left eye without knowing it. If the left eye was then closed they only saw three letters.

Another most simple experiment confirms this fact. We know that if a prism is held before the eye, the corresponding image is refracted and thus diplopia is produced. If the other eye is closed and there is no diplopia, the object is seen single and not double.

Hysterical patients with unilateral amaurosis should only see one image through the prism. Now, they saw two without any difficulty, hence, the amaurotic eye could see. Hysterical and suggestive achromatopsia are psychical, like amaurosis. The following is an experiment we owe to Dr. Parinaud. It was reported in M. Grenier's inaugural thesis. (*Des localisations dans les maladies nerveuses*, 1886.) For example, let us take the case of a hysterical patient with achromatopsia of the left eye. When looked at by this eye a square of green paper is gray, and when looked at by the other eye, green; each eye being alternately closed. If a prism is placed base upwards in front of the normal eye, and both eyes are opened, the patient will see two squares of paper and will see them, not one green and the other gray, but both green; that is to say, under these circumstances the achromatopic eye sees the color. If on the other hand, the prism is held before the achromatopic eye, the majority of patients will see both squares gray; both eyes will have ceased to see the color.

The author explains this fact on the hypothesis that the retina puts itself into relationship with the opposite hemisphere, in the vision of each eye separately, but that in binocular vision both eyes can put themselves into relationship with one or the other hemisphere, an hypothesis which has no basis either in experimental or anatomical data.

It is a question of a purely psychical phenomenon, that is, one in which the patient's imagination does all the work. If I put a green-colored cardboard before the normal eye of the subject and make him look at this cardboard through a prism, instead of seeing a gray image (given by the supposed achromatopic eye) and a green image (given by the normal eye) he will see two green images without any hesitation. This seems to prove,

the   age given by the left eye is
gr   a is purely psychical. If I
h   omatopic eye and make the
                                 instead of seeing a gray card
                                 ic eye), and a green card (image
                                 es both images gray.
                                 nows that the left eye sees objects
                                 so), because he is aware that the
                                 because he does not know that one
                                 by the other eye and thinks that the
                                 eye doubles the object seen by that
                                 and unconsciously, he thus suggests to
                                 iromatopic eye sees things gray, and as
                                 doubled by the prism, both images ought
to b.

In a thi.   cal case in my service, I have been able to confirm my interp. :tation, and to conclude that the whole phenomenon is subordinate to the imagination. The patient's left eye was achromatopic. A red object appeared gray to this eye, while to the right eye, it retained its red color.

I made her look through the prism with both eyes open. She saw the object double. I closed the left achromatopic eye and made her look through the prism with the right eye. She saw a single red object, which is exact, and agrees with optical laws.

On the other hand, if the right eye was closed and a red or green object placed before the left achromatopic eye, she saw it gray. If I then put a prism before the eye, instead of seeing a single gray object, she saw it doubled and in its own color.

The prism had re-established the true color in spite of all laws of physics and physiology. It had effaced the illusion by hindering the play of the diseased imagination. It is, then, solely a question of phenomena of unconscious auto-suggestion.

I have, then, demonstrated that suggestive and hysterical amaurosis and achromatopsia do not exist as so many organic material troubles. The phenomena are due to a mind illusion. The blindness of hysterical patients is a psychical blindness.

In my opinion, neuro-pathologists have wrongly given the name of psychical blindness, mind-blindness (*seelen blindheit* of the Germans), to the trouble constituted by the preservation of sight with loss of visual memory. The patient sees, but he no longer knows what he sees. He has lost the memory of what the objects seen signify. I propose to give this trouble the name of visual amnesia, and to reserve the name psychical blindness, for the blindness which I have just described. Psychical blindness is the blindness which comes through imagination. It is due to the destruction of the image by a psychical agency.

I add, further, that in all my hysterical cases, the symptoms of psychical amblyopia and achromatopsia disappear almost instantly upon hypnotic suggestion.

To conclude; hysterical and suggestive amaurosis have no anatomical localization. Their seat is not in the retina, nor in the optic nerve, nor in the cortical centre for vision. They are real, but exist only in the patient's imagination.

It is doubtless the same in regard to the other suggestive anæsthesias. This is easily shown in the case of deafness. I say to a somnambulist who has been hypnotized, " When you wake you will not see me ; you will not hear me ; you will be deaf and blind." I wake him; I speak to him, and whisper in his ear. He does not show any signs of understanding; his face remains inert. If I then say to him decidedly, perhaps once or several times, " You again hear," his face shows great astonishment ; he hears and answers me. It is in vain that I say, " You must have heard me all the time, since your pretended deafness vanished when I assured you that you again heard me." He is convinced that he has heard nothing, and does not know how his hearing came back. I repeat the experiment, each time with the same result. A person who is really simulating does not allow himself to be played with, with so much ingenuousness ; the patient deaf by suggestion hears, as the patient who is blind by suggestion sees, but each instant he neutralizes the impression perceived by his imagination, and makes himself believe that he has not heard.

I shall speak of another variety of hallucinations in Chapter IX., which I shall call retroactive hallucinations, and I shall lay particular stress upon this important question.

Sensorial and hallucinatory illusions, like suggestions of acts may be ordered to be carried out after a long interval of time. In Mme. G——'s case, of which I have spoken, I suggested that in five days, at the time of the visit, she would have a headache, which occurred. On another occasion, I said to her, " Next Thursday night " (six days) "you will see the nurse approach your bed, and she will upset a pail of water over your feet." The following Friday, at the time of the visit, she complained bitterly that the nurse had thrown water over her legs in the night. I called the nurse, who naturally denied it. The sister knew nothing about it. I said to the patient, "It is only a dream; Marie has done nothing to you. You know very well that I give you dreams." She asserted that it was not a dream, but that she had seen with her eyes, that she had felt the water, that she had been wet.

In some cases, suggestive phenomena are obtained at the end of a still longer interval. The following are two examples.

On Saturday, December 22, 1883, after hypnotizing Mme. G——, I suggested, "Three weeks from the coming Tuesday" (twenty-five days), "when I pass your bed on my morning rounds, you will see my colleague, M. V. P., with me. He will ask you how you are. You will give him the details of your sickness, and you will converse with him upon topics which interest you." When she woke, she remembered nothing. I never made the slightest allusion to this suggestion before her, and I had not told any of my pupils of it. During the interval she was hypnotized several times. Other suggestions were given. Her photograph was taken in different hypnotic attitudes. Tuesday, January 15, during my rounds, I stopped as usual, in a casual manner, at her bed. She looked to her left and bowed respectfully. "Ah, M. V. P." In a few minutes she replied, to an imaginary question, "I am much better; I have no more pain; unfortunately, my knee is still dislocated, and I cannot walk without support." She listened to another question from the imaginary speaker, then replied, "Thank you very much; you know that I nursed the children of M. B., the Mayor's assistant, your colleague. If you could speak to him of me, he might help in getting me into an hospital for the infirm." She listened again, then thanking him, bowed, and followed the image of my colleague to the door, with her eyes. I said, "Did you know that M. V. P. would come to see you to-day?" "No," she said. She assured me that she had had no idea, no presentiment of this visit. This, then, is a complex hallucination realized twenty-three days after suggestion.

I will relate the case of an old sergeant, S——, a somnambulist, to whom I said, during his sleep, in August, 1883, "What day in the first week in October shall you be free?" He replied

"Wednesday." "Well, then, listen carefully: the first Wednesday in October, you will go to Dr. Liébault" (who sent me this case) "and you will there see the President of the Republic, who will give you a medal and a pension." "I will go," he answered. I did not speak to him of it again. Upon waking he remembered nothing. I saw him several times in the interval, and gave him other suggestions, but never recalled the first to his memory. On October 3d (sixty-three days after the suggestion), I received the following letter from Dr. Liébault: "The somnambulist, S——, came here to-day at ten minutes of one. He greeted M. F——, who met him as he came in, and then went toward the left side of my library without paying attention to any one, and I saw him bow respectfully, and heard him speak the word 'Excellence.' As he spoke quite low, I went near him immediately. Just then he held out his right hand, and said, 'Thank your Excellence.' Then I asked him to whom he was speaking. 'Why, to the President of the Republic,' he said. I noticed there was no one near him. Finally, he turned away, bowed, and came toward M. F. A few moments after his departure, the witnesses of this strange scene naturally asked me about this fool,—as they thought him. My reply was that he was no fool, but was as reasonable as they or I. Another was acting through him."

I add that when I saw S—— again, several days later, he assured me that the idea of going to M. Liébault had come to him suddenly on October 3d, at ten o'clock in the morning; that he did not know on the preceding days that he had to go, and that he had no idea of the meeting which had taken place.

However singular, however inexplicable, may be these suggestive phenomena, which are realized after a long interval at a moment assigned in advance, and which are elaborated, or thought out by the mind, unknown to the subject himself, I do not hesitate to relate them. I should have hesitated in the presence of one isolated fact, but I have reproduced them so many times in different somnambulists, that I have not the least doubt of their reality. The interpretation of them belongs to the domain of psychology. I shall attempt it in a subsequent chapter.

CHAPTER III

Observations on different types of somnambulism.—Double personality in certain somnambulists.—Spontaneous dreams with or without preservation of the sense of reality.

WE have seen that the majority of people may, to some extent, be influenced by hypnotism, but that all cannot be put into deep sleep or somnambulism. In a report given me by M. Liébault prepared from a list of 2534 subjects whom he hypnotized, there were 385 somnambulists, that is 15.19 per cent. or one in 6.58. Some examples of induced somnambulism are here appended.

Observation 1.—M. S——, age, 40, pasteboard maker (the therapeutical observation upon whose case I shall give later), is a small, well-built man of mixed temperament, dull intelligence and slight cultivation, but well-balanced and without any nervous history, and who, about a year after a fracture of the vertebral column which was followed by cerebral disturbance, had paresis of the lower limbs and epileptiform attacks of which he was cured a few months ago. (Sept. 1883.) (See ob. 3).

For several weeks, I was only able to induce the third degree of hypnotism. Then he fell into a deep sleep. I can now put him to sleep in a second by a mere command. I command him to sleep deeply and he remains motionless in the position in which I place him. In the first séances he awoke spontaneously. At the present time, he keeps on sleeping indefinitely if I do not wake him. Once, I let him sleep for sixteen consecutive hours. I can put him into a complete or partial cataleptic condition by suggestion, and can keep his arms and legs up-raised as long as I wish, perfectly rigid and without fatigue. I can induce trismus or the forced separation of the jaws. I can keep the head bent over on the chest or inclined to one side in an irresistible contracture.

He answers all questions quickly, but like my other somnambulistic cases, shows no mental lucidity, not even the intellectual exaltation which is noticeable in some instances.

At my command he gets up, walks about the room, goes back to his chair or bed with his eyes shut, groping in the darkness. I tell him that he cannot walk any further and he remains as if nailed to the spot. I tell him that he can only walk backwards, and though he makes efforts to advance, he walks backwards.

Sensibility is totally destroyed. A pin may be drawn over his skin without causing the slightest reaction. His nostrils and the back part of his throat may be tickled, his conjunctiva may be touched and even electricity may be applied, but he does not react.

I can induce illusions of the senses. I make him drink water for wine and swallow salt for sugar. He sucks the salt and thinks it very sweet. This sensorial suggestion, however, does not always succeed perfectly. Sometimes he thinks the salt is a little salty as well as sweet.

I suggest acts to him. He dances, doubles up his fist, and at my command, searches the pockets of a person whom I point out, takes out what he finds, hides it in his bed and half an hour afterwards, still acting as I order him, looks for it again and replaces it, making excuses to the person robbed.

He accepts all the illusions and hallucinations which I suggest, whether they are to be realized immediately during his sleep or after waking up. Several post-hypnotic actions and hallucinations relating to his case have already been mentioned. I tell him his forehead itches, and he lifts his hand to scratch it.

I can make him see a cat jump up on his lap. He pets it and imagines that it scratches him, etc.

I wake him instantly by saying, "It is over." Sometimes he has no recollection of what he has done, said, and heard during the sleep. This is particularly the case, when I have said to him in sleep, "When you wake you will remember absolutely nothing." On the other hand when I have not taken the precaution of saying this to him he remembers everything he has done; he has swallowed sugar (it was salt), he has been walking, etc. One day, I made him dance with an imaginary partner, and drink imaginary beer; then I made him see the nurse on duty. The next day, the nurse told me that the patient was irrational, that he was telling everyone he had been to a ball the evening before, that I had offered him supper, and that he had met the nurse. The dream suggested in his sleep had been realized so vividly in his imagination, that upon waking, the recollection of it forced itself upon his mind as a reality.

Finally this subject is remarkable because of the facility with which the most diverse suggestions may be developed in the waking condition. We shall soon return to this most interesting part of his case.

Observation 2.—The second somnambulist whose history I wish to trace briefly, is a photographer, forty-four years of age, a native of Bordeaux and sent to me by M. Liébault.

He is thin, has a pained expression, protruding eyes, and appears to be in a precarious condition. He has three children, aged respectively, eighteen, nineteen, and twenty-one years, and lives apart from his wife on account of domestic unhappiness into which I did not care to inquire.

He has had no previous illness, and there is no venereal history. He says, that when he got up one morning, about ten years ago, he suddenly became aware of a peculiarity in his gait, characterized by a tendency to propulsion or impulsion forward. The phenomenon became progressively more marked. For five years he has walked irregularly, like a drunken man, stumbling to the right and left, so that the police have stopped him several times in the belief that he was drunk. C—— is however sober, and has committed no alcoholic excess. When he goes down-stairs, or when the weather is cold, the tendency to run forward, the irresistible propulsion, suddenly increases. He takes several hasty steps and then stops himself by swaying about. He has never had pains in his head, nor attacks of vomiting; but two years ago, and again about the first of last April, he suffered from vertigo, which came upon him like a thunderbolt, while he was walking, or when he got up. "It is like a feeling of intoxication," he says, "which only lasts a moment, about a quarter of a second." Since then this sensation of vertigo has disappeared rapidly in consequence of hypnotic suggestion. It also occasionally happens, especially in the evening, in a very brilliant light, that he is seized with diplopia, which lasts only an instant. He has passed water involuntarily five or six times in ten years. The last time was early in March.

He has never had seizures of any kind, and has never lost consciousness. Tactile and special sensibility are normal. The muscular force is preserved and the tendon reflexes are normal. The appetite, digestion, and other functions are not disturbed.

The intelligence is clear and memory good. C—— answers all questions clearly. He is naturally docile in disposition; his character is quiet and gentle, and he is simple and reserved in behavior. I believe that he has a tumor of the cerebellum.

C—— says that he has never been nervous. He sleeps well at night, remembers every act of his life and does not now seem to be subject to attacks of spontaneous somnambulism. Three years ago, however, he was in this condition on several different nights. This he proved by the fact that the next day he found his work finished without being able to remember having done it. Since then he has had nothing more of the kind.

He came to my *chef de clinique*, on March 20, after having been hypnotized many times by M. Liébault. I had only to put my two fingers before his eyes; in a few seconds he began to wink, his eyes closed, and he was hypnotized.

I lift his arms; he is in a condition of suggestive catalepsy. He is almost completely insensible, or becomes so if I assure him of the fact. He is pricked with a pin and does not react. I put him on the stool of an electric machine, and draw sparks from his body; he shows some reflex fibrillary contractions, but no pain. The nape of the neck and back of the head alone remain sensible. He admits that there is a painful sensation when the sparks are elicited from this region, and upon waking remembers that he felt some pain there.

In this somnambulistic state C—— is an accomplished automaton, obeying every suggestion and susceptible to all sensory or hallucinatory illusions.

I put him into complete or partial catalepsy. I paralyze one of his arms at will, and it falls motionless; or a leg, and he drags it as a hemiplegic patient would. I can induce movements by imitation. It suffices for me to stand before him, and rotate one arm about the other, clap my hands together, or separate them, put my fingers to my nose, or make any movement whatever with my legs, and he immediately imitates automatically every movement he sees, for he can open his eyes wide at the same time that he exhibits all these phenomena.

When I draw back from him and stretch out my hand, he follows me passively. He stops at my order. I suggest that he is fixed to the spot and cannot take another step, and he has to be pushed quite hard in order to be moved. I draw a line on the floor and tell him that he cannot pass it, and he struggles in vain to do so. I tell him that he cannot go forward any more, but only backward. He tries to advance, but can only move back.

Illusions can be induced instantaneously; I can produce uni- or bilateral blindness; he may be made to see with only one eye. A pin or a light held close to the other eye does not make him wink. It is a psychical or cerebral blindness; the pupil of the eye is not influenced by the suggestion; a light makes it contract, a suggestion of darkness does not make it dilate.

I can produce the various hallucinations of sight. I send him to sit in a chair where he finds an imaginary poodle; he touches it, is afraid it will bite him, and draws his hand away quickly. I make him pet a kitten. I evoke visions of people whom he has known. I show him his son, whom he has not seen for eight years. He recognizes him, and remains in a trance, his eyes fixed, a prey to the most lively emotions; tears flow from his eyes.

There are also distinct illusions of taste. I make him swallow a quantity of salt for sugar, and he finds it very sweet. I smear his tongue with sulphate of quinine, telling him that it is very sweet; but just before waking him up, I take care to assure him that the sweet taste will remain in his mouth. When he wakes, he perceives this taste. I put a pencil into his mouth, saying it is a cigar. He blows out puffs of imaginary smoke, and when I put the lighted end into his mouth, he feels it burn. I suggest that the cigar is too strong, and that he will feel badly. He is seized with coughing, is nauseated, spits, grows pale, and feels dizzy. I make him swallow a glass of water, pretending it is champagne. He thinks it is strong. If I make him take several glasses, he is drunk, and reels about. When I say, "Drunkenness brings gayety with it," he sings, and hiccoughs and laughs in a silly way. If I say "Drunkenness brings sadness with it," he weeps and laments. I make him sober again by holding imaginary ammonia under his nose; he draws back, contracting his nostrils and shutting his eyes as if suffocated by the odor. I make him sneeze several times successively by means of an imaginary pinch of snuff. All these sensations follow one after the other, rapidly and almost instantaneously. His brain accepts and perceives as soon as I express them. I can make him stutter. He cannot speak without stuttering. I send him to write my name on the board, suggesting that he can no longer write the consonants, he writes e-e; then that he cannot write the vowels, he writes b-r-n-m, etc.

In short, he carries out everything according to my command. I make him steal a watch out of some one's vest pocket. I make him follow me in order to sell it, and I take him to the Hospital Pharmacy, an imaginary pawn-shop. He sells it at the price offered, and follows me with all the appearance of a thief. On the way, I make him double up his fist at the nurse, and put his fingers up to his nose when he meets one of the sisters. He does all these things without any hesitation.

I provoked a truly dramatic scene one day, as I was anxious to see just how far the power of suggestion went with him. I showed him an imaginary person at the door and told him that he had been insulted by him. I gave him an imaginary dagger (a paper-cutter) and ordered him to kill the man. He hastened forward and ran the dagger resolutely into the door, and then stood staring with haggard eyes and trembling all over. "What have you done, unhappy man?" I said. "He is dead, he is bleeding, the police are coming." He stood terrified. He was led before an imaginary magistrate (my interne). "Why did you murder this man?" "He insulted me." "We do not kill the man who insults us. You must be complained of to the police. Did any one tell you to kill him?" He answers, "M. Bernheim did." I say to him,

"You are to be taken before the justice. You killed this man. I said nothing to you, you acted as your own master."

He was taken before my *chef de clinique*, who played the part of magistrate. "Why did you kill this man?" "He insulted me." "That is curious; one does not answer an insult by a dagger thrust. Were you in full possession of your faculties? They say that your mind is sometimes affected." "No, sir." "They say you are subject to attacks of somnambulism. Perhaps you had to obey some strange impulse under the influence of some one who could have forced you to act?' "No, sir, I acted from my own impulse because he insulted me." "Think, sir; it is a question of your life. Speak frankly in your own interest. How is it? Before the magistrate, you stated that the idea of killing this man was suggested to you by M. Bernheim." "No, sir, I acted entirely upon my own free will." "You know M. Bernheim well, you go to him at the hospital to be hypnotized." "I only know M. Bernheim, because I go to the hospital for treatment and he gives me electricity to cure my nervous trouble, but aside from this, I do not know him. I cannot tell you that he told me to kill this man because he has not told me anything." And the magistrate could not get the truth from him, because for him the truth was my last suggestion,—that he acted of his own free will. The significance of this experiment deserves thorough consideration from a psychological and medico-legal point of view.

When he awakened, or returned to his normal condition, C—— believed that he had been sleeping quietly in his chair, and had no remembrance of the drama in which he played the chief part. The terrible emotions which had seized him and the violent scenes called up before him, had left no imprint on his mind. He had been led about for hours in a somnambulistic condition, with his eyes open. He had been forced to do the strangest acts, and had done them resolutely. Finally, he had been led back to the place where he had been transformed into a somnambulist, and his true nature was restored to him. He remembered absolutely nothing of what had occurred in this automatic second life, which had been forced upon him by the will of another.

C—— is also a remarkable case on account of the facility with which hallucinations or post-hypnotic acts can be induced. Before he is actually asleep I suggest that when he wakes, he will see his portrait on the black-board. I do not wake him until an hour has passed, then he sees the portrait and thinks it a very good likeness. I suggest that he will see a big dog in each bed, and he is astonished at such a singular state of affairs. I suggest negative hallucinations; that upon waking for instance, he will not be able to see, hear, or feel any one but me, that everyone will have gone away and that I alone shall be with him when he wakes up. The assistants speak to him, touch him, give him his hat and cane, but he sees no one and answers no one. My honorable colleague, M. Victor Parisot, stops up his ears while I am talking to him, but he still hears and answers me. Of course, if I spoke in too low a voice, the mechanical obstruction of the ear would prevent his hearing. I take leave of him and one of my pupils brings him his hat. He appears not to see it, and does not take it, but goes to get it where he placed it. When I hold his hat, he takes it immediately and thanks me. The assistants make a circle around him just as he starts to go out. He walks directly against one of them, and stops before the obstacle without seeming to try to explain it. Some one stands in front of the door by which he is going out. He looks in vain for the knob and not finding it, thinks he has made a mistake, and goes to another door. Finally, we let him out. As soon as he is out of the room, he sees and recognizes everyone he meets.

In an interesting article published in the *Revue Philosophique*, in March, 1883, M. Charles Richet relates his observations upon somnambulistic cases, in which he has caused the patient to lose his feeling of personality by transferring it into another.

In C——'s case, nothing is easier than to induce illusions relative to his personality. I say to him, "You are six years old. You are a child. Go and play with the boys." He gets up, jumps about, makes a gesture as if taking marbles out of his pocket, arranges them properly, measures the distance with his hand, aims carefully, and runs to place them in order again. He keeps up his play indefinitely, with surprising activity, attention, and precision of detail. In the same way, he plays tag, and leap-frog, making jump after jump over one or two imaginary playfellows, increasing the distance each time, and with an ease which in the waking condition, would not be possible, because of his malady.

I say: "You are a young girl." He drops his head in a modest way, opens a drawer, takes out a piece of cloth and pretends to sew. Then he sits down in front of a table and begins to tap on it, as if he were playing the piano.

I say: "You are a general at the head of your army." He holds himself erect, and cries out: "Forward!" balancing his body as if he were on horseback.

I say: "You are a good and holy priest." He puts on a pious expression, walks to and fro reading his breviary, and makes the sign of the cross, as seriously as if it were all reality.

I can transfer him into an animal, by saying: "You are a dog." He gets down on all fours, barks, pretends to bite, and does not change his position, until I restore his own personality, or that of some one else, to him.

In all the alterations of personality, which are induced by suggestion, in many cases of somnambulism, the subject's own character is manifested. Each one plays his part with the qualities which are part of his personality, and with the aptitudes which belong to him.

C—— is naturally timid, and a poor talker. He speaks but little when acting the part suggested to him. When a personality beyond his power is suggested, he tries in vain to carry it out. On one occasion, I said to him: "You are a lawyer, you speak easily and fluently. The accused is before you; defend him. You are in court." He rises and begins: " The accused man whom I am to defend—" The rest does not come; he hesitates, and stops thoroughly confused; he hangs his head, and drops off to sleep again, as if exhausted by the impossible task set him.

Moreover, I have never seen the intellectual faculties exalted to an extraordinary degree, or new aptitudes suddenly created, by hypnotic suggestion, in any of my subjects, which is claimed by some to be the case. Doubtless, the concentration of the mind upon the suggested idea, may increase the natural sagacity, and develop a clairvoyance, limited to the sphere of the idea provoked, which may be greater than in the waking condition; but, up to the present time, I have never observed an intellectual phenomenon exceeding the normal in degree. I have not been able to make lawyers or preachers out of subjects not naturally endowed with the gift of eloquence.

I repeat the fact, that every somnambulist has his own individuality. Though an automaton, directed by a foreign will, he acts with his own machinery, and answers questions according to his own understanding.

Observation 3.—G——, a laundress, fifty-four years old, has locomotor-ataxia, with arthropathy of the left knee. She has attended our clinic since August, 1883. She is an excellent somnambulist, readily susceptible to suggestion, both in the waking and sleeping conditions. By simple affirmation, anæsthesia, paralysis, blindness, deafness, and complex hallucinations may be induced. Since the first trial of hypnotism in her case, there has been deep sleep, and the realization of all the hallucinations suggested. She has never had attacks of spontaneous somnambulism, crises of hysteria, nor any other nervous affections, except the lightning pains, and gastric disturbances caused by her tabetic trouble.

She understands any act which may be suggested, mimicks most expressively, and with astonishing correctness, and, like a true artist, identifies herself with the rôle forced upon her imagination.

The following is an instance of one of the hypnotic séances (April 14, 1886), the details of which were taken down *in short hand.*

"I am going to count up to six; when I count four, your eyes will close, and you will fall asleep." I count without looking at her. When I say four her eyes close, and she yawns and stretches several times. She is anæsthetic, and remains in suggestive catalepsy, retaining the rotatory movements communicated to her arms, etc.

"Well," I say, "here you are, as bright and gay as possible. When is your fête-day?"

"The 15th of August."

"To-day, the 15th of August, your fête-day!"

"Why, I did not know that it was to-day!"

"But you know very well that yesterday was the 14th."

"The time has gone very fast."

"See, it is fine weather; the sun is shining and the birds are twittering; you can smell the shrubs in bloom."

"Ah, yes!"

"Since it is your fête-day, perhaps you will drink some champagne. Here!"—She takes the imaginary glass and drinks, making all the movements of swallowing.

"It is very fiery," she says.

"You are lively after that!"

"Lively! Ah, yes! Ha, ha, ha! What am I doing! So small a glass to go to my head!"—She laughs and sings an air, and looks slightly inebriated.

"Every day is not a fête day, but one should not get as hilarious as that!"

She laughs. "There, hear the bells! I am so sleepy; champagne makes my head heavy!" She falls back on her pillow; her mind is excited by the imaginary wine.

I say: "Come, I will make you sober again. Here are some salts!" I put my hand under her nose; she draws back, contracting her nostrils, and snuffling vigorously. I hold the imaginary bottle under her nose again. She draws back again, pushes away my hand, coughs, and acts as if she were suffocating.

"You are stifling me!" she cries out.

I then give her the following suggestion for waking. "Two minutes after you wake, you will see a procession passing through the room, an altar and the holy sacrament. You will see Monseigneur, all the priests, and the sisters with the candles. You will join in singing the

Veni Creator. Then two nurses will come in, and you will hear them talking in an ill-behaved manner during the ceremony. When the procession has passed, you will go to sleep again. You will wake again in a minute, and your son, who is at Bourbon, will come to see you. He will bring his little boy, and you will think that he has grown. The boy will climb upon your bed, and you will give him some strawberries. You will offer some to these ladies here, also. When they have gone, you will fall asleep again, and when you wake, you will have a visit from M. B. (She had been his son's wet-nurse). He will give you news of your foster-child, and you will offer him a pinch of snuff."

As soon as I had made this suggestion, I said to her: "Whose dog is this on your bed?"—"Ah! it is my sister's; she makes a great pet of it. Well, you little rogue, go away! Who sent you here? Where is your mistress? Do you run away from her like this? Give me your paw; you are a good little dog. You want some sugar, do you, you little rascal?" She takes her bag from the stand by the bed, and looks in it for sugar. She finds a piece, breaks it, and gives him some, saying: "Oh, no, you know that is enough for you. Come, eat it." She watches him chew it up. "Now run home to your mistress; run fast, and don't get lost. He is a good little dog!"

"Now," I say, "you are twenty years old; you are a singer, and are going to make your first appearance at the Casino. You will sing a comic song."

"Oh! That is impossible! I am an old woman!"

"In two minutes, you will be twenty years old, you will feel yourself transformed."

She thinks, and in two minutes exclaims: "How pretty! how grand! It is beautiful, magnificent!"—She sits up, arranges her fichu, and puts on a smiling expression.—"Oh! there is the director! Whose turn is it?" And, speaking to an imaginary companion: "Is it yours, or mine? Well, I will go! What must I sing? I do not know what is on the programme. Well,—what difference does it make!"—She bows graciously three times, and sings, making expressive gestures: "*Mes Amours, je suis né en Bretagne*," etc. The song being finished, she bows, and puts out her hand to take something offered her. "Oh! the lovely bouquet, they give it to me because it is my fête-day,"—and turning to the audience, she bows again, saying: "Ah! you understood!"

"And now," I say to her, "you are a fine lady, driving in your carriage, with a footman."

She puts on an air worthy of the situation, leans back in her seat, folds her hands, and says in an appropriate voice: "What charming weather! Take me as far as the falls, Joseph. Go slowly." She bows and smiles at various people on the way, then says: "Now, go back, and drive slowly."

I say: "The horses are frightened and shy."—She calls out: "Be careful, Joseph; hold them in! Oh, oh, I will jump out! Hold them in firmly! I do not understand why you are not more careful. Quiet your horses. I shall dismiss you if you cannot do better."

I transform her into a corporal. She thinks up her part for a minute, then stands erect and says: "Attention recruits, stand erect! You must hold yourselves better than that! Stand in line! There, that is better! Attention! Present arms!" etc.

"Now eat this orange," I say. "Then an angel will come and blow on your eyes, to wake you."—She takes the imaginary orange, peels it carefully, putting the skin on the table by the bed, eats the quarters with a good relish, spits out the pits, and takes out her handkerchief to wipe her mouth. She then looks up, her face lights up, and she opens her eyes. She continues to look up for the angel who woke her.

"What are you looking at?" I ask.

"Nothing—I do not know."

"Have you been asleep?"

"I, asleep! I do not remember anything about it."

In two minutes she exclaims: "Oh, oh! look at the fine procession!" I tell her that it is only a dream which I have given her, and that there is nothing there.—She does not speak to me, but keeps on staring, in a surprised way.—"The altar is in front of me! There is Monseigneur, and all the dear sisters with the candles!"—I tell her in vain that it is a dream. She does not answer.—"The benediction is about to be pronounced! They are beginning to sing the *Veni Creator!* It is grand! Beautiful!"—Then she folds her hands, prays, and crosses herself. She bows humbly. "Thank you, Monseigneur!" Then looking around in an irritated way, she says: "Won't you go away? Is this the time to gossip? Just see these intoxicated nurses! Go away quickly! Are you not ashamed? Do you think that such conduct will be overlooked? They shall know how you have behaved, and the Sister Superior will discharge you."—She looks around at the door, and bows. —"The benediction is over!"

This whole scene appeared as an imposing reality, the incidents being regularly evolved as in a dream, but very much more rapidly than would be the case in reality.

The somnambulist falls asleep again, waking in a minute, and looking at the door on her right. Her face lights up and she stretches out her arms and embraces the empty air twice, crying out with emotion: "How do you do, my boy! What a surprise! Why did you not let me know? Oh, how he has grown! See, how he climbs up on the bed, the darling! Ah, he is a big boy!" She embraces him, and speaking to her imaginary son, says: "How did it happen that you came to-day,

Paul?"—She waits for his answer, and then replies: "Oh, yes! What, a basket of strawberries! They are the first of the season!" She laughs in a happy way, and tastes a berry.—"Will you allow me to offer you some, too, ladies?" She says, holding out the imaginary basket to two ladies present.—"What, are you going so soon? It was not worth the trouble to come! Well,—another time!" She embraces her son and grandson. "Kiss Gabrielle for me. Good-bye, my darling," and she follows them to the door with her eyes, throwing them kisses.

She falls asleep a third time, but awakes again, after a minute. She looks over at the door, and says in a surprised way: "See, M. B.! Good day, M. B. Are all well at your house? How is my little Louis? I always call him little Louis, because I knew him when he was so little; and now he is grown up! Yes, I have a cold. Won't you take a pinch of snuff? It does one good."—She makes the gesture of taking snuff, sneezes twice, and blows her nose.—"Oh, thank you, Monsieur. Please give my compliments to Mme., and kiss Louis for me." She follows him out of the room with her eyes, saying: "These visits are too short!"

I assure her that it is all a dream suggested by myself; that the procession, the visit from her son, and from M. B., only existed in her imagination. She will not believe me. "I have seen them and touched them, as I see and touch you!" Finally, I hypnotize her again, and take away all the impressions suggested. When she wakes, she remembers nothing.

Observation 4.—S——, thirty-nine years old, formerly a sergeant, is, at the present time, a workman in the great founderies. He was sent to me by M. Liébault, who had hypnotized him several different times. He was wounded on the head, at Patay, by the bursting of a bomb, and has a deep scar. He has had cystitis, in consequence of a stricture of the urethra, of which he is now cured. He is a man of sound intelligence, has no nervous history, sleeps well, and is not subject to attacks of spontaneous somnambulism. The only thing I notice in him, is a very marked, and almost general analgesia, without anæsthesia, which follows hypnosis.

He goes to sleep as soon as the command is given, or at least, shuts his eyes, and does not open them. "Are you asleep?"—"Partly so." —"Sleep soundly"—"Yes."—Anæsthesia, suggestive catalepsy, automatic movements, sensorial illusions, hallucinations, the execution of any acts commanded,—all succeed each other, punctually, with the precision characteristic of an old soldier.

I lift his arm: he stiffens it immediately. I close his hand gently; he contracts it with so much force, that a very decided command is necessary to make him relax the flexors.

I lift both his arms; he understands immediately, or thinks he understands what is wanted, and does what he has sometimes been made to do,—rotates his arms, one about the other, automatically, and with great rapidity.

I make him swallow a quantity of salt for sugar; he sucks it, and tastes it, without showing the least suspicion of what it really is.

I say: "You are now in the year 1870, a sergeant at the head of your company; you are at the battle of Gravelotte."—He thinks a minute, as if to arouse memories. They come back to him, form pictures in his mind, and force themselves upon him with striking vividness. He gets up, calls his men, commands them, marches, and places them for action. The enemy is at hand! He lies down, puts his gun to his shoulder, and shoots several times consecutively. Some of his men fall; he encourages the others. " Shelter yourselves behind this bush; we must retreat!" And he goes through all the movements of the struggle with the men, as memory revives them.

I make him imagine himself at the battle of Patay, where he was wounded. He falls, does not speak, puts his hand to his head, does not move. Then he comes to himself again, asks for a doctor, imagines himself being carried in an ambulance, calls a nurse to dress his wound, etc.

In living this part of his life over again, S—— doubles his personality, so to speak. He puts questions, and gives answers, all at the same time; he speaks for himself and for the others. I transfer him to Dijon, where he was on garrison duty.—"Hold! Corporal Durand! How are you?"—"Well, and you?"—"Where have you been?"—"I have just returned from a furlough."—"Let us go into the coffee-house!"—He gets chairs, asks his comrades to sit down, calls a boy, and orders beer, talking with his friends all the while, and speaking now for himself, now for them.

I say to him: "Where are you, S——?"

"I am at Dijon."

"Who am I?"

"You are Dr. Bernheim. But I cannot be at Dijon, for you are at St. Charles' Hospital, at Nancy. That cannot be! Here are my comrades! No, I do not know you."

I make him see his former colonel, General Vincendon. He rises and salutes:—"Good day, Colonel."

"Good day, my boy; are you well; is your wound cured? have you no medal, no pension?"

"No, colonel."

When he wakes, all that has occurred has absolutely disappeared from his memory.

Thus he dreams the drama that has been suggested to him, regarding himself as with his comrades in his former existence, repeating aloud what they say to him, what he answers, and gesticulating, as if he were at once the spectator and actor.

The subject of Observation 2 maintains his own rôle. He listens to the questions of his imaginary questioners, and gives his answers, without repeating the questions. He grows pale and trembles when he is wounded. S——, on the contrary, does not turn pale when wounded, neither does his heart beat more rapidly. It is another self he sees and feels acting in this strange division of his personality. He speaks to me, answers me, knows that he has been put to sleep in the hospital, and, at the same time, finds himself on the battle-field; the inconsistency does not strike him.

I have seen an analogous delirium in several cases of typhoid fever, where the patient's imagination was haunted by morbid dreams.

Do not phenomena of the same kind occur in physiological sleep? In our dreams, we believe ourselves back in our youthful days again. Deeply buried memories revive, and become pictures. We again behold people no longer living: we converse with them, but, at the same time, do not lose the sense of the present. Sometimes this feeling is so distinct, that we say to ourselves: "It is only a dream."—Maudsley says: "that through all our dream-wanderings, there is generally, deep down in us, an obscure feeling or instinct of our identity, for otherwise we should never know surprise in seeing that we are not ourselves, or that we are doing something extraordinary, or we should not have that sort of sentiment of personality, which is in us in all personal dramas in which we may take part. I believe that the organism preserves its identity, although our conscious functions may be of the most distracted order; although we may be asleep, our fundamental personality is felt more or less forcibly, in all conscious states, in the dream as in the waking condition. The patient in the insane asylum, who has the delusion that he is the All-powerful, asks a little favor humbly, at the same time that he is proclaiming his omnipotence. These are the consequences of a distracted identity."

The hallucinations of somnambulism are in reality nothing but induced dreams. The image produced is more or less real, the consciousness of identity may exist more or less confusedly, side by side with the dream, without the inconsistency striking the dreamer. S—— feels that he is near me, and under my control; at the same time he is on the battle-field, and repeats aloud the dream he is living through, but which has been suggested by me.

Side by side with the types of somnambulism just traced, examples of which I could multiply indefinitely, exists a rarer variety, in which the sleeper is attacked by spontaneous dreams, which may be directed and modified at will by the person in relationship with him. These dreams may be so vivid, that the feeling of reality, which is absolutely effaced, cannot be revived again.

Observation 5.—The following is the case of a young hysterical girl, whom I treated from October, 1881 until January, 1882. She has crises of hysterical convulsions, with lucid intervals, a complete hemianesthesia of the left side which was cured by the use of magnets, spastic paraplegia, transient contracture of the left arm, etc. Her intelligence is very clear, and between these crises, she is reasonable, not at all impressionable, and calm and deliberate in word and action.

She may be hypnotized in a few minutes by fixation. Her eyes close suddenly and she remains motionless. Suggestive catalepsy cannot be induced; if the limbs are lifted, they fall back again.

The following is an account of one of the séances.

I say to her, "Are you asleep?" She does not reply. I insist, and at last she answers, "No, I am not asleep." "Where are you?" She replies, "I am in the street." "Where are you going?" "I am going home." "Where do you live?" "In Etang Street with my mother." A moment after, I say, "Where are you now?" "You see very well, by the station." Suddenly she seems to be violently agitated by something. This, she explains upon waking, by stating that she saw a monument shake, and thought she would be crushed by it. "Well," I say, "here you are at your mother's." "How are you, Marie?" "I feel better," she says, thinking that she is answering her mother. "Are you to be always at the hospital?" "No, I have left; I am almost cured. They used electricity on me." "You would be very good," I say, "if you would help me iron this linen." "Ah, you weary me, I did not come to work."

At last, however, she yields to her mother's desire. She draws the counterpane off the bed, makes the gesture of dampening and starching it, takes up an iron, tries it to see if it is hot, irons with great care, and folds the spread several times, not forgetting any detail. Now I say to her, "You will do well to mend this stocking." She arranges the bedcover in the form of a stocking, makes the gesture of putting a darning ball into it, takes the knitting needle, picks up stitch after stitch with an astonishing appearance of precision, turns the stocking, reversing the stitches, etc. I make her sew. She turns down a hem in the spread she has in her hand, pretends to thread a needle, puts on her thimble, and hems, sticking in the needle and drawing in the thread, pricking her finger once, and putting it in her mouth to suck the drop of blood. She replaces the needle which has not a good point, by another, and does it all with a striking appearance of reality. "You have worked enough for your mother," I say, "let us take a walk together." She takes me for her friend Louise. "I should enjoy that," she says. "It is very warm, let us go and bathe," I say. She imagines herself going with me, describes the streets through which she passes, and the people whom she sees. I knock on the table three times. "What is that?" I say. "They are men breaking stones." We reach the baths. She makes the gesture of undressing herself, imagines that she is in the water, shivers, makes the regular motions of swimming with her outstretched hands, etc.

If I let her go on sleeping without paying any attention to her, she continues her dream spontaneously. Once after having left her alone for a few minutes, I saw her actively at work, washing linen, pulling it out of a little tub, dipping it in the water, soaping it on a board, plunging it again into the water, then wringing it out, etc.

As soon as she has awakened, she tells me all the details of her dream. She has been home, and has passed by the station on the way, where she had a fright. She has seen her mother, who said such and such things to her. She does not forget the slightest details, co-ordinating the incoherent acts in which I have made her take part, in logical order. If my students have sung softly while she slept, she speaks of them as musicians, or some bad singers she met on the way. Objects were laid on her forehead while she was sleeping to see if she could guess what they were. They are the people she has met on the way, who have stopped her to ask some question. In vain I say, "But it is a dream, you have been asleep. You have not been out of your bed." She does not believe it, the dream seems to her reality.

I can direct her dreams during this sleep, but am not able to make her conscious of reality. I say to her, "You are asleep." "Why, no," she says. "But you are paralyzed, you cannot walk." "You are making fun of me, as long as I am up, I can walk."

I have hypnotized her nearly every day and tried to remain in relationship with her during the hypnosis, by touching her hand or forehead, and by talking to her. I say, "Remember that you are asleep, that I am at the bed-side, and that you are paralyzed." At a given moment, her eyes close and she is beyond my influence. The remembrance of the reality has vanished. She is not sleeping, she is not paralyzed, she can walk; I am her friend or her mother.

No therapeutic suggestion has been of any use, as the patient is not in relationship with me in this respect. The various phenomena of hysteria,—contracture, paraplegia, transient trismus, aphonia, etc.—have persisted with slight modifications for better or for worse. The patient was discharged January 9, and was finally cured spontaneously. I only wish to describe the peculiar character of the somnambulism induced in her case.

Spontaneous dreams appear in other hypnotized subjects, but they vanish at the hypnotizer's voice; he retains control over the ideation and will of these subjects.

Observation 6.—A man thirty-seven years old, who had been suffering from gastralgia since 1872, came to consult me. I hypnotized him five times. By the aid of suggestion and the fixation of his eyes upon my fingers, he goes to sleep in two minutes; he is in the somnambulistic condition; suggestive catalepsy, automatic movements, complete anæsthesia and hallucinations are present.

If I stop directing him for an instant, he has spontaneous dreams. At one time, he remains motionless, trembling all over with an expression of fear upon his face. "He is coming! Here he is!" "What is there?" "The tiger! Do not you see him down there?" He imagines himself in a desert, and sees a tiger coming toward him. At another time, he thinks himself at Bar-le-Duc, with his brother, who is a wood merchant. He goes with him to the wood-yard and talks about business. I say, "You are at Nancy, yes, at Nancy in Stanilas Place." Then he imagines himself back again, and tells me everything he has seen on the walk, which I called up to his imagination.

In spite of his dream, he retained the idea of reality. He knew that I was present and that he was asleep. At one and the same time, he was asleep in Nancy and awake in a wood-yard in Bar-le-Duc. The contradiction did not strike him, he remained in relationship with the person who hypnotized him, during his spontaneous dream. If I lifted a leg, it remained up; if I made his arms rotate, one about the other, they continued the motion. I suggested that the epigastric and spinal pains would disappear. He said he was no longer conscious of them, and when he woke, they did not reappear.

This case of somnambulism, then, like the foregoing, is susceptible to spontaneous dreams if the subject is left to himself while in the hypnotic condition. It differs from the foregoing, in that the idea of reality remains with the subject and may be recalled by suggestion. The consciousness of his real personality, though it is distracted by the wanderings of imagination, is not obliterated, and the patient can be affected by therapeutic suggestions.

I give the following case, in which nearly all the suggestive phenomena mentioned in the preceding observations are wanting, as an illustration of still another type of somnambulism. Nothing but the closure of the eyes and absence of memory upon waking appear to distinguish this sleep from the waking condition.

Observation 7.—Mme. de X——, 56 years old, is a very intelligent woman. She has suffered for many years from chronic gastritis with dilatation of the stomach. I hypnotize her easily by simply holding her eyelids closed for a minute. She exhibits suggestive catalepsy to a certain degree. She keeps her arms up a while, but at last they fall spontaneously. I can induce rotatory automatism of the lower limbs by saying, "You cannot stop yourself," but the movement only lasts about ten seconds. I cannot induce either contracture, anæsthesia or sensorial suggestion. For example, if I say to her, "Hear the music," she hears nothing. If I say, "Swallow this draught," she answers, "You know, doctor, that does not work with me."

She retains much spontaneous activity during the sleep, discourses with me, initiating me into all the details of her sickness, or talking to me about outside and worldly matters. "Did I dream, doctor, of inviting you to drink tea that day?" etc. If she hears the maid walking about in an adjoining room, she talks to me about her. She acts exactly like a wide awake person, but she is sure that she is sleeping. I have hypnotized her more than fifty times, and have never been able to give her either a sensorial illusion, or a very clear hallucination. One day, however, I made her hear military music when she woke; she heard it as if it was far away and quite dreamy. She realizes certain suggestions of acts to be performed after waking. For example, I said on one occasion, "When you wake, you will rise from the arm-chair in which you are sitting, and go and sit down in the arm-chair opposite you." When she was waked, she looked around and said, "I do not know why, but my parlor is not in order to-day. I am not comfortable in this arm-chair," and, obedient to the suggestion, she went and sat down in the chair opposite. In this way, she tried to explain to herself the necessity she felt for changing her seat.

I can also suggest certain acts of the same kind which she is to realize during her sleep. For example, I say, "In three minutes, you will go and sit down on the sofa, and after you have been sitting there one minute you will wake." She obeys exactly.

I wake her, in the midst of a most animated conversation, by saying, "Wake up."

She remembers absolutely nothing. Everything is effaced from her memory. She does not know how long she has been asleep. Sometimes a single fact remains in her memory through auto-suggestion. She said to me one day, "You asked me in my sleep, if I always have acid eructations accompanied with a burning sensation. I said to myself then, when I wake up, I must not forget to ask the doctor, from what source the vichy water I take should come." She thus gave herself a suggestion to preserve this memory; everything else was gone.

Moreover, if I say before waking her, "You will remember absolutely nothing," I take away the possibility of remembering anything from her, even what she has suggested to herself.

I could multiply observations upon somnambulism without exhausting the subject. Everyone has his special individuality in the somnambulistic as in the waking condition.

In the preceding pages, I have roughly sketched the curious phenomena observed in induced sleep; phenomena which may be easily verified by any one who wishes to take the trouble. Subjects are doubtless met with, who simulate consciously, or who think they must simulate in order to be obliging. Doubtful cases also occur, which are not convincing. The conditions of sleep and of waking are separated by imperceptible gradations. Sometimes the operator is doubtful whether such and such a subject is really influenced. On the other hand, the subject who remembers everything he has heard, may think that he has not been influenced, but that he has been simulating.

Here as in everything else, experience teaches whether the influence obtained is real or not. A man of large knowledge and intelligence, whom I hypnotized for some time, on account of a nervous affection, fell into sleep of the third degree at the first séance. Suggestive catalepsy was present and memory was preserved on waking. I asked him if he slept. He thought so, without being absolutely sure, though he heard everything. To my questions, why he had not once opened his eyes, and why he had not lowered his arms when I raised them, and if he could have done so, he answered: "I do not know whether I could have done it. I had no idea of doing it. The desire was wanting." I was convinced that he had been influenced. He was influenced so decidedly at the following séance, and at all the others since that time, that he fell into a deep sleep with absolute loss of memory upon waking. I observe similar facts daily.

After a single observation, positive or negative, judgment should not be lightly pronounced. I can honestly say, that I have made my observations coolly, without any predisposition to either side, and without enthusiasm. But when after many hundred observations in all classes of society, in the hospital and in the city, I have seen constant, uniform phenomena induced, and when, on the other hand, I know that everyone who has studied the question in an unbiased manner, has observed facts identical or analogous to those I have observed, am I to admit that all our subjects have leagued together to mystify us? Certain minds have a horror of the marvellous. They are right: but they are wrong when they consider as marvellous and systematically deny, facts which they have not verified, just because these facts do not agree with the *à priori* conceptions in their minds. The facts are undeniable: the interpretation of them follows; if that is faulty, do not blame the facts, but the insufficiency of our knowledge of psychology and nervous physiology.

CHAPTER IV

Circulation and respiration in hypnotism.—Changes observed by authors are due to the emotion of the subjects.—Influence of the hypnotic suggestion on the functions of organic life: retardation and acceleration of the pulse influence; upon the vaso-motor circulation; inflammation, blisters, hemorrhages produced by suggestion.

ONE word more about the circulation and respiration in hypnotism.

According to Braid, the pulse and respiration are at first slower than normal; but as soon as the muscles are put into activity a tendency to cataleptiform rigidity is produced, with increase of the pulse rate and rapid and laborious respiration. According to his experiments, the increase of the pulse rate caused by the muscular effort which the person makes normally, in order to keep his legs and arms extended for five minutes, is about twenty per cent. In the hypnotic condition it is one hundred per cent. If, then, all the senses are excited, if the muscles of the head and neck are put into a cataleptiform condition simultaneously with the limbs, there is a rapid fall to forty per cent. (that is, twice as much as the increase during the normal condition). If the muscles are allowed to relax again, the subject still remaining in the hypnotic state, the pulse falls rapidly to its rate before the experiment, and even below it. Further, during the cataleptiform rigidity the pulse is slow and small, and at the same time, a sudden injection of the ocular conjunctiva of the capillaries of the head, neck and face occurs. Braid thinks that the rigidity of the cataleptic muscles prevents the free transmission of blood to the extremities, and thus causes an increase of the cardiac action and hyperæmia of the brain and spinal cord.

Other authors have, like Braid, observed modifications of the cardiac and respiratory functions. In a case of hypnotic lethargy reported in a thesis at Strasburg, Pau de St. Martin noticed the increase of the pulse and respiration, the diminution of the vascular tension and profuse perspiration.

By means of more precise methods, Heidenhain reached the

same results, and noticed besides an augmentation of the salivary secretion, and recently Tamburini and Seppili, with the graphic method and Mosso's plethysmograph, observed that at the time of transition from the waking condition to the hypnotic sleep, the respiratory movements became irregular, unequal, and more frequent, the cardiac and vascular pulsations increased, and the face was congested.

Dr. Hack-Tuke observed an acceleration of the cardiac and respiratory movements in one case; in another, on the contrary, both remained unaffected.

In forming their conclusions, it seems to me that these observers have not taken into consideration the method used to induce hypnosis, and the emotional conditions under which it is obtained.

The subjects, being asked to fix their eyes upon a brilliant object, or upon the operator's eyes, make a more or less intense effort in so doing. To the muscular fatigue of the eye and the psychical concentration there is added a certain moral emotion, especially when submitting to the experiment for the first time; hence, an irregular, increased, and sometimes panting respiration. The pulse is agitated by the emotions, and clinicians call it a medical pulse. The congestion of the face, the muscular twitchings, and the uncomfortable sensations experienced by some subjects do not seem to me to be due to any other cause.

None of these symptoms are manifested by patients who are hypnotized by the quiet suggestion method, and who retain their tranquillity of mind; nor by those who having already been hypnotized several times go to sleep with confidence and without emotion or agitation. Under these conditions I have observed neither increase nor diminution of the pulse rate, nor of the respiratory movements. I have recorded the pulse by the sphymograph before, and during hypnosis, and have found it to be the same at both times. Neither have I noticed the marked acceleration, which according to Braid, is produced by the cataleptiform rigidity which occurs in the extension of the limbs. It appears to me that no appreciable difference exists between the waking and the hypnotic conditions.

Can the functions of organic life, which under ordinary conditions are beyond the influence of the will, be modified by suggestion? M. Beaunis has performed some physiological experiments, in order to determine this question. He has tried to vary the frequency of the heart-pulsations in somnambulists by suggestion, registering them by physiological methods. To this end, the sphymograph, with Marey's transmission, is applied over the left radial artery; an electric clock inscribes the seconds on the registering cylinder. The following are the results obtained in two cases of somnambulism: In one the average number of pulsations to the minute, before hypnotic sleep, was ninety-six, and during sleep, ninety-eight and four-tenths, and the suggestion of decrease gave ninety-two and four-tenths to the minute. Then the pulse having returned to the normal condition and registering one hundred and two per minute, the suggestion of increase brought it to one hundred and fifteen and five-tenths. Upon awaking it was one hundred and two-tenths. The decrease and increase in the pulsations followed immediately upon the suggestions. In the other case, the suggestion of decrease in pulse rate gave an analogous result.

Suggestion may act upon the vas-motor circulation. In certain subjects a fixed spot on the body may be made to appear red. M. Beaunis said to a somnambulist, "When you wake up you will have a red spot where I now touch you." In ten minutes the patient waked. The spot indicated began to look slightly red, growing more and more so, and after lasting from ten to fifteen minutes it gradually disappeared. This condition may be made to persist a long time by means of suggestion.

In certain cases even more can be done. A blister can be raised by hypnotic suggestion. M. Focachon, an apothecary at Charmes, has shown us the phenomenon in two cases of somnambulism, which he brought to Nancy, in order that we might verify the experiment. At eleven o'clock in the morning, while the subject was asleep, eight postage stamps were applied to the left shoulder and the suggestion was given that a blister was being applied. The subject was allowed to sleep during the entire day, being waked only at meal-time. She was watched all the time. She was hypnotized for the night with the suggestion that she would not wake until seven o'clock in the morning. Next day, at a quarter past eight the bandage was taken off. The postage stamps had not been disturbed. Over an area of from four to five centimetres in diameter, the epidermis appeared thickened, modified and yellowish white. It was not raised however, and no blister was apparent; but it was thick, wrinkled and in a word, presented the condition which immediately precedes an actual blister. This region of the skin was surrounded by an intensely red zone with swelling. The person went back to Charmes with M. Focachon. At four o'clock in the afternoon four or five phlictenulæ had developed. Fifteen days later the blister was still at the height of suppuration.*

M. Focachon tried the same experiment in an another case, successfully. The blister was raised in forty-eight hours.

M. Dumontpallier endeavored to reproduce this phenomenon. He observed a notable rise in temperature, but no blister.

Finally, hemorrhages and bloody stigmata may be induced in certain subjects by means of suggestion.

MM. Bourru and Burot of Rochefort have experimented on this subject with a young marine, a case of hystero-epilepsy. M. Bourru put him into the somnambulistic condition and gave him the following suggestion. "At four o'clock this afternoon after the hypnosis, you will come into my office, sit down in the arm-chair, cross your arms upon your breast and your nose will begin to bleed." At the hour appointed the young man did as directed. Several drops of blood came from the left nostril.

On another occasion the same investigator traced the patient's name on both his fore-arms, with the dull point of an instrument. Then, when the patient was in the somnambulistic condition he said, "At four o'clock this afternoon you will go to sleep, and your arms will bleed along the lines which I have traced, and your name will appear written on your arms in letters of blood." He was watched at four o'clock and seen to fall asleep. On the left arm the letters stood out in bright red relief, and in several places there were drops of blood. The letters were still visible three months afterward, although they had grown gradually faint.

Dr. Mabille, director of the Insane Asylum at Lafond, near Rochelle, a former pupil of excellent standing, repeated the experiment made upon this subject at Rochefort, after he was removed to the asylum, and confirmed it. He obtained instant hemorrhage over a determined region of the body. He also induced an attack of spontaneous somnambulism, in which the

---

* Prof. Forel recently made a number of experiments upon somnambulists with a view to producing vesication by suggestion, but without success. There was generally, however, a patch of distinct erythema at the point where the blister was to have been produced.   C. A. H.

patient doubling his personality, so to speak, suggested to himself the hemorrhagic stigmata on the arm, thus repeating the marvellous phenomenon of the famous stigmatized auto-suggestionist, Louise Lateau.

These facts, then, seem to prove that suggestion may act upon the cardiac function, and upon the vaso-motor system Phenomena of this order, however, rarely occur. They are exceptional and are obtained in certain subjects only. I have in vain tried to reproduce them in many cases. These facts are sufficient to prove, however, that when in a condition of special psychical concentration, the brain can influence even the organic functions, which in the normal state seem but slightly amenable to the will. Experiments might be instituted to determine to what degree imagination may influence certain functions in the waking condition. We know how greatly micturation and defecation are influenced by will, idea and imagination. By concentrating the mind upon the phenomenon, can we not also produce an increase of heat in certain regions of the body, perhaps even without hypnosis? This is a question for experiment to answer by seeking to determine a local increase of temperature through psychically induced vaso-motor congestion.

CHAPTER V

Suggestion in the waking condition.—Production of the same phenomena by simple affirmation in subjects who can be hypnotized and in those who cannot be hypnotized.—Transfer of hemianæsthesia in a case of hysteria.—Sensorial suggestions.—Hallucinations.—Suggestive modifications of the visual field.—Auto-suggestion in ecstasy.—A question of priority.

I NOW approach the study of some facts observed in regard to *suggestion in the waking condition.*

I have shown that many subjects who have previously been hypnotized, may manifest susceptibility to the same suggestive phenomena in the waking condition, without being again hypnotized, however slight may have been the influence of a small number of previous séances. (One, two or three séances.)

Here, for example, is the case of X——, one of my patients who is accustomed to being hypnotized, and who is subject to light somnambulism. Without putting him to sleep, I say directly, "Close you hand. You cannot open it again." He keeps his hand closed and contractured and makes fruitless efforts to open it. I make him hold out his other arm, with his hand open and say, "You cannot shut it." He tries in vain to do so, brings the phalanges into semiflexion, one upon the other, but can do no more in spite of every effort.

I say, "Now your closed hand opens and your opened hand closes," and in a second or two, the phenomenon takes place and the hands remain motionless in this new position.

Automatic movements succeed very well in his case. I say, "Rotate your arms; you cannot stop them." He turns them one about the other for an indefinite time. I add, "Do all you can to stop them. Do not try to oblige me, stop them if you can." He struggles to bring both hands together so as to strike one against the other. It is useless. They fly apart like springs forced by an involuntary mechanism. I stop one of his arms, the other keeps on turning. As soon as I release the one stopped, it resumes its place and continues the rotatory movement. In the same way, I induce trismus, wry-neck, suggestive paralysis of a limb, etc.

This is not a unique observation; the same thing is manifested by many patients susceptible to hypnosis, who are not in the least hysterical, and even by those who do not pass into a deep sleep but only into that of the second or third degree. Some of them at least, show exactly the same phenomena in the waking condition as in the hypnotic state; some exhibit suggestive catalepsy with muscular contraction, or a varying contracture only; others, catalepsy with automatic movements; others, at the same time, suggestive sensitivo-sensorial anæsthesia; and others still, all suggestive phenomena up to hallucinations. I do not have to assume a deep authoritative voice nor frighten my patients with a look, in order to obtain the suggestive phenomena. I speak pleasantly, in the simplest manner possible, and obtain the effect, not only in the docile, obliging patients who have no will, but in well-balanced, clear-headed patients, possessed of strong will and some of them even of a spirit of insubordination.

Modifications of sensibility may be obtained, in some cases, by suggestion in the waking condition.

The following is a remarkable instance. There is in my service, a young, hysterical girl (whose case is related farther on) afflicted with sensitivo-sensorial hemianæsthesia of the left side, and capable of being hypnotized into deep sleep.

In the waking condition, she is susceptible to catalepsy or suggestive contracture. I can effect transfer of the hemianæsthesia from the left to the right side, without hypnotizing and without touching her.

I say, "You will again have feeling in your left arm and hand. The sensibility will come back entirely." I direct her attention to the return of this sensibility, in a commanding manner. In three minutes she feels a sharp pain in her shoulder, and sensibility returns to the shoulder at this moment, though not to the forearm. The right shoulder is insensible. The pain spreads rapidly from the centre to the periphery, down the fore-arm and into the fingers, and then disappears. This lasts from several seconds to a quarter of a minute. Sensibility comes back with the spreading pain. It is restored completely to the upper left limb but destroyed in the right. A transfer has taken place and this transfer has not been suggested. The return of sensibility to the left side alone was suggested.

I effect the transfer between the lower limbs simultaneously; if the suggestion is commanding enough, successfully, if it is less authoritative, less efficaciously. Similar transfer from left to right occurs most frequently in the special senses, smell, taste, sight and hearing, and without special suggestion.

The transfer back again may be immediately provoked, and successively, as many times as we wish.

I can produce crossed sensibility, in the upper left limb and the lower right limb, for example, and *vice versa*, the other limbs remaining anæsthetic.

By strongly accentuating the suggestion and keeping the patient's attention fixed upon both arms and legs, which is sometimes, but not always possible, I provoke the return of sensation without transfer. Both sides are then sensible. If, on the contrary, the suggestion is insufficient, the spreading pain and sensation stop half way. The arm and the upper half of the fore-arm, for example, alone are sensible, the wrist and hand remaining anæsthetic.

The anæsthesia is more rapidly produced than the restoration of sensation. The latter requires at least a minute, the former is instantly obtained. I prick the left hand with a pin, and the patient reacts quickly (the eyes being closed to avoid deception). Then I say, "You no longer feel anything," and I prick the hand again; there is immediate and complete analgesia.

Transfer or restoration of sensation may be effected by a still more efficacious method, which, so to speak, embodies the functional re-establishment in a visible and tangible phenomenon.

I make the patient raise the anæsthetic arm with the hand closed. It remains in a cataleptic condition. Then I say, "Your hand will open, you arm will fall back again and you will again have feeling in it." In less than a minute, the hand opens suddenly, as if by a painful electric shock; the transfer of sensation has taken place. A transfer of contracture occurs at the same time, if I have suggested it; the other hand closes and the arm becomes cataleptic.

Instead of contracting the hands in flexion, I can contract them in extension and suggest their closure. The same effect is produced.

I prevent the transfer and restore the sensation of the anæsthetic limb, keeping it in the healthy limb at the same time, by the following method. I lift both arms and both legs, and keep them in a cataleptic condition with the hands closed. Then I say, "Your hands will open, your legs will fall back again and you will feel all over." In a few instants, the hands open, the legs fall back again and sensation is general.

Finally, if while inducing these suggestive phenomena, I say, and repeat authoritatively, "Sensation is returning without pains, you have no pain," the patient recovers sensation without sudden or spreading pains.

I may add, that after a variable time, hemianæsthesia of the left side reappears spontaneously.

I have performed and repeated all these experiments daily for several weeks, in the presence of my students and several of my associates and colleagues, who have been able to verify them, as they have been all the facts which I have already stated, and have still to state.

In one of my somnambulistic cases (S——, whose history I have already given), I can obtain all possible modifications of sensibility in the waking condition. It suffices to say, "Your left side is insensible." Then if I prick his left arm with a pin, stick the pin into his nostril, touch the mucous membrane of his eye, or tickle his throat, he does not move. The other side of his body reacts. I transfer the anæsthesia from the left to the right side. I produce total anæsthesia, which was, on one occasion, so profound that my *chef de clinique* pulled out the roots of five teeth which were deeply embedded in the gums, twisting them around in their sockets for more than ten minutes. I simply said to the patient, "You will have no feeling whatever." He laughed as he spit out the blood and did not show the least symptom of pain.

This subject, moreover, takes all suggestions without being hypnotized. He may be walking when I say, "You cannot go any further," and he remains as if fixed to the spot. I say, "Do all you can to move on, you cannot advance." He bends his body forward, but does not succeed in lifting his feet from the floor. I can provoke any attitude and any contracture I please in him, and he will keep it for an indefinite time. He is susceptible to any hallucinations suggested. I say to him, "Go to your bed, you will find a basket of strawberries there." He goes, finds the imaginary basket, holds it by the handle and eats the strawberries, just as we have seen subjects do in post-hypnotic cases.

G——, a boy fourteen years old, was admitted to the hospital

on account of a catarrhal nephritis of which he was rapidly cured. He is of lymphatic temperament, intelligent, has had a good primary education, and shows no signs of any nervous trouble. I have hypnotized him four or five times. He goes into somnambulism, performs any actions suggested during sleep, has no remembrance of anything upon waking and is susceptible to post-hypnotic hallucinations.

In the waking condition I can induce suggestive catalepsy of the upper limbs and automatic rotation of the arms, one about the other, without his being able to stop them, as in examples already cited.

I only emphasize the sensory phenomena in this case. After having assured myself that his sensation is normally perfect, and that both hands react quickly when pricked, I say, " Your right hand has no more feeling in it. Your left hand only can feel," and I stick the pin some distance into the right hand. It does not react, but the other shows pain when it is pricked. Then I say, " But no, it is the left hand which has no feeling," and instantly the phenomenon supervenes; the right hand is sensible again. In the same way I induce anæsthesia of the face and nostrils, etc. The sense organs may also be influenced by affirmation. After satisfying myself that his vision is normal I say to him : "You see well, and at a great distance, with your left eye, but your right eye is defective and distinguishes only very near objects." Then I ask him to read printed letters, three millimetres in height. The left eye reads eighty centimetres off, the right only at twenty four centimetres.

I bring about transfer by suggestion, saying, " The right eye sees very far away, the left eye only very near to." The right eye reads at eighty centimetres, the left at twenty-four. These distances are only measured when the patient says he can see clearly.

His hearing is very good. The right ear hears the ticking of a watch at ninety-four centimetres, the left ear at eighty-seven.

I say to him, "You hear very clearly, and at a long distance with the left ear, but your right ear hears only with difficulty and very near to." I measure the distance at which the ticking of the watch is perceived, and get eighty-seven centimetres for the left ear, and two only for the right. I suggest the transfer which immediately occurs. These measurements are taken by my *chef de clinque*, while I hold the boy's eyes tightly closed, which seems to me to exclude any chance of mistake.

I suggest complete deafness of one side. He says he does not hear the watch when held to the ear of that side. I transfer the deafness to the other side. I suggest complete bilateral deafness. He assures me that he does not hear anything when the watch is held to both ears. When I have restored his hearing, he says he has not heard the slightest noise while I was speaking, and only read what I wished to say by the motions of my lips. Verification is of course impossible here. I can only be guided by the subject's assertion.

In G—— (Marie, whose case I have already related), I can induce catalepsy, automatic movements, anæsthesia and hallucinations in the waking condition. I wish only to speak of the anæsthesia. After having ascertained that sensation throughout the body was perfect, I said to her, "You have absolutely no more feeling in your right upper limb, it is just as if dead." With her eyes closed she no longer reacts to the pin. She does not know whether her arm is up or on the bed; her muscular sense is gone. In order to exclude all idea of deception, I use Dubois-Raymond's apparatus, varying the intensity of the current by alternately separating and approximating the coils of the induction apparatus. A rule graded into centimetres indicates the degree of separation of the coils. Now I had already determined that the tingling caused by the electricity was perceived by this subject when the separation between the ends was five centimetres, and that the pain became unendurable, the patient drawing back the arm suddenly, when the separation was from three to two centimetres. These figures remained absolutely the same when her eyes were tightly closed, so that she could not have observed the degree of separation, and I have proved this several times. By this means I determined that the pain is really perceived and not pretended.

This being granted, I provoke anæsthesia by affirmation and place the electrodes on her arm with the greatest current attainable with the greatest approximation of the coils. The painful sensation thus produced is normally absolutely unbearable. "The pretence of an equal analgesia," said my colleague, E. Victor Parisot, who desired to verify this experiment, "would be more remarkable than the production of analgesia." Now the patient showed no sign of reaction, and assured me that she felt nothing in her arm, and the electrodes were applied to her arm indefinitely, until I said, "Your arm is again sensible." In an instant she drew it back. I can produce the same analgesia by affirmation anywhere on her body. This experiment has been repeated before several of my colleagues, under careful control. I frequently repeat it when I happen to be passing by the patient. In the same case all possible hallucinations may be evoked without first hypnotizing.

The observations which I have mentioned are not exceptional. Many subjects are susceptible to suggestion and hallucination in the waking condition.

I will finish this chapter by presenting the following fact which belongs to a class of conceptions (*suggestive therapeutics*) which I shall treat later.

A young man was sent to the Society of Medicine at Nancy by Dr. Spillmann. He was syphilitic, had vegetations on his penis, and presented some interesting hysterical conditions, among others, a persistent amblyopia of the left eye. Under the influence of an interrupted current, suggested and tried by my colleague, M. Charpentier, the acuteness of his vision which was reduced to one-sixth, became normal again, and the visual field increased from ten to twenty-five degrees in each meridian.

Subsequent hypnotic suggestion enlarged each one of the meridians still more (from eight to ten degrees), and this improvement was still observed at the end of a week.

Then, as my colleague and I wished to see what effect suggestion would have in the waking condition, united with pretended electrical treatment, we applied the electrode to the temple for about fifteen minutes, without allowing the current to pass. Now the visual field, measured by M. Charpentier, was increased seven degrees internally, twenty-five externally, and twenty in the vertical meridian. Its extent was greater than that given as normal. (See observation farther on.)

Relative to these experimental facts, I give without comment the following quotation from Dr. Charpignon.*

"Among the martyrs of Christianity many escaped pain through the ecstasy which came from the ardor of their faith, a phenomenon well-known to their executioners, who increased

---

* Charpignon: *Etudes sur la Médecine Animique et vitaliste.* Paris, 1864.

their fury and improved their inventions for punishment. In the same way, at the time of the tortures of the Inquisition certain individuals became insensible under the influence of their faith in the somniferous virtue of some talisman. Upon this point I will give the following passage, an extract from *Secrets merveilleux de la magie naturelle et cabalistique*. (In — 12, Lyons, 1629.) "Some rascals trusted so strongly in the secrets they possessed to make themselves insensible to pain, that they voluntarily gave themselves up as prisoners, to cleanse themselves of certain sins. Some use certain words pronounced in a low voice, and others writings which they hide on some part of their body. The first one I recognized as using some sort of charm, surprised us by his more than natural firmness, because after the first stretching of the rack, he seemed to sleep as quietly as if he had been in a good bed, without lamenting, complaining or crying, and when the stretching was repeated two or three times, he still remained as motionless as a statue. This made us suspect that he was provided with some charm, and to resolve the doubt he was stripped as naked as his hand. Yet after a careful search nothing was found on him but a little piece of paper on which were the figures of the three kings, with these words on the other side: 'Beautiful star which delivered the Magi from Herod's persecution, deliver me from all torment.' This paper was stuffed in his left ear. Now although the paper had been taken away from him he still appeared insensible to the torture, because when it was applied he muttered words between his teeth which we could not hear, and as he persevered in his denials, it was necessary to send him back to prison."

One word more on a question of priority, before finishing this chapter.

I was the first to mention these phenomena of suggestion in the waking condition in my report to the Congress for the Advancement of Science, held at Rouen, in August, 1883. Since then these phenomena have been verified by Bottey, Dumontpallier, Charles Richet and by observers in general.

Fourteen months after my communication, Charles Richet, in a paper entitled, *De la suggestion sans hypnotisme*, seems to claim priority in the discovery, and mentions a communication made by himself to the Biological Society, in 1882 (No. 3).

This communication was concerning a person who without being hysterical, and without the aid of hypnotism, showed remarkable symptoms of contracture when pressure was exerted on the muscles, the contracture disappearing upon a slight excitement, such as insufflation or sudden noise. Further, if a light oscillatory movement was impressed upon the hand for half a minute, the patient could not stop it voluntarily; it kept up indefinitely.

The author refers to the reflex medullary excitability intensified to such a degree that the psychical centres can no longer exercise control over the spinal cord. This then is all that M. Richet says. He did not see that it was a question of suggestion. His communication is entitled, *Notes sur quelques faits relatifs a l'excitabilité musculaire.* He passed *close by a fact* without getting the real signification of it.

It was not until 1884, after I had shown that phenomenon of *paralysis, contracture, sensitive and sensorial anæsthesia, sensorial illusions,* and *complex hallucinations* may be obtained by *suggestion* in a great number of subjects susceptible to hypnotism, *without hypnosis,* just as absolutely as with it, that enlightened by the facts I had published, he at length comprehended the significance of what he had seen, and published a new paper entitled: *De la suggestion sans hypnotisme.* (Biological Society, October 11, 1884.)

I should add further that after having demonstrated these facts, I found them mentioned by Braid under the name of " Phenomena of the waking condition," in a treatise entitled, *The power of the mind over the body*, published since 1846, and later in an additional chapter to his *Neurypnology*, in 1860. They have been confirmed in America under the name of *Electro-biology*. I have, then, only called attention to these phenomena; and I was moreover, the first to notice suggestive anæsthesia and analgesia in the waking condition, of which Braid has made no mention.

CHAPTER VI

Reply to critics.—The three phases of hypnotism according to the school of the Salpêtrière.—Experiments of transfer.—Experimental illusions.—The real image and the hallucinatory image.

IN the preceding pages, I have endeavored to outline as faithfully and exactly as possible, the different manifestations from simple drowsiness to the most pronounced degree of deep somnambulism, which can be induced in the various hypnotic conditions.

I now wish to answer several criticisms which have been made upon the observations carried on at Nancy, and at the same time to show in what respect and why the results we obtain differ from those observed by the school of the Salpêtrière.

M. Charcot, who has made his experiments principally upon hysterical cases, considers the hypnotic condition developed in them to be a real neurosis, essentially made up of three states or periods, each having its own very distinct differential characteristics, and states that the operator may make the subject pass at will from one to the other, by means of certain skilful manipulations.

The first is the lethargic state. It is obtained either by fixation upon an object or by pressing lightly upon the eye-ball through the closed eyelids. The lethargy thus induced is characterized essentially by the appearance of deep sleep, relaxation of the muscles, anæsthesia, often complete, and the abeyance of the intellectual life. In this stage, suggestion is impossible. But a certain muscular hyper-excitability is noticeable; any muscle excited by pressure or light friction, contracts; pressure upon ulnar nerve provokes the ulnar attitude (griffe cubital), and pressure upon the facial nerve is followed by distortion of the features of the corresponding side of the face.

The second is the cataleptic condition. To make a subject pass from the first to the second stage, it is only necessary to raise the eyelids. If one eye only is opened, the corresponding side of the body alone passes into the cataleptic condition, the other side remaining lethargic. The cataleptic subject retains any position into which he is put; the neuro-muscular hyper-excitability has disappeared.

In this condition, suggestions can be induced through the muscular sense. For example, if the subject's hands are brought together as if to throw a kiss, the face assumes a smiling expression; if joined as in prayer, the face becomes grave and the subject kneels down. The subject can be made to pass from the cataleptic to the lethargic condition by closing his eyelids. Finally this condition can be directly induced without being preceded by lethargy, through the nervous shock caused by a very brilliant light or a violent noise.

The third stage is that of somnambulism. It can be primarily induced by fixation or by other methods. Lethargy or catalepsy can be transformed into somnambulism, by light or repeated friction of the top of the subject's head. This condition is characterized by a more or less marked habitual anæsthesia, hyper-acute sensibility, and above all, by the susceptibility of the subject to all suggestions.

The neuro-muscular hyper-excitability does not exist in this stage. Permanent contractions cannot be induced by mechanical excitation of the muscles or nerves; but by means of light contact, or by gently breathing upon the skin, etc., a special contracture may be induced, "differing from the contracture of the lethargic state in that it cannot be relaxed by the excitation of the antagonistic muscles, and from cataleptic immobility in that it resists, when one wishes to alter the position." (Binet and Féré.)

Somnambulism can be transformed into catalepsy by opening the subject's eyes, or into lethargy, by closing the lids and pressing lightly upon the eye-balls. These three phases constitute what is called "*le grand hypnotisme*," or the great hypnotic neurosis.

The Nancy school has been reproached with having rushed suddenly into the field of psychical phenomena instead of having first studied the somatic, physical characters of the subjects hypnotized. They say that we have confused and confounded all the different conditions without discerning them; in short, that we have not mentioned whether our patients were in the lethargic, cataleptic, or somnambulistic condition.

I reply that if we have not taken the three phrases of hysterical hypnotism, as Charcot describes them, for the starting-point of our researches, it is because we have not been able to confirm their existence by our observations. The following is what we constantly observe at Nancy. When a patient, hysterical or not, is hypnotized by no matter what method, by fixation upon a brilliant object, or upon the operator's fingers or eyes, by passes, vocal suggestion, or closure of the eyelids, there comes a moment at which the eyes remain shut. Often, but not always, they are rolled up under the upper lid. Sometimes a twitching of the lids occurs, but this is not constant. We neither observe the existence of neuro-muscular hyper-excitability nor exaggeration of the tendon reflexes. Is this state that of lethargy? I insist upon it, that in this condition, as in all hypnotic conditions, the hypnotized patient hears the operator. His attention is fixed upon him and his ears are prepared to catch any sound. He frequently answers questions; indeed, this is almost always the case, if it is insisted upon, and he is told that he can speak. Then although he remains motionless and insensible, with his face as expressionless as a mask, and to all appearance isolated from the outer world, he hears everything. Upon waking, later, he may or may not remember all that has passed. The proof is that without touching him and without blowing on his eyes, he is awakened by simply saying, once or twice, "Wake up."

In this condition, the subject is capable of manifesting the phenomena of catalepsy or somnambulism without the necessity of subjecting him to any manipulation, provided the degree of hypnotization is deep enough.

In order to cause a limb to assume the cataleptic condition, it is not necessary to open the patient's eyes or to subject him to a brilliant light or to a loud noise, as is done at the Salpêtrière. It is sufficient to lift the limbs, keeping them up for some time and asserting that the patient is unable to lower them again. They remain in suggestive catalepsy and the subject hypnotized, whose will or power of resistance is enfeebled, passively maintains the position imposed upon him.

It is unnecessary to rub the crown of the head as is done at the Salpêtrière, in order to demonstrate somnambulistic characteristics in patients who are capable of showing them. To speak to the patient is enough, and being susceptible to suggestion, he performs the action or realizes the phenomenon suggested. Passes or breathing upon the skin bring about no contracture of the underlying muscles, in our subjects, when suggestion is not used. We have not observed that the act of opening or of shutting the eyes, or of rubbing the top of the head modify the phenomena in any way, or that these actions develop the phenomena in subjects incapable of manifesting them by suggestion alone.

We have simply observed that there are variable degrees of susceptibility to suggestion in hypnotized subjects. Some manifest only occlusion of the eyes, with or without a general drowsiness; others exhibit beside this, a relaxation of the limbs with inertia or inaptitude for spontaneous movements; others still, retain the attitudes impressed upon them—(suggestive catalepsy). In short, suggestive contracture, automatic obedience, anæsthesia and provoked hallucinations mark the progressive development of this susceptibility to suggestion. One subject out of about six or seven hypnotized, reaches the highest degree of somnambulism, with amnesia upon waking, and when he does not reach this degree immediately by hypnotization alone, none of the manœvres we have tried can develop it. Continued suggestion alone has been able to produce it. The degree of hypnotic suggestibility has always seemed to us to depend upon individual temperament and the psychical influence exercised; not in the least upon the manipulation employed.

This is what I have constantly observed in the several hundred people whom I have hypnotized. None of my colleagues' at Nancy, nor M. Liébault, who has hypnotized more than six thousand persons during the last twenty-five years, have ever observed anything to the contrary.

I have never been able to induce in any of my cases, the three phases of the Salpêtrière school, and it is not for want of trial. I add, that even in three hospitals in Paris, I have seen subjects hypnotized in my presence and they acted as our subjects do, and the doctors who were treating them fully confirmed our observations.

Once only did I see a subject who exhibited perfectly the three periods of lethargy, catalepsy and somnambulism. It was a young girl who had been at the Salpêtrière for three years, and why should I not state the impression which I retained of the case? Subjected to a special training by manipulations, imitating the phenomena which she saw produced in other somnambulists of the same school, taught by imitation to exhibit reflex phenomena in a certain typical order, the case was no longer one of natural hypnotism, but a product of false training, a true *suggestive hypnotic neurosis.*

Even if I am mistaken, and these phenomena are met with primarily, and without any suggestion, we must recognize that this "grand hypnose" is a rare condition. Binet and Féré say that only a dozen of these cases have occurred at the Salpêtrière in ten years. Should these cases, opposed to thousands of cases in which these phenomena are wanting, serve as the basis for the theoretical conception of hypnotism?

It would be a curious thing in the history of hypnotism to see so many distinguished minds misled by an erroneous first conception, and carried into a series of singular errors which no longer permit them to see the truth. Grievous errors they are, for they hinder progress by obscuring a question which is so simple that everything explains itself, when it is known that suggestion is the key to all hypnotic phenomena!

From this point of view, there is nothing more curious to read than the many transfer experiments of MM. Binet and Féré. These authors conclude from their experiments, that the application of a magnet to a hypnotized subject can transfer to the side to which it is applied,—for example, to the upper left limb,—such phenomena as anæsthesia, contracture, paralysis, etc., which have been provoked on the opposite side,—for example, in the upper right limb. In the same way, the magnet is supposed to transfer sensorial anæsthesia, hallucinations of the senses, of smell, hearing, sight, taste, and touch. This transfer is supposed to take place without the intervention of suggestion, by a simple physical phenomenon in which the subject's brain, considered as the psychical organ, takes no part.

These authors think they have eliminated suggestion because they have made their experiments in the conditions known as lethargy and catalepsy. They say, "These are unconscious states in the 'grand hypnose,' states in which the condition of the senses and intelligence renders the subject a complete stranger to what is going on around him. Experiment, however, shows that in these conditions the magnet transfers a large number of phenomena." This is a fundamental error, which has been the source of all the experimental illusions of these authors.

I repeat that the subject remains conscious in all degrees of hypnotism, as we have observed in thousands of cases in Nancy.

If, in the twelve only cases in which, during the space of ten years, the phenomena of what is called "*great hypnotism*," to distinguish it from what is known as the "*little hypnotism*," *of the Nancy School*, have been observed ; if in these cases, an apparent unconsciousness during what is called the lethargic state has been noticed, I believe that it was only an illusion. The subject, unconsciously educated in this suggestion, cannot react in this condition, because *he believes* he cannot, because *the idea has been introduced into his brain*, that as the necessary manipulation has not been made upon him, he cannot emerge from this state, and cannot accept any suggestion. Nothing is easier than to artificially create an analogous condition in all somnambulistic cases.

This granted, I have tried to reproduce MM. Binet's and Féré's experiments. I have tried a great many times on a great many subjects, in the presence of several colleagues, among them, MM. Beaunis and Charpentier, and should never have succeeded unless suggestion had been employed.

For example, here is an experiment which I made with M. Beaunis. We hypnotized a nurse in our service who was susceptible to somnambulism. She had never been present, either as witness or subject of the kind of experiment which I wanted to try on her. I put the upper left limb into the cataleptic condition in the horizontal position, the thumb and index finger stretched out, the other fingers bent ; the right arm remained relaxed.

I applied a magnet to it for eight minutes. No phenomenon occurred.

Then, turning to M. Beaunis, I said, " Now I am going to try an experiment. I shall apply the magnet to the right hand (on the unaffected side), and in a minute you will see this arm lifted and take the exact attitude of the left arm, while the latter relaxes and falls."

I placed the magnet just where it was at first, and in a minute, the suggested transfer was realized with perfect precision. The subject's face was expressionless. It was a lifeless mask.

If then, without saying anything more, I put the magnet back against the left hand at the end of a minute, the transfer occured in inverse order, and so on consecutively.

In the same subject, I can provoke wryneck by the contracture of the muscles of one side of the neck. I bring the magnet to the opposite side, *without saying anything*. In a minute, the head turns toward the side where the magnet is, and there is wryneck of the opposite side. The transfer has taken place.

A single statement to the effect that the transfer would occur, made to M. Beaunis in the subject's presence, sufficed to ensure the occurrence of the phenomenon on every subsequent occasion and for all positions, because the idea of the phenomenon had penetrated into the subject's mind, which was intelligent and attentive, in spite of her apparent inertia.

Afterwards I said, "I shall change the direction of the magnet, and the transfer will take place from the arm to the leg."

At the end of a minute, the arm fell, and the leg was raised. I put the magnet against the leg, *without saying anything*, and the transfer took place from the leg to the arm.

If, without saying anything to the subject, I replace the magnet by a knife, a pencil, a bottle, a piece of paper, or use nothing in its place, the same phenomenon occurs.

The next day, I repeated these experiments on another somnambulist who had been present the day before, and, without saying anything to her or to any of the persons present, they succeeded marvellously; the idea of the transfer had been suggested to her mind by the circumstances of which she had been a witness.

Moreover, after I had repeated this transfer from one arm to the other several times, on discontinuing the alternate applications of the magnet, the transfer recurred twice spontaneously (*consecutive oscillations*), doubtless, on account of *the idea* the person had that the experiment was being continued. Before this, I had tried several times to obtain the transfer in this subject, but without result, so that the idea of the phenomenon could not have penetrated into her mind.

MM. Binet and Féré state, also, that the transfer of localized phenomena such as the attitude of the limb in catalepsy, paralysis and hallucination, is accompanied with a localized pain in the head, generally appearing first on the side to which the magnet is applied, then passing to the other side. "The position of this pain is constant for the same limb, and the same sense, and should accord precisely with the corresponding cortical centre. Thus the transfer of the positions and of the paralysis of the upper limb, determines a pain which is localized at the level of the inferior extremity of the second frontal convolution, and of the corresponding region of the ascending frontal; for the movements employed in the articulation of words, inferior and anterior to this position; for the lower limb, about the upper part of the fissure of Rolando; for sight hallucinations, in the upper part of the inferior parietal lobule in the region where hemianopsia and word blindness have been localized; for hallucinations of hearing, in the anterior region of the sphenoidal-lobe."

Here is another one of these authors' experiments.

"Wit (the same somnambulist who served for all these transfer experiments) is in the somnambulistic condition. We suggest to her to count up to one hundred. When waked, she begins to count. A ten-armed magnet is placed near her right arm. When she gets as far as seventy-two, she stops, stutters, and can count no farther, and, in a minute, cannot even speak. She can readily stick out her tongue, however, and understands everything that is said to her. She is very lively and laughs continually; her head is turned to the left. In ten minutes, the magnet is applied to the left side. After about two minutes, her left arm begins to tremble, and her speech comes back. Her first words are, 'That makes me act foolishly.' Then she feels an inclination to cry, at the same time turning her head to the right.

"It is easy to account for what has happened," say these authors; "we have caused a peculiar excitement of the left brain, or, more exactly, of the convolution of Broca, by suggestion, which manifests itself outwardly by the act of counting aloud. The magnet has caused the transfer of this excitement to the symmetrical area of the right brain. The corresponding convolution on this side does not subserve speech; the patient is silent." (*Revue Philosophique*, January, 1885.)

I defy any one to reproduce these phenomena under conditions in which suggestion cannot play a part; and it is upon experiments of this kind that M. Binet builds up psychological theories, which he speaks of as *experimental!*

Is it worth while to say, that I have never observed the transfer, spontaneously accompanied with a localized pain in the head, in any of my hypnotic cases? But each time I stated that there would be a pain at such or such a part of the head, the subjects felt it. A second hypnotized subject sometimes manifested it spontaneously, when he had seen it exhibited by the first. Neither have I been able to determine, without suggestion, any phenomena by pressure exercised upon certain points of the cranium. For example, here is one of my somnambulistic cases hypnotized. I press upon the different points of the cranium successively; no result. I say, " Now I am going to touch that part of the cranium which corresponds to the movements of the left arm, and this arm will go into convulsion." Having said this, I touch an arbitrary part of the head; immediately the left arm is convulsed.

I say, "I press harder, and paralysis will take the place of excitement." The arm falls motionless. In the same way, I provoke convulsions localized to one side of the face.

I state that I am going to induce aphasia by touching the region corresponding to speech. I touch any part of the head, and the subject no longer replies to our questions; he answers as soon as I take my hand off his head. Then I state that I shall touch the head in such a way that irritation will result, instead of paralysis; speech will then be easier and the person then answers my questions in the following manner. " What is your name?" —"Marie—Marie—Marie—Marie." " How are you?"—" Well —Well—Well "—etc. " You have no pain?"—" None at all— none at all—none at all," etc.

It is well to add that many somnambulists possess extremely acute perception. The slightest indication guides them. Knowing that they should carry out the hypnotizer's thought, they make an effort to divine it. If the transfer experiments have been repeated many times with the same subject, he readily guesses that he should transfer such and such a phenomenon, and without anything being said before him, he can divine whether the transfer should occur or not, by the expectant attitude of the operator or by some other indication.

If I rather insist upon these facts and lay stress upon my critical observations, I do so in order that the doctrine of hypnotic phenomena may be perceived in its very origin.

I also wish to describe here, some experiments upon hallucinatory images which were made with the aid of my colleague, M. Charpentier. Nothing shows better that these experiments how readily suggestion takes effect and how deceptive is observation.

It is possible to suggest to many somnambulists during their sleep that they will see such and such things upon waking, and the hallucination may be realized with such vividness that the subject confounds it with reality. Now, MM. Féré, Binet, and Parinaud have concluded from their experiments, that this image acts like a real image, obeying the laws of optics. For example, they contend that a prism doubles it, or again, if cards are colored red and green by suggestion and these colors are superposed by one of the known methods, the patient sees gray as the resulting color produced by the mixture of these two complementary colors.

Are these results accurate? Does the image suggested, act as they allege, like a real image? Is it objective? Does it traverse the peripheral apparatus of vision, the retina and the optic nerve, up to the visual centre of the cerebral cortex? Or is it only a subjective image awakened directly as a memory in the visual center and evoked by the subject's imagination?

We have made some experiments calculated to decide this question and shall describe them in the order in which they were made.

As subjects, we have chosen non-hysterical women of medium intelligence and good judgment, who were susceptible during sleep to all grades of suggestion; that is to say, to anæsthesia, catalepsy, sensorial illusions, hypnotic and post-hypnotic hallucinations. All of them could be put into a condition of complete analgesia during their sleep. They did not move if their nostrils were tickled and there was no question of simulation in the matter. What is more, and we insist upon this fundamental precaution, all these experiments were performed *without saying a word, even in a low voice*, that could put the hypnotized subjects on the right track; because, and nothing can be more easily demonstrated, they hear in all degrees of the hypnosis, and often note everything with a delicacy of perception which is, at times, highly remarkable.

This premised, the following are the facts.

Louise C—— seventeen years old, healthy, is easily hypnotized by simple closure of the eyelids and an injunction to sleep. We prepare a disc of white card-board, and suggest to her that upon waking she will see the left side of the disc red and the right side green. She sees these two colors distinctly upon waking. We then put this card-board on a rotating disc and make it rotate rapidly. We know that when two primary colors fall thus simultaneously upon the retina, they are perceived as one color. Now, the two colors mentioned would, when blended, appear as yellow, but if we ask L—— what color she sees, she designates white.

2d. Having hypnotized her again, we suggest that she will see another disc, half yellow, half blue. When she wakes, we show her the same disc perfectly white, but she sees the two suggested colors. We make it rotate. She sees white again.

3d. While she sleeps, we prepare a real blue and yellow disc and she perceives it thus upon waking, and when rotated it again appears white to her.

4th. A perfectly blue disc appears red and yellow to her by suggestion. When rotated, it always appears white.

5th. The same blue disc is suggested to be blue and violet. When rotated, it appears white.

6th. A white disc is suggested to be red and yellow. When she wakes, she sees the two colors distinctly. On the opposite side of the card board out of Louise's sight, we had marked with a pencil the part suggested yellow, and the part suggested red. To displace the two colors, we turned the disc around, unknown to the subject, and asked her to indicate them. We repeated this experiment several times, and each time Louise pointed out, rapidly and exactly, the red and the yellow halves, as marked on the reverse side. But we perceived an opening, with a seam, in the center of the card-board, which might answer as a guiding mark. This we removed. Louise could not localize any longer. She pointed out the red and yellow at random, to the right or left, up or down. Her indications no longer agreed with the mark on the disc.

The second series of experiments was made with Rose A——, a girl eighteen years old, two months convalescent from typhoid fever, and like the preceding subject susceptible to all degrees of suggestion.

1st. During her sleep it is suggested that a white disc will appear half red, half yellow. When she wakes up, she sees the two colors clearly. When the disc is rotated, she sees yellow and red together.

2d. A white disc appears yellow and blue by suggestion. It is turned in another direction unknown to her. Rose localizes the yellow and the blue by chance. When the disc is rotated she sees both yellow and blue.

3d. A disc really red appears yellow and blue by suggestion. If the disc is displaced without her knowledge, she localizes the two colors by chance. She sees both yellow and blue, when it is rotated.

4th. A white disc appears red by suggestion. The disc being placed on a sheet of white paper, Rose is asked to fix her eyes on it for two minutes. Then it is lifted suddenly and she is asked what color she sees. She says only white. After a few seconds she thinks she sees the red appearing, but she does not see the complementary color green, which would appear after gazing at an actually red object.

A third series of analogous experiments was made with Mme. G——, forty-seven years old, troubled with arthropathy of the right knee, secondary to locomotor ataxia. She is a very intelligent woman and highly suggestible, like the two preceding cases.

1st. A white disc appears red and yellow by suggestion. If we turn it another way, she localizes the two colors by chance. When rotated, she sees two colors at once.

2d. The same result is obtained with the same disc suggested to be red and green, or yellow and violet.

3d. A white disc is suggested to be half red, half white. When she wakes, she says she sees the red half very distinctly. She is told to fix her eyes on the disc for some time and then is asked the color of the other half. She always states that it is white and not green, the color complementary to red.

4th. In the waking condition she is shown a disc, one half of which is really red and the other green. Then it is rotated. She recognizes perfectly the yellow color, the result of the mixture of the two colors.

Then we put her to sleep and suggest that upon waking she will see this same red and green disc. We wake her and show her a white disc. She sees it as red and green. We rotate it, she sees white first, then both red and green.

We hypnotize her again and suggest that when she wakes she will see the same red and green disc, but that when we rotate the disc, the two colors will blend into a single one which we shall indicate.

When waked, she sees the red and green disc again. When rotated, it appears to her yellow, as she had seen it before being hypnotized.

5th. Before being hypnotized she is shown a blue and orange disc. During sleep we suggest that she will see this same disc, and that in rotating it rapidly, she will see but one color.

When she wakes, she sees (on a really white disc) the two colors, the union of which on a rotating disc makes her see fire color, which she compares to a sunset. The union of the two colors really gives gray.

6th. Before being hypnotized, she is shown a disc two thirds red and one third yellow. Upon waking she sees these same colors by suggestion, on a disc which is really blue. When we rotate the disc, she sees a dirty gray or a gray-blue color. The real color formed by the mixture of the two is orange.

All these experiments agree. The suggested image does not act like a real image. The mixture of the suggested colors does not occur as is the case with differently colored rays of light impinging upon the retina. If it occurs, it is according to the will of the subject's imagination and contrary to optical laws.

We have made the following experiments in order to confirm and verify this conclusion.

We suggest to our hypnotized subjects that upon waking they will see some object, a light, for example, one or two metres in front of them.

When awakened they see the light. Then, we put a cylinder before their eyes, which contains a doubly-refracting prism, and which should, therefore, make an object appear double. Now the majority of subjects do not see the light double.

Then, if they are made to look at the *real* light through the prism, they see it double. If they once know that the prism has the property of doubling objects, they see this same duplication for the suggested image also. We said the *majority*, because one of our somnambulists, Rose (after submitting four times to this experiment), saw the image double at first sight, without having known, apparently, the property of a prism. This series of experiments will show that we have not been slow to discover that certain subjects recognize the doubling of the image, because they deduce it psychically from the doubling of the real objects which traverse the field of the prism.

To continue the recital of our experiments.

According as the cylinder containing the prism is turned in one direction or the other, the two *real* duplicated objects are seen side by side on the same horizontal line, or, on the contrary, one above the other, on the same vertical line. We mark by points on a register, the position of the cylinder corresponding to the horizontal or vertical juxtaposition of the two images.

At a given distance in front of the subject, we place some object, a bottle, for instance, which we make him look at through the prism. He sees a double image. We ask him to turn the cylinder in such a way as to bring the two images side by side, then one above the other. His indications agree with the points on the register. He understands the handling of the prism now, and takes in thoroughly what he sees.

Then we hypnotize him and take the bottle away, while he is

asleep, suggesting that he will see it in the same position as before, when he wakes up. When he wakes, he does in fact see the imaginary bottle, and through the prism, a double image. We tell him to turn the prism, so as to produce two images, horizontally side by side, then vertically, one over the other. His indications are then purely imaginary, and no longer correspond to the points of the register.

Every time we replace the fictitious bottle by a real one, unknown to the subject, he gives exact indications corresponding to the registered points, thinking that he sees the same bottle each time. Every time that we remove the real bottle and suggest one in its stead, the indications become imaginary again.

It sometimes happens, however, that after a certain amount of experience, a subject gives exact indications deduced from the vertical and horizontal duplication of the real objects seen through the prism.

To avoid this source of error, we have suggested the appearance of a letter or number on a totally white wall without any object between it and the subject. The subject sees it single with his eyes, and through the prism, double, if he knows that the prism duplicates. The two images are juxtaposed or superposed, but with four subjects submitted for the first time to this experiment, the indications never corresponded to those given by a real object. The duplication occurs by chance, contrary to all rules, through the suggestion given by the imagination.

This manner of experimenting is not always sufficient to exclude error. To be perfectly convincing, the experiments must be repeated and varied. One must be on guard against everything.

We have used two cylinders of similar appearance: one containing a doubly refracting prism, the other plain glass. After placing one of our somnambulists before a white wall and suggesting that she would see the number six on it when waked, we waked her. She saw this number and when made to look at it alternately through the two cylinders, the effect of each being unknown to her, she recognized the doubling power of the prism each time, and even guessed the horizontal or vertical direction of the duplication frequently.

Four other somnambulists gave imaginary indications. The

first one, submitted to the same experiment at another time of the day, saw nothing more corresponding to optical laws.

In consequence of this, we ask ourselves if there may not be two different results here. Sometimes the duplication of the object may occur in the person's imagination only, varying according to her caprices. The effect of the prism may be hidden, so to speak, by the eyes of the imagination. At other times, on the contrary, she may *really* see the suggested image, single or double, just as the glass would represent a veritable object, the effect of the *prism* dominating and not allowing the imagination to wander into a deceptive suggestion.

The following fact may also give some support to this hypothesis. We put two cylinders one inside the other, each containing a doubly refracting prism. By making the two cylinders turn one about the other, the prisms are juxtaposed in such a way as to present the object double or quadruple. Now the first somnambulist whom we made look through this glass at the number six, suggested on the white wall (the glass being placed so that it could quadruple), saw four images at the first glance. The glass being then changed for duplication, she saw only two images.

This indication would appear striking to a superficial observer. It seems evident, however, that the images were not real, but suggested by some guiding mark, because the somnambulist always placed the four images horizontally side by side, while they should have been superposed, two above two.

To avoid guiding marks, we have placed this somnambulist out in the open air, and having hypnotized her have suggested that she would see a balloon very high up in the air when she woke. The sky was blue and cloudless, and she saw the balloon. We made her look alternately through the two glasses, only one of which doubled. Another somnambulist has been subjected to the same experiment. We have convinced ourselves that each time they directed the prism toward the balloon for the first time, they gave false indications. The indications did not become exact until they had found a chimney, a roof or some object to answer as a guide.

Of course, it is well to know that somnambulists sometimes (not always) display an astonishing sagacity in elucidating the problem set them. They want to solve it, they endeavor to do so, and all their attention being concentrated upon the question, they consciously or unconsciously find in the slightest sign, a crack in the wall, an almost imperceptible line, a guide, which, coming under the influence of the prism, suggests the same effect to them for the subjective image. If they have once found this indication, or once recognized a difference in weight, dimension, or brightness, between the simple and the prismatic glass, they are no longer deceived; they deceive in good faith.

To thwart any surprise of the senses and to exclude absolutely anything liable to guide the imagination, we have acted in the following manner. We took two subjects into a dark room and having hypnotized them, suggested that they would see a lighted candle on the mantel-piece when they awakened. They saw it very distinctly. We then asked them to look at this fictitious candle through the two prisms which we put alternately in the positions of doubling and quadrupling. The experiment was repeated at least twenty times with each subject. We had proved previously with a real candle, that the objects were distinct and that there were no sources of error. Under these conditions their indications were erroneous and it was perfectly evident that when so restricted that their eyes could not fix upon any point of indication, they saw the image single, double, triple or quadruple, solely according to the fancy of their *auto-suggestion*.

We give the following experiments as conclusive.

We suggested to Mme. G—— during sleep, that she would see a red wafer on her white bed-spread when she woke (there was nothing on the bed), and at the same time an orange hung at the foot of her bed. When she woke she saw both objects. If she looked at the wafer through the two prisms, she saw it by chance, single, double, triple, or quadruple, the positions of the prisms never agreeing with what they should have been for a real object. On the other hand, if she looked at the imaginary orange hung at the foot of the bed through the glass, she was no longer deceived. Her indications agreed with the optical position of the glass. Why this difference? Because in the first case, she did not see any point of indication on the white bed-spread, while when she looked at the orange her imagination was enlightened by the real objects around it, which were doubled or quadrupled by the glass, and then the fictitious image followed logically the example of the real image, unknown to the subject.

If we first made her see an orange quadrupled by the prism (according to the position of the glass), and afterwards directed the glass upon the wafer, she would quadruple the latter also, but never gave the four images the respective positions which the prism demanded. If on the other hand, we asked her to look through the glass at the wafer first, she was deceived; she saw it doubled for example, instead of quadrupled. If afterwards she turned the glass from the wafer to the imaginary orange, the latter, owing to the points of indication between her and it, appeared quadrupled, and this greatly astonished Mme. G—— who is an intelligent woman and understands the fact very clearly, that if a prism quadruples one object it quadruples all the others also.

Before hypnotization, we made another one of our somnambulists, Mme. X——, see a piece of orange skin which M. L—— was holding in her hand at the foot of the bed. Then having hypnotized her, we suggested that she should see the same piece when she woke, and when waked, she saw the fictitious piece of skin, though M. L—— held nothing in her hand. Then we requested that she should look through the glass (arranged to quadruple), and asked if it caused any change. (She had no idea of the property of the glass.) She stated that she saw a whole orange, one only. Her imagination had evidently suggested this change to her. Then, unknown to the subject M. L—— took the real piece of skin in her hand again. Mme. X—— saw it clearly, without the glass, thinking it to be the same one (fictitious) she saw at first. We made her look through the glass again, and this time she saw four pieces of skin distinctly. This experiment was repeated several times with her and always succeeded. The fictitious piece of skin when looked at through the glass was transformed by the imagination into an entire orange; the actual piece was transformed into four pieces, according to the properties of the prism.

Such are the facts, and we could add others. All have been carefully verified. They have left no doubt in our minds; they have forced upon us this conviction, easy to foresee, that the suggested image is a fictitious image, and that it answers to no material representation in space. A prism can double only rays passing through it from a *real* object. It cannot double an image perceived behind it in the cerebral centres. The hallucinatory image may be as distinct, as bright, and as active to the subject as reality itself, but, borne entirely in the subject's imagination, he sees it as he conceives it, as he interprets it, as conscious or unconscious memory brings it up again in the sensorium. It is a psychical cerebral image and not a physical one. It does not pass by the peripheral apparatus of vision, has no objective reality, follows no optical laws, but obeys solely the caprices of the imagination.

I should acknowledge that M. Binet has mentioned the existence of points of indication which served as a material substratum for hallucination in his article "Hallucinations" in the *Revue philosophique*. But if this is true, do these experiences constitute, as the author believes, a method of making the phenomenon *objective*, the method which he reproaches me with having neglected? Hallucination has no objective characteristics, but only subjective ones, rendered objective by the imagination.

And now, may I be permitted to again say to MM. Féré and Binet, and to all who may desire to repeat their experiments:

1st. Take inexperienced subjects who have not been used in this kind of experiment, who have not assisted in such experiments made upon others and have not heard them talked about ;

2d. Make the experiment without speaking a single word before the subject, even in a low voice, because in all degrees of hypnotism he hears and notes everything with a sharpness of perception, which is often quite remarkable.

I maintain that the conclusion will not be doubtful, and I feel convinced that after these experimental counter-proofs, the young contributor to the *Revue Philosophique*, better enlightened upon the question, will have the courage to rectify some of his criticisms.

CHAPTER VII

Historical sketch.—Mesmer and mesmerism.—His condemnation by the learned societies.—Husson's report.—Abbot Faria and sleep by suggestion.—Alexandre Bertrand's doctrine.—Gen. Noizet's experiments and the fluidic doctrine.—Second period: Braid and Braidism.—Analysis of the doctrine.—Grimes and Electro-biology in America and in England.—Durand de Gros' experiments and doctrine.—Dr. Charpignon's moral medicine: his fluidic doctrine.—Braidism in France: Prof. Azam's communication.—Application to surgical anæsthesia.—Experiments and doctrine of Dr. Liébault of Nancy: hypnotic sleep compared with ordinary sleep.—Hypnotism in animals: Kircher, Czermak, Preyer, Wilson, Beard.—Induced somnambulism in France: Chas. Richet's experiments.—Induced sleep in cases of Hysteria: Charcot's and Dumontpallier's experiments.—Hypnotism in man in Germany: experiments of the Danish magnetizer, Hansen; Rumpf's physiological theories; Preyer's chemical theories; Schneider's, Berger's and Heidenhain's psycho-physiological theories.—Prosper Despine's theory.—Recent publications.

I HAVE published the phenomena of suggestion as I have observed them, so that any one wishing to repeat my experiments might be able to do so. I have stated only that which I have seen and verified and which has been verified by others a number of times. I hasten to add that I have seen nothing which has appeared to me opposed to the physiological and psychological conceptions already established by science. Is it necessary to say that I have observed nothing of a marvellous nature, such as clairvoyance, prevision of the future, spiritual insight, sight at a distance or through opaque bodies, transposition of the senses or instinctive knowledge of remedies?

For a long time the truth has been drowned in a flood of hazy practices and chimerical absurdities; so that the history of magnetism appears as one of the greatest vagaries of the human mind. Scientific men rejected what was opposed to reason; classic science repelled that which was alien to it. Only a shameless charlatanism, which fell into disgrace, continued to profit by public credulity.

All was not worthless, however, in the foolish and arrogant conceptions of mesmerism. A few earnest persons insisted in seeing a grain of truth in the midst of the errors, and in distinguishing the kernel from the chaff. To-day, magnetism is dead together with alchemy, and hypnotic suggestion is born of magnetism as chemistry is born of alchemy.

I shall not go back to the history of Mesmer and of mesmerism. It has been written by Figuier and by Bersot, and delineated by the master hand of Dechambre in the *Dictionnaire encyclopédique des Sciences Médicales*. Who has not heard of the *baquets* of Mesmer, of the patients standing silently in rows around these *baquets*, of the magnetizer's animal current meeting with the current from the pit and after a time causing different nervous or hysteriform troubles, or troubles analogous to those of somnambulism, veritable convulsionary scenes? And who has not heard of the doctrine of a universal magnetic fluid which is capable of receiving, propagating and communicating all the impressions of movement by which a mutual influence is exerted between the celestial spheres, the earth and animated bodies! The learned societies, the Academy of Science and the Royal Society of Medicine condemned the new doctrines after examining them. "From a curative point of view," said the latter, "animal magnetism is nothing but the art of making sensitive people fall into convulsions. From a curative point of view, animal magnetism is useless and dangerous."

In spite of the discredit which the interested charlatanism of Mesmer threw upon his practices, magnetism continued to have its followers; moreover it became modified by his pupils. The Marquis of Puységur, the most celebrated of all these pupils, magnetized by means of passes, by contact, and by the use of glass rods, and the influence of a magnetized tree. By these means he really induced the condition known as somnambulism, our actual knowledge of which appears to be inseparably connected with his name. According to his interpretation, the essence of animal magnetism lay in the action of the will upon the vital principle, the focus of electricity, that is of movement.

Numerous magnetic societies were gradually founded in the principal cities of France. In Strasbourg, the Society of Harmony, consisting of more than 150 members, published the result of their work for several years.

The disturbances incident to the revolutionary period and the wars of the Empire directed thought into other channels. Nevertheless, innumerable books and essays for or against magnetism, continued to attract attention.

When order and quiet were again established, the question came to the front once more. Public courses were instituted; the official world and the learned societies showed less opposition. In 1820, Dupotet carried on a series of experiments at the Hotel-Dieu, and afterwards at the Salpêtrière. In 1825 Dr. Foissac sent a note to the Academy of Science and to the Academy of Medicine, requesting them to pass judgment upon him. At his request these societies again began the investigation of animal magnetism. Six years after, on June 21, and 28, 1831, Husson's report was read before the Academy. "The favorable conclusions of this report," says Dechambre, "give a general idea of the state of magnetism about 1831, as it had been moulded by the action of the times and the many tests through which it had passed."

To-day, when the question seems to have escaped from clouds of theory and the charlatanism which enveloped it so long, it is interesting to go back and read the conclusions reached in this remarkable report, which contains and recognizes the value of the majority of the facts, as we have described them, in a reasonable way.

The following are some of these conclusions.

Contact of the thumbs and hands, the frictions or certain movements called passes, which are made a short distance from the body are the means used to put different persons in relationship, in other words, to transmit the action of the magnetizer to the person magnetized.

The time necessary for the transmission and testing of the magnetic action is from half an hour to one minute.

After a person has been magnetized several times, it is not always necessary to use contact and passes in order to magnetize afresh. The hypnotizer's gaze, or his wish only, have the same influence over the subject.

More or less remarkable changes ordinarily occur in the perceptions and faculties of individuals who fall into the somnambulistic condition through the effect of magnetism.

(*a*). In the midst of the noise of confused conversation, certain subjects do not hear anything but the magnetizer's voice. Many reply in a precise way to questions asked them by the magnetizer or by persons with whom they have been put into magnetic relationship; others converse with all the people around them. It is rare, however, that they hear what happens about them. Most of the time they are complete strangers to external and unexpected noises, such as the resounding of brass vessels struck near them, the falling of furniture, etc., even when made near their ears.

(*b*). The subject's eyes are closed, and it is difficult to force the lids open with the hand. This painful operation shows the eye-balls sometimes rolled up and sometimes down.

(*c*). The sense of smell sometimes seems to be destroyed. The subject may be made to inhale the fumes of muriatic acid or ammonia without showing any ill feeling, and without even suspecting it. The contrary holds true in certain cases and odors are noticed.

(*d*). The majority of the somnambulists we have seen, were completely insensible. Their feet, nostrils and the corners of their eyes could be tickled with a feather, their skin pinched so that it bled, a pin could be run under their nails to a considerable depth without their being aware of it. Finally we saw one somnambulist who was insensible during one of the most painful surgical operations, and in whom neither the face, nor the pulse, nor the respiration denoted the slightest emotion.

We have only seen one case, which, magnetized for the first time, fell into somnambulism. Sometimes the somnambulism did not appear until the eighth or tenth séance.

On waking, the subjects say that they have totally forgotten all the circumstances of the somnambulistic state, and they never recall them. On this point we have no other guarantee than their declarations.

In order to estimate the relationship of magnetism to therapeutics justly, it would be necessary to observe the effects of it on a large number of individuals, etc. This not having been done, the commission had to limit itself to the statement that it had observed too small a number of cases to dare pass judgment upon the question.

Some of the patients magnetized have not felt any benefit from it, others have been more or less improved. In one case there was a suspension of habitual pain, in another a return of strength, in a third, epileptic seizures were postponed for several months, and a fourth completely recovered from an old and serious paralysis.

Regarded as a means of inducing physiological phenomena or as a therapeutic agent, magnetism ought to take rank as one of the resources of medicine; consequently physicians only should make use of it and direct its employment as is done in the countries of the North.

The Academy did not dare to print Husson's report. They let him shoulder the responsibility of his own opinions. The probity of the writer was above suspicion, but he got a reputation for credulity which long remained attached to his name.

Several years later, in 1837, a magnetizer named Berna made

experiments relative to the transfer of sight, before a new commission, appointed by the Academy. Nobody was convinced. Dubois made a negative report. Burdin, the elder, another of its members, offered a prize of three thousand francs to the person who could read without the help of his eyes and without a light. The candidates came, but the prize was not awarded. At the end of October, 1840, the date of the adjournment of the assembly, the Academy decided that it would no longer answer communications concerning animal magnetism. So again in this case, the truth contained in Husson's report was drowned in the chimerical absurdity of the marvellous.

We have now reached the second period of the history of animal magnetism. The doctrine of a magnetic fluid regarded either as a universal fluid or as an emanation from the human organism, animal heat or electricity, was unable to bear the test of scientific investigation. The persons commissioned by the learned societies had all been impressed by the influence of the imagination in the production of the phenomena. Deslon himself, Mesmer's first pupil, wrote in 1870, "If M. Mesmer possessed no other secret but that of being able to benefit health through the imagination, would this not always be a sufficient wonder? For, if the medicine of the imagination is the best, why should we not make use of it?"

About 1815 an Indian Portuguese Abbot from the Indies, who had become celebrated under the name of the Abbot Faria,* gave a series of strange mystic lectures, in which he taught that the cause of somnambulism lies in the subject and not in the magnetizer, and that the sleep cannot be produced against the subject's will. He assembled about sixty persons every day and

---

*The following are the statements made by Gen. Noizet about him. "The Abbot-Faria was a man endowed in many respects with superior understanding. All Paris has had an opportunity of witnessing his experiments; nevertheless few persons have been convinced. When they branded him with the name of charlatan, all was said. Many persons were persuaded beforehand that they would see sleight-of-hand tricks and only visited him once. All persons upon whom the experiments succeeded they regarded as accomplices. If, in an assembly of several persons, it happened that one of them experienced some influence and fell asleep or became somnambulistic, the effect was at first astonishing to those who could not doubt its reality; but afterwards the impression became weaker, and the power of the word charlatan was sufficiently great to make them forget what they had seen, and even the person who had felt the influence, deluded himself like the others, and in the end believed that nothing out of the way had happened to him. The shame of having something in common with a man called a charlatan frequently made them deny the truth, and

tried his experiments on eight or ten of the number among whom one, two, and sometimes more fell into a state of somnambulism.

The person to be magnetized was seated in an arm-chair and was requested to close his eyes and collect his thoughts. Then, all at once, the magnetizer said in a strong and imperative voice, "Sleep," repeating the command three or four times if necessary. After a slight shock, the subject sometimes fell into the condition which Faria called lucid sleep.

The doctrine of suggestion was created at least as an explanation of the mechanism for the production of sleep, if not as an interpretation of the so-called clairvoyant phenomena, which are manifested in this sleep.

In 1819, Alexandre Bertrand, a former pupil of the Polytechnic School, and a doctor of medicine, announced a series of public lectures on animal magnetism. He attributed all the effects he observed to the properties of a magnetic fluid, that is, he was a mesmerist.

At the same time an officer (afterwards Gen. Noizet), a follower of Abbot Faria, who had been deeply impressed by the facts which he observed, denied the fluid theory and admitted the existence of no other force but that of the imagination, the conviction of the person who experienced the effects.

He allied himself with Bertrand, whom he finally converted to his belief. "Too much so perhaps," adds Gen. Noizet, "in that he (Bertrand) rejects even the little I took from his system."

Bertrand's definite opinions were published in his *Traité du Somnambulisme et des différentes modifications qu'il présente*, written in 1823. According to his views the phenomena are due

---

they even dared to state that a plan had been laid to deceive the audience and the juggler himself. No one who knows the weakness of the human heart should be astonished at what I state. I have been the more impressed by this, as I have had occasion to verify it for myself.

"It actually happened one day however, that an actor simulated somnambulism and deceived the Abbot Faria. From this moment charlatanism was more loudly cried than ever, as though it was a charlatan's part to expose himself to such contempt, and to allow himself to be thus taken in by an unknown person. His experiments were no longer attended, and it was considered absurd to believe in them. Nevertheless, I believe in them, and shall never blush to proclaim the truth. I do not declare myself the champion of the Abbot Faria, whom I hardly knew. I do not know what his morality was, but I am certain that he produced the effects which I have reported."

to the peculiar form of nervous exaltation to which he gave the name of ecstasy. The possessed patients of Loudun, the magnetized persons around Mesmer's *baquets*, and the somnambulists, were in this ecstatic condition; a condition which is characterized by loss of consciousness, moral inertia, and loss of memory on waking, instinctive knowledge of remedies, thought transmission, and sight without the help of the eyes, and an exalted state of the imagination.

It is a singular thing that Gen. Noizet, after having rescued Bertrand from his first (mistaken) conceptions, dominated by his spiritualistic ideas and striving to reconcile the opposed fluidic and anti-fluidic doctrines, soon fell back on the fluidic theory himself. It is by this hypothesis of a vital fluid that the author explains the interesting phenomena which he relates in a memoir addressed to the Royal Academy of Berlin in 1820. (*Mémoir Sur le somnambulisme et le magnétisme animal.* Paris, 1854.)

Although the doctrine of suggestion had its precursors, it was not until the year 1841 that it was definitely established and demonstrated by James Braid, of Manchester.* To him is due the discovery of hypnotism, and the words *Braidism* and *Braidic suggestion* have remained in science to commemorate a new doctrine which arose in the face of Mesmerism.

Braid proved that no magnetic fluid exists and that no mysterious force emanates from the hypnotizer. The hypnotic state and its associated phenomena are purely subjective in their origin, which is in the nervous system of the subject himself. The fixation of a brilliant object so that the muscle which holds up the upper eyelid becomes fatigued, and the concentration of the attention on a single idea bring about the sleep. The subjects can even bring about this condition in themselves, by their own tension of mind, without being submitted to any influence from without. In this state, the imagination becomes so lively that every idea spontaneously developed or suggested by a person to whom the subject gives this peculiar attention and confidence, has the value of an actual representation for him. The oftener these phenomena are induced, the more readily and easily can they be induced, for such is the law of association and habit. If the hypnotizer's will is not expressed by his words or his gest-

---

* Braid: *Neurypnology.* Translated from the English by Jules Simon, with a preface by Brown-Séquard. Paris, 1883.

ures, or if the subject does not understand them, no phenomena appear. The attitude which is given the hypnotized subject, the position into which the muscles of his limbs or face are put, may give rise to sentiments, passions, and acts corresponding to these anatomical attitudes, in the same manner that the suggestion of certain sentiments or passions may give rise to a correlative mimicked attitude or expression.

This part of Braid's work cannot be attacked. Observation confirms it on all points. But is this true of the phreno-hypnotic experiments in which, by manipulation of the neck and face, he pretends to excite certain corporeal and mental manifestations, according to the parts touched, and in this way to stimulate through the medium of the sensory nerves of the head, organs localized in the brain corresponding to the different passions, benevolence, imitation, theft, etc?

I believe with Brown-Séquard "that Braid did not guard sufficiently against the effects arising from suggestion when he believed that he had found proofs of the verity of the phrenological doctrines in his subjects. It is easy for any one to see how Braid committed the faults which I mention, if he realizes that a single word spoken to the hypnotized subject from a distance, is sufficient to suggest a whole series of ideas to him, or to develop the most varied sentiments or acts."*

Moreover it seems to me that at the end of his life Braid felt some doubt about his experiments relative to phreno-hypnotism. In his last memoir, a remarkable *résumé* of his work addressed to the Academy of Sciences in 1860, at the time of the experiments of Azam and Broca, he passes by his phreno-hypnotic researches in silence. He contents himself with saying that his experiments on the emotional phenomena induced by contact with the scalp, led him to conclude that the results obtained neither proved nor disproved the phrenological organology. He explains his error relative to the correlation which he supposed to exist between the frontal integument and the memory, by the fact that contact with the forehead of a hypnotized subject gives rise to a more efficacious suggestion by driving away distraction and reveries, and so enabling the subject to fix his attention better on the question, and answer it correctly.

---

* *Preface to the Treatise on Nervous Sleep or Hypnotism*, by James Braid. Translated from the English by Jules Simon. Paris, 1883.

HYPNOSIS AND SUGGESTION 113

Braid's experiments did not make much stir in England; in France they were hardly known.

It was in America that the doctrine of magnetism was to reappear under a new name. About 1848 a New Englander by the name of Grimes induced analogous phenomena, without having heard of Braid's discovery it seems. He showed besides that these phenomena could be induced in certain subjects, in the waking condition, by simple vocal suggestion, which fact Braid had already mentioned in 1846, in a memoir, entitled: *The Power of the Mind over the Body.* Emotion, sensation, the passions, and even the exercise of the organic functions, could be modified by a foreign will without the induction of hypnotism.

This doctrine, designated by Grimes as *electro-biology*, was propagated in the United States by a multitude of professors "the majority of whom," says Dr. Philips, from whom I borrow these details, "were, unfortunately, not fitted for scientific investigation." In 1850 Dr. Dods delivered twelve lectures on this subject of "*Electrical Psychology*" before the Congress of the United States, in reply to a semi-official invitation, signed by seven members of the senate. He published these lectures under the title of *The Philosophy of Electrical Psychology*, etc., N. Y.

The new method was applied successfully in inducing insensibility in surgical operations, as well as in the treatment of diseases.

In 1850 it spread to England, and Dr. Darling was one of its first disseminators. Electro-biology caused hypnotism to be forgotten for an instant, but it was not long before it was recognized that the phenomena observed in the waking condition rank in importance with Braid's discovery, and the most distinguished English savants, J. H. Bennet, Simpson, Carpenter, Alison, Gregory, Dr. Holland, the physicist David Brewster, and Dugald Stewart the psychologist, published numerous confirmatory observations.

In France the public were indifferent to all these researches. Official medicine knew neither Braidism nor Electro-biology. Dr. Durand de Gros, under the name of Dr. Philips,* was the

---

* Being proscribed on Dec. 2d, he had to change his name in order to reënter France.

only one who called the attention of physicians and savants to these phenomena, through his oral and experimental lessons given in Belgium, Algeria, and at Marseilles, during the year 1853. In 1855 he published a treatise entitled: *Electro-dynamisme vital*, the abstract, theoretical conceptions of which, were too obscure to appeal to the medical public. Later, in 1860, appeared his *Cours théorique et pratique du braidisme ou hypnotisme nerveux*, in which the author's thought and method were presented with great clearness.

Braid had proved that the concentration of the attention and thought, obtained by fixation of the gaze, were the determining causes of the hypnotic state, but he did not try to fathom the physiological and psychological mechanism of the phenomena. Durand de Gros tried to go further, and to explain the relation which exists between this concentration of thought (the first point of departure of the Braidic modification), and the appearance of insensibility, catalepsy, and ecstasy; that is, in a word, the profound and general revolution of the economy which is its culminating point.

The following is the author's theory, as he himself gives it. A general and sufficiently intense activity of thought is necessary for the regular diffusion of nervous force in the nerves of sensibility. If this activity ceases, the innervation of these nerves is suppressed, and they lose their ability to conduct external impressions to the brain. In fact, we know that idiots are more or less anæsthetic, etc. On the other hand, sensation is the necessary stimulus to mental activity.

From this it follows, that in order to bring about insensibility it suffices to suspend the exercise of thought, and, in order to suspend this, it is necessary to isolate the senses from the external agents which act upon them. It is not possible to suspend the actions of the mind, but they may be reduced to a minimum, by submitting them exclusively to a simple, homogeneous, and continuous sensation; thus, its sphere of action is reduced to a simple point. The cerebral ganglion-cell continues to secrete its nervous force, but that only consumes a very small part of the whole amount; hence its nervous force accumulates in the brain until congestion takes place. This is the first part of the Braidic operation, which produces what the author calls the *hypotaxic condition*. This condition being once produced, the impression glides in as far as the brain through the half open door of the sensorium along the path of sight, of hearing, or of muscular sense, and the point to which this excitation is transferred immediately emerges from its torpor, to become the seat of an activity which the tension of the nervous force increases with all its power. Thus it is that the general arrest of innervation will all at once succeed an excessive local innervation, which, for example, will instantaneously substitute hyper-æsthesia for insensibility, and catalepsy, tetanus, etc., for relaxation of the muscular system, etc.

The available nervous force may be called to this or that functional point of the center of innervation, by directing toward this point an impression, which arouses its peculiar activity. To accomplish this, a mental impression is employed, that is to say, an idea is suggested. This constitutes the second stage of the Braidic operation, which Durand de Gros calls *ideoplastic*. The idea becomes a determining cause of the functional modifications to be induced. The mental excitation reproduces the sensations previously induced by means of organic excitations. These sensations, which are originated by means of an idea, are called sensations of recollection.

The experiments of Dr. Philips (Durand de Gros), did not succeed in dispelling the discredit into which magnetism had fallen with the medical public, and Braidism remained forgotten. It is, however, necessary to mention Dr. Charpignon of Orléans, who, about 1841, took a great interest in the subject of magnetism and emotional medicine in the treatment of nervous disease. His memoir entitled: *De la Part de la Médecine morale dans le traitement des maladies nerveuses* (1862), received honorable mention from the Academy of Medicine. The phenomena of hypnotic suggestion, and of suggestion in the waking state, which are there described, thus obtained the official sanction of this learned body for the first time. It was in reality a return to the summary decision of October 1, 1840. The memoir was published in 1864, under the title of: *Etudes sur la médecine animique et vitaliste*.

Dr. Charpignon admits, that, in addition to the moral influence, there exists a magnetic influence, which has just as much of a fluid nature as the luminous, caloric, and electric forces, and that this influence transmitted from the one organism to another through the terminations of the peripheral nerves, is, in certain individuals, a means of modifying the nervous and vital functions.

We must also mention Victor Meunier who, in 1852, in the journal *La Presse*, had the scientific courage to popularize the knowledge which official science then condemned.

In 1859, Braidism really made its entrance into France. A communication of Prof. Azam, of Bordeaux, to the surgical society, published in the *Archives de Médecine* (1860), gave it great, but ephemeral popularity. He became acquainted with the phenomena induced by the English physician, through a colleague who had read Carpenter's article on *Sleep* in *Todd's Encyclopædia*, and repeated the experiments upon a number of persons in good health successfully.

Demarquay and Giraud-Teulon (*Recherches sur l'hypnotisme ou sommeil nerveux*, Paris, 1860), and Gigot-Suard (*Les Mystères du magnétisme animal et de la magie dévoilés ou la Vérité démontrée par l'hypnotisme*, Paris, 1860), published some interesting observations. Surgeons, especially, sought for an anæsthetic agent in hypnotism, capable of replacing chloroform, and a satisfactory observation (on the incision of an ischio-rectal abscess by Broca and Follin) was presented to the Academy of Science in 1859. Some years afterward, Dr. Guérineau, of Poitiers, announced to the Academy of Medicine that he had amputated the thigh under hypnotic anæsthesia (*Gazette des hôpitaux*, 1859).

The use of hypnotism for the production of surgical anæsthesia was by no means a new thing. Dr. Charpignon reviewed the following facts, relative to operations practised during hypnotic anæsthesia, in the *Gazette des hôpitaux* in 1829. The removal of a breast by Jules Cloquet in 1845; in 1846, the amputation of a leg, and the extirpation of a gland, both painlessly performed by Dr. Loysel of Cherbourg; in 1845, a double thigh amputation by Drs. Fanton and Toswel of London; in 1845, the amputation of an arm, by Dr. Joly of London; and in 1847, the removal of a tumor of the jaw, by Drs. Ribaud and Kiaro, dentists of Poitiers.

In spite of these fortunate trials, surgeons soon showed that hypnotism only rarely succeeds as an anæsthetic, that absolute insensibility is the exception among hypnotizable subjects, and that the hypnotizing itself generally fails in persons disturbed by the expectation of an operation. Braidism seemed to be denuded of practical interest, and fell into oblivion.

If Lasègue had carried his researches a little further, he would have been able to resuscitate Braidism permanently. In an essay entitled: *Des Catalepsies partielles et passagères* (*Arch-génér. de médecine*, 1865), he proves that the simple closure of the eyes, in certain hysterical and even in certain non-hysterical subjects, induces degrees of sleep varying from drowsiness to complete lethargy accompanied with anæsthesia. These various grades are accompanied by a cataleptic rigidity of the limbs, which suddenly ceases when the subject is awakened, and regains the sense of sight.

But Lasègue went no further; he did not think of identifying these phenomena with the phenomena of hypnotic sleep, as Braid had described them.

In 1866, Dr. Liébault, who had been studying the question for a number of years, published a book entitled: *Du Sommeil et des états analogues considérés surtout au point de vue de l'action du moral sur le physique.* This is the most important work that has ever been published upon Braidism. As a partisan of the doctrine of suggestion, which he had pushed further than Braid had, and which he had applied with success to therapeutics, and as an enemy of the marvellous and of mysticism, the author sought to interpret the phenomena observed from the psycho-physiological standpoint.

His doctrine resembles that of Durand de Gros. The concentration of the mind on a single idea, the idea of sleep, facilitated by the fixation of the gaze, brings about the repose of the body, the deadening of the senses, their isolation from the external world, and finally the arrest of thought, and an unvarying condition of consciousness. Suggestive catalepsy is the consequence of this arrest of thought. His thoughts concentrated, the subject remains in relationship with the person who has put him to sleep. He hears him, and receives impressions from him. Being incapable of passing from one idea to another by himself, his mind remains fixed on the idea which has been last suggested to him. If, for example, this idea is that of extension of the arms, he keeps them extended.

Ordinary sleep does not differ from hypnotic sleep. The one is, like the other, due to the fixation of the attention and of the nervous force upon the idea of sleep. The individual who wishes to sleep, isolates his senses, meditates, and remains motionless. The nervous force concentrates itself, so to speak, at one point of the brain upon a single idea, and abandons the nerves of sensation, motion and special sense.

But the *ordinary sleeper is in relation with himself only*, as soon as his consciousness is lost. The impressions conducted to his brain by the nerves of sensibility or of organic life, may awaken diverse memory-sensations or images, which constitute dreams. These dreams are spontaneous, that is to say, suggested by himself.

The *hypnotized subject* falls asleep, with his thought fixed, *in relationship with the hypnotizer;* hence the possibility of the suggestion of dreams, ideas and acts, by this foreign will.

The loss of memory on waking from deep hypnosis, comes from the fact that all the nervous force collected in the brain during sleep, diffuses itself anew throughout the whole organism when the subject wakes, and this force, diminishing in the brain, makes it impossible for the patient to recall what he was conscious of before, after he has come to himself.

In ordinary sleep, or in a light grade of hypnotic sleep, the nervous force collected about the seat of the fixed idea is less. The other portions of the nervous system are not as inactive, the dreams are led in by peripheral impressions. Moreover, the waking is not sudden, but gradual. The nervous force accumulated in the brain, diminishes gradually, and when thought begins to be established, it grasps the recollection of the end of the sleep at least.

The work of the physician of Nancy was passed by unheeded, and hypnotism continued to be simply a scientific curiosity. People were satisfied to know that fixation upon a brilliant object produced sleep with anæsthesia in some subjects, and in others catalepsy, and the researches were carried no further.

In Germany, in 1873, Czermak * published his observations on the hypnotic condition induced in animals. As early as 1646, Athanasius Kircher had shown that a hen, placed with its feet bound before a line traced on the earth, remains motionless for a certain length of time; it retains the same attitude even when the ligature is removed, and when it is excited. Czermak obtained the same phenomena without the use of the ligature, and without tracing the line on the ground: it sufficed to keep the animal motionless for some time, with his neck gently stretched over the abdomen. Other animals, birds, salamanders,

---

* *Beobachtungen und Versuche über hypnotische Zustände bei Thieren.* (*Arch. f. Physiologie*, VII., p. 107, 1873.)

lobsters, pigeons, rabbits, and sparrows were hypnotized, and some were made cataleptic simply by fixation upon an object, a finger, match, etc., placed before their eyes.

Preyer * considered this state due to fear, and called it cataplexia. The contracture of tritons when seized, the effects of lightning, surgical shock, paralysis due to violent fright, the unconsciousness of animals wounded by fire-arms, might be phenomena analogous to those produced by hypnotizing animals, and might be due to the excitation of the regulating apparatus of central innervation by an intense tactile impression. In horses similar hypnotic conditions have been observed. In 1828 Constantine Balassa, † a Hungarian, called attention to the method of shoeing horses without danger of violence. By looking him square in the eyes, the horse is induced to draw back, to lift his head, and stiffen the cervical column, and he can be influenced to such a degree that he does not budge even if a gun is fired off in his neighborhood. Gentle friction with the hand across the forehead and eyes, might be used as a valuable auxiliary means of calming and quieting the gentlest horse, as well as the wildest.

In England, in 1839, Dr. Wilson produced a condition, which he called trance, in the animals of the London Zoological Gardens. Finally, more recently, in 1881, Beard, ‡ of Boston, compared these phenomena exhibited by animals in so-called trance or trancoidal states, with hypnotism in man, and showed that they may be obtained by various methods: fear (the attitude impressed on animals which renders them incapable of resisting, dorsal decubitus, ligature), magnetic passes, fixation with the eyes, bright light (fishing by torch-light, insects drawn to a candle), music; all methods which disturb the psychical equilibrium, and concentrate the cerebral activity upon a single idea.

In 1875, Charles Richet § resumed his experiments on man

---

* *Die Kataplexie u. d. thier. Hypnotismus.* (*Sammlung physiol. Abhandl., von W. Preyer.* 2 *Reihe*, 1 Heft. Jena, 1878.)

† *Methode des Hufbeschlages ohne Zwang.* Wien, bei Gerold, 1828.

‡ Beard, Geo. M., *Trance and trancoidal states in the lower animals.* (*Journal of comparative medicine and surgery,* April, 1881.)

All these facts of Czermak's, Preyer's, Balassa's and Beard's are extracts from a *General Review of Hypnotism*, by Möbius, of Leipzig. *In Schmidl's Jahrbücher,* Band 199, No. 1, 1881.

§ Chas. Richet, *Journal de l'anatomie et de la physiologie,* 1875. *Archives de physiologie.* 1880. *Revue Philosophique,* 1880 et 1883.

and studied induced somnambulism anew. He showed that by the so-called magnetic passes, by fixation upon a brilliant object, and by other empirical procedures, a neurosis, analogous to natural somnambulism, is obtained. It is difficult to obtain the first time, but almost always appears if one has patience enough to try several séances. Moreover, according to Richet, this magnetic neuropathy offers little in the way of therapeutic applications.

This author has had the merit of having called the attention of the medical world to the phenomena of hypnotism; he is one of those who has studied and best brought out the psychical phenomena of somnambulism.

In 1878, Charcot * studied somnambulism, induced in hysterical patients. His memorable researches are well known; the production of catalepsy with anæsthesia by fixation upon a bright light, and, in this condition, phenomena of suggestion, that is to say, the attitude impressed on the limbs reflecting itself by the expression of the physiognomy (smiles, prayers), the sudden disappearance of the light, replacing the catalepsy by a sleep with relaxation, or lethargy, the muscular hyper-excitability manifesting itself in this condition (the contracture of a muscle by slightly stimulating it, or its nerve), finally the friction of the head, transforming this lethargic state into somnambulism, with the possibility of walking, answering questions, etc.

Bourneville and Regnard have described and illustrated these experiments in the *Icongraphie de la Salpêtrière*. Charcot and his pupils did not formulate any theory for the interpretation of these phenomena. The interesting results of Dumontpallier, communicated to the Society of Biology, are also known.

In 1879, the question was again taken up in Germany A Danish magnetizer, named Hansen, a man unacquainted with medicine, travelled through the principal cities, giving public representations. I saw him at Strasbourg and at Nancy. He hypnotized according to Braid's method. Out of twenty persons in the audience, who submitted to his experiments, voluntarily, he found four who were susceptible of being thrown into catalepsy, and of receiving all sorts of suggestions. These

---

* *Comptes rendus de l'Académie des sciences*, 1881. *Progrès médical*, 1878, 1881 et 1882.

experiments were repeated by the professors of the University towns;—at Chemnitz by Weinhold,* Ruhlmann, and Opitz, at Breslau, by Heidenhain, Grützner, Berger and others.

Diverse theories sprang up: some purely physiological, like the theory of Rumpf,† who admitted the existence of reflex changes in the cerebral circulation, giving place to phenomena of cerebral hyperæmia or anæmia; others purely chemical, like that of Preyer, ‡ who believes that the concentration of thought causes an exaggerated activity of the cerebral ganglion-cells, from which result readily oxydizable products, such as the lactates, which make the brain drowsy by the abstraction of oxygen from its different parts. The rapidity of the hypnosis and the instantaneousness of the awakening, cannot be reconciled with these theoretical conceptions.

Finally, other doctrines are psycho-physiological. Schneider,§ of Leipzig, looks for the interpretation of the phenomena in the exclusive and abnormal concentration of the mind upon a single idea; the intellectual excitation, the exaggerated acuteness of the senses, and the vivacity of the imagination, might be due to the fact that the psychical activity concentrates itself upon a small number instead of being spread over a large field, a theoretical view already put forth in France, as we have seen, by Durand de Gros and by Liébault. Berger, of Breslau, also believes that the concentration of the whole thinking being upon a single idea gives rise to an inertia of the will, which constitutes the basis of the hypnotic condition; the cataleptiform rigidity might be a concomitant phenomenon, due to the fact, that the psychological excitation spreads itself to the excito-motor centres of the brain.

Heidenhain, of Breslau, gives an analogous hypothesis. He admits that the feeble and continued excitation of the nerves of special sense, acoustic or optic, brings about a suspension in the activity of the cells of the cerebral cortex; to this is added ex-

---

* Weinhold, *Hypnotische Versuche. Exper. Beitrage zur Kentniss des sogen. tierischen Magnetismus*. Chemnitz, 1880.—Ruhlmann, *Die Exper. mit dem sogen. thier. Magnet. Garten-laube*, No. 819. 1880.—Opitz, *Cheméitzer Zeitung*. 1879.—Heidenhain, *Der sogen. thier. Magnet.*, etc. Leipzig, 1880.—*Breslauer arztl. Zeitschr.* 1880.—Grützner, *Ibid.*—Berger, *Hypnot. Zustande.* (*Ibid.* 1880-1881.)

† Rumpf, *Deutsche med. Wochenschr.* 1880.

‡ Preyer, *Die Entdeck. des Hypnotismus.* Berlin, 1881.

§ Schneider, *Die psych. Ursache der hypnot. Erschein.* Leipzig, 1886.

altation of the activity of the reflex motor centres, lying subjacent to the cortex, perhaps, because the cortex is paralyzed, and its inhibitory action over the reflex is therefore wanting; perhaps, because in consequence of this same paralysis, all centripetal irritation transmitted to the brain spreads itself over a more circumscribed nervous domain, and for this reason acts more efficiently upon this excito-motor region.

M. Espinas, * Prof. of the Literary Faculty of Bordeaux, develops analogous physiological views. He made a special study of the sleep in hysterical subjects, and holds that in these subjects the nervous system is in a state of unstable equilibrium, and that rapid exhaustion of the higher centres follows prolonged and depressing sensations.

In terminating this historical review, let me call attention to the theory of Dr. Prosper Despine † of Marseilles, who has published one of the most interesting scientific studies on somnambulism. There exists, says the author, an automatic cerebral activity which manifests itself without the concurrence of the ego; for all nervous centres possess, in accordance with the laws which govern their activity, an intelligent power, without any ego, and without personality. In certain pathological cerebral states the psychical faculties may manifest themselves in the absence of the ego, of the mind, of consciousness, and may give rise to acts similar to those which normally are manifested through the agency of the ego. This is automatic cerebral activity. That which manifests the ego, on the contrary, is conscious cerebral activity. In the normal condition, these two activities are intimately bound together, they are but one, and always manifest themselves conjointly; in certain pathological nervous states they may be separated and act alone.

Somnambulism is characterized, physiologically, by the exclusive exercise of the automatic activity of the brain during the paralysis of its conscious activity. Hence, the somnambulist's ignorance of all that he has done in the somnambulistic condition does not arise from forgetfulness, but from the non-participation of the ego in these acts. In the following chapter we shall see whether this opinion has any foundation.

---

* Espinas, *Du sommeil provoqué chez les hystériques*, Essai d'explication psychologique de ses causes et de ses effets.—*Bulletin de la Société d'anthropologie de Bordeaux*, t, l, 1884.

† P. Despine, *Etude scientifique sur le somnambulisme.* Paris, 1880.

Admitting the doctrine (hypothetical) of Luys, that the different layers of the gray substance of the cortex possess different functions, and that the most superficial layer subserves sensation, while the middle layers subserve the intellectual faculties, and the deepest, the transmission of will for action,—the author believes he is bound to deduce from it that active somnambulism would be physiologically determined by the nervous functional paralysis of the most superficial layer of the gray substance of the convolutions, with persistence of the activity of the middle and deepest layers; but if the middle layer is similarly paralyzed, there occurs inactive somnambulism, which does not manifest any psychical activity.

In a study of Dr. Ladame, of Geneva, published in 1883, entitled *La Névrose hypnotique ou le magnetisme dévoilé*, there is a clear and complete exposition of the subject as understood at that time. Mention must also be made of the publication of M. Emile Yung, of Geneva, which appeared in 1883, entitled *Le Sommeil normal et le Sommeil pathologique*. (O. Doin, editor.)

Since my first publication which appeared in 1884, and which was soon followed by M. Liégeois's essay on *La Suggestion hypnotique avec le droit civil et criminel*, the question of hypnotism has been studied and discussed with great ardor. Special treatises on the subject have been published by Dr. Bottey,* Prof. Beaunis,† Dr. Cullerre, ‡ MM. Binet and Féré, § Dr. Gilles de la Tourette, ‖ and by MM. Fontan and Ségard. ¶ We must also make mention of the inaugural thesis of M. Louis Sicard,** of Montpellier; of M. Alphandery,†† of Paris; of M. Brullard ‡‡ of Nancy; and of the inaugural thesis of M. Barth. §§

For very interesting psychological and physiological studies,

---

* Bottey, *Le Magnétisme animal*. Paris, 1885.
† Beaunis, *Du Somnambulisme provoqué*. Paris, 1886.
‡ Cullerre, *Magnétisme et Hypnotisme*. Paris, 1886.
§ Binet et Féré, *Le Magnétisme animal*. Paris, 1886.
‖ Gilles de la Tourette, *L'Hypnotisme et les états analogues au point de vue médico-légal*. Paris, 1887.
¶ Fontan et Ségard, *Éléments de médecine suggestive*. Paris, 1887.
** Louis Sicard, *Contribution a l'étude de l'hypnotisme et de la suggestion*. Thèse de Montpellier, 1886.
†† Alphandery, *La Thérapeutique morale et la suggestion*. Thèse de Paris, 1886.
‡‡ Brullard. *Considérations générales sur l'état hypnotique*. Thèse de Nancy, 1886.
§§ Barth, *Le Sommeil non naturel : ses diverses formes*. Thèse d' agrégation, Paris, 1886.

we are indebted especially to M. Delboeuf,* M. Azam, † Prof. Enrico dal Pozzo,‡ of Pérouse, and Prof. Morselli, § of Turin. Among the authors who have written upon the question from a forensic point of view, I shall mention Prof. Lilienthal, ‖ of Zürich ; Dr. Giulio Campili, ¶ of Pérouse, and Dr. Paul Garnier,** of Paris.

The therapeutic applications have been brought to notice by Dr. Auguste Voisin,†† Prof. Desplats,‡‡ of Lille ; Dr. Vizioli,§§ in Italy ; Prof. Forel,‖‖ of Zürich ; and Dr. Von Renterghem,¶¶ of Amsterdam.

The *Elements of suggestive medicine*, by Drs. Fontan and Ségard of Toulon, contain ninety-nine clinical observations which show the efficacy of suggestion.

The *Revue Philosophique*, directed by M. Ribot, the *Revue de l'hypnotisme*, founded by Dr. Bérillon, the *Mémoires de la Société de Biologie* and the *Archives de neurologie*, contain a large number of interesting studies and observations. The numeration of all the publications which have appeared on this subject during the past years, would occupy too much space.

---

* Delboeuf, *Une visite à la Salpêtrière.* Bruxelles, 1886. *De l'origine des effets curatifs de l'hypnotisme. Etude de physiologie expérimental.* Paris, 1887. Articles in the *Revue Philosophique* and the *Revue de Biologie.*

† Azam, *Hypnotisme, double conscience et altérations de la personnalité.* Paris, 1887.

‡ Enrico dal Pozzo di Mombello, *Un Capitolo di Psicofisiologia. Conferenze.* Poligno, 1885.

§ Enrico Morselli, *Il Magnetismo animale.* Torino, 1886.

‖ Von Lilienthal, *Der Hypnotismus und das Strafgerecht.* Berlin et Leipzig, 1887.

¶ Guilo Campili, *Il grande ipnotismo nei rapporti col diritto penale e civile.* Torino 1886.

** Paul Garnier, *L'automatisme somnambulique devant les tribunaux.* Paris, 1887.

†† Auguste Voisin, several publications in the *Revue de l'hypnotisme.* Paris, 1886 et 1887.

‡‡ Desplats, *Applications thérapeutiques de l'hypnotisme et de la suggestion.* Lille, 1886.

§§ Vizioli, *La Thérapeutique suggestive.* (*Giorn. di neuropatologia.* Sept. et Dec. 1886.)

‖‖ Forel, Einige therapeutische Dersuchen mit dem Hypnotismus bei Geisteskrankheiten. (*Correspondenz-blatt fur Schweizer Aerzte*, 1887.)

¶¶ Von Renterghem, *Hypnotisme en Suggestie in de Genees, Kundige Praktijk.* Amsterdam, 1887.

CHAPTER VIII

The author's theoretical conception of the interpretation of the phenomena of suggestion.—Automatism in daily life; reflex acts; automatic instinctive acts.—Automatism in the new-born child, and in the adult.—Moderating influence of the mind.—Sensorial illusions rectified by the mind.—A. Maury's experiments.—Hypnagogic hallucinations.—Credulity.—Sensorial suggestions by imitation.—Automatic obedience.—Influence of the idea upon the act.—Despine's doctrine—Abolition of the state of consciousness.—Continuity of the state of consciousness.—Exaltation of reflex ideo-motor, ideo-sensitive, and ideo-sensorial excitability.—Negative suggestion.—Inhibition.—Sleep by suggestion, from fatigue of the eyelids, from occlusion of the eyes, from monotonous, feeble, continuous impressions.—Suggestion without sleep.—Chambard's classification of the various periods of hypnotic sleep.—Objections.—Attempted interpretation of latent memories, and of suggestions *à longue échéance.*—Answer to M. Beaünis's objections.

WE have shown that the phenomena which are present in the hypnotic and waking conditions, are not due to a magnetic fluid, to an emanation from one organism to another, but that the whole explanation lies in suggestion:—that is, in the influence exerted by an idea which has been suggested to, and received by the mind. The most striking feature in a hypnotized subject is his automatism. The cataleptic condition is the result of suggestion. The subject retains the attitude in which he is placed, and continues the movements communicated to his limbs. He perceives the sensations impressed upon his mind. He believes that the visual images which are suggested, are realities, and refers them to the outer world.

At first sight it seems as if we had to deal with an abnormal and unphysiological condition. In the waking condition, the subject only perceives that which he actually sees, does only what he wishes, and obeys only his spontaneous and personal suggestions. This is our first impression. On reflection, however, we see that this is not an absolute contradiction, that nature does not violate her laws, and that the same laws which govern the normal organism govern the organism which is experimentally and pathologically modified.

In every-day life many acts occur automatically, involuntarily and unconsciously, on our part. The spinal cord exercises its peculiar functions without our consciousness. The complex phenomena of vegetative life,—circulation, respiration, nutrition, secretion, excretion, the movements of the alimentary canal, and the active chemistry of the organism, are quietly carried on by means of a mechanism which acts without our voluntary effort. We know that an impression transmitted along a sensory nerve may be reflected through the gray horns of the cord, without traversing the brain; involuntary motion follows the unperceived impression or sensation. This is spinal reflex action, and is an illustration of the automatism of the spinal cord. Tickling of the sole of the foot gives rise to reflex movements, even when the spinal cord is injured and no longer transmits stimuli to the brain. A decapitated frog continues to execute adapted, appropriate and defensive movements with its forelegs and trunk, and if a drop of acetic acid is put on the surface of the skin, the hind leg is drawn up in such a way as to scratch the irritated spot. If the region of the flanks be pinched between the points of a forceps, the frog brings the extremity of the corresponding hind leg in front of them, and, pressing his toes upon them, makes repeated attempts to push the forceps away. (Vulpian.) In this case there is no cerebral interference. The involuntary animal mechanism is capable of executing complex acts, designed to protect the organism from the external world. Is it not the same with a man, who, absorbed in profound meditation, functionally decapitated, as Mathias Duval says, unconsciously and without subsequent memory brushes away a fly which alights on his hand, by means of simple, perfectly co-ordinated, reflex acts?

The brain may intervene to give the primary impulse; the act continues, even when thought and will are otherwise occupied, exclusively by means of spinal automatism. When we are walking, and various ideas distract the mind, we forget that we are walking. Our steps continue, simply by means of a reflex process. The contact of the sole of the foot with the ground is sufficient to bring about the phenomena of muscular co-ordination, which effects the act of progression, through a centrifugal path in the spinal cord. Being thus relieved of the necessity of constantly watching the execution of this complex activity of an inferior, automatic mechanism, our brain works with perfect liberty in other directions. We habitually walk in a mechanical way, to such an extent that we often pass the limit assigned by the will, which directed our first step, provided that this will, by interrupting our preoccupation, does not intervene to arrest our steps. It is the same with swimming, fencing, horseback riding, and music. The artist who plays through a long piece without stopping, frequently allows himself to be absorbed by foreign ideas; his thoughts are no longer upon the music: his fingers wander over the key-board, and he plays on mechanically, under the direction of medullary stimuli succeeding each other spontaneously.

Moreover, that which the mind has lost track of, spinal automatism may resume. The artist no longer remembers all the phrases of a musical composition. His recollection has become defective; he is incapable of playing the piece through, in consequence of his mental confusion. The spinal memory, if I may use the expression, supplements the cerebral memory. The fingers frequently recover the difficult arrangements of stops and movements on the key-board, and accomplish them precisely, even when these movements assimilated, so to speak, by the spinal cord, have become a mechanical operation, owing to their frequent repetition.

The phenomena of automatic activity of the nervous centres may be *instinctive*. Acts occur naturally, without ever having been acquired, by means of the spontaneous, unconscious initiative of the brain and spinal cord. "The most remarkable of these acts," says Despine,* " are those which manifest facial expression, gestures, and bodily attitudes, imitative acts, which are habitually associated with various and indistinct feelings, and which are carried out by everyone, although they have never been learned. To these acts also belong the different inflections which the voice takes under different circumstances, and the movements of the head which are made by some musicians when they are playing, as well as by some of their hearers.

" Hate, anger, pride, cunning, admiration, etc., bring about in all persons who experience them, the same muscular contractions, and consequently a similar expression. And this is true, not only of man, but of animals. These various acts, accomplished by the automatic mechanism of the nervous centres, are so pre-established by law, that they are found to be always identical in all individuals submitted to the same exciting causes.

---

* *Etude scientifique sur le somnambulisme.* Paris, 1880.

"Another effect of this automatic arrangement, is seen in affectation. It is thought that the phenomena which constitute it, are voluntary and studied. This is a mistake. A person is affected in manner in consequence of an exaggerated facility for following what happens in thought, which the automatic nervous organs possess. The voice takes the most varied inflections, according to the slightest changes in the feelings. The muscles of the face produce the greatest variety of contractions. The limbs and the body move in a thousand ways. This disposition is observed especially in woman."

To these instinctive acts, we may add certain movements which may succeed the impressions received and perceived by the sensorium, and which are none the less due to automatic, cerebral activity. A disagreeable odor, which makes us close our nostrils, a sudden noise, which causes us to turn the head, an arm directed against us, which makes us extend the hand to push it away, are all examples of defensive movements adapted to the repulsion of a danger, or of a hostile impression. The impression has been perceived by the olfactory, auditory, or visual centres, but has been received in the raw state, if I may use the expression. It has not had time to be elaborated and interpreted by the psychical centres of the hemispheres. The defensive movement has been committed unconsciously, involuntarily and without deliberation. We cannot help performing it. Before the will-power comes into play, the reflex reaction is instantly transferred from the sensory bulbar nucleus where it has been perceived, to the motor centres, corresponding to the complex movement which has to be carried out in the instinctive, that is, the non-deliberate interest of self-preservation.

As my distinguished friend, M. Netter, has well shown in his excellent work,* the cerebro-spinal activity is almost exclusively automatic, both in the animal throughout life, and in the newly born child. The life of the nervous system is in a manner almost exclusively concentrated in the medulla, the spinal cord, and its intra-cranial prolongations. Voluntary acts do not exist, and, nevertheless, complicated acts, such as suction, are accomplished solely by the reflex mechanism of the cerebro-spinal centres. Anatomy confirms this observation. Parrot has shown that the brain of the newly-born child, which has a gelati-

---

* *L'Homme et l'Animal devant la methode experimentale.* Paris, 1883.

nous consistency, and is of a uniformly gray color, contains hardly any nerve fibres. The excitable parts of the cortex and the so-called motor area, do not exist in man and animals before the occurrence of voluntary acts (Soltman). The white color, corresponding to the completed structure of the nerve fibres (the axis-cylinder covered by its medullary sheath), only appears later. Hence, anatomically and physiologically, the brain is embryonic. Not until the end of the first month, does the substance of the occipital lobe begin to grow white, and only about the fifth month do the anterior regions begin to develop. This development is not completed until about the ninth month (Parrot.)

Hence, consciousness, will, and the psychical faculties of the brain, become active and are developed gradually through the progress of years and education. The automatic cerebro-spinal activity, which alone dominates the organism during the first months, and which predominates throughout life in animals, is associated in the human being with conscious and deliberate activity. The automatic phenomena always persist and recur in all the acts of life, sometimes isolated, often dominated and modified by consciousness. The child is impulsive, it acts from instinct, that is to say, it is entirely given over to its automatism. It jumps, laughs, screams, makes faces, cries, according to the impressions it receives. It sings, when a familiar air awakens in it the idea of song. We see a troop of young school-boys; a regiment passes with drum and band, and the boys are thrown into step as though moved by a spring. They march to the music, fatally impelled by an instinctive suggestion.

"It is impossible," says Gratiolet, "to be seized by a vivid idea, without the whole body being placed in harmony with this idea." Even we, at more advanced years, and, indeed, at every time of life, accompany exhilarating music with gesture and voice; and does not the idea of dancing suggested to the mind by music, tend to produce involuntary, corresponding motions of the body and limbs? We should be forced to relax our habitual restraint for a trifle, if the condition of mind developed by education, the reserve imposed by custom, and our introspection, did not intervene as moderating and regulating influences, to impose a check to the cerebral automatism awakened by sensorial suggestion. Are not all our every-day acts ruled by education and by social conventionality? Are they not the result of the domination which our consciousness, directed by habit, exercises over our unpremeditated instincts, over our animal nature? And in fact, are not savages in a state of prolonged infancy, unconditionally surrendered to the automatism of the nervous system which controls them, until the civilization resulting from a philosophical education, or a suitable religion has created in the embryonic mind, a new state of consciousness, a force regulating instinctive acts?

It often happens in the most enlightened self-controlled man, that a perceived impression is so intense that it is transformed into an automatic act before the moderating influence of consciousness has had time to prevent it. A soldier violently struck by a superior, forgets himself and strikes back. His action follows the perceived impression instantly,—it is a reflex act. The soldier regrets it, for it exposes him to severe punishment. But reason comes too late; anger is blind and does not reason.

As a psychical organ, the brain not only intervenes to moderate reflex action, but also intervenes to correct, to interpret, and to rectify, impressions imperfectly transmitted by our sensory organs, or suggested by an external influence. The wind blowing through a crack produces the auditory impression of a sigh; the mind interprets it, and refers it to its true cause. A vision startles us during our reveries, but consciousness itself again triumphs and re-establishes the truth. Are we not all susceptible to illusions and suggestions, on account of the imperfection of our conscious being, and of our sense-impressions? What happens in our dreams, when our dull senses no longer rectify the rushing incoherent ideas which make the most fantastic things appear to us as realities, and in which we believe because our judgment is absent and no longer exercises any control,—this happens in some persons in the period of mental concentration which precedes sleep. Alfred Maury has made an interesting study of these phenomena upon himself, being decidedly subject to certain kinds of hallucinations which he calls hypnagogic hallucinations. "My hallucinations," says he, "are more numerous and particularly vivid, when I am disposed to cerebral congestion, which is frequently the case. As soon as I suffer from headache, or have nervous pains in the eyes, ears, or nose, the hallucinations attack me before my eyelids are closed. If I do difficult work in the evening, the hallucinations never fail to appear. After having spent two consecutive days in translating a long and very difficult Greek passage, I saw before falling asleep, images which were so numerous, and which followed each other so rapidly, that I sat up in bed in actual fear, in order to dissipate them.

"It is not necessary that the attention should be long diverted in order that the hypnagogic hallucination may appear. A second, or perhaps less, suffices. I have often observed this myself. Soon after lying down, my attention becomes distracted. Images immediately appear before my closed eyes. The appearance of these hallucinations brings me back to myself and I resume the course of my thoughts, soon after to fall a prey to the new visions, and this happens many times in succession, until I fall fast asleep. One day I had the following singular experience. I was reading aloud an account of a trip through Southern Russia. I had hardly finished a certain paragraph, when I instinctively closed my eyes. In one of these short moments of somnolence, I saw hypnagogically, but with the rapidity of lightning, the vision of a man, clad in a brown robe and with a cowl on his head, like one of the monks in Zurbaran's pictures. This image called me back to myself as soon as I had closed my eyes and stopped reading. I suddenly opened them again and resumed the course of my reading. The interruption was of such short duration, that the person to whom I was reading did not perceive it, etc."*

Who has not had more or less marked hallucinations of this kind, when the attention is distracted, when the mind, losing distinct consciousness of the ego, becomes the play of visions evoked by the imagination? Blind to the truth, the mind is delivered over completely to the fictitious conceptions which beset it, until consciousness once more takes the ascendency, disperses these disturbing dreams, and re-establishes the truth.

Our errors, illusions, and hallucinations, are not all spontaneous or consecutive to an imperfect sensorial impression; they may be suggested to our minds by others, and they are sometimes accepted without being challenged.

For have we not all a certain amount of credulity, which inclines us to believe what we are told? Says Durand de Gros, "The credulity which theologians call 'Faith' is given us in order that we may be able to *believe upon simple affirmation*, without exacting rational or material proofs as evidence. This

---

* *Sleep and Dreams.* Paris, 1878.

is a most important moral bond. Without it, no education, no tradition, no history, no social code, would be possible, for all evidence would go for naught, and the most vehement assurances of our best friend, breathlessly announcing that our house is on fire, or that our child is drowning, would find us as cool and immovable as if he had contented himself with saying, 'It is a fine day,' or, 'It is raining.' Our mind would remain fixed and imperturbable in the balance of doubt, and actual evidence would be the only means capable of bringing it out of this condition. In a word, *to believe* without *credulity* would be as difficult as *to see* without *vision*, that is it would be radically impossible." *

When an assertion is made, our first impression is to believe it. The child believes what it is told. Daily experience, the habit of correcting errors which are imposed upon us, the second nature with which social education furnishes us, gradually weakens this inborn credulity, this naïveté of youth. Like all the innate feelings of the human soul, this credulity always survives to a certain extent. Say to some one, "There is a wasp on your forehead," and mechanically he puts his hand on the spot. Indeed, there are persons who even believe they feel the sting.

An idea may originate in the mind through imitation, and may give rise to a corresponding sensation. For example, we see a person scratching himself, and the idea of itching, the fear of having gotten upon us the insect which we saw upon our neighbor, is often sufficient to produce the *sensorial image* of itching, and we feel the necessity of scratching some part of the body. The first itching suggests a second somewhere else on the body. The necessity of emptying the bladder is felt at the sight of a person making water; and yawning is contagious. Nervous habits, nervous cough, and sometimes vomiting, chorea, hysterical convulsions, and certain vicious habits of children, are among the pathological states which may be developed by imitation. Not unfrequently the pupil unconsciously acquires his master's gestures, intonation, and certain of his peculiarities of expression.

Some people are very susceptible to these sensory suggestions; They are endowed with lively imaginations, that is to say, they have a great aptitude for mentally creating an image of the sug-

---

* Philips, *Cours théorique et pratique de Braidisme.* Paris, 1860.

gestions induced by speech, vision, and touch, and this image projected to the exterior through the peripheral nerves of the corresponding organs, reproduces an actual sensation, as vivid as if it had an objective cause in these same organs; for example, the pain of a stump, which is referred to a member which no longer exists. Such may be the effect of imagination. Charpignon says, "When I think of an acid fruit, I represent to myself an apple yielding under a knife, or being crushed by my teeth, my mouth waters, and I experience a sensation almost as distinct as if the object itself had been the cause of it."

Do we not all possess a certain cerebral docility which makes us obey commands? We tell a child to walk, and he lifts his leg mechanically. Say to a person, "Close your eyes," and many persons will close them without reflection. The idea suffices to bring about the corresponding movement automatically, and sometimes even, contrary to the will. A well-known experiment shows the influence of an idea upon the act. I hold the end of my watch chain between two fingers at the height of my forehead; the watch hangs vertically suspended and moves to the right or left, backwards or forwards, or in a circle, according as I conceive the idea of these successive movements. I try in vain not to interfere voluntarily, but am unconscious of the motion which my hand imparts to the chain. Simply the idea of motion is enough to occasion it. Is not this the secret of table turning, which has turned so many heads for more than thirty years? Involuntarily and unconsciously everyone imparts a slight movement to the table, and the sum of all these unconscious movements, results in the tipping of the table.

Doubtless, the impression produced by an order given by one who has no authority over us, is too weak to make the mind carry it out automatically, without first estimating its expediency. Our judgment questions it, and our reason opposes the instinct of passive obedience. But when the mind is dulled by somnolence, or lost in reverie, this no longer holds true. The absent or distracted attention no longer allows of control, automatism gains the mastery, and we involuntarily obey.

"One evening," says Maury, "I was dozing in my chair, and I still heard vaguely, when my brother said to me, in a loud voice, 'Get a match, the candle has gone out.' It seems that I heard the words, but without knowing that it was my brother who had uttered them, for in the dreams which I then had, I imagined that I went to look for a match. Awaking a few seconds afterwards, I was told what my brother had said. I had already forgotten that I had heard him, although at the time I answered. My answer was purely mechanical. However, in my dream, I believed that I was looking for a match upon my own account, and I did not even suspect that I was carrying out an order."

The following remarks, which I quote from Chambard,* show in an entertaining way how a frequently repeated act is aroused by a suggested idea. " When Dr. Veron was director of the opera, he invited the ballet-dancers and their mothers to dinner on a certain occasion. When the rich repast was over, the respectable matrons fell asleep. A queer idea, worthy of a clever man, originated with the host. ' Dance, if you please!' he exclaimed in a loud voice. Mechanically, but in perfect harmony, the sleeping women executed the traditional figure, thus betraying the exercise of a profession at which their daughters blushed, and to which not one of them would have owned a few minutes before."

These considerations, which it seems to me unnecessary to amplify, are sufficient demonstration of the fact that the normal, physiological state shows, in a rudimentary manner, phenomena analogous to those which are observed in hypnotism; that nature does not contradict herself, and that there exists in our cerebro-spinal nervous apparatus, an automatism by which we accomplish certain highly intricate acts, unconsciously and involuntarily, and through which we submit to a certain extent to orders which are given us, to movements which are communicated to us, and to sensory illusions which are suggested to us. They also demonstrate that the condition of consciousness intervenes to modify or neutralize automatic action, and to rectify or destroy false impressions insinuated into the nervous centres.

Suppress consciousness, suppress voluntary cerebral activity, and we have somnambulism. Such at least is the opinion of P. Despine. " Somnambulism," says this author, " is characterized physiologically, by the exercise of the automatic activity alone of the brain, during the paralysis of the conscious activity, which manifests the ego."

According to this doctrine, the hypnotized subject would move as the decapitated frog swims: he would be an unconscious

---

* *Etude symptomatologique sur le somnambulisme.* (*Lyon medical*, 1883.)

mechanism, at the mercy of the hypnotizer. If I lift his arm, it remains passively raised, as though fixed in the position imposed, for his personal will no longer exists to put it back into place. I say, "Your arms are revolving, you cannot stop them." The idea of the suggested movement is accepted by the mind which is deprived of initiative, and this idea automatically engenders the movement, which continues, because the ego is weakened, and unable to arrest the automatic action directed by an external influence.

I say, "Your hand feels hot," and the idea of warmth being induced into the mind, and accepted without control, calls forth a memory-sensation of heat, which is projected along a centrifugal path to the periphery of the hand.

Or, I say, "You are sad," and sad feelings take possession of the mind;—"You are gay," and bright ideas arise. I direct the movements, sensations and feelings of the hypnotized subject, who no longer possesses a conscious personality, who yields without a struggle to modifications of his relationship with the external world, and of his intellectual life, which my will dictates to his mind.

Does the doctrine thus formulated conform to the facts? Is it correct to say with P. Despine, that involuntary cerebral activity may be put to sleep with the hypnotized subject, and that the ego does not participate in his acts? I think not.

In the primary degrees of sleep, consciousness and will exist, as we have stated in our description of the hypnotic manifestations. In a case of this sort, the only phenomenon manifested after hypnotization is the closure of the eyes: the subject observes everything, laughs, even aids in the maintenance of the catalepsy of his eyelids or of the arms if it exists. He makes ineffectual efforts to open his eyes, or to put down his arm. He says, "I try in vain and I cannot." Intelligent subjects on awaking, can often give a complete account of all their sensations during sleep. One man said to me, "I heard everything, and I was even able to struggle, my hand was closed in contracture, and I tried hard to open it, my arms revolved one about the other, and I tried every means of stopping them. I brought my hands nearer together, so that one should hit against the other. I thought I had succeeded in stopping them at last, when all at once they flew apart like a spring, in spite of me, either spontaneously, or at the slightest word spoken by you." I lay one of his fingers on his nose and say, "You cannot take it away again," He tries to do it. As he finds it impossible to pull it away directly, he tries to do so by sliding it up and down. He almost succeeds when I say, "Your finger is stuck there," and it immediately adheres throughout the whole length of his nose. He still tries to pull his finger away, and though he knows perfectly well why it sticks fast, he cannot remove it.

Despine states that "The somnambulist's ignorance of what he does when in the somnambulistic condition, does not come from forgetfulness, but from the non-participation of the ego in his acts." I have seen somnambulists, however, who recall their acts when they wake. It is sufficient to say to them, "You will remember everything when you wake," and the memory of what has occurred is retained. If they are told when they wake, "You are going to remember everything," the memory of what they have done in the somnambulistic condition comes back to them. Moreover, they are perfectly self-conscious while in this condition;—they answer the questions addressed to them;—they know that they are asleep. When I tell S—— that he is on the battle-field, he recalls the scenes in which he assisted; a truly active intellectual work goes on within him; his thoughts, consciously evoked memories, become images of which he cannot rid himself. "Hallucination," says Lélut, "is the transformation of thought into feeling.' The suggestions which I induce in the waking condition, are created in a conscious being, who knows what he is doing, and who remembers what he has done. I develop a hallucination in S—— without hypnotizing him. He says that he is perfectly self-conscious. The suggested hallucination is the only abnormality evident in his mind. He goes and comes, speaks, and carries out all his ordinary, everyday actions, spontaneously and thoughtfully. I have created a susceptibility to hallucination;—I have made an organic automaton.

Consciousness and will are doubtless weakened in cases of profound sleep. The more intense the sleep is, the less the subject's spontaneity, and the greater the docility to suggestions. But this profound sleep, and weakness of the will and consciousness, are not necessary for the manifestation of suggestive phenomena. This important fact indisputably follows from the preceding considerations.

The one thing certain is, that a *peculiar aptitude for transforming the idea received into an act* exists in hypnotized subjects who are susceptible to suggestion. In the normal condition, every formulated idea is questioned by the mind. After being perceived by the cortical centres, the impression extends to the cells of the adjacent convolutions; their peculiar activity is excited; the diverse faculties generated by the gray substance of the brain come into play; the impression is elaborated, registered, and analyzed, by means of a complex mental process, which ends in its acceptation or neutralization; if there is cause, the mind vetoes it. In the hypnotized subject, on the contrary, the transformation of thought into action, sensation, movement, or vision is so quickly and so actively accomplished, that the intellectual inhibition has not time to act. When the mind interposes, it is already an accomplished fact, which is often registered with surprise, and which is confirmed by the fact that it proves to be real, and no intervention can hamper it further. If I say to the hypnotized subject, "Your hand remains closed," the brain carries out the idea as soon as it is formulated. A reflex is immediately transmitted from the cortical centre, where this idea induced by the auditory nerve is perceived, to the motor centre, corresponding to the central origin of the nerves subserving flexion of the hand;—contracture occurs in flexion. There is, then, *exaltation of the ideo-motor reflex excitability, which effects the unconscious transformation of the thought into movement, unknown to the will.*

The same thing occurs when I say to the hypnotized subject, "You have a tickling sensation in your nose." The thought induced through hearing is reflected upon the centre of olfactory sensibility, where it awakens the sensitive memory-image of the nasal itching, as former impressions have created it and left it imprinted and latent. This memory sensation thus resuscitated, may be intense enough to cause the reflex act of sneezing. There is also, then, *exaltation of the ideo-sensorial reflex excitability, which effects the unconscious transformation of the thought into sensation, or into a sensory image.*

In the same way the visual, acoustic and gustatory images succeed the suggested idea.

Negative suggestions are more difficult to explain. If I say to the hypnotized subject, "Your body is insensible, your eye is blind," the impression transmitted by the auditory nerve to the centre of tactile or visual sensibility, creates the image of the tactile or visual anæsthesia; the cutaneous nerves receive the stimulus; the retina receives the image; retinal vision exists, light makes the pupil contract: but the cerebral perception of the tactile impression, or of the retinal image, no longer exists. It seems as if it might be a *reflex paralysis of a cortical centre*, which the suggested idea has produced in this case. Moreover, these nervous actions of arrest are well known, if not well explained, to physiology and pathology. Stimulation of the pneumogastric stops the beating of the heart; a violent emotion paralyzes us; a severe injury produces bodily insensibility (surgical shock); speech fails from the effect of a deep impression; and sudden functional blindness is manifested in cases of hysteria.

The organism possesses dynamic mechanisms, by the aid of which control or activity may be suddenly suspended. This is what Brown-Séquard calls *inhibition*. The control or activity may on the contrary be re-enforced, and Brown-Séquard calls this *dynamogeny*. "This inhibitory or dynamogenic faculty belongs to different parts of the nervous system, and may be exercised either in a direct or reflex manner." As an example of inhibition, Brown-Séquard cites the arrest of the heart from the irritation of the abdominal sympathetic ganglia, the arrest of respiration from the irritation of the laryngeal nerves, the inhibition of mental activity or loss of consciousness, by simple puncture of the medulla, the heart continuing to beat; the reflex amaurosis following a lesion of the trigeminus and other nerves, or the partial section of the restiform bodies in rabbits.* The negative suggestions of which we have spoken, belong under the same order of facts.

The mechanism of suggestion in general, may then be summed up in the following formula: *increase of the reflex ideo-motor, ideo-sensitive, and ideo-sensorial excitability.* In the same way,

---

* Brown-Séquard says,—" The initial act by the aid of which an individual is thrown into hypnotism, is itself but a peripheral (from one of the senses or from the skin), or central (by the influence of an idea or of an emotion) stimulus, which produces a diminution or augmentation of power in certain parts of the brain, the spinal cord, and other parts of the nervous system, and Braidism or hypnotism is nothing else than the very complex condition of the loss or increase of energy into which the nervous system and other organs are thrown under the influence of the primary peripheral or sensorial stimulus. Hypnotism is then essentially only the collective effect of acts of inhibition and of dynamogeny." (*Gazette hebdomadaire*, 1883, p. 137.)

through the effect of some influence, strychnine for example, the sensitive-motor excitability is increased in the spinal cord, so that the least impression at the periphery of a nerve is immediately transformed into contracture, without the moderating influence of the brain being able to prevent this transformation. In the same way in hypnotism, the ideo-reflex excitability is increased in the brain, so that any idea received is immediately transformed into an act, without the controlling portion of the brain, the higher centres, being able to prevent the transformation.

This is only a formula, I know; I do not pretend to advance a theory. In the realm of psychology the cause and essence of phenomena escape us. If I am not mistaken, this formula, such as it is, helps us to conceive of a mechanism which the mind cannot strictly explain. It seems to me that a little light rises from this theoretical conception, imperfect as it is; we understand that these curious phenomena may exist normally in the waking condition, in certain subjects, whose paths of intra-cerebral reflectivity are more distinct and more easily traced, and in whom the condition of consciousness which moderates the reflex automatism, is at the same time weakened. We also know that subjects who have been hypnotized often, may contract an increase of this ideo-reflex excitability through habit, that is to say, through the frequent repetition of the phenomena induced; the paths most frequently followed, present the easiest and most rapid way of diffusing the nervous force; the impression follows these paths from preference, even in the waking condition; and for this reason subjects trained and educated by former hypnotizations, without being again hypnotized, may manifest the same phenomena, and carry out the same acts, under the influence of the all-powerful suggestion.

Sleep itself is born of a conscious or unconscious suggestion. The subject who has made up his own mind that he is going to sleep, or who has been assured of the fact by word or gesture, concentrates his thoughts upon this idea, and gradually experiences all the symptoms of sleep,—heaviness of the eyelids, dimness of sight, insensibility of the limbs,—he isolates his senses, avoids all external impressions, his eyes close, and sleep has appeared.

The various methods of hypnotization act partly in a suggestive way; fixation upon a brilliant object, the convergent strabismus of the eyes, develops fatigue and a heavy feeling in the eyelids, which insinuates the idea of sleep; the closure of the eyelids is an invitation to sleep. It is said that the women of Brittany put their babies to sleep by hanging a little glass ball to the top of the cradle, so that it shines in front of their eyes. Certain practices used in order to produce religious ecstasy are referable to this suggestion, visual fatigue. For instance, the contemplation of an imaginary point in space, or of the end of the nose, practiced by the devotees of India; the contemplation of their umbilicus, which is practised by the Mount-Athos monks, or "*omphalo-psychiens.*" Let us add that in the majority of persons, the monotonous wearying and continuous impression of one of the senses, produces a certain intellectual drowsiness, the prelude of sleep. The mind, entirely absorbed by a quiet, uniform, and incessant perception, becomes foreign to all other impressions; it is too feebly stimulated; and allows itself to become dull. "If the mind," says Cullen, "is fixed upon a single sensation, it soon reaches a condition in which there is total absence of impressions, or in other words, the condition which nearest approaches sleep."

The prolonged and monotonous sound of tambourines struck in the same cadence and in the darkness of night, produces ecstatic hypnotism in Arabs of the Aissaoua sect. The impression made upon the hearing by the continual murmur of the waves, or by monotonous and slow utterance, induces sleep. "The child is hypnotized through its sense of hearing, by the monotonous songs sung by its nurse; the regular oscillations of its cradle hypnotize it through its *muscular sense* by communicating a long series of weak shocks, each one like the last and separated by equal intervals. Incantation with charms (*carmina*), the simple and unvarying rhythm of which murmurs in the captive's ear, without speaking to his intelligence, ought to be considered as a particular form of Braidism which is exercised upon the sense of hearing instead of upon sight." (Dr. Philips.)

There is no fundamental difference between spontaneous and induced sleep. M. Liébault has very wisely established this fact. The spontaneous sleeper is in relationship with himself alone; the idea which occupies his mind just before going to sleep, the impressions which the sensitive and sensorial nerves of the periphery continue to transmit to the brain, and the stimuli coming from the viscera, become the point of departure for the incoherent images and impressions which constitute dreams. Have those who deny the psychical phenomena of hypnotism, or who only admit them in cases of diseased nervous temperament, ever reflected upon what occurs in normal sleep, in which the best balanced mind is carried by the current, in which the faculties are dissociated, in which the most singular ideas, and the most fantastic conceptions obtrude? Poor human reason is carried away, the proudest mind yields to hallucinations, and during this sleep, that is to say, during a quarter of its existence, becomes the plaything of the dreams which imagination calls forth.

In induced sleep, the subject's mind retains the memory of the person who has put him to sleep, whence the hypnotizer's power of playing upon his imagination, of suggesting dreams, and of directing the acts which are no longer controlled by the weakened or absent will.

Moreover, owing to this paresis of the psychical activity of the voluntary regulator of the cerebro-spinal automatism, the latter becomes exaggerated and dominant. Thus sleep favors the production of suggestive phenomena, by suppressing or weakening the moderating influence, but it is not indispensable to their production. I repeat the fact that it is itself a phenomenon of suggestion. Certain subjects who reach the condition in which the cataleptiform closure of the eyelids occurs, resist the idea of sleep. In one case in my service, I cannot induce either sleep or closure of the eyelids, but by affirmation alone I can induce the closure of the contractured hand. Hypnotism is not then the *necessary* prelude to suggestion; it facilitates suggestion when it can be induced; but other suggestions may sometimes succeed when the suggestion of sleep is inefficacious.

At the beginning of this study, we showed that the hypnotic condition exhibits various degrees. M. Chambard has classed the periods of hypnotic sleep in a different way, in an interesting memoir, the work of an ingenious mind. This division is partly based upon Alfred Maury's conception regarding the succession of the phenomena which border upon physiological sleep.

Sight first disappears: the other senses are at first exalted, afterward they cease to perform their functions; taste is the last to disappear.

The intellectual functions, which become more active for the moment, being no longer distracted by sensorial impressions, finally undergo dissociation; the faculties of *co-ordination*, decision, and direction, are the first to disappear; will, attention, and judgment follow, and finally memory disappears. The *imaginative* faculties, the faculties of suggestion and impulsion, are the only ones which persist for a time, leaving the brain accessible to dreams, hallucinations, and curious conceptions.

These are obliterated in their turn. For an instant, the *ego* alone watches over the intellectual faculties and the deadened senses; then it suddenly vanishes. Sleep is complete.

Provided with these data, M. Chambard classifies the degrees intermediate between the deepest sleep and waking, in the following manner.

1st. The most profound degree is *lethargy:* the hypnotized subject is at first under its sway, then, rousing himself more or less completely, he reaches one of the intermediate degrees.

In the lethargic state the subject is inert, unconscious, and without any relationship with the outside world: the functions of vegetative life alone continue.

The functions of relationship re-appear; in the first place, those which created an unconscious bond between the organism and the impressions from without; this is known as *automatism;* every sensorial or sensory stimulus causes simple or complex movements, the same movements which it would cause in the waking condition, if the faculties of co-ordination did not interpose to prevent or to moderate them.

2d. *Motor automatism* gives place to the phenomena described by Charcot under the name of neuro-muscular hyperexcitability. The brain being still absent, as far as function is concerned, the reflex excito-motor action is increased still more, as in the decapitated frog.

3d. These functions of relationship, which are unconscious or at least but slightly conscious, grow more active. The tactile, acoustic, and muscular senses are gradually aroused. This is known as *passive somnambulistic automatism.* The subject continues any movements communicated to his limbs (*motor inertia*), carries out any acts in relation with the sensory or sensorial impression (*motor suggestion*), reproduces articulate sounds, the movements which he sees or hears (*automatic imitation*), and executes orders (*automatic obedience*).

4th. Memory and the faculties of the imagination are aroused in their turn. This is known as *active somnambulistic automatism.* The brain is deprived of spontaneity, and is accessible to dreams which differ from ordinary dreams, in that the psycho-motor and psycho-sensorial phenomena are of an unconscious character. In this state there are dreams in which the subject walks about, professional, instinctive, and passionate dreams, dreams in which memory is revived, intelligent dreams (during which the subject performs intelligent acts, writes, and plays upon the piano, etc.), and suggested dreams.

5th. The faculties of co-ordination are imperfectly aroused; the imaginative and instinctive faculties still rule the scene, and have the advantage over the first or reasoning faculties. This is known as the *somnambulistic life*. The subject appears to be awake, performs his every-day acts, but his weakened will and exalted imagination leave him susceptible to suggestions and obedient to acts commanded.

6th. Finally, the faculties of co-ordination re-appear entirely; the equilibrium is re-established, and the awaking is complete.

This ingenious conception does not appear to me to conform to the facts.

From all observation, and from descriptions of the phenomena, we may deduce the fact that active somnambulism (Chambard's active somnambulistic automatism and somnambulistic life), implies the most profound influence, the most advanced degree of hypnotism, and the most widely separated from the waking condition. All the other phenomena, moreover, motor-automatism, motor-suggestion, automatic imitation and obedience are found in the active somnambulists. The same subject whom we hypnotize daily, often reaches only the stage of motor automatism in the first séances; it is only through repeated hypnotizations that he gradually acquires the aptitude for carrying out the hallucinations and dreams suggested. It is then only that amnesia upon waking exists; a proof of more intense psychical modification than that of the preceding degrees, in which the subject was fully aware of the cause of his catalepsy and retained an exact recollection of it. Moreover the subjects who only manifest motor-automatism are not pure automatons; they hear and remember that they have heard when they wake; they often reply to questions; they try to resist suggestions, and struggle against the attitudes or movements which are commanded; consciousness is not destroyed; the will is still alive, but is powerless against the exaggerated automatic action.

Even in active somnambulism, the psychical faculties are not destroyed; the somnambulistic subject also resists certain suggestions, and refuses to perform certain acts; he reflects before answering certain questions, and carries on active intellectual work. Moreover, acts, illusions, and post-hypnotic hallucinations commanded during the hypnosis, are carried out when the subject wakes, when consciousness and the faculties of co-ordination have certainly resumed their control. Finally, the manifestation of these same phenomena in the waking condition in a subject who is *compos sui*, and astonished that he cannot struggle against the automatism which dominates him, shows clearly that consciousness and will may survive all degrees of hypnotism.

As to lethargy, that is to say complete inertia,—the reduction of the organism to vegetative life,—this I have not observed. Although they appeared inert, all my hypnotized subjects were in relationship with the outer world through the agency of some one of their senses; vocal suggestion has always been sufficient to arouse them.

The division of the hypnotic condition into degrees, such as I have stated, seems to me to conform more closely to the data furnished by observation.

The slightest influence is manifested by simple drowsiness, accompanied with closure of the eyelids.

If the *susceptibility to suggestion* is greater, the motor function is the first to yield to its effects; suggestive contracture and finally suggestive automatic movements appear upon the scene. Automatic obedience, anæsthesia, sensorial illusions, and finally induced hallucinations, mark the progressive steps in the development of this susceptibility to suggestion, the culminating point of which is active somnambulism and the somnambulistic life.

I shall not try to interpret the mechanism of all these hypnotic phenomena more thoroughly.

There is however, one among these phenomena which is particularly interesting. It has appealed in vain to all the lights of psychology for some attempt at interpretation;—I refer to suggestions which are to be carried out after a long interval of time (*suggestions à longue échéance*).

Let us try in our turn to throw a little light upon this obscure question.

It seems to me necessary to develop a few considerations relative to *latent memories*, before touching on this question.

The study of hypnotic phenomena makes the existence of

latent memories, I do not say unconscious memories, evident. Impressions are stored in the brain during hypnotic sleep. The subject is conscious of them at the moment he receives them. This consciousness has disappeared when he wakes. The memory is latent for the moment, as are many, indeed all memories which sleep in the brain from the time when we begin to live and think. But these latent memories of the hypnotic condition may be aroused or may wake spontaneously by means of certain influences. Let us give a few examples.

1st. On one occasion, one of my somnambulists was photographed in the waking condition, then she was hypnotized and her photograph was again taken in different suggested attitudes; —anger, fright (imaginary serpent), gayety (drunkenness), disdain (sneering students), ecstasy. The subject remembered nothing when she woke. I hypnotized her several days later, and said, "When you wake, you will open the book by your bedside, and will find your photograph in it." I said nothing else. When she woke she took the book, opened it, found her photograph (imaginary; there was none there), and asked if she might keep it and send it to her son. "Do you think it is like you?" I asked.—"Very like me, but my expression is a little sad." "Well," I said, "turn over the page." She turned it over, and recognized her photograph (imaginary) taken in an attitude of anger. —"Turn over again." She kept on turning over the pages in succession, and recognized her photographs in the different attitudes of fear, gayety, disdain, and ecstasy, as distinctly as if they really existed. She described each one of the attitudes to me precisely, just as she saw it, and just as it had been taken during her sleep, without remembering having had a photograph taken at all, or the suggestion corresponding to each one. She seemed very much astonished when I told her that I had communicated these attitudes to her during her sleep. Thus, the latent memory of acts performed during somnambulism had been aroused by a sort of association of idea-memories.

2d. I can produce suggestive phenomena of transfer in a hypnotized somnambulist. For example, I put his left arm into the cataleptic condition in the horizontal position, and, as I bring a stethoscope up to the other arm, I say that the catalepsy is going to be transferred to this side. In a minute this arm is stretched out horizontally, while the left falls motionless. If I bring the stethoscope near the left arm, it assumes the horizontal position, and the other falls motionless, and so on. I can also induce wryneck, paralysis, and suggestive contracture, and transfer them from one side of the body to the other; simply by means of the idea suggested to the subject that the stethoscope produces this phenomenon. It is a remarkable fact that upon waking the subject remembers nothing, and yet, if I put one of his arms in a horizontal position and hold the stethoscope near it, the phenomenon of transfer takes place. The wry-neck, paralyses, and contractures, are transferred in like manner, to the subject's great astonishment, for he does not know how it happens, and does not remember that the same phenomena have been induced during his sleep. He realizes them spontaneously in the waking condition. It must be added, that during hypnosis I have not suggested the reproduction of the phenomena in the waking condition. In like manner, I say to him in his sleep, "If I touch your forehead, you will burst out laughing. If I touch the back of your head, you will sneeze. If I touch the right side of your head, your left arm will be convulsed." After I have obtained these phenomena by suggestion, I awaken the subject. Without saying a word I touch his forehead, and he laughs; I touch the back of his head and he sneezes; I touch the right parietal bone, and his left arm makes convulsive movements. The memory of the reflex which I suggested during his sleep is unconsciously retained in the waking condition. I have succeeded in these experiments with a large number of subjects.

3d. I have proved that some somnambulists who have been rendered analgesic during their sleep, have become so in the waking condition as well, after a certain number of séances;—they have no pain when pricked with a pin. It is perhaps a phenomenon of the same nature in these cases,—the phenomenon of analgesia suggested by latent memory.

4th. I cite another fact which has not been mentioned before, and which is of interest to all psychologists. A somnambulist is hypnotized; I speak to him, I make him speak, I make him work; I give him hallucinations, I wake him in half an hour, or in an hour at the most; he remembers absolutely nothing of what has passed; he will remember nothing spontaneously. Now, nothing is easier than to recall to any somnambulist the memory of all the impressions he has received in his sleep, *and this experiment succeeds in all cases of somnambulism.* In order to do this I have only to say, "You will remember everything that has happened, everything that you have done during your sleep." If necessary, I lay my hand on his forehead to concentrate his attention ; he thinks deeply for an instant, *without falling asleep*, and all the latent memories arise with great precision ; he repeats my words as well as his own, relates his acts, gestures, and hallucinations successively ; nothing is forgotten. I have aroused the latent memories by a simple affirmation.

In the waking condition the active and reasoning part of the brain (we will call it the higher centre, in order to have a fixed idea, but we must not attach any precise anatomical signification to the term), this part, I say, interferes and controls ; it moderates or neutralizes the imaginative or automatic part (we will call this the lower centre). In sleep this influence ceases. The higher centre of the brain becomes dull. The cerebral activity is concentrated upon the imaginative and automatic centres ;—in other words, the intellectual control is diminished. (We have already developed this conception.)

If we admit, then, with Durand de Gros, and Liébault, that during sleep all or almost all the cerebral activity, all the nervous force, if we will, wanting in the higher centre of the brain (faculties of control), is concentrated in the lower centre (automatic centre),—what is the result ? That all the phenomena induced during sleep, conceptions, movements, sensations, images, all the impressions produced are created by means of all this concentrated and accumulated nervous force.

What happens at the waking period ? The subject resumes his self-control. The concentrated nervous activity is again diffused through the higher centres of the brain, and to the periphery. Then the impressions which were perceived during sleep, become faded as it were, because, having been perceived by means of a great quantity of nervous light, if I may be permitted this comparison, they are no longer bright enough to be conscious when this light ceases to be concentrated upon them ; they are latent, as too faint an image is latent.

We see a somnambulist ; she goes and comes, obeys orders, converses, works, and is entirely conscious. We would swear that she is awake. After half an hour's active conversation I suddenly say, " Wake up." She goes on talking after she wakes. She remembers nothing, absolutely nothing. It is a singular phenomenon. Everything has faded from her memory. The nervous force which was concentrated in certain parts of the brain is now diffused throughout; the light being distributed elsewhere, no longer illumines the preceding impressions; a new state of consciousness exists. I put the somnambulist to sleep again; the old state of nervous concentration re-appears, and with it the old state of consciousness, the faded impressions return; the latent memories revive.

The facility with which some subjects pass thus from one state of consciousness to the other is astonishing. I simply close their eyes and talk to them: "What is your name?"—"Paul Durand."—"How old are you?"—"I am thirteen years old."—"You have no ill-feelings?"—"No, I feel perfectly well all over."—"Do you go to school? What do you study?"—"I study Arithmetic, History, French, etc."—"Wake up." The child wakes up. "What did I say to you?"—"You have not spoken to me."—"What? I did speak to you, did you not hear me?"—"I heard nothing. You said nothing to me."—"Close your eyes." He shuts his eyes. "What did I say to you just now?"—"You asked me what my name was, how old I was, if I was well, and what I was studying at school."—"What did you reply?"—"I said that my name was Paul Durand, that I was thirteen years old, that I was perfectly well, that I study Arithmetic, History, and French."—"Open your eyes." He opens them. "What were you just saying to me?"—"I have not spoken to you." I have tried this experiment a great many times with many subjects, and especially with children.

Simple closure of the eyes is in many cases enough to determine a new state of consciousness. Being no longer impressed by the material objects upon which it fixes its attention, the mind falls into a passive condition; looking about no longer with his eyes, the subject no longer looks about with his mind, if I may so express it. The nervous activity abandons the higher centres of attention, and concentrates itself upon the automatic centres; the new impressions, evoked in this centre after the cerebral influx has spread elsewhere, are as if implanted upon a special state of consciousness. The subject looks about with his eyes open; the material images make an impression upon the brain, and by calling its nervous activity to the surface, causes the psychical concentration to cease. The centres which perceive the impression by means of an accumulation of nervous force, only retain a diminished nervous force, the state of consciousness is modified, the impression is faded, to again appear if the same state of consciousness is again induced by the simple occlusion of the eyes.

A phenomenon of the same kind is produced in us instinctively. What do we do when we wish to recall a memory, or to create a profound impression in ourselves, to register it in our minds so that it may be aroused at a given moment? We concentrate our thoughts, we shut our eyes, we close the sensorium to all other impressions; and we thus revive the latent memory, or engrave the desired impression deeply upon our minds. It soon disappears when the cerebral activity is again diffused over a great many objects, over the whole nervous periphery; but it readily reappears, if the cerebral activity is again concentrated; the memory gains, so to speak, in depth and distinctness, what it loses in continuity.

Is it not for the same reason also, that the memories of childhood, stored in a younger, more impressionable and more credulous mind, a mind which is less preoccupied with many ideas, is more readily concentrated, and in which the faculties of automatic activity predominate,—that these memories are more deeply engraved and are more readily recalled. In old age, when memory is weak, childish memories are always retained, re-appear at intervals, and are never entirely effaced, while the impressions of adult age often disappear never to return, even when they have been retained a long time. Let us add that almost all children may be hypnotized, and that the number susceptible to induced somnambulism is much greater than among adults; three times as great according to M. Liébault.

The hypnotic condition is not an abnormal one, it does not create new functions nor extraordinary phenomena; it develops those which are produced in the waking condition; because of a new psychical modality, it exaggerates the normal susceptibility to suggestion, which we all possess to some extent; our psychical condition is modified so as to carry out the images and impressions evoked with greater boldness and distinctness.

When we are deep in thought, and our mental activity is concentrated upon memories, old impressions revive, old images re-appear before our eyes, often as distinct as reality; we remain absorbed in the contemplation of the past, we live our past life again, we dream, our thoughts are turned inward upon ourselves, so deeply that a sudden sensorial excitation, an unexpected noise, a friend's voice, recalls us to ourselves and snatches us from the contemplative life,—a veritable hallucination in the waking state. We come to ourselves, our psychical activity is again diffused to the surface, and our memories instantly fade: we can no longer remember the object of our passive reveries. Who has not experienced this? The same thing happens, if our minds are concentrated upon an idea instead of upon a memory-image: we can no longer recall the object of our abstract meditations. The state of consciousness is modified. Is this not a condition comparable to the induced hypnotic condition which is spontaneously and involuntarily evoked in us? The soldier who does not feel his wound in the heat of combat, Archimedes killed while he was meditating on abstract problems, dead to all else,—are not these examples of nervous concentration by means of an idea, an emotion, like to that which hypnotism induces; and are we not all, often without our knowledge, in an analogous condition?

Perhaps in reality there are neither one nor two states of consciousness, but infinitely varying states. All degrees of variation may exist between the perfect waking condition, and the condition of perfect concentration which constitutes somnambulism. Our minds are peopled with memories which have been stored up there since childhood. All these memories are latent, for if they were all aroused our understanding would be in a veritable state of chaos; but each one of these memories may be revived when the same state of consciousness which produced it is again induced.

If these data of observation are thoroughly grasped, it will be easy to understand the ideas which I am going to present upon the interpretation of suggestions *à longue échéance.* Some somnambulists have the faculty of carrying out a suggestion made in the somnambulistic condition, at the day or hour indicated, several weeks or even months after the suggestion. This memory of the command given, apparently latent during a long interval, revives at the moment fixed upon with mathematical precision, and the subject executes the act or carries out the hallucination commanded, without knowing its origin.

I know of no other attempted explanation of this strange phenomenon which is so indisputably real; some, unable to explain, have denied it, obstinately refusing to bow before the evidence of facts; others, like the abbot who wrote upon hypnotic phenomena in *l' Universe*, not being able to find any plausible explanation, have looked upon it as supernatural,—evil spirits rising from the infernal regions to aid the operator. Some are wanting in scientific spirit; others err because modesty and humility are lacking. To deny what we cannot understand, to invoke the aid of God or the devil to explain what our poor human minds cannot conceive, is an evidence of a certain mental self-sufficiency, which is not characteristic of strong minds. The transmission of the tones and inflections of the human voice by means of a wire and a vibrating plate, is a marvellous phenomenon, which we can demonstrate much better than we can explain. The problems of infinity, eternity without beginning, of limitless space, appear to our human understanding like enigmas of which it can conceive no solution, and yet the solution exists. All phenomena of the psychical order are mysteries, the mechanism of which escapes us, and which nevertheless are carried out. Let us be contented to remain humble, feeling our insufficiency, and let us resign ourselves modestly not to overstep the limits of our intelligence.

If I dare to give an attempted interpretation here, or at least a few ideas which may help the conception of the phenomenon I mention, it is not because I pretend to be able to solve the question: my conception is perhaps not the true one. I may at least show that a certain conception of the phenomenon is possible, and thus free the question from that mysterious and supernatural appearance which is repugnant to all scientific minds. May not the suggestions *à longue échéance* be explained by means of an organic modification imprinted upon the nervous substance, which is the sub-stratum of psychical phenomena? Shall we say that in the hypnotic condition the brain has the property of receiving the imprint of the suggested idea, and of undergoing a modification analogous to that of a mechanism in which the spring is wound up or stretched in such a way as to produce the recoil at a given moment, like an alarm clock arranged to strike at a set hour? This seems to me a conception which does not rest upon any known anatomical or physiological fact.

As an argument in favor of this comparison of the psychical apparatus which governs memory, to the alarm clock, we could cite the fact that many persons are able to wake themselves at the hour which they set before going to sleep. The mind would then have the property of regulating its sleep in advance for any number of hours it might choose.

But the explanation seems to me to lie elsewhere. The man who goes to sleep with the idea of waking at a fixed hour, retains this idea during his sleep; for natural sleep does not necessitate the abolition of thought and consciousness, any more than artificial sleep does; we are self-conscious during sleep, we think, we dream, we work. Many subjects talk in their sleep and answer the questions put to them. I have often said to subjects whom I found sleeping naturally, "Do not wake up, continue to sleep." Then I lift the arms; they remain passively in suggestive catalepsy. I give a suggestion for waking. They execute it without remembering anything, without knowing that I spoke to them. Gen. Noizet and M. Liébault have mentioned the same fact. Natural sleep is transformed into hypnotic sleep; or better, I have put the subject into relationship with me; for, in my opinion, nothing, absolutely nothing differentiates natural and artificial sleep; we can experiment with natural as we experiment with artificial sleep. One of my patients, an intelligent man, whom I hypnotized for several months, only reached the third degree of sleep; that is I could induce catalepsy, contracture, and automatic movements, but neither anæsthesia, hallucinatory suggestions, nor amnesia upon waking. He remembered everything which was done and said while he was asleep. One day he told me that his brother was in the habit of talking to him in his sleep when they roomed together at his father's house, and that he answered him without remembering anything about it upon waking; to such an extent he added, that when his brother wanted to get some information which he did not wish to give, he extorted it from him, so to speak, while he was asleep.

I then said to him, "If you can talk thus in your natural sleep without remembering about it when you wake, I ought to be able to put you to sleep artificially in the same way." And I suggested to him to sleep as he did, naturally, without any remembrance upon waking. In fact, from this time on, I induced profound sleep accompanied by amnesia, anæsthesia, suggestive, hypnotic, and post-hypnotic hallucinations. Generally all subjects who talk and answer questions in their sleep, are susceptible of being put into somnambulism artificially.

I repeat that sleep, whether it be artificial or spontaneous, does not mean the abolition of the intellectual faculties; it is a cerebral condition other than the waking, one which it is difficult to define, the study of which still remains for psychologists,—a condition in which the phenomena of automatic life predominate, but in which the so-called reason, or reasoning faculties may be roused and concentrated upon a special point, upon a class of ideas. Concentration, the fixing of the nervous force upon the phenomenon,—the image or idea suggested,—is what appears to dominate. Moreover this concentration may be turned successively upon different objects; dream succeeds dream in a sleeping subject; many and diverse suggestions are communicated to somnambulists, and are instantly executed by them. The nervous concentration changes its object at the hypnotizer's will; the focus shifts its place, if I may so express it, but the same concentration continues to exist.

Without developing this view, which I leave to psychologists, let us be content to know that the mind may still think and work during sleep. It does not work involuntarily; we are conscious of it, as the somnambulist is conscious of what he is doing, only it is *another state of consciousness*, for nervous force is distributed otherwise than in the waking condition; it is concentrated upon a fixed idea or upon the centres of imagination; and upon waking memory has faded away, as the memory of acts performed in artificial sleep fades away. Who has not had the experience of going to sleep with the idea in his head of a problem, or of an abstract solution which has slipped his memory, and of awaking with the solution ready? The mind keeps up its intellectual work during sleep, and sometimes carries it on more easily owing to a special psychical concentration. In some cases this work during sleep is accomplished in a visible manner; the subjects rise, go and come, write, play the piano, or do some manual work, and when wakened are very much astonished at what they have done, without having the least recollection of it—these are *active sleepers or somnambulists.*

Why does the sleeper awake spontaneously at the hour set?
Because he goes to sleep with the idea of waking at such or such an hour, and thinks about it all night, voluntarily and consciously; his attention is fixed upon this idea. If he has an

accurate idea of time, as some people have, and can tell exactly at any time during the day what o'clock it is—or if he hears the clock strike, he wakes spontaneously.

If he has no idea of time,—what happens? He is preoccupied with the idea of not missing the hour, and he wakes several times during the night, and lights the candle each time to make sure; which seems to be evidence of a perfect state of consciousness during sleep. Our ideas are conscious while we sleep: they become latent when we wake; we do not remember that we dreamt all night of not missing the hour, and we think that we waked spontaneously or unconsciously.

It is by means of this class of facts that I try to account for the mechanism of suggestions *à longue échéance*. The somnambulist, who at the end of three months should carry out an act suggested during sleep, manifests no idea of the command which has been given him during these three months; and when he has executed it, he believes and states that he had no idea relative to this act in the interval. Has the memory of the impression stored in the brain by sleep, in reality been latent? Or, at least, has it been latent during all this time? I do not think so.

Let us review the facts which have already been given.

1st. The impressions perceived by somnambulists during their sleep seem absolutely effaced; everything is a dead letter. Memory is revived, however, if the subject is assured that he is going to recall everything; he puts himself spontaneously into the condition of psychical concentration necessary for recollection.

2d. In certain subjects the impressions produced simply while the eyes are closed, are effaced when the eyes are opened, and re-appear when the eyes are again closed.

It is important to have witnessed these striking phenomena, to have seen how easily memories are instantaneously destroyed and revived in somnambulistic cases, to have seen subjects perfectly healthy in body and mind whom suggestion has put,—I do not say into sleep, but into another condition of consciousness. These subjects talk, walk about, work, a second after, when they are awake again and in their former conscious condition, all memory of their preceding life seems to be destroyed forever. They are convinced that nothing has happened. In another second memory is revived;—and thus by the most simple proceeding we can alternate these two states of consciousness, and artificially reproduce this double life, which was manifested spontaneously in the case of the famous Fetida, observed by Azam. In order to grasp all they import, we must have seen these curious psychical phenomena. And we cannot refrain giving the subject thought, when like phenomena are spontaneously and involuntarily induced in somnambulists. They pass from one state of consciousness to the other easily, the memories of the second state being effaced in the first. Put an idea into their minds when they are in the condition known as somnambulistic, an idea which should be manifested on a certain day. During the condition known as the waking condition, the idea seems to be effaced; but it does not remain latent until the day fixed upon. It revives and regains consciousness every time that the same nervous concentration, the same psychical state, is reproduced. If their attention is self-concentrated, and their minds self-absorbed in an idea or an image, it is sufficient to produce a sort of passive somnambulism, passive only in that it cannot be made to change the condition. And this is so true, that many somnambulists are susceptible to suggestion in the waking condition; every idea formulated, every image called forth, is carried out by them in the waking condition; hallucinations may be communicated by word alone; they are somnambulists normally, and without being, so to speak, prepared.

The operator cannot avoid working on this condition of special psychical receptivity.

There is, then, reason for thinking that the somnambulist often goes spontaneously into the somnambulistic condition of consciousness, in which the impressions which were lodged in the mind in a previous and similar condition may be revived. He then recalls the order he received, the suggestion which was commanded; he knows that such and such a phenomenon should be carried out on such and such a day; he takes his measurements, so to speak, he re-enforces the idea of not forgetting it, of carrying it out at the desired moment, as the natural sleeper re-enforces the idea of not missing the hour set for waking. This idea is then a perfectly conscious one in the somnambulist's mind. But when his mind is no longer concentrated, when we speak to him, when we recall his nervous force to the exterior, we restore him his full self-possession, we give him back his condition of normal consciousness, as when we tell a child to open its eyes and look out with its mind. The concentration no longer exists, the memory is again destroyed or latent: and at the very time the somnambulist has executed the suggested act, he believes in good faith that the idea has newly and spontaneously dawned in his mind;—*he no longer remembers that it is a memory.*

I have been able to verify the question directly in two cases of somnambulism. While one of the patients was asleep I said, "Next Thursday (five days), you will take this glass on the night-stand, and put it in the valise at the foot of your bed." Three days after, when I hypnotized her, I asked, "Do you remember what I told you?" She replied, "Yes, sir, I must put the glass in my valise Thursday morning."—"Have you thought about what I told you since?"—"No."—"Think."—"I thought of it the next morning at eleven o'clock."—"Were you awake or asleep?"—"I was drowsy."

I hypnotized the other patient one morning and said to him, "To-morrow morning when I make my rounds, you will ask me if you are to keep on taking the bromide of potassium; you will ask me as if to obtain information, without knowing that I told you to ask me." The next morning Dr. Voisin honored me with his presence at my clinic. I had forgotten the suggestion myself. I was leaving the patient's bedside when he called me back, and asked if he should continue taking the bromide. "Why do you ask?" I said. "Because I must soon leave the hospital, and I want to know if the bromide does me good." — "Why do you ask me just now?" — "I do not know, the idea just came into my head." I then hypnotized him again and asked, "Why did you ask me if it was necessary to continue taking the bromide?" — "Because I wanted to know if it did me good." — "But why did you ask on this particular morning?" — "Because you told me yesterday to ask you the question this morning." — "Have you dreamed since yesterday morning that I hypnotized you and that you were to ask me this question?" — "I dreamt of it last night. I dreamt that I had pains in my legs, and that I ought to ask you if I was to go on taking the bromide." I waked him, and he no longer remembered anything about this. He believed that the idea of asking me this question had come to him spontaneously.

Thus the suggestion which has been stored in the mind during sleep, and which remains as a latent memory upon waking, is susceptible of becoming conscious again spontaneously; and if the suggestion is not to be carried out for several weeks, the idea only remains latent and unconscious until the time fixed upon.

To sum up:

1st. The impressions produced by artificial or induced sleep are always conscious at the time they are produced.

2d. The consciousness of these impressions, which is effaced when the subject wakes from the induced sleep, may always be evoked by simple affirmation.

3d. Latent memories of the hypnotic condition may awake spontaneously in certain states of psychical concentration.

4th. The idea of suggestions which are to be carried out after a lapse of time (*à longue échéance*), only remains unconscious up to the time set for their realization; the consciousness of the idea stored in the mind during the hypnotic state may be aroused at times, as other latent memories are in the same states of psychical concentration.

My colleague, M. Beaunis, does not accept this theory.* "If the suggestion," says he, "is spontaneously recalled in the interval, instead of remaining latent up to the time fixed upon, there is the same difficulty; the explanation reduces it, but does not solve it."

To reduce a difficulty is to solve it partly; to reduce it sufficiently is to solve it totally. I have said that somnambulists who are susceptible to suggestions *à longue échéance* are all eminently suggestible, even in the waking condition; they pass from one state of consciousness into the other very easily; I repeat the fact that they are somnambulists spontaneously, without any art of preparation. Self-absorbed and concentrated, they are in a state of consciousness in which they recall the suggestion communicated to them. If we speak to them, we call their cerebral activity to the outside, we produce another state of consciousness in which they no longer remember, in which they do not know that they have a memory.

Thus the suggestion which is to be executed may be present in their minds a great part of the day; only the subject no longer knows this when we speak to him.

If this is an accurate conception, the suggestion which is to be

---

* Beaunis, *Le somnambulisme provoqué.* Second edition. Paris, 1887, p. 241.

carried out after an interval of time is no more difficult to interpret than the suggestion which is to be carried out immediately upon waking.

M. Beaunis does not accept my explanation of the awakening at a set hour. "If the sleeper," says he, "thought of waking at such and such an hour, either consciously or unconsciously, he would preserve some memory of it. We remember a dream, which has nevertheless done nothing but pass through our minds, and would we not remember an idea upon which our attention has been immovably fixed?" But this is exactly what constitutes the essence of deep sleep or somnambulism,—amnesia upon waking. The somnambulist may remain for hours with his mind concentrated upon one single idea, for example, upon a problem to be solved: he remembers nothing when he wakes. Doubtless in the less profound degrees of natural or induced sleep, we remember our dreams; certain light sleepers may, as the hypnotized subjects of the first degrees, remember the ideas which have passed through their minds; they may remember that their minds have been occupied with the idea of not missing a certain hour. But in this case, like the hypnotized subjects who retain memories, they lack what is for them the criterion of sleep; they believe that they have not slept.

M. Beaunis sees the phenomena of *unconscious cerebration* in all these facts. I confess that I have not this conception except in so far as it relates to the phenomena of vegetative life; the mind interferes in the processes of circulation, respiration, and nutrition, unknown to us. But thought, at the moment it is produced, is always a phenomenon of consciousness; the hypnotized subject who robs because he was suggested to do so, the fool who kills, know that they steal and that they kill. If they are not responsible, it is because their moral conscience is perverted by imperative conceptions, and because madness and suggestion dominate their being; they cannot prevent themselves from striking. The state of consciousness is modified, as it may also be modified by vivid moral emotions, such as anger. When the subject returns to his normal condition, and is no longer under the power of suggestion, no longer angry, no longer insane, and returns to his habitual state of consciousness, he may have forgotten everything. The act, nevertheless, was conscious, although the memory of it may be now effaced. There are latent ideas, but there are no unconscious ideas.

CHAPTER IX

General applications of the doctrine of suggestion.—Moral and psychological standpoint.—Education.—Legal stand-point.—Criminal suggestions.—Observation.—Retroactive hallucinations.—The Tiza-Eslar affair.—Instinctive imbecility.—Reply to M. Paul Janet.

THE doctrine of suggestion, as we have established it according to the facts gained from observation, raises the most throbbing questions on all sides. In psychology it means revolution. Though still in its infancy, what problems is not this study called upon to solve? To what degree may not suggestion influence the most widely different minds, chosen from among the intelligent classes, refined by the power of education, as well as from the lower classes where less cerebral resistance is offered? To what extent may not the subject's instincts, tastes, and psychical faculties be modified by a prolonged and cleverly managed suggestion, whether in the waking or in the hypnotic condition? Have we not, indeed, a veritable suggestion in the waking condition in the child's education, in the notions and principles inculcated by word and example, in the philosophical and religious teachings by which it is surrounded from the earliest age,—a suggestion which often works with an irresistible force if practiced methodically, directed in a uniform manner, and not thwarted by contradictory ideas or examples? Mature men, whose minds have been rendered liberal by personal experience, in spite of the intelligent action of their reasoning powers often reserve a stock of old ideas from which they cannot escape, because, through previous and long continued suggestion, these have become part of the mind, although they may seem to disagree with its present working. M. Liébault says: " Without being aware of it, we acquire moral and political predispositions, prejudices, etc., etc., we are impregnated with the mental atmosphere about us. We honestly believe and defend as we would our own welfare, social and religious principles which may be opposed to common sense, not to say reason. These principles were held by our ancestors, they are also national, and they descend from father to son. It is impossible to destroy them by argument, and dangerous to do so by force. Their fallacy is pointed out in vain. Man thinks by imitation, and however absurd his thoughts may be, they form part of the man, and are finally transmitted from generation to generation, as instincts are."

What suggestion may accomplish in the waking condition with the minds of the young, hypnotic suggestion accomplishes forcibly by its power to suppress all mental control in the person hypnotized. Can we say truly, as Durand does, that Braidism furnishes us with a basis for an intellectual and moral orthopædia, which will some day surely be introduced in educational establishments and penitentiaries?

How many are the applications from the judicial and medico-legal stand-point! When we see a subject who is in a spontaneously or artificially induced somnambulistic condition, a docile instrument in the hands of another, with no will of his own, when we see him submit to all influences, and perform any acts, we cannot help being deeply affected. And when, after he is awakened from hypnotic sleep, we see him execute an order, believing he is doing something of his own initiative, we cannot help repeating with M. Ribot,[*] Spinoza's saying: "Our illusion of free will is but ignorance of the motives which make us act."

It is the duty of moralists, psychologists, and medico-legal practitioners, to scrutinize courageously great questions of this kind, which force themselves upon the human conscience.

I wish to show by one example only, to what degree the phenomena of psychical suggestion, as demonstrated by experiment, may be criminally employed. The following, according to P. Despine, is an extract from the records of the Draguignan assizes of July 30 and 31, 1865.

"On the 31st of March, 1865, a beggar came to the village of Guiols (Var.). He was twenty-five years old, and lame in both legs. He asked for hospitality at the house of a man named H——, who was living in the village with his daughter. The daughter was twenty-six years old, and had always borne a perfectly moral character. The beggar, named Castellan, pretending to be a deaf mute, made them understand by signs that he was hungry. They asked him to supper. During the meal he acted

---

[*] Ribot, *les Maladies de la volonté.* Paris, 1883.

in such a strange manner that he attracted the attention of his hosts. He pretended not to empty his glass until after he made the sign of the cross upon it and upon himself. During the evening, he made a sign that he could write. Then he wrote the following sentences: 'I am the son of God, I am come from Heaven, and my name is Our Lord! You shall see my small miracles, and later, you shall see greater ones. Fear nothing from me, I am sent from God.' He pretended to foretell the future, and declared that civil war would break out in six months. These absurd actions made an impression upon the witnesses, and Josephine H—— was deeply affected by them. She went to bed dressed, fearing the beggar. He spent the night in a hay-loft, and the next day after breakfasting, went away from the village. He soon returned, after making sure that Josephine would be alone during the day. He found her busy with household cares, and conversed with her for some time by the aid of signs. Castellan employed the whole morning in exercising a sort of fascination over this girl. The witness declares that while she was leaning over the fire, Castellan bent over her, making circular signs and signs of the cross on her back. (She had a very haggard look; perhaps he had put her into the somnambulistic state.) At mid-day they sat down to the table together. The meal had hardly begun when Castellan made a gesture as if to throw something into Josephine's plate. The girl fainted. Castellan carried her to her bed, and there outraged her. Josephine was conscious of what happened, but, restrained by an invincible force, could make no movement nor utter a cry, although her will protested against the crime committed upon her. (She was then in a condition of lucid lethargy.) When she had come to herself again she could not release herself from Castellan's control, and at four o'clock in the afternoon when the man left the town, the unhappy girl, drawn by an influence against which she struggled in vain, left her father's house and followed this beggar, for whom she felt only fear and disgust. They spent the night in a hay-loft, and next day went toward Collobrières. M. Sauteron met them in a wood, and took them to his house. Castellan told him that he had run away with this young girl, after having betrayed her. Josephine also told him of her unhappiness, adding that she wanted to drown herself from despair. On April 3d, Castellan, followed by the girl, stopped at a farmer's named Coudroyer. Josephine did not cease lamenting and deploring the unhappy situation in which the irresistible power of this man held her. Fearing further outrage, she asked to sleep in a neighboring room. Castellan approached her just as she was going out, and caught her by the hips. *She immediately fainted.* Then, according to the declarations of the witnesses, although she was like a dead person, they saw her go upstairs at Castellan's command, counting the steps and laughing convulsively. It was proved that she was at this time completely insensible. (She was in the somnambulistic condition.)

"The next morning, April 4th, she came down stairs in a condition resembling insanity. She talked irrationally, and refused nourishment. She called upon God and the Virgin Mary. Castellan, wishing to give a new proof of his power over her, ordered her to go round the room on her knees, and she obeyed. Touched by the unhappy girl's sorrows, and indignant at the audacious way in which her seducer abused his power, the inhabitants of the house drove the beggar out, in spite of resistance. He had hardly got out of the door when Josephine fell down as if dead. They called Castellan back. He made various signs over her and restored the use of her senses. Night came and she again went with him to his room.

"The next day they went away together. No one dared to prevent Josephine from going with this man. All at once she was seen running back. Castellan had met some hunters, and while he talked with them, she had escaped. She begged in tears that she might be hidden, and that they might snatch her from this influence. She was taken back to her father, not seeming to possess her full reasoning powers.

"Castellan was arrested. He had already been condemned for misdemeanor. He seemed to be naturally gifted with rare magnetic power. To this must be attributed the influence he exercised over Josephine. Her constitution was marvellously influenced by magnetism, as has been proved by diverse experiments to which expert physicians have subjected her. Castellan recognized that his magnetic passes were the cause of Josephine's fainting turns, which preceded the violation. He confessed that he had had criminal connection with her twice, at a time when she was neither asleep nor fainting, but when she could not have given full consent to the culpable actions of which she was the object. (That is to say she was in a condition of lucid lethargy.) The violation during the second night they spent at Capelude took place under the following conditions: Josephine had no suspicion of the crime of which she was the victim, and it was Castellan who told her about it in the morning. At two other times he abused her in the same manner without her being suspicious of the fact. (That is to say she was in the somnambulistic sleep.)

"Since she has been delivered from this man's influence, Josephine has recovered her reason. In her testimony before the court, she said, ' He exercised such an influence over me with his gestures, that several times I fell as if dead. He could then do what he pleased with me. I understood what I was the victim of, but I could neither speak nor act and I endured the most cruel torments.' (She alluded to the turns of lucid lethargy; when she was in the somnambulistic condition, she had no consciousness of what had happened.)

"Three physicians, Drs. Hériart, Paulet, and Théus, were summoned to enlighten the jury upon the effects of magnetism. They confirmed the conclusions of the medico-legal report prepared by Drs. Auban and Roux, of Toulon, on this occasion. Castellan was sentenced to twelve years hard labor."

At the time when these things occurred, the phenomena of somnambulism were not understood as they are to-day. Our readers will doubtless appreciate all the details of this curious observation.

Here, the psychical condition of the unhappy victim, due to criminal manœuvres, can be easily established; but what of the unconscious suggestions, the origin of which remains doubtful?

My colleague, M. Liégeois, professor of law at Nancy, has made a special study of suggestion in relation to civil and criminal law in a memoir which has been very favorably received.

He has made a large number of experiments necessary for the establishment of the possibility of suggesting crimes, which the subjects of such suggestion may carry out, ignorant of the real motive power which guides their hand.

The following is a statement of one of his experiments:

M. Liégeois says: I am to blame for having tried to have my friend, M. P., formerly a magistrate, killed, and this, serious as it was, in the presence of the commissary general of Nancy.

I armed myself with a revolver and some cartridges. I took a subject at random from among the five or six somnambulists who were at M. Liébault's that day; and to remove any possible idea of play, which the subject to be experimented with might conceive, I loaded the pistol, and fired one shot in the garden. Then I came in again, showing the assistants a card just pierced by the ball.

In less than a quarter of a minute, I suggested to Mme. G—— the idea of killing M. P. by a pistol shot. Absolutely unconscious, and perfectly docile, Mme. G—— approached M. P. and fired the pistol.

The commissary questioned her immediately. She confessed her crime with complete indifference: she killed M. P. because she did not like him. They could arrest her. She knew very well what awaited her. If they took away her life, she would go into the other world as her victim had done, whom she saw there stretched out on the ground bathed in his own blood. She was asked if I had not suggested the idea of the murder which she had just committed. She assured us that this was not so, that she was led to it spontaneously, and that she alone was to blame.

I have spoken of post-hypnotic suggestions, to which many deep sleepers are susceptible. In such cases, acts or hallucinations may be provoked which will take place several days, even several weeks after the subjects are awakened,—actions from which they will not be able to escape, and of whose origin they will be ignorant.

We may produce even greater results. Since these facts were established, I have proved that true *retroactive hallucinations* may often be developed. We can suggest to subjects that at some period, now past, they saw such and such an act committed, and the image created in their minds seems like a living memory, which governs them to such an extent as to appear an incontestable reality.

For example, here is the case of a somnambulist, Marie G——, an intelligent woman of whom I have already spoken. I hypnotize her into deep sleep and say, "You got up in the night?" She replies, "Oh, no." "I insist upon it; you got up four times to go to the water-closet, and the fourth time you fell on your nose. This is a fact, and when you wake up no one will be able to make you believe the contrary." When she wakes I ask, "How are you now?" "Very well," she answers, "but last night I had an attack of diarrhœa. I had to get up four times.

I fell, too, and hurt my nose." I say, "You **dreamed** that. You said nothing to me about it just now. Not one of the patients saw you." She persists in her statement, saying that she has not been dreaming, that she was perfectly conscious of getting up, that all the patients were asleep;—and she remains convinced that the occurrence was genuine.

On another occasion, while she was sleeping, I asked what house she lived in, and who else lived there. Among other things, she told me that the first floor was occupied by a family, —mother, father, and several little girls, and an old bachelor who lived with them. Then I gave her the following suggestion: "On August 3 (three months and a half ago), at three o'clock in the afternoon, you went into the house where you live. When you reached the first floor, you heard cries coming from a room. You looked in through the key-hole. You saw the old bachelor committing rape upon the largest little girl: you saw it. The little girl was struggling, she was bleeding, and he gagged her. You saw it all, and you were so distressed that you went to your apartment and did not dare to say anything. When you wake up you will think no more about it. I have not told the story to you; it is not a dream; it is not a vision I have given you during your hypnotic sleep; it is truth itself; and if inquiry is made into this crime later on, you will tell the truth." I then changed the course of her ideas, and gave her brighter suggestions. When she woke, I did not dare to speak of the fact. I asked my friend M. Grillon, a distinguished lawyer, to question the woman three days later, as if he were a judge deputed to do so. She related the facts to him in my absence, giving all the details, the names of the criminal and the victim, and the exact hour of the crime. She gave her evidence energetically. She knew the gravity of her testimony. If she was summoned before the assizes, she would tell the truth in spite of her feelings. If it were necessary, she was ready to swear before God and man! As I approached her bed after her evidence was given, the lawyer, assuming the privilege of a magistrate, made her repeat the evidence before me. I asked her if it was really true; if she had not been dreaming; if it was not a vision like those I was in the habit of giving her during her sleep. I tried to persuade her to doubt herself. She maintained the truth of her testimony with immovable conviction.

After that I hypnotized her in order to take away this suggestion. "Everything you told the judge was a mistake," I said, "you saw nothing on August 3d. You know nothing about anything of the kind. You will not even remember that you have spoken to the judge. He has asked no questions and you have told him nothing." When she waked I said to her, "What did you say to M—— just now?"—"I said nothing"—"What, you said nothing!" replied the magistrate. "You told me about a crime which occurred on August 3, in the house where you live. You saw the person named X——, etc."

Marie was disconcerted. The news of the crime took away her breath. She had never heard of it. When M—— insisted, telling her that she herself had mentioned this crime, she could not understand. She was violently affected by the news that she would be summoned to court as a witness, and to calm her I had to hypnotize her again and wipe out the memory of this truly frightful scene. When she woke again, the memory of all that had passed was effectually erased from her mind, and the next day when talking with her, I purposely led her to speak of the people in the house where she lived. She spoke of them naturally, as if we had never mentioned them when together.

More still may be proved. We have observed that certain subjects capable of being hypnotized are susceptible to illusions or varying hallucinations by *simple affirmation in the waking condition*, without the necessity of re-hypnotizing them. They are also susceptible to retroactive hallucinations. What occurs pathologically in the insane when they imagine themselves as having been present at such and such a scene, as having committed such and such an act, as a murder or a robbery, and when they enumerate all the details of a crime in which they have been actors and spectators—all this may be artificially carried out in certain persons with frightful ease by affirmation simply.

I say to one of my somnambulistic cases, S——, "Last night you saw by your bedside Dr. G——, my *chef de clinique*. He felt ill and vomited. You gave him your handkerchief to wipe his mouth." He is convinced that this happened. The suggested idea forces itself upon his mind, like a real retrospective image. When S—— meets Dr. G——, an hour afterwards, he says to him,—"I saw you last night: you were pretty sick."—"Why, you astonish me, I was not in the hospital."—"I certainly saw you; it was five minutes of four. You were sick: it was just a little indisposition which you could not help."

I said to the same subject on another occasion,—"You went out of the room this morning. You went to the chapel and looked through the key-hole. Two men were fighting," etc. He saw it. The next day I called him into my office, where I had somebody who pretended to be a police commissioner. He related the facts, described the workmen; one had a broken arm, he saw him carried into the surgeon's room on a stretcher; he was the one who began the quarrel. He declared himself ready to give evidence in court, and to take his oath. The pretended commissioner insinuated, while I was out of the room, that perhaps it was all an illusion, an idea which I had suggested to him. The subject seemed vexed by this observation and maintained energetically that he had seen it, and spoke only of what he had seen. I add that this man enjoyed good reasoning powers. He was a former patient, who, when cured, took the office of assistant nurse in the service.

These are not isolated facts. M. Liégeois made numerous experiments of the same kind upon other hypnotizable subjects in the waking and sleeping condition, at the same time that I made mine. The conclusions he reached agree with mine.

I was inspired with the idea of these experiments by a recent trial which excited public opinion very much.

The Tisza-Eslar affair is well known. A young girl, fourteen years old, who belonged to the reformed faith, disappeared. Nineteen Jewish families lived in this Hungarian village. The rumor soon spread that the Jews had killed the girl for her blood. It was the eve of the Passover feast;—they had mixed her Christian blood with their unleavened bread. A corpse was later found in the Theiss, and was recognized by six people as that of the girl: but the mother remained incredulous, and other witnesses chosen by her, refused to recognize the body. The anti-semitic passion was aroused. Public opinion was decided, and thirteen unhappy Jews were arrested. The judge, a great enemy of the Jewish race, busied himself in confirming with active ferocity the conjecture which blind hatred had conceived. The sacristan of the synagogue had a son thirteen years old; he was summoned before the judge. The child knew nothing of murder, but the judge, wishing by all possible means to establish what he believed or wanted to be the truth, gave him into the hands of the commissioner of public safety, who was expert in extorting confessions. The latter took the boy to his house.

Several hours later the child had confessed; his father had allured the girl into his house, and had then sent her to the synagogue. The boy Moritz, heard a cry, went out, looked through the key-hole of the temple door, and saw Esther stretched on the ground; three men held her. The butcher cut her throat and caught the blood in three basins.

The child was isolated for three months under the care of a guardian who never left him. When he came before the assembly he persisted in his confessions. The sight of his father and twelve co-religionists threatened by the gallows, the most earnest supplications to tell the truth, tears and curses,—nothing moved him. Without hesitating he repeated the same things in the same terms; he had seen. We know that justice triumphed in the end, causing all the friends of Hungary and of civilization to rejoice.

How are the child's statements to be explained? Two hypotheses are possible. Terror, violence, threats have been able to force the lying disposition, and everyone knows how in children, and even in adults, persistence in a lie becomes obstinate opinion, through the sole fact of having lived for weeks with the habit of this lie. Add to this the flattery that follows, and the promise of a rose-colored existence as a reward for perseverance in a forced lie. This is possible. Yet I cannot willingly conceive of moral perversion so monstrous, so rapidly developed, in a child, who, up to that time, had shown no evidence of bad instincts.

That terror should force false testimony from persons of weak mind, is in the nature of things. But that a child, in the presence of a suffering and imploring father, deaf to all supplications, can maintain his evidence, knowing that it will bring capital punishment, that, notwithstanding, he can continue to maintain his little story, which he knows to be invented, is a rare example of moral monstrosity.

The following is the other hypothesis. The child is led before the judge. Humble, debased in the eyes of the poor, among whom he has been brought up, he trembles before the personage representing force and justice. Alone, face to face with the commissioner of public safety, into whose hands he has been delivered, he is terrified. The commissioner persuades him convincingly that the Jews are a cursed race, who consider it a pious duty to spill Christian blood, that it is their custom to sprinkle the unleavened bread of the passover with this blood, and that this is not the first trial of the kind. In colored language full of assurance, he relates the circumstantial and realistic details of analogous scenes. The imagination of the poor nervous child, fascinated by terror, is deeply impressed. He is all eyes, all ears, and his reasoning faculties are paralyzed by emotion. The narrator's word makes an impression upon his weak mind, and little by little, the profound and persistent impression becomes an image. Under the influence of this vigorous suggestion the hypnotized brain constructs the scene which the commissioner makes out of whole cloth. It is all there. The child sees the victim stretched out, held by three people, the sacrificer plunging his knife into the throat, the blood flowing; the child has seen; retroactive hallucination has been created, just as it is experimentally created in deep sleep, and the memory of the fictitious vision is so vivid that the child cannot escape it. Such a dramatic scene, vigorously sketched by a romancer, forces itself upon the imagination with as much vividness as reality itself.

I do not know whether this hypothesis is the true one. The simple fact of the child's rapid conversion, due to the skilful working of his instructors, seems to denote a mind susceptible to suggestion. The psychical study of this witness by a commission of physicians thoroughly conversant with these facts, would without doubt have enabled them to measure the suggestibility of his brain, to prove whether he was hypnotizable, and perhaps bring the truth to light.

The facts just related were given in the preceding edition of this work. The following are new confirmatory observations.

Joseph François S——, a young man of twenty-two, had worked as a compositor in the printing house of Berger-Levrault. He came under my notice for a sciatic trouble, dating back eight days. I recognized that he was hypnotizable, susceptible to hallucinations, and suggestible in the waking condition. At one séance he was cured of his sciatica by suggestion.

He is an almost beardless youth of lymphatic temperament, and was exempt from military service on account of a delicate constitution. At the same time he is well formed and has never been sick. He has never had attacks of spontaneous somnambulism, nor any other evidences of nervous affection. He is quiet, intelligent, and well-educated, honest and industrious. He went through the classes of the Franciscan School, during the year 1882 to 1883. He attended the chemistry course at the high school twice a week. He has been working as compositor for seven years, and was earning lately three and a half francs per day. He has never committed any excesses. His father, a shoemaker, is sixty years old, and a hale old man. His mother, too, who is the same age, is a healthy woman. He has two brothers, both strong and well nourished, and a sister, twenty-nine years old, who is also strong, and has three vigorous children. He knew of no nervous trouble in his family. On the 21st of last March, in the presence of Dr. Schmitt, substituting professor in the faculty, in my service, I said to S—— (without hypnotizing him and without having hypnotized him before), "you see this gentleman? you met him yesterday in the street talking with several people. As you passed him he approached you, struck you several times with his cane, and took the money which was in your pocket. Tell me how that happened?" S—— instantly said: "Yesterday at three o'clock in the afternoon I was walking along Academy Place. I saw M—— talking in a loud voice with several people. Suddenly, I cannot tell why, M—— came up to me, hit me several times with his cane, put his hands into my pockets and took my money away from me."—"Is that really true?" I asked. "I have just made you tell that."—"It is perfectly true."—"Look here, you know very well that I hypnotized you, and gave you a suggestion."—"But this is true; it is not a suggestion."—"What is your profession?" I asked.—"I work in Berger-Levrault's Printing House. I set the type for the *Revue médicale de l'Est.*"—"Well, do you know who this gentleman is?"—"No, I do not know him."—"It is Dr. Schmitt, the chief editor of the *Revue médicale de l'Est.* You are not going to maintain that a doctor like this gentleman, has struck and robbed a poor boy like you?"—"It is true: I do not know why, but I cannot say otherwise, for it is true."—"See here, you are an honest boy; you are religious."—"Yes, sir."—"One does not accuse a man without being absolutely sure of what he has done. If the police commissioner questioned you, what would you say?"—"I would tell the truth. He struck me with his cane, and took my money away."—"And you would swear to it? Are you sure enough of yourself to swear? Think. Perhaps it is simply an idea, an illusion, a dream."—"I would swear before Christ."—"Perhaps it was some one resembling this gentleman."—"It was this gentleman; I am absolutely certain."

HYPNOSIS AND SUGGESTION

Three children were with us during this conversation.

One of them, Adrian V——, fourteen years old, is tubercular and has moist rales at both apices of the lungs. He says that for five years he has had colds all winter, but has never had any evidences of nervous trouble, and no spontaneous attacks of somnambulism.

He is very susceptible to suggestion and hallucination in the waking and sleeping conditions. He is intelligent, can read, write, and cipher. His memory is remarkable. He is a gentle, honest child, has been in the service a long time, and is loved by the sisters and the patients.

His father, an alcoholic case, abandoned his mother last September. The mother is very strong, as are also his brothers and sisters. None of them have any nervous affection.

I said to this child, " You heard this young man's story this morning?"—He replied without hesitation, "Yes, sir."—" What was it about?"—" That a gentleman had struck him and taken his money away."—" Where was it?" I asked.—" In the hospital."—" Why, no," I said, "that is not right, because he has just told us that it happened in Academy Place." Without being disconcerted, the child said,—" I no longer remember where it happened, but he told me that he had been struck and robbed."—" When did he tell you that?"—" This morning at half past seven."—" Enough," I said; " it is not necessary to tell me untrue things;" and I pretended to be angry. " M—— has told you nothing. I made you say it. You are honest and religious: it is not necessary to make up stories to be obliging."—" I assure you, sir, that he told me about it this morning."—" If the commissioner asked you, what would you say?"—" I would say what was told me."—" Would you swear to it?"—" I would swear to it."

Another child present was Joseph L——, fourteen years old. He is delicate, having had a stroke of infantile paralysis, but suffers from no other nervous troubles. His father, mother and one sister are strong and healthy. He is quite intelligent, and reads and writes correctly. He is susceptible to suggestion in the waking and sleeping conditions.

" You were present," I said to him, " when M—— told how he had been struck and robbed?" He replied without hesitating, "Yes, sir."—" When did he tell it?"—" This morning at half past seven."—" See here, you need not repeat that like a parrot, because you have just heard it. But did you hear it from the gentleman's own lips this morning?"—"Yes, sir, this morning at half past seven."—"You swear to it?"—"I swear it."

Finally, in the next bed, there is a child nine years old, G——, who is convalescent from pleurisy. He has a good constitution, with no nervous inheritance. Father, mother, two sisters and a brother are all well and strong. This child is also very susceptible to suggestion, though to a less degree than the others.

"Did you hear it too," I asked him? He hesitated. "I do not remember very clearly."—I insisted. "Think hard," I said; "he related the story before you this morning. Do not worry, do not be afraid, you can tell it if you know it." He thought several moments then stated, "It is true, I heard it."—"When?"—"This morning at half past seven."—"What did you hear?"—"That a gentleman had struck him and had taken away his money."—"Are you very sure that you heard him tell it? A moment ago you did not remember. You must not say so if you are not certain of it. You just heard it told, but you did not hear it this morning?"—"Yes, sir, I am perfectly certain I did."

The next day S—— left the hospital. I had him come into my office before his departure and said to him, "See here, my friend, tell me the truth. Yesterday, you accused Dr. Schmitt of having struck you with his cane and taken your money. Confess that you were joking, and that such was not the case. You thought you were pleasing me by pretending to believe what I said to you. Now that we are alone, tell me there is nothing in it." He replied, "I swear to you that it is true. I was passing along Academy Place. He came up to me with his cane, struck me several times and took the money out of my pockets. I had but ten sous, and I have them no longer." "Why should a doctor take a few sous away from a poor boy? That is not credible."—"I do not know why, but he took them from me."

The following is a similar case:

V—— Louis, is a man thirty-seven years old, who has been tubercular since 1872. Both apices are consolidated. The affection runs a subacute course. There is no well authenticated neuropathic history. Clinical examination reveals an ordinary phthisical process, but nothing further. He had been in the hospital several weeks, when one day, being honored by a visit from Prof. Forel of Zürich, an eminent colleague who is working in psychiatry, and who was desirous of attending my clinic in order to study the question of hypnotism, I experimented upon some new subjects. I tried V——, and found him an excellent somnambulist, susceptible to suggestion in the waking and sleeping conditions.

Some time after this, on the 3d of April, my honored colleague, M. Victor Parisot, being with me on duty, I said to the man without hypnotizing him; "Do you know this gentleman?"—"No sir."—"Did you go out yesterday?"—"Yes sir."—"Well, think; you met this gentleman. When passing, you came too close, so as to hit him with your elbow, and he struck you with his cane. You remember it very well." After a few moments he said, "Oh, yes, sir; it was in Jean-Lamour Street; I was going home. M—— hit me with his cane so that it hurt me very much."—"Are you perfectly sure? I have made you say so."—"It is perfectly true; it is the same gentleman."—"It is a suggestion. I have made you dream it."—"No, sir, it is really true. I felt the pain in my leg distinctly and I feel it still." He persists in his positive affirmation.

In the same room opposite him is a patient, T. Nicholas, thirty-four years old, a plasterer, who has been in the hospital two years for mitral insufficiency. He has no nervous trouble, and is very susceptible to suggestion in the waking and sleeping conditions. I asked him questions at a distance. "Is it true that V—— told you that story yesterday evening?" Without hesitating,—"Yes, sir; yesterday evening when he came in he said to me, 'I have just been struck with a cane by a gentleman coming down Jean-Lamour Street.'"—"What gentleman?"—"He did not say who, he did not recognize him."—I went up to his bed and said to him, "Look here, my friend, you need not say anything of which you are not sure. Do not state it to be obliging. He was not struck by a cane: it was only a suggestion I gave him."—"He told me about it last night, however."—"At what time?"—"At half past four, when he brought me an Easter egg." And he shows me an Easter egg in his drawer. A remarkable coincidence. The retroactive hallucination provoked in T—— was associated with the real fact in his mind. His statement was corroborated by this incontestable fact; the egg was there! What weight this would add to testimony given in court!

Still another fact.

Last November, when I resumed work after my vacation, I passed by a large, fat, servant girl, Josephine T——, twenty-two years old, and quite stupid. She was affected with articular rheumatism, but not at all of nervous constitution. Her bed was next Mme. G., a laundress, fifty-four years old, who had locomotor ataxia, and was a very intelligent and highly suggestible person. Speaking of the former case, the students said to me, "This girl is a good somnambulist like her neighbor."

Then, without hypnotizing her, I said point blank, "What was the trouble between you and your neighbor yesterday morning? She threw her crutches at your head and struck you on the nose. You remember it very well." She seemed a little surprised at first. I repeated the sentence. "Ah! yes, sir," she said, after an instant, "it was after breakfast; we were chatting a little. All of a sudden she grew angry and threw her crutches at me. She hurt me very much; I have a bruise on my nose yet."—"Look here, stupid," I said, "you dreamed it; I have just made up the story."—"No, I have not dreamed it; I am not stupid. She threw her crutches at my head. I told her that I should tell M. Bernheim."—"You have been dreaming." She became angry. "I know what I say. I am not confused. All the patients saw it and can tell you so," and she calls upon all her neighbors successively as witnesses. There was a general burst of laughter in the room.

Her neighbor G—— was convulsed with laughter. Josephine T—— was furious, made faces at her, and shook her fist. The scene lasted for twenty minutes. Finally, I said to the woman G——, "What are you laughing at?" She pointed to her neighbor. "But," said I, "is it not possible that this is true? You may have forgotten about it. Think." Her face immediately grew serious. "Yes, it is true. Why is she always bothering me? I confess that I was angry, I could not command myself for a moment. I threw my crutches at her head." "And you also used bad language." "Heavens, I forgot that. I called her——. I beg your pardon, you must not bear any grudge against me. Was it necessary for you to tell M. Bernheim all that?"—"Assure yourself," I said to her, "that all this is not true. It is a suggestion I gave you."—"No, sir, it is true." And she persisted in her assertion, convinced of its reality, so much so that when I started to leave her bed she became restless, and said to me, " She is furious, I am afraid she will beat me in revenge." " Do not be afraid," I said, " I am going to put her asleep and take away the memory of all that has happened." I did so, and Mme. G—— was reassured.

I could multiply these cases, but will finish with the following, which I observed on the 8th of April. The case was that of Charles R——, an Italian mason, twenty years old, who was in the hospital for tubercular pleurisy;—a boy of lymphatic temperament, without any nervous history, but very susceptible to suggestion. I said to him, " Were you in the yard when two drunken nurses had a fight? One had his leg broken, and had to be taken to the surgeon's; the other had a nose bleed." He answered, " I do not know. I was not there." I said, " You told me about it this morning. You were in the yard yesterday at three o'clock," and I repeat the story, emphasizing the details. In about two minutes the hallucinatory memory has dawned on his mind. He saw it. " They were the two nurses on the surgical side; the elder had his leg broken; he was the one who began the fight. They called each other bad names. The policemen came, etc."

I asked him for the man's name, in order to give it to the police commissioner, who was coming to question the witnesses of the scene. He should tell what he had seen and should take his oath.

All these experiments were made independently of one another in different rooms. None of the subjects had been present at similar experiments. There had been no chance for suggestion by imitation.

I add that I made all these insinuations quietly, without trying to force them upon the subject, or making great effort to provoke a favorable reply. Some cases were affected by the suggestion immediately. In others it required several seconds, two minutes at the most, for the hallucinatory image to be evoked. After their affirmation I insisted upon pointing out to them that they were mistaken, and pretended to be angry with them. The false evidence was persisted in, because the subjects saw; a retroactive hallucination had been created.

Some subjects relate the facts with surprising accuracy of detail. Like a professional liar, they invent out of whole cloth, with imperturbable coolness and perfect conviction. Their imagination suggests all the circumstances of the self-conceived drama. They remind one of apparently lucid cases of insanity, who invent a thousand calumnies, create discord wherever they can, and tell groundless stories about Peter and Paul with absolute good faith, and with a refinement of detail that make them seem credible. The world believes in malice and in moral perversity where there is sometimes only mental insanity; instincts perverted by sickness engender in these highly imaginative people retroactive hallucinations that force themselves upon their minds as realities. Like the subjects we experiment with, they do not lie, yet are led into error by the weakness of their reasoning powers.

People will ask, "What proof have you of your subject's veracity? Are they not acting to oblige you?" I reply, "I have no certain proof, but I have repeated these experiments with numbers of different subjects; I know these subjects to be honest, as they have been in the hospital some time; their expression, their behavior, intonation of voice and manner of relating a story, all denote conviction and sincerity."

Dr. Motet has mentioned similar facts. He has lately called the attention of the Academy of Medicine to the false evidence given by children in court. He cites the Tisza-Eslar affair, which he interprets as I have done. He shows that these children act in good faith through auto-suggestion. Doubtless Dr. Motet had no knowledge of the facts and experiments I had published in my book, because he does not cite them. His opinion has more value coming as it does, to confirm what I had stated independently.

As we have seen, it is not children alone that can give false testimony sincerely and in good faith. It can also be done by serious adults, who understand the significance of what they say, and do not speak lightly.

I repeat that it is a true retroactive hallucination which dictates the evidence to them. The picture of the fictitious scene exists in their own minds; *they have seen with their own eyes.*

Is there any need of emphasizing the importance of the experimental facts just related, from the social and legal point of view? To study them is to enlighten justice, to forewarn society against grave judicial errors which may result from ignorance; for to attract attention to these phenomena of suggestion is often enough to liberate the truth.

In order to reassure those who may be troubled by my statements, I give some indications which may serve to establish the differential diagnosis between true evidence, and evidence falsified through suggestion.

1st. False witnesses or accusers do not seem to me to act as honest ones do. The memory of the suggested event does not appear to be as persistent as the memory of the real event; the impression is not as continuous. The recollection of it becomes latent or dim again, unless it is aroused. Here is a young man, who, according to my suggestion, accuses some one of having robbed him. When I question him, he states the fact positively and with evident conviction, but if during the day he meets his pretended robber, he will not approach him with the idea of making accusations, of reproaching him with the robbery, or of denouncing him to justice, unless a special suggestion on this point has been given. We may say that the created retroactive hallucination is latent in the normal condition, and does not awaken again until I call it forth by questioning. This constitutes a veritable suggestion, which provokes the hallucination by developing a special state of consciousness in which the subject perceives it.

2d. The magistrate should question the witness without forewarning him, without trying to put him on the right track, and without letting him see what his own opinion is. People have been aroused against the abuses of hypnotism. They have cried out, and rightly, against the idea of making use of hypnotic suggestion to obtain confessions from the accused. But does the magistrate know that he is liable to give suggestions to certain subjects unconsciously, and with a frightful facility?

3d. Witnesses may give suggestions to one another. If one of them makes an affirmation forcibly and convincingly, and relates facts in such a manner in the presence of others, some among them will be influenced, will accept the witness' word, and will make a picture of the event in their own minds, similar to that which has just been presented to them. Each witness, therefore, should first be questioned alone, and it should be definitely decided that no reciprocal suggestion has taken place in previous conversations. The agreement of several witnesses about the details of a fact is not always an argument in favor of its reality, even when the witnesses are known to be acting in good faith. There may be some among them who have made, and some who have received suggestions. Nothing is more false than the saying: *Vox populi, vox Dei.*

4th. A well-informed magistrate can measure the suggestibility of a doubtful witness by a process of clever questioning. He will appear to accept the witnesses' word, will insist upon the incidents, and will suggest details which betray the witness' suggestibility if he confirms them.

For example, he will say to him, "You said that when X—— took away your money, he let a piece fall, and picked it up again. Do you remember this circumstance?" If the accuser falls into the trap and confirms it, the question is decided.

5th. The medical examination of a witness by a physician who is conversant with the subject, will, I believe, in a majority of cases, enable the fact to be established as to whether suggestion is present or not. In fact, in all cases where my experiments have proved successful, the subjects were hypnotizable (by our method), and susceptible to suggestion in the waking and sleeping conditions; in the majority of these cases catalepsy was produced by simple affirmation, and in some hallucinations could be induced.

Such are the facts which I submit to the consideration of my colleagues. I have studied them without prejudice, and without passing the limit of strict and rigorous observation.

The study of suggestion opens up new fields in medicine, psychology, and sociology. Poor human imagination is exposed on all sides to good or bad, salutary or pernicious impressions. All criminals are not guilty; all untruths are not lies; there are those who mystify, and those who are mystified unconsciously: there are people who deceive themselves.

Scientific men will not accept my statements until they have verified them, and those who, from prejudice, systematically refuse to examine the facts, because they do not accord with their *a priori* ideas;—those who judge without having seen, and without wishing to see;—those who have enough self-confidence to assume that the conceptions of their own minds are identical with the truth, and that facts should bow before them, will also believe that I am mistaken.

They have not reflected upon these words of Claude Bernard's:

"Men who have excessive faith in their theories or ideas, are not only ill-adapted to making discoveries, but they also make very bad observations. The results of experiment must be accepted as they present themselves to us, with all their surprises and irregularities."

I have endeavored to show that hypnotism does not really create a new condition : there is nothing in induced sleep which may not occur in the waking condition, in a rudimentary degree in many cases, but in some to an equal extent. Some people are naturally susceptible to suggestion. From a psychological point of view, they are normally in the condition called hypotaxic or charmed, which makes them incapable of taking care of themselves, and enfeebles or suppresses all their moral resistance. Men, in many respects distinguished, and endowed with artistic qualities or brilliant intuitions, are often only grown up children, having all their intellectual power concentrated, as it were, in one or two faculties of the imagination. Everyone has heard of infant prodigies; lightning calculators, for example, like Mondeux and Inaudi, who solved the most complex problems mentally, by means of a prodigious natural power of abstraction, but who were incapable of intellectual efforts in other directions. Here, at least, an immense talent, bordering upon genius, compensates for the discord of cerebral functions. Many people have not this compensation.

Who has not seen those disinherited beings, who, not deprived of intelligence, are capable of assimilating current ideas, and even able to shine in the parlor, exhibiting illustrations of their worth and fulfilling their social duties properly when well guided, but who are in reality wholly without initiative and will power, without moral resistance, and are carried along with the wind, that is, wherever suggestion blows them? I freely affirm that they are affected with instinctive imbecility.

Under the name of instinctive imbecility, foolish actions, moral insanity, or reasoning mania, alienists describe "a morbid condition which is shown less by intellectual delirium, by disorder in ideas and expressions, than by extravagance of sentiment and action which appear to be the result of instinctive, automatic, thoughtless impulse, without the intervention of reflection or reason, as in the case of a man possessed of all his senses."—(A. Foville.) "These patients are foolish," says Trélat,—" but they do not appear foolish, because they express themselves clearly. They are fools in their actions rather than in their words. They have sufficient power of attention to allow nothing happening around them to pass unnoticed, to leave nothing heard unanswered, and to commit no omission in carrying out any project. Their want of reasoning power is wholly internal and is not apparent to the outside world. It is among these that we find a large number of beings who are considered sometimes as insane, sometimes as malefactors, and who have alternately been inmates of asylums and of prisons."

We recognize this in those who have an unusual power in discussion, who have the gift of repartee, and who are constantly seeking an opportunity for displaying their mental brilliancy. "Among patients of this sort," says Gueslain, "we find some capable of nonplussing sound logicians. Their controversies at times could not be more witty. I call to mind a lady who was a real torment to me as well as to everybody in the establishment. Every time she took part in conversation I had to struggle against her witty attacks. All her answers were passed through the crucible of analysis, and that with a penetration truly astonishing to everyone."

Side by side with this instinctive insanity, I class instinctive imbecility; and under this head range those already spoken of, who are not fools, who commit no unreasonable acts spontaneously, and who have no monomaniacal impulses. They are mentally-clear imbeciles; they talk well, reason correctly, are sensible, and sometimes brilliant in conversation; they can use *finesse* and intelligence in accomplishing projects they have conceived; but the instinctive, sentimental part of the moral being which directs the every-day acts is as if atrophied. They have no moral spontaneity; they do not know how to behave, and, like somnambulists from a psychical point of view, obey all suggestions, submitting readily to all outside influences. This psychical condition exists in variable degrees, from simple instinctive weakness to absolute instinctive idiocy. Under good guidance these beings, deprived of moral sense, may fulfil a happy and useful career. Others are stranded in the mud, or before tribunals.

For example, let us take a young girl brought up with good principles, and considered by everybody to be sweet and honest. She marries. The first years pass happily; she seems to be a devoted wife and a good mother. A young man takes her fancy. Her husband, engrossed with the struggle for existence, neglects her; she gives herself up to this young man.

Later, the husband meditates vengeance against the man, who, after seducing his wife, has set up a rival establishment which flourishes, while his own goes to pieces. In order to gratify his revenge, he captures his wife's mind anew, persuades her that his rival is the cause of their unhappiness, insinuates that he must be killed, and that her moral well-being is at the expense of this murder. She yields to his suggestion. Gentle in disposition, giving in when threatened, she arranges a rendezvous with her former lover—and coldly, on a pretense of renewing the relationship which has been broken off, she takes him to her husband, who assassinates him. No remorse, no regret stirs her conscience. She does not seem to suspect the enormity of her crime.

Nothing in her previous history foretold this monstrous perversion of the moral sense. To the jury, the mistress of her boarding-school states that she was the most docile and best disciplined pupil. A witness, at whom some of the audience laughed because they did not understand him, said of her;— "She was soft dough, and turned to evil as readily as to virtue." Translated in psychological language, she was susceptible to suggestion. I add that the moral sense did not counterbalance her excessive suggestibility. It was less a perversion, perhaps, than a natural absence of the moral sense. It was instinctive imbecility.

I do not claim that my interpretation is the true one; it suffices that my proposition is plausible. Moreover, far be it from my thoughts to imply that all criminals are foolish or unconscious actors; every deed should be studied with its circumstances, with its causes, with its antecedents, with the moral condition of the person who perpetrated it. For, who would venture to claim that the degree of culpability is to be measured alone by the gravity of the act committed?

But I must stop. I desired to treat but briefly a question which involves the gravest interests of justice and society, leaving the care of further scrutiny and deduction to those more competent than myself. It has seemed to me that the experimental study of hypnotic phenomena could throw some light upon this field of moral responsibility, still so obscure. This dangerous ground must be ventured upon with prudence and reserve. I have disclosed my doubts and my scruples; I dare not tell my convictions.

The first part of this book published (excepting numerous additions) in 1884, called forth considerable criticism. The eminent philosopher, M. Paul Janet, wrote a series of articles for the *Revue Politique*, in which he reproached the observers at Nancy with several imperfections of method. This is the answer which I believed it my duty to give M. Paul Janet.*

"When M. Liégeois read his memoir, *De la suggestion hypnotique dans ses rapports avec le droit civil et criminal*, before the Academy of Moral and Political Sciences, the assembly, which it must be said was little prepared for studies which were up to that time foreign to its domain, was deeply stirred. Some of your colleagues denied the statements. The observer at Nancy was deluded by simulation, they said. Others, fearing the consequences of deducing facts not in accord with their preconceived ideas, refrained from investigating them.

"To the honor of this learned body however, many of the sound minded, you among the number, dared to look the question coolly in the face, and to accept, as demonstrated, certain facts elsewhere sanctioned in science by noted medical authorities.

"You have read some recent publications upon the subject, you have seen some experiments at the Salpêtrière, you have acquired some oral information, you have formed an opinion upon hypnotic suggestion. But without being sufficiently enlightened upon the subject, without verifying what is going on outside of your immediate surroundings, you publish your opinion. You state what, according to your idea, is exact, and what is subject to doubt. You point out the method which ought to be followed, and wish to call the attention of the observers at Nancy to defects in the methods they follow.

"Allow me, highly honored master, to reply to some of your deductions. I shall do so with the respectful deference due to your character and talent, but also with the perfect freedom of conviction with which the love of truth alone inspires me.

---

* This reply to the articles M. Paul Janet published in the *Revue Politique* was intended for the same *Revue*. M. Yung, after having submitted it to M. Janet, refused to insert it, finding it "too technical, too physiological," for a literary journal.

I then substituted for it simply a letter, short and courteous, without any scientific detail, simply answering the criticisms of which my memoir *De la Suggestion dans l'etat hypnotique et dans l'etat de veille* had been the object in the *Revue*. M. Yung readily acknowledged the interest I had shown in replying, but was unwilling to insert my answer in his journal.

"You accord boundless faith to all the work issuing from the School of the Salpêtrière. You accept only with a certain reserve that which is produced elsewhere. There, everything is demonstrated to your mind. There, thanks to the truly scientific method, nothing is contestable. 'We leave the most simple and elementary facts to rise to the most complicated ones, the physical and apparent facts for the more hidden psychological facts which are more difficult to interpret.' At Nancy, on the contrary, you seem to say, we neglect the most elementary and plain physical phenomena, and try above all to make the most extraordinary and the most striking facts stand out in relief. We push suggestion too far perhaps, and perhaps also the physician's imagination counts for something in the therapeutic results, or the psychological phenomena which we pretend to develop.

"My reply is to this fundamental objection, for it is the directing idea of your study.

"No one regards the work of the Salpêtrière School more justly than I do. I am too much a pupil of M. Charcot, I owe him too great a part of my medical education, not to render the homage which is due to the eminent master whose name will always be an honor to the French School of Medicine.

"But I do not accept blindly—does the master himself do so? Does he accept all the scientific assertions coming from all the pupils which succeed one another upon this fruitful field of observation? Science advances slowly over thousands of difficulties; new facts daily appear to contradict or to modify the acquisitions which we believed to be assured only the day before; real truth is long in disengaging itself from the dross which hides it.

"If I have not accepted the three phases of hysterical hypnotism as M. Charcot describes them, lethargy, catalepsy, and somnambulism, for the point of departure in my studies, it is because I have not been able to confirm their existence by my own observations.

"As I stated before the Biological Society, suggestion, that is to say the penetration of the idea of the phenomenon into the subject's mind by word, gesture, sight, or imitation, has seemed to me to be the key of all the hypnotic phenomena that I have observed. The phenomena said to be physiological or physical, have seemed to me in large part if not entirely, psychical phenomena. I do not claim to explain by suggestion the facts stated by other observers. I only hold to my statement, that I have not been able to produce them without suggestion. Therefore, was it necessary to take as a starting point for my researches the elementary, physical, and apparent facts which you mentioned, but which I have not been able to demonstrate myself? Have I then fallen from the truly scientific method because I have reasoned only from what I have seen?

"Moreover, if I admit that these facts of a purely physical or physiological order may be exact and constant, is it true to say that they are simpler, and more elementary, and easier of interpretation than the psychological facts which we have observed? Is it true, that one can rise from the most simple ones to others more complex and delicate? I answer, not at all, because these facts are of an absolutely different order.

"Suggestive phenomena have their analogies in normal and pathological life. Nature produces them spontaneously. Paralyses, contractures, anaesthesia, sensorial illusions and hallucinations, are present in natural somnambulism, in hysteria, in mental alienation, in alcoholism, and in other intoxications. They are present in us all in normal sleep. Hypnotized naturally, we are all susceptible to suggestions and hallucinations by our own impressions or by impressions coming from others. M. Alfred Maury has thoroughly studied these hallucinations which are called hypnagogic, and which appear in the period preceding sleep. Some people are also beset by them during the period immediately subsequent to the awakening.

"We reproduce artificially that which is liable to be produced spontaneously.

"Far from considering these facts as marvellous, I have tried to reconcile them with the analogous facts which exist in the physiological condition. I have called upon the automatism of daily life, reflective and instinctive acts, credulity, imitation, and the influence of idea over action; I have risen from suggestion in the normal, to suggestion in the hypnotic condition, and if you will re-read chapter eighth of my memoir (Chapter VIII. of this book), you will there find my ideas, which you yourself have published after me in other terms.

"I add that all observers have confirmed the psychological phenomena which we, as well as M. Richet and others, have related. No one disputes them. On the other hand, we have not been able to verify the phenomena which are supposed to be physical.

"These have no analogy in normal and pathological life. No lesion, no experiment upon the scalp, has ever produced a contracture, a paralysis, or a partial somnambulism upon the part of the body corresponding to the underlying cortical region of the brain. Is this a simple fact easy to interpret, that by touching the skin an effect is produced which is transmitted across the scalp, the cranium, and the meninges, to the brain, to localize itself in the zone corresponding to that where the hand was applied?

"No interpretation exists in the present condition of science. If the fact were confirmed, it would be necessary to turn back to the hypothesis of a fluid or of an emanation of some kind, disengaging itself from the operator's hand, and capable of traversing the membranous and osseous envelops of the brain; it would be necessary to turn back to mesmerism, and admit two absolutely distinct orders of phenomena in the hypnotic condition: suggestive phenomena (and these are easier to conceive of); and fluid phenomena (and these are absolutely impossible to interpret, and can in no way serve as a basis for the conception of the former). At Nancy we have studied only phenomena of suggestion.

"A second fault in method which we may have committed, and which in your opinion was calculated to increase public astonishment, is to have carried on our experiments with healthy subjects and not with subjects characterized by some disease. This objection will astonish all scientific men. I am not aware that physiologists choose sick animals in which to observe the phenomena of the living organism, and that psychologists begin by studying pathological minds in order to analyze the faculties of the understanding. And shall we, studying phenomena of induced sleep, devote ourselves to cases of hysteria, in which the symptoms of normal hypnotism may be perverted by abnormal or pathological reactions? When a hypnotized hysterical subject is seized with general convulsions, or with a limited contracture—with trismus for example, as I have seen—when she passes from the hypnotic sleep into the hysterical sleep, as I have also seen, in addition to other characteristics, do you think that research into the phenomena connected with the hypnotic condition would be facilitated by the addition of those connected with hysteria? For the hypnotic condition and the hysterical condition are absolutely different things. And here I touch upon a question which among them all has the greatest hold upon your heart.

"Yielding to the evidence of facts, you wish to accept the reality of hypnotic suggestions; but, obedient to a certain set of ideas, you think that suggestion can only be provoked in nervous subjects, that the hypnotic condition is a neurosis, the congener of hysteria, which, exceptionally and under a rudimentary form, may be provoked in ordinary subjects, but which, characterized by all its features, requires an hysterical or neuropathic ground to work on. You seem to think that when we state that we have had nothing to do with hysterical or neuropathic cases, it is forcing the truth a little for the sake of provoking not only astonishment but fear. You endeavor to show that my precise observations only treat of patients with nervous affections; that for all others the diagnosis would be ' badly defined, badly charterized.'

"I reply to this personal argument. Doubtless many of my observations relate to nervous affections, for the reason that I submit nervous affections especially to hypnotization, using it as a therapeutic means to an end. It is not my custom to hypnotize all patients indifferently. I choose those to whom I believe it may be beneficial. For this reason, nervous cases are in the majority, but I assure you that a very large number of observations refer to subjects who are not at all nervous. On one occasion, I hypnotized nearly a whole ward full of patients in M. Liégeois's presence. The majority of them were recovering from phthisis, emphysema, and rheumatism; only two out of twenty were hysterical.

"Among my observations, you mention the case of an old sergeant who worked in the founderies, and had been wounded in the head at Patay, by the bursting of a bomb. You mention him as affected with *very grave nervous troubles*. I say in vain ' that his intelligence is clear, that he has no nervous history, that he has no attacks of spontaneous somnambulism.' In spite of my words, you affirm ' very grave nervous troubles,' which do not exist. Again, you qualify as neuropathic, a case of gastralgia, because I speak of rachialgia, and you define rachialgia as an affection of the spinal cord, which is not exact. The spinal column is no more the spinal cord, than the cranium is the brain.

All physicians know that affections of the stomach are accompanied with spinal pain, and that this sensibility does not imply any medullary trouble. Our case had no such trouble.

When I speak of a sailor employed on a railroad as affected with chronic articular rheumatism, and add, 'He is an intelligent man, well-balanced, quite cultivated, not in the least nervous or credulous,' and that I have been able to put him into deep somnambulism and induce hypnotic and post-hypnotic suggestions, I state, as it seems to me, a well-defined, well-characterized fact. I could furnish further details, describe the state of his joints, trace out completely the growth of his rheumatism, question his heredity, and load the case which I desired to mention with details which are useless to the end in view; but I have told all that I need tell.

"I relate the case 'of a very intelligent man, not at all nervous, of high social position, and very healthy,' to whom I successfully suggested a post-hypnotic olfactory hallucination during sleep. I relate some of the phenomena of suggestion in the waking and sleeping condition, produced in a convalescent boy, fourteen years old, affected with catarrhal nephritis;—'A boy of lymphatic disposition; intelligent, having had a good primary education, showing no nervous trouble.' I could have specified a hundred like facts. However, you do me the honor to believe that I am quick to discern the nervous perturbations of the organism, and that I have enough scientific coolness not to allow myself to compromise with the truth.

"Doubtless we all have nervous systems; we all possess a certain nervous impressionability. In order to act upon the psychical being, a certain disposition, a certain cerebral receptivity is required for hypnotic suggestion. The subject must know how to concentrate his mind, and how to saturate it, so to speak, with the idea of sleep. But this special disposition, which is possessed to a certain degree by many people, is not at all the exclusive characteristic of neuropathy and hysteria. It is true to say that it is often very strongly marked in hysterical cases, since they are sometimes put in somnambulism by nothing at all. In any case, that is far from being constant. There are hysterical patients who, as you say, are difficult to hypnotize. Among cases of neuropathy there are also refractory subjects. The insane, cases of melancholia, and of hypochondriasis, and people of mobile imagination, who do not know how to concentrate their attention, those who are entirely absorbed by emotion, whose minds are preoccupied by various ideas,—all these oppose a conscious or unconscious moral resistance to suggestion. The wish or the idea of sleep must be present. Common people, soldiers, artisans, those who are accustomed to passive obedience, and those who have docile dispositions, have seemed to me the quickest to receive suggestion. Intelligent, well balanced men of sanguine and lymphatic disposition, who know how to concentrate their attention without preoccupation or retrospection, sleep better when they wish to, than certain neuropathic men who cannot fix their minds upon anything.

"In reality, ordinary sleep does not differ from hypnotic sleep. To be subject to my influence it is sufficient that a person goes to sleep voluntarily and naturally before me, with his thoughts fixed on me. I recently found a poor phthisical patient asleep. I had never hypnotized her. Touching her lightly with my hand I said, ' Do not wake, sleep, continue to sleep, you cannot wake.' In two minutes I lifted both arms. They remained cataleptic. After having said that she would wake up again in three minutes, I left her. At the time indicated she waked, and I went back to talk to her. She did not remember anything. Here then was a natural sleep, during which I was able to put myself into relationship with the sleeping subject, and that alone constituted the hypnotic sleep. How was it possible to establish the relationship? I suppose that the patient began to wake, but that my command to continue sleeping prevented the complete awakening. The patient passed into the sleep called hypnotic, that is, she was in relation with me. A mother finds her child asleep, she speaks to it, the child answers; she gives it a drink, the child drinks, then goes off again into its inertia, and upon waking has forgotten all. The child has in reality been hypnotized, that is, it has been in relationship with its mother. I believe that all men can be hypnotized, but we do not know the methods by which this can be done. When a sure and constant soporific agent shall be discovered, provoking sleep rapidly without modifying the psychical disposition, so that the subject may sleep with his thoughts fixed on the person present,—then perhaps no one will escape from the suggestive influence of others, as no one escapes from the hallucinatory suggestions provoked by his own impressions in the normal sleep.

"You go so far as to think that the success of M. Liébault's

HYPNOSIS AND SUGGESTION

experiments has created a sort of suggestive epidemic at Nancy, as epidemics of somnambulism, of magnetism, and of mesmerism are created. And to support this opinion you say that in the Paris hospitals spontaneous somnambulism is very rare, while at Nancy very much more of it seems to be met with of late. That is not accurate information. Spontaneous somnambulism is as rare at Nancy as at Paris. I have never seen it at our hospitals, and neither have my colleagues. Our hypnotized subjects never have attacks of spontaneous somnambulism.

"As to artificially induced sleep, M. Chas. Richet obtains it as easily in Paris as we do in Nancy. Dr. Bremaud also obtains it readily at Brest. I myself have recently successfully experimented in a Paris Salon upon a young man twenty years of age, and upon two men forty years of age. None of them were at all neuropathic, and yet I do not believe that I imported the microbe of the epidemic from Nancy to Paris. One of these experiments deserves to be related, as it is particularly instructive. It was the case of a handsome, well developed boy of more than ordinary intelligence, and positive character, the first to be promoted in one of our large schools for superior scientific instruction. Wishing to be enlightened upon the question of hypnotism, he himself asked to be put to sleep, promising to submit in earnest, and without resistance. In less than two minutes his eyelids closed. Suggestive catalepsy, contracture and automatic movements were present. Upon awaking he said he had heard everything, but as he had promised to obey without resistance, he had obeyed. 'Could you have resisted?' I asked. 'When I lifted your arms could you have dropped them, in spite of my affirmation to the contrary?' 'I think so,' he said, 'but I am not certain. Once I began to lower my arm (which in fact had been noticeable) but as I was about to do it, a feeling of remorse took hold of me. I lifted it again saying to myself, no, I ought not to lower it.' Was this the result of a wish to be obliging?

"The young man did not himself know what to think. Half an hour later he begged me to hypnotize him again, as he was curious, and wished to be enlightened. In less than a minute, he was again influenced. I lifted his legs and arms. They remained up. Then I said to him, 'Now, make the experiment; try to lower your arms and legs. If you can, if you have the will-power, use it, but I warn you that you cannot do it."

He tried in vain, and in spite of all his visible efforts, did not succeed in modifying the suggested attitude. I made him turn his arms one about the other. 'Try to stop them; I say you cannot.' In fact, he could not stop this rotatory automatic movement. When he was awakened he was convinced that it was not only the result of a wish to be obliging, but there was also present a material impossibility of resisting the suggested action.

"I have repeated this experiment with a great number of subjects.

"Chas. Richet, relating analogous examples, has described this singular psychical state well. Many imagine that they have not been influenced, because they have heard everything. They believe in good faith that they have been pretending. It is sometimes difficult to show them that they were not able to pretend.

"This digression supports my conclusion: that hypnosis is not a variety of hysteria, is not a morbid condition which takes hold of neuropathic cases. It is a physiological condition, as natural sleep is, from which it can be derived. It can be induced to a certain degree in the majority of subjects. The most intense degree, profound somnambulism, is neither rare nor difficult to obtain.

"Must we conclude that these facts will inspire terror in the masses, that people are destined to universal hallucination, and that a look cast upon a passer-by is sufficient to hypnotize him? This is an exaggeration against which as a moralist and a philosopher you have wisely forwarned the public.

"No magnetizer exists. No magnetic fluid exists. Neither Donato nor Hansen have special hypnotic virtues. The induced sleep does not depend upon the hypnotizer, but upon the subject; it is his own faith which puts him to sleep. No one can be hypnotized against his will, if he resists the command. I am glad to join you in re-assuring the public against all chimerical fear which a false interpretation of the facts might produce.

"Is this saying that justice and human morality have no reason to be moved by these facts, that all is said, that all is foreseen, that all is for the best in the best judiciary organizations? It would be prejudice perhaps to shut one's eyes to a pregnant truth. You have no hesitation in saying that lawyers and philosophers have greatly profited by these studies, and that

M. Liégeois must be thanked for having brought the question before an academic tribunal.

"Induced somnambulism is manifested in extreme cases; those in which the act suggested forces itself with an irresistible sway. But nothing happens in the profound sleep which has not its analogy, its diminutive, if I may so express it, in the waking condition. Sleep exaggerates physiological automatism, it does not create it. Between the fatal suggestion and the absolutely voluntary determination, all degrees may exist. And who can analyze all the suggested elements which, unknown to us, come into the actions we believe to be of our own initiative?

"Truth is never dangerous; ignorance alone is disarmed. You speak of universal hallucination. It existed, when it was not known, when no one suspected the singular facility with which artificial hallucination could be realized. It existed when a naïve faith in sorcery blinded the best minds, as if implanted in the human brain by suggestion;—when meetings of witches, sorcery, nightmares, malicious spirits, and all phantoms evoked by the imagination were considered as realities, when trembling science did not dare, in face of the funeral pile, to beard all-powerful religious superstition. What crimes, what catastrophes, what judicial errors might have been spared poor humanity, if scientific truth had been able to show itself! The history of the devil, of witchcraft, of evil possessions, the history of demoniacal epidemics, these collective suggested hallucinations weigh like a frightful nightmare upon the centuries which precede our own, and in our day still, what superstitions suggested by the blinding of a coarse faith will disappear like shadows under the torch of scientific truth!

"To conclude this too long reply, allow me to add, honored master, that I have deeply meditated upon these words of Bacon's: 'The human mind does not sincerely receive the light thrown upon things, but mixes therewith its own will and passions; thus it makes a science to its taste; for the truth that man most willingly receives, is the one he desires.'"

PART II

THE APPLICATION OF SUGGESTION TO THERAPEUTICS

CHAPTER I

Imagination as a therapeutic agent.—Talismans and amulets.—The therapeutic effect of magnets.—Report of the Royal Society of Medicine upon the magnetotherapy of Abbot Lenoble.—Medicinal magnetism falls into discredit, and is again revived.—Various practices, ancient and modern; the healers.—Observations upon cures effected through the influence of the imagination.—Observations upon the miraculous cures at Lourdes.—Therapeutic suggestion.—The hypnotic condition exalts susceptibility to suggestion.—Cures obtained by the ancient magnetizers.—Braid's doctrine; his theoretical ideas upon the mechanism of the cures.—M. Liébault's method; suggestion by speech.—A general picture of the results obtained; the various methods of suggestion.—Failure inherent in the disease or in the subject.—Auto-suggestionists.

What a powerful worker of miracles is the human imagination! Upon it is based the therapeutic virtue of talismans and amulets.

"From the time," says Charpignon,* "that stones were worn attached to the breastplates of the Jewish priests and to the girdles of the priests of Cybele, from the time that beetle-shaped, hand-shaped, and circular stones were worn by the Orientals, Greeks, and Romans, down to the cameos of our modern ladies, all these objects have represented the magic talisman of ancient and mysterious power."

"Paracelsus, the great partisan of occultism, recognized," this author goes on to say, "the cause of the effects produced by magnets and similar objects, for he wrote these wise words: 'Whether the object of your faith be real or false, you will nevertheless obtain the same effects. Thus, if I believe in St. Peter's statue as I would have believed in St. Peter himself, I will obtain the same effects that I would have obtained from St. Peter;—but that is superstition. Faith, however, produces

---

* Charpignon, *Etudes sur la Médecine animique et vitaliste.* Paris, G. Baillière, 1864.

miracles, and whether it be a true or a false faith, it will always produce the same wonders.'"

Let us compare the words uttered by Pierre Ponponazzi of Milan, an author of the sixteenth century, with these. They are given by Hack Tuke.*

"We can easily conceive the marvellous effects which confidence and imagination can produce, particularly when both qualities are reciprocal between the subjects and the person who influences them. The cures attributed to the influence of certain relics, are the effect of this imagination and confidence. Quacks and philosophers know that if the bones of any skeleton were put in place of the saints' bones, the sick would none the less experience beneficial effects, if they believed that they were near veritable relics."

The magnetic stone which the Egyptians used in the preparation of their prophylactic amulets, has cured gouty pains, headaches, toothaches, and hysteria, from time immemorial. In the last century, the artificial magnets made by Father Hell, the celebrated astronomer of Vienna, and used in the form of magnetic armatures, cured spasms, convulsions, and paralyses. As applied constantly by Abbot Lenoble they were no less efficacious in grave nervous affections.

Let us dwell a little upon the subject of magneto-therapeutics, because, together with the metallo-therapeutics of Burcq, it has been a true forerunner of hypnotic therapeutics; the medicinal magnetism of Father Hell preceded the animal magnetism of Mesmer: and modern magneto-therapeutics has led to therapeutic suggestion.

Abbot Lenoble, who succeeded, by means of the most perfect methods, in making artificial magnets of a power before unknown, and in testing their therapeutic application, established a depot for his magnets in Paris, in 1771. He announced that certain pieces, such as bracelets, and magnetic crosses, were to be applied to the wrist, to the chest, etc. In 1777, he confided the care of verifying the exactitude of his assertions to the Royal Society of Medicine. The Royal Society entrusted Andry and Thouret with the repetition of these experiments. The remarkable report

---

* Hack Tuke, *Le Corps et l'Esprit. Action du moral et de l'imagination sur le physique.* Paris, 1886.

made by these authors, and entered in the Society's memoirs, is marked with the stamp of a judicious and truly scientific spirit.

Andry and Thouret reported forty-eight cases in which the magnet was tested by them, or in their presence. The cases observed comprised toothache, nervous pains in the head and loins, rheumatic pains, facial neuralgia, tic douleureux, stomach spasms, spasmodic hiccough, palpitation, different kinds of tremor, convulsions, and hystero-epilepsy, etc.

Among the effects observed, a large number occurred a short time after the application of the magnet. In some cases, sharp neuralgic pains in the face were each time soothed by the contact of the magnet. Spasmodic and convulsive symptoms disappeared rapidly after its application; a nervous cough was instantly soothed, and did not re-appear. In one case, convulsive movements of the arm, and contracture preventing the use of the hand, ceased, or were notably diminished in the course of a day. Rheumatic pains were soothed, and in cases where they returned after the removal of the armature, they disappeared upon replacing the armature. In others, similar pains, calmed by the action of the magnet, appeared again in different parts of the body; they were dissipated by the local application of certain magnetic pieces. Moreover in cases of toothache, the application of the magnet was sometimes followed by prompt and obvious relief. Sometimes too, when a magnet did not soothe the pains or other symptoms against which it would have been efficacious in other patients, relief was gained by prolonging the application, or by using a stronger magnet. Finally, this agent has at times seemed to augment troubles, and to create sensations not before experienced.

In one case, the application of a magnetic head-band was followed by headache and fever, which ceased when the band was removed. An epileptic patient experienced slight but recurrent attacks of syncope, which ceased as soon as the magnetic pieces were removed; the epileptic attacks also seemed to increase in intensity. Another patient, with nervous paralysis, had the same syncope a short time after the application of the magnet. Various sensations were noticed each time the magnetic applications were renewed, sensations of heat in the affected parts, vertigo, nausea, palpitation, headache, itching, twitching, intestinal movements, etc. To sum up,—without excessive enthusiasam, in the light of irrefutable facts, the commissioners of the Royal Society of Medicine recognized in medicinal magnetism a real and efficacious agent, not against organic affections, but against nervous troubles of various kinds, the exact nature of which remain to be determined.

Following Andry and Thouret, several good observers, among whom may be mentioned Marcellin, Halle, Laennec, Alibert, Cayol, Chomel, Récamier, and Alexandre Lebreton, tested the truth of the majority of these observations. Trousseau says in the *Dictionnaire de Médicine* of 1833,—" as for us, who have sometimes made use of the magnet, we can state that this therapeutic agent exercises an influence over the parts with which it comes into contact, an influence which it is impossible to refer to the patient's imagination. I have seen neuralgic pain modified, attacks of nervous dyspnœa rapidly checked, etc. Laennec is gratified with the effects of the magnet in the treatment of angina pectoris. I have been able to gather two facts myself, which prove that, if the magnet does not cure disease, it can at least moderate its intensity. Incontestable cures have been performed in cases of rheumatism, temporary it is true, as they almost always are; and in support of this we can cite the history of a French marshal, whose rheumatic pains could only be relieved by the use of magnetic armatures." In spite of Trousseau's words, all these experiments were lost in profound oblivion. The discredit attached to the practice of animal magnetism which, instead of prospering as it might have done on the ground of scientific observation, had turned with Mesmer into a dangerous charlatanism,—this discredit seems to have enveloped the practice of magneto-therapeutics also. The magnet lost its place in the therapeutic armamentarium. When, thirty-five years ago, Dr. Burcq brought his doctrine of metallo-therapeutics before the medical world, he only met with incredulity. He had to wait until 1876, before his voice found an echo in the Salpêtrière. Metallo-therapeutics, and with it magneto-therapeutics, was resuscitated. Among the numerous therapeutic virtues assigned to metals and magnets, one only was proved and put beyond doubt; esthesiogenic virtue. The magnet, like the metals, often restored lost sensibility.

I have myself begun a series of researches to distinguish the value of magneto-therapeutics in different nervous affections; these researches have been published in the *Revue Médicale de 'Est*, 1881.

In certain cases I have demonstrated a real, though not constant efficacy, in regard to various conditions. But, in the course of these researches, I learned the suggestive method used by M. Liébault, and I showed that constant and rapid therapeutic effects could be obtained in another manner. What the magnet produces, simple suggestion always produces, and I asked myself if the therapeutic virtue of metals and magnets might not be simply a suggestive virtue. One of my observations, which is detailed further on, speaks for this view. However, I do not wish to state positively that this is the case. It is a question for future observation to answer. It is certain that suggestion plays a very great rôle in the dynamic effects obtained. The medicine of magnets and metals is perhaps only a medicine of the imagination, and, if Trousseau had been able to see what can be done by the imagination in hypnotic sleep, he would doubtless not have attributed the therapeutic influence of magnets to another mechanism.

And now, without further emphasis, the possible efficacy of various practices employed for the cure of disease, and which have succeeded each other from ancient to modern times, will be readily understood. We may cite the invocations of the Egyptian priests to obtain a cure from each god for those submitted to his influence; the magic formulas, which taught the use of herbs against disease; the medicine of Esculapius' descendants in the Asclepiads, or temples of this god. We may also mention Paracelsus' sympathetic powder; Perkin's metallic tractors, the pseudo-metallic (wooden) but none the less efficacious tractors of Drs. Haygarth and Falconer, and in our own times homeopathic medicine, and the medicine of Mattei. Is it necessary to speak of the king's touch, of the miraculous cures at the tomb of Deacon Pâris, and of the no less miraculous cures of Knock, in Ireland, and especially of Lourdes, in France? Or is it necessary to mention the numerous healers, of whom some were honest and believed themselves to be endowed with supernatural powers like certain magnetizers, and who used suggestion without knowing it, as, for example, the Irishman Gréatrakes, the German priest, Gassner, the Abbot Prince of Hohenlohe, Father Mathew, the peasant healer in the environs of Saumur, the Zouave Jacob, and many others whose fame does not extend beyond the region where they exercised their mysterious power.

Does not suggestion claim a share in the efficacy of certain pharmaceutical, hydro-therapeutic, and electrical means of medication? "Dr. John Tanner," says Hack Tuke, "has recommended the application of electro-magnetism to the tongue exclusively, for the treatment of hysterical aphonia. He states that he has used this treatment in more than fifty cases, without being once unsuccessful. He particularly cites four cases. In the first, the return of the voice was made evident by a loud cry; in the second, the voice returned immediately; in the third, it was recovered and again lost in the space of ten minutes, but re-application of the treatment brought about a permanent cure; in the fourth case, there was also instantaneous return of the voice." Dr. Tanner adds the following remarks: "Before using electro-magnetism, it is extremely important to persuade the patient *that he will be cured:* if the persuasive efforts are useless, it is probable that the treatment will be inefficacious."

In a witty study, dedicated by Dr. Lisle to the medicine of the imagination, in the *Union Médicale* (24th and 26th Oct., 1861) and entitled, *Homéopathie orthodoxe*, this influence of the moral over the physical is skilfully presented. For the sake of the reader who may wish to examine into this subject closely, we must also mention Virey's article on Imagination in the *Dictionnaire des sciences médicales*, in sixty volumes, the works of Padioleau (*Médecine morale*), and of Charpignon (*Etudes sur la Médecine animale et vitaliste*); M. Liébault's book (*Du Sommeil et des Etats analogues considérés surtout au point de vue de l'action du moral sur le physique*); and especially Hack Tuke's recent work (*Le Corps et l'Esprit. Action du moral et de l'imagination sur le physique*).

Before touching upon the heart of our subject, which is therapeutic suggestion, let us give a few observations upon cures obtained through the influence of the imagination, according to these authors; facts, which although well known everywhere, it is well to have before our eyes, because they show that what we are doing has always been done. Therapeutic suggestion is not new; what is new, is the mode of applying it methodically, and its final adoption in general medicine.

Sobernheim, cited by Charpignon, tells the story of a man with a paralysis of the tongue which had yielded to no form of treatment, who put himself under a certain doctor's care. The doctor wished to try an instrument of his own invention, with which he promised himself to get excellent results. Before performing the operation, he introduced a pocket thermometer into the patient's mouth. The patient imagined it to be the instrument which was to save him; in a few minutes he cried out joyfully that he could once more move his tongue freely.

Among our cases, facts of the same sort will be found. A young girl came into my service, having suffered from complete nervous aphonia for nearly four weeks. After making sure of the diagnosis, I told my students that nervous aphonia sometimes yielded instantly to electricity, which might act simply by its suggestive influence. I sent for the induction apparatus. Before using it I wanted to try simple suggestion by affirmation. I applied my hand over the larynx and moved it a little, and said: "Now you can speak aloud." In an instant I made her say a, then b, then Marie. She continued to speak distinctly; the aphonia had disappeared.

"The *Bibliothèque chosie de médecine*," says Hack Tuke, "gives a typical example of the influence exercised by the imagination over intestinal action, during sleep. The daughter of the consul at Hanover, aged eighteen, intended to use rhubarb, for which she had a particular dislike, on a following day; she dreamt that she had taken the abhorred dose. Influenced by this imaginary rhubarb, she waked up, and had five or six easy evacuations.

The same result is seen in a case reported by Demangeon. (*De l'Imagination*, 1879). "A monk intended to purge himself on a certain morning. On the night previous he dreamed that he had taken the medicine, and consequently waked up to yield to nature's demands. He had eight movements."

But among all the moral causes, which, appealing to the imagination, set the cerebral mechanism of possible cures at work, none is as efficacious as religious faith. Numbers of authentic cures have certainly been due to it.

The Princess of Schwartzenburg had suffered for eight years from a paraplegia, for which the most celebrated doctors in Germany and France had been consulted. In 1821, the Prince of Hohenlohe, who had been a priest since 1815, brought a peasant to the princess who had convinced the young prince of the power of prayer in curing disease. The mechanical apparatus which had been used by Dr. Heine for several months to overcome the contracture of the limbs, was removed. The prince asked the paralytic to join her faith to both his and the peasant's.—"Do you believe you are already helped?"—"Oh, yes! I believe so most sincerely."—"Well! Rise and walk."

At these words, the princess rose and walked around the room several times, and tried going up and down stairs. The next day she went to church, and from this time on she had the use of her limbs. (Charpignon).

The reader of course understands that this was one of those very common nervous paralyses which often exist only in idea, (ideal paralysis), and which are at times susceptible to cure through violent emotion.

The same thing may occur in hysterical contractures. Charcot says, "Deep moral emotion, a concurrence of events which strikes the imagination vividly, the return of monthly periods which have not occurred for a long time, etc.—are frequently the cause of these prompt cures."

In this hospital I have seen three cases of this kind, of which I will give a brief résumé:

1st. The first case was a contracture of a lower limb, dating four years back at least. On account of the patient's bad behaviour, I was obliged to give her a vigorous talking to, and to assure her that I would send her away if she did not do better. The next day, the contracture disappeared entirely.

2d. The second case was also one of contracture limited to one limb. The hysterical crises, properly so-called, had been absent a long time. The woman was accused of robbery, and the contracture, which had lasted more than two years, suddenly vanished on account of the moral shock which this accusation produced.

3d. In the third case, contracture had taken a hemiplegic form; the right side was affected, and the upper limb especially. The cure came suddenly, eighteen months after the appearance of the contracture, being brought about by a very animated controversy.

In this connection, Charcot cites an article by Littré, published in the *Revue de philosophie positive*, and entitled, *Un fragment de médecine rétrospective* (*Miracles de Saint Louis*), in which is found the history of several cases of paralysis cured after pilgrimages to Saint-Denis, to the tomb where the remains of the King, Louis IX., had just been placed.*

---

* Charcot, *Leçons sur les maladies du systeme nerveux*. Paris, 1872–73.

I give a résumé of some of the histories of cures which took place at Lourdes, and which have been collected by M. Henri Lasserre.

Catherine Latapie-Chouat fell from an oak tree in Oct., 1856. Her arm and hand were badly dislocated. The reduction of the dislocation was performed successfully; but, in spite of the most intelligent care, the thumb, index, and middle fingers, remained fixedly bent, and it was neither possible to straighten them nor to make them move in any way. The idea of going to the Massabielle grotto, six or seven kilometres away from her home, came into her mind. She got there at daybreak, and after praying, went to bathe her hand in the marvellous water. Her hand immediately *straightened out;* she could open and shut her fingers, which had become as flexible as they were before the accident.

Among our cases, analogous examples of contracture of the hand will be found, even cases of organic origin, maintained by a functional nervous state, and instantly cured by the use of suggestion.

Marie Lanou-Domeugé, twenty-four years old, had been troubled with incomplete paralysis of the whole left side for three years. She could not take a step without help. Hearing the Massabielle spring spoken of, the peasant sent some one to Lourdes one day to bring a little of this healing water from the source itself. She was helped to get up and dress; two people lifted her and she stood, both of them supporting her by the shoulders. Then she stretched out her trembling hand and plunged her fingers into the glass of healing water, made a large sign of the cross, put the glass to her lips and drank the contents slowly. Then she straightened herself up, shook herself, and cried out in triumphant joy; " Let me go! Let me go quickly! I am cured." And she began to walk as if she had never been paralyzed.

We also relate the story of an old woman, who for two months had not been able to stand, and who walked after two séances of hypnotic suggestion.

According to the doctors' reports, a child five years old, named Tambourné, had showed symptoms of the first stage of coxalgia for two months; very sharp pains in the knee, dull ones in the hip, external rotation in the foot, lameness, then inability to walk without the greatest pain. The digestive functions became disordered. The child could not take any nourishment, and in consequence became very thin. He was taken to the grotto in his mother's arms and bathed in the miraculous water. He fell into a sort of ecstatic state. His eyes were wide open and his lips were apart. "What is the matter with you?" asked the mother. "I see the good God and the Holy Virgin," he replied. When he came to himself again, the child cried out,—"Mother, my sickness has gone. I do not feel any more pain. I can walk." He walked back to Lourdes, and has been well ever since.

M. Charcot recently gave a clinical lecture upon nervous coxalgia, and said: "We know by the observations of different authors, that these psychical arthralgias, whether of traumatic origin or dependent upon some other cause, are sometimes suddenly cured in consequence of a deep emotion, or of a religious ceremony forcibly striking the imagination."

In May, 1858, Mlle. Massot-Bordenave of Arras, fifty-three years of age, was seized with an illness which deprived both her feet and hands of part of their strength and power of movement. The fingers were semiflexed. She could not cut her own bread. She went on foot to the grotto, and bathed her feet and hands. She left cured, her fingers had straightened out and become flexible again.

In January, 1858, Mlle. Marie Moreau, sixteen years old, had some trouble with her eyes. It was an amaurosis. The sight of one eye seemed to be lost entirely, and the other was in a very bad condition; all medicines had failed to help her. A nine days' prayer was begun on November 8. At ten o'clock in the evening, the young girl dipped a linen bandage into the Lourdes water, and put it over her eyes. When she woke and took the bandage off the next morning, the eye which had been in a bad condition was entirely well, and the eye which seemed to have lost the power of sight was again normal.

We know that complete amblyopias and amauroses of an hysterical nature exist, even without the presence of hysterical crises. Among our observations will be seen rapid cures of amblyopia by the application of a magnet, or by suggestion. Braid also tells of a remarkable case of nervous amblyopia of traumatic origin, which was almost cured by a single hypnotic séance.

Mlle. de Fontenay, twenty-three years old, had a paralysis of her lower limbs for nearly seven years. It developed after two falls, one from a carriage and one from a horse, which had given her a great shock, and had provoked uterine disease. Two seasons at Aix, homeopathy, hydro-therapeutics, the actual cautery; all these different forms of treatment had failed. From the end of January, 1873, she could no longer stand on her feet. She had, moreover, sharp internal pains, and attacks of nervous irritation. On the 21st of May, 1873, she went to Lourdes. During the course of a nine days' devotion, her strength gradually came back; after the devotional season was over, July 3, she could follow the procession on foot. But the day after Pentecost, the paralysis reappeared. She tried a season at Aix again in vain, at Brides, at Bourboule, and came back to Autun feeble, paralyzed, and demoralized. Under the influence of religious suggestions, her imagination was gradually exalted again. On May 4, 1874, Bernadotte appeared to her in a dream, and promised her that she should be cured. In August, she accompanied the Abbot of Musy to Lourdes, who was himself miraculously cured of a paraplegia. She was plunged into the pond several times, and then taken to the cave in a carriage. This was on August 15, the anniversary of the Abbot Musy's cure, and at the same place where he was cured. During mass read by the abbot, she felt a slight pricking in her limbs; after the mass was over, she rose; she was cured.

This is another instance of nervous paraplegia cured by faith. The first religious suggestion had had only a temporary result. The second, given under conditions calculated to deeply impress the imagination, found the soil better prepared, and a better developed psychical receptivity; the psycho-therapeutic action was lasting.

By relating these observations of authentic cures obtained at Lourdes, by trying, in the name of science, to rid them of their miraculous character, by comparing religious suggestion with hypnotic suggestion, simply from this point of view, I do not intend either to attack religious faith, or to wound religious sentiment. All these observations have been gathered together with sincerity, and verified by honorable men. The facts exist; the interpretation of them is erroneous. Religious convictions are eminently respectable, and true religion is above human errors.

I come now to the study of therapeutic suggestion. If, in the waking condition, violent moral emotions, lively religious faith, everything which strikes the imagination, can drive away functional troubles and work cures, it must nevertheless be said that active therapeutics does not often reap advantage from this means. In the waking condition, many imaginations are refractory to the suggestive shock of the moral emotions. Credulity is moderated by the superior faculties of the understanding. Hypnotism, like natural sleep, exalts the imagination, and makes the brain more susceptible to suggestion. The strongest minds cannot escape from the hallucinatory suggestions of their dreams. It is a physiological law, that sleep puts the brain into such a psychical condition that the imagination accepts and recognizes as real the impressions transmitted to it. *To provoke this special psychical condition by means of hypnotism, and to cultivate the suggestibility thus artificially increased with the aim of cure or relief, this is the rôle of psychotherapeutics.*

The brain, influenced by suggestion, tends to realize the phenomena commanded with an energy varying according to the individuality; in some it is already docile in the waking condition; it becomes so in almost all cases when the hypnotic condition, or a condition analogous to it, has put to sleep or dulled the faculties of reason, judgment, and control which moderate and restrain the cerebral automatism. Then the brain, more powerfully impressed by the formulated order, accepts the idea and transforms it into action. We have seen hypnotic suggestion cause paralysis, contracture, anæsthesia, pains, cough, nausea, etc.; we have seen these dynamic effects of suggestion persist when the subject is awakened, or appear only after the awakening (post-hypnotic suggestion). The brain refuses to perceive the centripetal impressions of tactile, visceral, or sensorial sensibility; it refuses to set the motor cells of the spinal cord into activity; hence, psychical motor paralysis, anæsthesia, blindness, deafness, *which are phenomena of inhibition.* Or, on the contrary, it perceives the centripetal impressions with greater vividness. It sends extra activity to the motor cells; hence, sensitiveness and sensorial hyperæsthesia, and more energetic muscular work, or contracture; these are *dynamogenic phenomena.* Other psychical (moral emotions), or experimental (experiments of Brown-Séquard) proceedings may put both the cerebral mechanism of inhibition and of dynamogeny into play; as, for example, paralysis of speech produced by fear, (*vox faucibus hæsit*), or the increase of strength caused by anger or unusual excitement.

Observation having thus shown what the simple hypnotic suggestion can perform in the healthy condition, it was natural to apply these qualities to pathological states, and to make use of the nervous activity concentrated by means of suggestion, in neutralizing morbid phenomena. It was natural to say to oneself—if, in a hypnotized subject, anæsthesia, contracture, movements, pains, can be produced at will by an analogous mechanism, it ought to be possible in some cases to suppress anæsthesia, contracture, or paralysis caused by disease, to increase the weakened muscular force, to modify favorably, or to restore the functional force perverted or diminished by the pathological condition, as far, of course, as the organic condition permits this restoration.

It would seem that an idea so simple as this would have forced itself upon the attention of the first physicians who learned to recognize suggestion. But it has been a long time coming to the front.

In the early days of mesmerism, therapeutic effects were obtained. "Some among the patients magnetized," says Husson's report, "have felt no benefit. Others have experienced a more or less marked relief. In one case there was suspension of habitual pain, in another return of strength, in a third cessation of epileptic attacks for several months, and in a fourth the complete cure of an old and serious paralysis." Mesmer, Puységur, Dupotet, and many other magnetizers obtained cures without knowing what they were doing. Rostan was able to say, in spite of the Academy: "There were very few physicians, very few physiologists, who denied that magnetism determined changes in the organism and that it could act with some power in curing disease."

As long as magnetic phenomena were considered the effect of a fluid acting upon the organism, it was to this fluid action that the cures were attributed. Magnetism, by its mysterious influence upon the vital principle, re-established functional harmony; it was beneficial, like warmth, light, and electricity.

Since Braid's time, the hypothesis of a magnetic fluid has had but few adherents; hypnotic suggestion has replaced magnetism. It is the subject's imagination alone which is rendered active and which causes all the phenomena.

It is a singular thing that Braid, who was the first to establish the doctrine of suggestion (caught sight of for a moment by Bertrand) upon firm foundations, thought no more of applying suggestion itself in its most natural form,—*suggestion by speech*,— to bring about the hypnosis and the therapeutic effects. He induced sleep by fixation upon a brilliant object; he brought about therapeutic effects by means of *special manipulations*.

These manipulations are based upon this fact, that the cataleptiform rigidity of a limb produces, according to Braid, an acceleration of the pulse, which becomes small and wiry. This acceleration of the pulse caused by the effort to hold the limbs stretched out for five minutes, is much greater in the hypnotic than in the normal condition. If the muscles are made to relax while the subject is still under the influence of the hypnosis, the pulse declines rapidly to its rate before the experiment, and even below it.

This understood, Braid varies the manipulations according to the object in view. "In order to diminish the force of the circulation in a limb and reduce its sensibility, it is necessary to set the muscles of this limb in activity, leaving the other limbs relaxed. If we wish to increase the force and the sensibility of a limb, it must be kept relaxed and the other limbs must be put into catalepsy. If we wish to obtain a general depression, after one or two of the limbs have been extended for a short time we must put them back carefully into the normal position, and let the entire body rest. To obtain a general excitation, all the limbs should be rendered cataleptic, whence arises difficulty in the free transmission of blood to them, and consequently an augmentation of the cardiac activity, rush of blood to the brain, and excitation of the nervous centres."

Further, in keeping a particular organ in action while the others are quiet, there is a considerable augmentation of its activity by concentration of its nervous energy; in keeping the other organs in activity, and the one which is too active quiet, its activity is diminished.

"Whether I am wrong or right in my theoretic views," the author adds, "one cannot doubt that in numerous cases I have succeeded in the use of hypnotism as a curative agent, and the happy results of the operation have been so immediate and so clear that one could not overlook the relation of cause and effect. Nevertheless, it seems to me to be proved that the success depends in great part upon the impression produced by the modification in the circulation."

Braid relates about sixty cases of cure or benefit obtained through his method. Though the facts may hold, his theoretic views are certainly erroneous. I have not been able to confirm the accuracy of his statements relative to the modifications of cardiac activity induced by catalepsy. Were they otherwise exact, these modifications would not be sufficient to explain cures as sudden as those which were observed.

It is singular enough, that after having proved so well that the source of all hypnotic phenomena is in the subject's imagination, that all these phenomena are purely psychical, Braid did not dream of explaining the curative effects obtained by this same psychical influence. The founder of the doctrine of suggestion, Braid, forgetting his directing idea, did as all his predecessors had done, and as many of his successors still do; he made use of suggestion without knowing it. His patients knew that they were hypnotized with the idea of curing them in view; this idea remained with them during their sleep; they knew that the manipulations which were made were designed to free them from their troubles; this was a therapeutic suggestion.

Braid does not seem to have had any successors in his own country. Dr. Charpignon, in France, is one of those who have most deeply studied the influence of faith and of suggestion in the hypnotic condition. But side by side with the moral influence, he believes in the influence of a magnetic fluid which tends to restore the destroyed harmony.

In reality we must come down to 1860 to find the doctrine of suggestion entirely freed from all the elements which falsified it even in the hands of Braid himself, and applied in the simplest manner to therapeutics. Durand de Gros, like the Abbot Faria, had already employed simple vocal suggestion, speech, in the production of hypnotic phenomena. M. Liébault conceived the idea *of applying the same vocal suggestion to therapeutics.*

The patient is *put to sleep by means of suggestion*, that is by making the idea of sleep penetrate the mind. He is *treated by means of suggestion*, that is by making the idea of cure penetrate the mind. The subject being hypnotized, M. Liébault's method consists *in affirming in a loud voice the disappearance of his symptoms*. We try to make him believe that these symptoms no longer exist or that they will disappear; that the pain will vanish, that feeling will come back to his limbs, that the muscular strength will increase, and that his appetite will come back. We profit by the special psychical receptivity created by the hypnosis, by the cerebral docility, by the exalted ideo-motor, ideo-sensitive, ideo-sensorial reflex activity, in order to provoke useful reflexes, to persuade the brain to do what it can to transform the accepted idea into reality.

Such is the method of therapeutic suggestion of which M. Liébault is the founder. He was the first to clearly establish that the cures obtained by the old magnetizers, and even by Braid's hypnotic operations, are not the work either of a mysterious fluid or of physiological modifications due to special manipulations, but the work of suggestion alone. The whole system of magnetic medicine is only the medicine of the imagination; the imagination is put into such a condition by the hypnosis that it cannot escape from the suggestion.

M. Liébault's method was ignored a long time, even by the physicians at Nancy. In 1884, Chas. Richet was satisfied to say that magnetism often has advantages, that it calms nervous agitation, and that it may cure or benefit certain insomnias.

Since 1882 I have experimented with the suggestive method which I had seen used by M. Liébault, though timidly at first and without any confidence. To-day it is daily used in my clinic; I practice it before my students; perhaps no day passes in which I do not show them some functional trouble, pain, paresis, uneasiness, insomnia, either moderated or instantly suppressed by suggestion.

For example, a child is brought to me with a pain like muscular rheumatism in its arm dating back four or five days; the arm is painful to pressure; the child cannot lift it to its head. I say to him, "Shut your eyes, my child, and go to sleep." I hold his eyelids closed and go on talking to him. "You are asleep and you will keep on sleeping until I tell you to wake up. You are sleeping very well, as if you were in your bed; you are perfectly well and comfortable; your arms and legs and your whole body are asleep and you cannot move." I take my fingers off his eyelids, and they remain closed; I put his arms up, and they remain so. Then, touching the painful arm, I say, "The pain has gone away. You have no more pain anywhere; you can move your arm without any pain; and when you wake up you will not feel any more pain. It will not come back any more. In order to increase the force of the suggestion by embodying it, so to speak, in a material sensation, following M. Liébault's example, I suggest a feeling of warmth *loco dolenti.* The heat takes the place of the pain. I say to the child, "You feel that your arm is warm; the warmth increases, and you have no more pain."

I wake the child in a few minutes; he remembers nothing; the sleep has been profound. The pain has almost completely disappeared; the child lifts the arm easily to his head. I see the father on the days following; he is the postman who brings my letters. He tells me that the pain has disappeared completely, and there has been no return of it.

Here, again, is a man twenty-six years old, a workman in the founderies. For a year he has experienced a painful feeling of constriction over the epigastrium, also a pain in the corresponding region of the back, which was the result of an effort made in bending an iron bar. This sensation is continuous and increases when he has worked for some hours. For six months he has only been able to sleep by pressing his epigastrium with his hand. I hypnotize him. In the first séance I can only induce simple drowsiness; he wakes spontaneously; the pain continues. I hypnotize him a second time, telling him that he will sleep more deeply, and that he will remember nothing when he wakes. Catalepsy is not present. I wake him in a few minutes; he does not remember that I spoke to him, that I assured him that the pain had disappeared. It has completely disappeared; he no longer feels any constriction. I do not know whether it has re-appeared.

Next in order is the case of a workman fifty years old, who has already been in the hospital several times. The observations referring to his case will be given later on. For several days he has had an ulnar neuritis, characterized by contraction in flection of the three last fingers of his hand, a complete anæsthesia in the entire ulnar region, twinges of pain along the path of the nerve, and pain along the olecranon groove. I hypnotize him; in a few seconds he falls into a condition of complete relaxation; suggestive catalepsy and somnambulism are present. At different times I suggest the relaxation of his hand, the return of sensibility, the cessation of the pains. I run a needle into his forearm, saying, "You are going to feel." In a few minutes the feeling has come back again and the fingers unbend. When he wakes all phenomena of the neuritis have vanished.

These examples relate to actual observations. However singular they may appear they are nevertheless facts.

Morbid phenomena do not always yield at a first séance.

Sometimes the pain persists, or is simply diminished; it may gradually disappear after two or more séances. In other cases it may be diminished when the subject wakes, and may continue growing less until it disappears without a new hypnotization. If not, a new suggestion may succeed, especially if a deeper sleep be induced. The pain, taken away for the moment, may return in several hours or still later, and may only yield definitely after a variable number of hypnotizations. Finally, only certain troubles among those complained of, may be effaced; the others resist the attempt. We can understand that the effect obtained is subordinate both to the subject's suggestibility, and to the psychical cause which determines the symptoms.

Muscular pains, the painful points in phthisis, certain dynamic contractures, even though bound up with organic affections of the nervous centres, certain movements which remain after chorea, incontinence of urine, which children suffer from at night, etc.,—often disappear as if by enchantment after a single suggestion, or after several.

It is not always necessary to have deep sleep for the manifestation of a rapid action; simple dullness is sufficient in some cases; certain subjects are suggestible in the waking condition. For example, one of my patients, whose history I shall give in detail, had a contracture in flexion of the hand, the result of an old hemiplegia. For a year he was not able to hold it open; he was a great snuff-taker, but could not use this hand for this purpose. I hypnotize him and suggest that his hand is pliant again, that he can open and shut it. He tries during his sleep, and succeeds easily in stretching and bending his fingers. "If it could only last," he says. I assure him that it will last. And so it does. When he wakes, the stiffness has disappeared. He remembers everything he did during his sleep; he does not think he has been asleep. At another séance the next day, however, I put him into a profound sleep. He was somnambulistic, with no remembrance of anything upon waking, and eminently suggestible.

Generally the action is more rapid and complete in profound

sleep. *It is in somnambulism that suggestion reaches its maximum efficiency*, and that cures are often instantaneous and seem miraculous. Certain subjects resist for many séances; they only fall into somnolence; the effect obtained is slight or doubtful. By persevering for a longer or shorter time, several days or even several weeks, with hypnotizations which give but little result, some subjects can be put into a deeper sleep, and then the therapeutic action of suggestion may be rapid and lasting.

The *mode of suggestion* should also be varied and adapted to the special suggestibility of the subject. A simple word does not always suffice in impressing the idea upon the mind. It is sometimes necessary to reason, to prove, to convince; in some cases, to affirm decidedly; in others, to insinuate gently; for in the condition of sleep just as in the waking condition the moral individuality of each subject persists according to his character, his inclinations, his special impressionability, etc. Hypnosis does not run all its subjects into a uniform mould, and make pure and simple automatons out of them, moved solely by the will of the magnetizer; it increases the cerebral docility; it makes the automatic activity preponderate over the will. But the latter persists to a certain degree, the subject thinks, reasons, discusses, accepts more readily than in the waking condition, but does not always accept, especially in the light degrees of sleep. In these cases, we must know the patient's character, his particular psychical condition, in order to make *an impression* upon him.

Contact by touch, friction, movements imparted to the affected region, and suggested warmth, often co-operate efficaciously. As noted in one of my observations, I have seen the use of electricity upon the painful part, thus materializing the suggestion into a new sensation, succeed where simple affirmation had been insufficient. At other times, success is obtained by evasion. One of my patients, a good somnambulist, had an unconquerable distaste for meat. I had in vain suggested that she would eat it with pleasure; she absolutely refused to accept the suggestion, she did not even wish to taste meat during her sleep. I made her change her personality; she was no longer herself; and then she ate the meat with the greatest appetite. But this mode of suggestion is only applicable to a restricted number of somnambulists, who constitute the minority.

In some cases, a nervous habit can only be broken by a strong diversion, or by a vigorous forcing. One hysterical woman went into somnambulism easily, but in this condition she often complained of discomfort, pain and oppression; then sometimes an attack of hysterical sleep in which the patient ceased to be in relationship with me, replaced the hypnotic sleep. Affirmation alone did not succeed in dissipating this uncomfortable precursor of a crisis. I succeeded by means of a musical diversion: I made her hear a wonderful suggestive orchestra; and as she adored music, her face became radiant, she beat time with her hand, and all the discomfort vanished.

A neurotic patient complains of pain in her legs. She cannot walk. Suggestion soothes the pain during sleep; but upon waking she feels too weak to walk; there is some pain still. I put her into somnambulism again and say, "You are cured; you are at home. Get up, attend to your housekeeping; work, since you have been cured." She gets up, walks very well, takes up a towel and a duster, and also a broom which is brought to her, begins to dust, and does not complain of anything. Upon waking she walks very well. Thus, by a powerful diversion, or by transforming passive *into active somnambulism*, the efficiency of suggestion may be increased.

We have a case of convulsive, painful, dorso-lumbar tic in our service; several times a minute the man's body is agitated by clonic movements which throw him forward. He positively cannot walk. Nothing does any good. This condition lasts for weeks. When he wants to walk, the movements repeat themselves obstinately, and he is obliged to stop and lean against something in order to keep from falling.

I hypnotize him; he only reaches the third degree of sleep; he is sitting on a chair. Simple suggestion does not always succeed in arresting these movements, but if I make him walk, either in the sleeping or waking condition, affirming energetically that he has no more trouble, if I make him walk quickly without stopping to rest, the movements cease, and he goes about for hours without feeling any tendency to the tic. *The active forcing suggestion* succeeds where simple suggestion fails.

Therapeutic suggestion is not infallible, though it gives good results in a very large number of cases. It may fail even when it is intelligently and persistently managed. The cause of the failure is inherent *sometimes in the disease, sometimes in the subject*.

I do not speak of incurable diseases, certain manifestations of which may, however, be favorably acted upon by suggestion. Even in affections which are not very serious and which seem to be simply functional, psycho-therapeutic hypnosis fails at times, although the subject may be perfectly susceptible to suggestion. I remember an Italian mason who, in consequence of a contusion, had a violent pain in the lumbar region for several weeks. No bruise could be found, no lesion could be seen; the pain alone persisted, yielding neither to rubbing, blistering, nor electricity. Suggestion, kept up persistently for a long time, could do nothing, although the man was easily put into a deep sleep and appeared to be very susceptible to suggestion.

The lesion, although not perceptible, may exist, and its disturbing action may be such that the brain is powerless to perform acts of inhibition or of dynamogeny, even when it is put into the most favorable psychical conditions. The stimulus which incessantly excites the motor or aesthesodic cells, constantly renews the contracture or pain; the brain tries in vain to neutralize the existing functional trouble; the *organic cause, stronger than the suggestion*, annihilates the dynamic effects.

Sometimes the subject resists. We have noticed that even in hypnotic sleep his will is not always destroyed; *he refuses to accept the suggestion*, or if he accepts it for a moment, the influence does not remain with him. Melancholic, hypochondriac, and certain neuropathic cases, often rebel against hypnotic sleep; they do not allow themselves to be influenced. What is told them makes no impression; or if the hypnotic suggestion succeeds with some, the therapeutic suggestion remains inefficacious. I recently had to treat a young woman who was hypochondriacal. Among other troubles she had a violent pain in the epigastrium, which she believed to be connected with uterine cancer, although she had been repeatedly told that there was no lesion there. I succeeded in hypnotizing her often enough, and sometimes even in obtaining a profound sleep. I hypnotized her for ten days; by energetic suggestion I succeeded in quieting the pain. Upon waking, she was obliged to confess that she had no more, or scarcely any pain. But she hastened to add that the pain would return; and in fact it did come back, involuntarily evoked by her diseased imagination.

In the Laennec hospital, in Dr. Legroux's service, I recently saw a man who had been troubled with a sort of tic douloureux of the lower limbs for several years. It was sufficient to touch the limbs, and especially the sole of the foot, and strong convulsive movements of flexion and extension were determined, following each other frequently, prolonged for a certain time, and accompanied with intense pains which forced the patient to cry out. M. Legroux succeeded in neutralizing this pain by simple suggestion in the waking condition. By assuring the patient that the pains had ceased, he could both touch and rub the sole of his foot indefinitely without producing the least pain. But as soon as the poor man was left to himself, to his own suggestions, the pains and convulsion re-appeared. This man had not walked for a long time, but I could make him walk by a vigorous hypnotic suggestion. I forced him to get up and walk in spite of the resistance he offered. In vain did he tell me he was tired; I obliged him to walk quickly about the room for several minutes. He lay down again, saying that his trouble would return, that it was incurable, that he knew very well he would have to pay dear for the effort he had just been making. There was no doubt in his mind about the re-appearance of the tic douloureux. Could he be cured by a suggestion obstinately prolonged both in the waking and sleeping condition, by continuous forcing? I believe so, without stating it as a fact. With this sort of patient, auto-suggestion is stronger than a suggestion from some one else. They listen to their inner feelings, they call them up, they are in relationship only with themselves; they are *auto-suggestionists*.

At the present time I have a remarkable case in my service. I will give it briefly; it is a fine example of local hysteria.

A young girl, twenty-six years old, came into the surgical clinic twenty months ago for a tibio-tarsal sprain. My colleague, M. Weiss, put an apparatus on her. When he took off the apparatus at the end of several weeks, he saw that the swelling of the foot had gone down, but that the entire limb was rigid and painful. He asked me to look at the case; there was contracture and excessive hyperæsthesia to the slightest touch. Our diagnosis was hysterical contracture provoked by traumatism. She did not show and had never shown any other hysterical symptoms.

I tried to hypnotize her; she gave herself up to it with bad grace, saying that it would do no good. I succeeded, however, in putting her into a deep enough sleep two or three times. But the painful contracture persisted; she seemed to take a malicious delight in proving to the other patients in the service that it did no good, *that she always felt worse*. Then, after a few séances, I was no longer able to hypnotize her. The apparatus was put on again. Three months later, without any cause, and as if to confirm the diagnosis, she had retention of urine, and from this time on, the retention persisted together with the contracture; a catheter had to be used regularly three times a day. I again tried to hypnotize her; to free herself from my experiments she simulated sleep.

The persistent contracture, however, brought about retraction of the tendon of Achilles, and talipes equinus. Chloroform had to be administered several times, in order to have the foot straightened out, and finally the tendon of Achilles had to be cut. The contracture of the knee at last yielded spontaneously; the contracture in the leg and foot still exists, and an apparatus now holds the foot flexed.

I tried intimidation, electricity, and various methods, against the retention of urine, but all in vain. Nothing did any good. I have used gentle means lately. I have hypnotized her again; she gave herself up to it well, and went into a profound sleep, without any simulation. She is distressed on account of her situation; she wishes to be cured. She gets angry when she is accused of acting with bad grace. In March of this year, after I had hypnotized her several times, and tried to inculcate the idea that she would soon be cured, she seemed at last to accept the idea; she even fixed upon the day in her sleep, when she should urinate spontaneously;—in fifteen days, on a Wednesday. The prediction did not come true. The retention persisted.

Here it is certainly a question of contracture and psychical paralysis. The inrooted idea, *the unconscious auto-suggestion*, is such that nothing can pull it up again. When the treatment was begun she seemed to be convinced that hypnotism could not cure her. Is it this idea, so deeply rooted in her brain, which neutralizes our efforts and her own wish to be cured?

I have tried to show failure side by side with success, the shadow side by side with the light. Psychotherapeutic suggestion may fail, as other agents do; but it often succeeds when other means have failed; it often accomplishes marvels, I do not say miracles.

I am now going to give quite a large number of observations on suggestive therapeutics. They are not chosen observations. By publishing only those where the cure has been complete and instantaneous I could embellish the picture and astonish my readers much more. I keep to the strict truth, and present the idea as faithfully as the present results given by therapeutic suggestion show it. Among our observations, some show rapid and radical cures, others show slow and gradual ones, others again show suggestion suppressing certain symptoms of the trouble only, still others show it struggling a long time with obstinate troubles, which though improved, keep returning persistently, and in this persevering and prolonged struggle between mind and body, it is sometimes one, sometimes the other, which prevails.

Up to the present time, only a few physicians have followed the Nancy School in its trials of suggestive therapeutics according to M. Liébault's methods. We must mention M. Auguste Voisin, who, at the Blois and Grenoble Congresses, called attention to its application to the treatment of mental disease. A very much agitated hysterical patient was calmed by hypnotic suggestion, and moral sentiments and sentiments of affection were awakened, at least for a short time, in her. Three new observations, given in the *Bulletin général de thérapeutique* (April 15, 1886), are entitled:

1st. Hystero-epilepsy. Erotic delirium, with hallucinations of sight and hearing. Treatment by hypnotic suggestion. Cure.

2d. Melancholic delirium. Hallucinations of sight and hearing. Refusal of nourishment. Cure by hypnotic suggestion.

3d. Hysteria. Hysterical insanity. Hallucinations of sight and hearing. Ideas of suicide. Hemianæsthesia and hemidyschromatopsia. Cure by hypnotic suggestion.

New observations have been published since by the author in the *Revue de l'hypnotisme.*

We must mention still another interesting observation on suggestive therapeutics successfully used in a case of hysteria, published by M. Séglas (*Archives de Neurologie*, Nov. 1885), and one published by M. Lombroso (*lo Sperimentale*, Nov. 1885).

M. Desplats of Lille, M. Bérillon, M. Debove, and M. Delbœuf, have cited a certain number of facts relating to suggestive therapeutics. M. Fontan, Professor at the Toulon School, and M. Ségard, Chef-de-Clinique in the same school, have published in their *Eléments de médecine suggestive,* ninety-nine most interesting observations, which throw brilliant confirmation upon the facts stated by the Nancy School.

In Germany, M. Berger (*Breslauer Zeitschrift,* 1880) reports that an hysterical contracture of the fingers was cured while the patient was in the hypnotic condition.

Preyer, (*der Hypnotismus,* Berlin 1882) says that his assistant, Dr. Creutzfield, has stopped neuralgic pains by means of hypnotism.

Dr. Fisher (*der sog. Magnetismus oder Hypnotismus,* Mainz, 1883) has observed a similar result. Rieger (*der Hypnotismus,* Jéna 1884) says that he has also obtained very good effects by means of it, notably in the case of a young girl with contracture.

Dr. Wiebe, from whom the preceding citations are borrowed, has had recourse to hypnotism as a therapeutic means four times, in Prof. Baumler's service at Fribourg in Bresgau.

The following are the results he obtained. (Berl. Klin. *Wochenschr,* 1884, No. 3):

In three of these cases, hypnotism acted as a prompt and lasting cure; in the fourth, the effect was not complete, but nevertheless it was useful. In the first case, hypnosis cured anæsthesia; in the third clonic convulsions were stopped, and in the fourth, clonic convulsions were benefited.

I borrowed these facts from a sketch of hypnotism by Prof. Lépine in the *Revue mensuelle* (1884, p. 829).

Among the physicians who have applied hypnotism to therapeutics, we must yet mention Prof. Achille de Giovanni (*Clinice medica della Universita di Padowa,* 1882). The following is a résumé of his observations, taken from the *Revue de médecine* (1883):

1st. Persistent rachialgia in a patient, who was much weakened, and of a nervous constitution. The rachialgia had been preceded by contracture of the lower limbs, cured by massage. Sleep was easily induced. The patient was hypnotized every day for a week; the rachialgia grew better, then disappeared. There was simultaneous improvement in her normal condition.

2d. A woman, eighteen years old, troubled with a neurosis, between which and hysteria the author makes a distinction. After intermittent fever and a dangerous attack (about the nature of which the author is doubtful), arthralgia developed, with contracture in the right leg and arm, without any apparent lesion. This contracture grew better, and then was entirely cured by the application of electricity over the homologous groups of muscles of the opposite side. Attack of fever without any known cause. Incomplete hemianæsthesia of the right side, glossalgia, labio-glosso-pharyngeal paralysis, a crisis of hystero-epilepsy; neuralgia in the shoulder, with ecthyma, boils, ganglionic congestion. The first trials of hypnotism did not induce sleep, but a tremor of the upper and lower limbs; at the third séance there was sleep and no tremor. From this time on the patient rapidly improved. In fifteen days, with one, two, and three séances a day, she was cured.

4th. Patient had alopecia areata, great muscular weakness, pain in the knees, and certain nervous troubles. The patient was hypnotized in order that a piece of the skin could be obtained for microscopical examination. The operation was performed unknown to the patient, and without any pain.

5th. A young man, suffering from acute coxalgia with pain in the knee, and whom it was impossible to move or even to touch, was hypnotized; in that condition he was examined easily. Upon waking he said that the pain in his knee had disappeared.

In spite of these isolated facts, suggestive therapeutics has few adepts. I should be happy if the observations which I am about to relate, could help to spread abroad the new method instituted by M. Liébault.

I

ORGANIC AFFECTIONS OF THE NERVOUS SYSTEM

OBSERVATION I.—*Hemiplegia of the left side, with sensitivo-sensorial hemianæsthesia, dating back one year.—Transient hemiplegia of the right side.—Lesions in each hemisphere.—Post-hemiplegic bilateral tremor simulating insular sclerosis.—Reflexes of both sides exaggerated, and contracture of the left limbs.—Hemianæsthesia, tremor, and trepidation cured by a single application of the magnet to the face.—Return of the contracture of the left limbs with flexion of the hand; twenty months later, the contracture is cured by hypnotic suggestion.—Diminution of the sense of oppression.—Death at the end of three years.—Autopsy.*

A MAN came into my service at the hospital last December, who at first sight seemed to have insular sclerosis. His limbs trembled a good deal, and as soon as he wanted to move them the tremor increased in proportion as he accomplished the desired motion. On closer examination it was immediately found that he had a sensitivo-sensorial left hemianæsthesia, and the conclusion was that it was not a question of insular sclerosis, but of a bilateral post-hemiplegic tremor. The following is his history:

H—— is forty-six years of age. At the present time he is wasted by disease, and emphysematous, but was formerly strong and well. On December 3, 1879, he went to bed feeling badly, and when he got up at three o'clock the next morning to milk the cows, he had an attack of vertigo, thought everything was moving around him, and fell unconscious. He was taken to the hospital of St. Nicolas-du-Port, and did not come out of the coma for four days. He had left-sided hemiplegia, with facial deviation and difficulty of speech. About the 15th of January his left arm grew rigid, and a tremor came on which soon extended to the left leg and has grown progressively worse.

On January 18 the patient still kept his room; the hemiplegia had slightly decreased, and he could pronounce a few words. This same day, when he wished to go to bed, and started up for that purpose, he had a giddy feeling again, thought everything was turning around him, and fearing that he would fall, sat down on the floor, then lay down, and a few instants afterwards became unconscious. He was taken up and put to bed. He became conscious again in three hours, but was not able to speak a word for four days. His right arm was paralyzed during this time.

This right hemiplegia was of short duration; the tremor in the left arm continued, and on the 26th of the month the right arm was affected in the same way, after having first showed a certain degree of rigidity. The aphasia lasted until the beginning of March without any appreciable improvement, and then disappeared quite rapidly. Hemiplegia of the left side persisted to a certain extent; the patient dragged his left leg and let the sole of the foot slip over the ground; he felt as if he were walking upon cotton, and no longer felt his clothes on the left side of his body; his sight grew weaker; he was deaf in the left ear. The tremor remained in all four limbs and progressed slowly. He had sudden spasms in his limbs at times. His other functions were well performed. Last November, the patient, who had complained of dyspnœa on going upstairs, for two years, was seized with a cough with expectoration and a permanent feeling of oppression. He came into the hospital where he was treated for a bronchitis lasting fifteen days.

On December 26, 1880, the following notes were made; tremor extended to all four limbs, more marked on the right than on the left side, more intense in the upper than in the lower limbs; movement rhythmical, ceasing when the limbs are in repose, increasing in extent, especially at the extremities of the limbs, in proportion to the complexity of the movement; emotions and peripheral stimuli bring it on when the limbs are in repose.

The left hand is closed; the patient cannot open it entirely; the three first fingers are partly bent in toward the palm of the hand, almost at right angles; the thumb and little finger are brought nearer together; the interosseous spaces are more marked on the dorsal surface; the thenar and hypothenar eminences appear diminished in size. *The patient cannot use this hand and cannot hold anything in it.* In the elbow the movements of extension are limited. Shoulder movements are made with a certain stiffness. On the right side, all movements are performed without any stiffness, and the patient can close his right hand with considerable force, but cannot lift a glass to his mouth without going through a series of extensive zigzag movements.

In the lower limbs the tremor is less marked, the patient performs all the movements he is told to without ataxia, and walks without either incoördination or tremor; in the movements of the left knee slight stiffness is noticeable. The tendon reflexes are exaggerated; there is ankle-clonus and the knee-jerk is increased. The ankle-clonus is more marked on the left side and is accompanied by a less strong trepidation at the end of a few moments, first in the opposite limb, then in the upper right limb, and finally it sometimes spreads to all four limbs.

General sensibility is destroyed on the left side for touch as well as for pain and temperature. On the right side it is present, but a little diminished. The following are the distances between the two points of the compass at which two distinct sensations on this side are obtained, expressed in centimetres.

Arm, 3, 5; fore-arm, 4.—Hand: palm, 1, 5; back 2, 5; ends of fingers, 1.—Thigh: anterior surface 4, 5.—Calf, 8.—Back of foot, 9, 5; sole, 3.—Thorax; anterior surface, 5, 5.—Abdomen 3.—Cheek, 2, 5.—Forehead, 1, 5. There is moreover a certain degree of analgesia on this side. The muscular sense (idea of position of the limbs) is abolished on the left side.

Special senses: *the left eye only distinguishes light from darkness*, has no perception of objects or of colors, *no visual field.* With the ophthalmoscope, slight posterior staphyloma; some pigmented spots on the inferior parts of the papilla. The right eye has its normal visual field, and distinguishes objects and colors; myopia from posterior staphyloma. (Examination made by Professor Charpentier.)

The left ear does not perceive the ticking of a watch held up against it. *The left half of the tongue is anæsthetic,* and insensible to colocynth. *The left nostril does not react* to the odor of acetic acid. On the right side, hearing, taste and smell are preserved.

The intelligence is clear; there is neither cephalalgia, vertigo, nor abnormal feeling in the limbs; the articulation of words is normal.

The feeling of oppression is intense. The thorax is convex in front;

vesicular murmur is exaggerated on both sides near the sternum. Inspiration is hard and dry; expiration prolonged and sibilant in front. Behind, the breathing is vesicular. There are numerous dry rales. *Diagnosis: focal lesion* (hemorrhagic or necrotic softening) *double and symmetrical, more extended on the right side, involving the internal white capsule, its posterior third particularly; consecutive irritation of the pyramidal tracts,* whence the exaggeration of the tendon reflexes, and the post-hemiplegic tremor. Pulmonary emphysema and bronchitis.

On December 25, a magnetic bar is applied along the external surface of the leg, the negative pole above, and is left in place for twenty-four hours. The patient is not conscious of any abnormal sensation.

28th.—It is observed that tactile sensibility and sensibility to heat and to pain have reappeared in the leg, but are very dull. A second twenty-four hour séance. In the night there are pricking sensations in the limb lasting four hours.

29th.—The prick of a pin on the sole of the foot is perceived, and causes reflex movements.—The sensibility in the leg is dull, and is still more so in the thigh. Anæsthesia persists in the other regions. During the day, there are several shooting pains in the calf of the leg and in the great toe.

30th.—Sensibility is present in the lower limb, but is dull.

31st.—At eight o'clock in the evening there is a third séance; the magnet is applied to the left side of the face, the negative pole to the temple, the positive pole against the thorax at the level of the third rib, and is fixed by a band. A few minutes later the patient says he feels *shooting pains in the frontal region and in the eyes, especially on the left side, and sees yellow rays and black spots.* At four o'clock in the morning, when the ward is lighted, the patient states that he can see distinctly with this eye.

January 1st.—When making rounds we observe that *all the varieties of sensibility have reappeared on the left side of the body. The left eye sees, and the left ear hears the ticking of a watch held at a distance of seventeen centimetres to the left, and twenty-six centimetres to the right. Taste and smell are again present on the left side.*

2d.—This result continues. The left arm feels two points of the compass, when separated three centimetres; the right arm, eighteen millimetres; the left leg, two centimetres; the anterior surface of the thigh, eighteen millimetres; on the back and thorax the sensibility is equal on both sides of the body. *The left visual field, measured by M. Charpentier, measures from fifty to seventy-five degrees, and is equal to that of the right side.*

3d.—Very slight pain in the left leg. A few spots of acne from iodide of potash (has been taking one gram of iodide of potassium daily since

December 26). *The tremor in the upper limbs has very visibly diminished.* The patient *opens his left hand* slowly, but completely; *he can hold a glass in his hand*, and lift it to his mouth, which he has not been able to do since February, 1880. *He can dress himself and use this hand*, which he could not do before.

4th.—Perfect sensitivo-sensorial sensibility continues. The tremor has further diminished since yesterday. The hand lifts the glass to the mouth directly, sometimes almost without tremor, at other times with slight tremor as it nears the mouth. The tremor has almost totally disappeared on the right side. The muscular force of both hands has increased considerably. The paresis of the lower limbs persists; the patient always takes short steps, sliding along on the soles of his feet. The tendon-reflexes persist but are no longer generalized.

5th.—The magnet is applied to the left leg from five in the evening until the next day; pricking sensation in the leg and thigh, pains in the hip and knee, which disappear rapidly. The tendon-reflexes persist, but are diminished; on the right side, there is no ankle-clonus, and the knee-reflex is feeble; on the left side it remains localized in the limb.

The left hand preserves its functions, opens and shuts more slowly than the right hand and with a certain stiffness, but can do everything nevertheless, can button and unbutton, etc. The tremor persists, but to a very slight extent, and does not interfere with the functions of the limb. Sensibility remains throughout. Such is the patient's condition to-day (April 15, 1881). Unhappily for him, the emphysema and oppression persist. The chest is filled with sonorous, sibilant, and mucous rales, and it is to be feared that he will succumb to the pulmonary disease.

June 5th.—The patient is still in the hospital; the dyspnœa persists; it is combated by blisters, dry cupping, and iodide of potassium. The cure of the hemianæsthesia is lasting. The left side of the body and the sense organs preserve their sensibility. The tremor in both limbs is reduced to almost nothing.

The muscular contracture alone has again increased during the last month; the left hand is deformed, the first phalanges bent over upon the metacarpus at an obtuse angle, the other phalanges extended, the fingers separated; the patient slowly and laboriously succeeds in opening the hand completely and in closing it; a resistance is noticed when some one else tries to open or close it; nevertheless the patient can use this hand. He can for example hold a glass, and lift it to his mouth easily. Flexion and extension of the elbow are accomplished with a certain stiffness. It is noticeable that the patient drags his left leg slightly when he walks; there is also slight resistance in the knee movements; the lifting of the toe of the foot does not produce any trepidation; striking the patellar tendon gives the knee-jerk; the left leg describes a much greater arc than the right leg if its tendon is struck with the same force.

To sum up. The curative action of the magnet upon the hemianæsthesia, and upon the tremor and reflex trepidation continues at the end of five months. The contracture of the upper limb, due to the progressive sclerosis of the pyramidal tract, is alone reproduced. On the right side the limbs perform their functions normally without contracture or trepidation.

The patient remains in the hospital on account of his pulmonary emphysema; his condition remains almost stationary.

October 22d.—Contracture is again present in the upper limb, especially in the flexors of the fingers; the first phalanges are flexed upon the metacarpus, the others are in demiflexion; the patient can no longer open his hand spontaneously; it can be opened, though it offers a certain resistance, but it shuts again like a spring; the limitation in the movements of the elbow and shoulder also exists, to a less degree. The patient no longer uses this limb. The right hand performs its functions well; he can lift a glass to his mouth easily with it, but it again shows slight tremor, which becomes a little more exaggerated as the glass is brought to the lips. Nevertheless it does not prevent him from drinking and he does not spill a drop. The articulations of the lower limb are also a little stiff. The restored sensibility is still present. For two weeks, walking has been painful and almost impossible; the patient drags himself painfully to get over a short distance. The attacks of dyspnœa are more intense; mucous and sibilant rales are present throughout both lungs.

The results which I had seen with M. Liébault, and those which I had obtained on this same day with a patient in my service (See Obs. 2), influenced me to try hypnotization. *I hypnotize the patient by means of suggestion;* he falls into a sleep of the second degree. I suggest to him that his hand is cured, that he can again move it easily, that the tremor in the hand has ceased, and at the same time that his dyspnœa is less and that he breathes better. *During his sleep, I tell him to open and shut his hand; he opens and shuts it alternately with a little stiffness;* but little by little it becomes more supple and the movements of flexion and extension grow easier. "If that could only last!" he says in his sleep. I assure him that it will last. When he wakes, he remembers everything that I told him; the restored movements remain; he opens and shuts his hand with the greatest ease. The right hand hardly trembles during the movements, and the left hand lifts a glass to his lips without any tremor. On the dynamometer the needle indicates thirty-six for the left hand and forty for the right.

October 3d.—*The benefit obtained has continued.* Since the séance of yesterday, the patient has walked easily with the aid of a stick. *There is no tremor whatever of the right hand*; the left preserves its limberness. *The dynamometric force has increased;* for the left hand it is forty-seven; for the right, fifty.—New hypnotic suggestion. This time the patient goes into somnambulism, without memory upon waking. The dynamometer continues to register forty-seven and fifty. *Moreover the patient states that he has less oppression.*

4th.—Same condition. Has had almost no feeling of oppression. Has slept well during the past two nights, while the preceding nights were very bad.

5th.—Same condition. The hand continues limber. Slight stiffness remains in the shoulder. Has slept from six o'clock to midnight; has had no dyspnœa. There are fewer sibilant rales in the chest. The dynamometer registers thirty-eight for the left hand. There is slight stiffness in the left knee and hip. When the patient walks the leg is almost rigid, bends a little at the joints, and shows some tremor. He cannot stand on the left leg alone. Tendon reflexes of the foot and knee are present.

Hypnotic Suggestion.—The condition of the limb is about the same when the patient wakes; the foot and knee phenomena persist.

6th.—The stiffness in the lower limb seems to have diminished a little; the tendon-reflexes persist. The leg is stiff when the patient walks. However, by resting one hand on the bed he can stand alone upon the left leg, which he was unable to do before. *He was able to walk yesterday afternoon without a cane for the first time.* He has slept well and has no feeling of oppression.

Hypnotic suggestion: somnambulism. I suggest the complete relaxation of the limb, the disappearance of the tremor and dyspnœa. During sleep, *the tendon-reflexes of the foot are diminished and cease* at command, after having been excited about ten times. Upon waking, *he can stand for a second without aid* and walks without a cane. The tendon-reflexes of the foot persist.

7th.—Has slept well, without any dyspnœa. Walked yesterday without a cane. The hand and shoulder are supple.—*Suggestion.*

The tendon-reflexes are diminished, but reappear through the action of cold. He says he walks better, but the legs are still stiff, and the toes are slightly so in extension.

The improvement continues during the days following.

12th.—The tendon-reflexes are only slightly exaggerated and the patient walks better.

16th.—He walks almost all day, and no longer has any dyspnœa. Four weeks ago he kept his bed because of a sense of suffocation : now he has nothing more of the kind and is up all day.

20th.—He keeps on improving; has no more attacks, sleeps, and no longer has exaggerated tendon-reflexes.

The cure holds its own as far as the cerebral affection is concerned. For two years the patient goes and comes, and walks with very little dragging of the leg; we keep him in the hospital on account of his emphysema.

We thought that he would soon succumb; he lived on until April 4, 1885. I am convinced that he owed this prolongation of his life to hypnotic suggestion. The frequent attacks of oppression were invariably calmed by means of it: when he passed a sleepless night on account of the orthopnœa, I hypnotized him the next day, and, thanks to suggestion, the following nights were quiet; the dyspnœa was reduced to a minimum. The organic evolution of the emphysema, however, gradually brought about oppression, with permanent cyanosis. About the end of September, 1884, the patient could not leave his bed, and this was so until his death.

Autopsy.—*Considerable pulmonary emphysema*, with splenization of the inferior lobes. Dilatation of the right heart.—Atheromatous patches in the aorta.—Venous congestion of the liver and kidneys.

Examination of the brain.—Distinct sub-arachnoid oedema.

Left hemisphere.—*Focus of yellow softening* 0^m, 012 in width and 0^m, 018 in antero-posterior diameter, *upon the convexity of the occipital lobe*, immediately behind the fissure which separates this lobe from the interior parietal lobule.

Right hemisphere.—By making horizontal sections, until the level of the upper surface of the corpus striatum is reached, *a spherical cavity is reached which contains serous fluid* and is lined by a yellow, smooth, serous, false membrane, which is easily detached. This cavity exposed, measures 0^m, 025 from before backward; 0^m, 03 in width, and 0^m, 02 in height. At this level the focus is situated *immediately behind the posterior extremity of the optic thalamus*, near the internal capsule, and touching externally and in front the posterior segment of the insula near its superior border, with its anterior portion. This segment, cut very thin, presents an orifice 0^m, 003 in diameter, which opens into the cavity which is found in the sections following.

A second section about a centimetre below, shows *the optic thalamus and the corpus striatum softened in their posterior third, together with a portion of the intermediate white capsule.* The length of the softened area at this level is four centimetres, one centimetre and a half of which has preserved its white color, the rest of the tissue being soft and yellow. The white capsule is softened through an antero-posterior extent of 1.8 centimetres.

In a third section about a centimetre below, the cavity is seen to be prolonged *into the posterior third of the white external capsule of the claustrum;* its external wall is made up of the gray substance of the posterior third of the lobule of the insula. The external white capsule measures five centimetres and a half in length at this level. The focus takes up 2.3 centimetres of its extent. At this level, *almost all the posterior portion of the external segment of the corpus striatum is destroyed:* the two internal segments, to the extent of seven millimetres from their posterior extremity, present a yellowish tint. Finally, in the same section, the lesion extends into the internal capsule, as far as the origin of the posterior third; the tissue is there softened to the extent of five millimetres from before backward, and the lesion reaches the external border of the optic thalamus, upon which it encroaches to a depth of from four to five millimetres.

A fourth section below shows nothing further.

The hardened mid-brain, medulla, and spinal-cord, do not present any descending degeneration of the pyramidal tract.

This case is of great interest from different points of view. It is an instance of a focus of central softening having given rise to an incomplete left hemiplegia with complete sensitivo-sensorial hemianæsthesia, post-hemiplegic tremor, and secondary contracture.

At the end of a year, the application of a magnet to the left side of the face brought back the sensibility of the whole body and of the special senses, in a few hours; during the days following, the sensibility kept on improving, the muscular force increased considerably, the muscular stiffness disappeared for the moment, the tremor which hindered the upper limbs from performing their functions diminished to a point where it no longer interfered with the lost prehensile function, and at last disappeared entirely. The contracture alone attacked the muscles again gradually, at the end of four months, especially those of the upper limb, and the hand was again closed. Twenty months later this contracture, together with the exaggeration of the tendon-reflexes, yielded distinctly to hypnotic suggestion.

A fundamental question presents itself. *Has the magnet a special therapeutic virtue*, or has it only acted as a suggestive influence in an individual who, as we have seen, was eminently suggestible, even in the waking condition? Is it faith in the power of the magnet, is it the expectant attention of the subject turned in upon itself and suggesting to itself the return of sensibility, which has put the cerebral mechanism of cure into activity? The question does not yet seem to be definitely decided.

Whatever it may be, however, can the disappearance of such persistent phenomena as these, hemianæsthesia, tremor, exaggeration of the tendon-reflexes, and contracture, be explained either by a special action of the magnet, or by the psychical action of suggestion; phenomena which seem at first sight to be directly induced by the organic lesion?

Has the centripetal conductivity of the sensory impressions interrupted by the focus in the posterior third of the internal capsule, been able to re-establish itself by other paths, or by the *white fibres of this region which are still intact* and are seen in the third section, near the base of the brain? Is it by means of the fibres of the sensory crossway, *which are still preserved*, that the magnet, the suggestive influence, or any other influence has been able to restore the muscular and tactile sensibility? This is possible.

We must note too, that the anterior portion of the internal capsule was not destroyed, and that the medullary bundle had not been affected by descending degeneration. It was then a question of a *purely dynamic irritation of this bundle*, caused by the neighboring lesion. We know besides that the secondary contracture is not, as Charcot says very clearly, the result of the direct activity of the pyramidal tract. But the lesion or the irritation of this bundle is reflected, thanks to the direct anatomical relations which seem to exist between them, into the motor cells of the anterior horns. Hence, the contracture or increase of muscular tone; hence, the exaltation of the excito-motor reflex action of the spinal-cord, as shown by the exaggeration of the tendon-reflexes. If this condition of irritation stretches by diffusion to other ganglionic elements of the region, an exaltation of the activities of this system will be the result. Each stimulus transmitted from the brain to a group of motor cells, instead of localizing itself there, may radiate to one or several neighboring groups; hence the result, that intentional movements will be complicated with more or less disordered involuntary movement, and the hemi-tremor or hemi-chorea will be seen to reappear according to the degree of this spinal-cord exaltation, and according to the manner of the reaction, which varies with each individual. The tremor, contracture, and trepidation are then three phenomena due to a common pathogenic mechanism, the exaltation of the gray ganglionic excito-motor substance associated with the pyramidal tract.

Has the magnet, acting in the first place by suspending these phenomena simultaneously with the anæsthesia, acted directly upon the spinal cord, the exaggerated excitability of which it has diminished? I do not think so. The tremor and contractture disappeared after the return of sensibility. I am inclined to think that the disappearance of these symptoms was associated with the restoration of the tactile and muscular sense;—but by what mechanism?

Physiologists admit that the brain has a regulating influence over the reflex excitability of the cord. Warned by the impressions which reach it, of what is going on in the muscles and organs set in activity, of the position of the limbs, of the degree of contraction in the muscles, of the vitality of the movements, etc., the brain may act in knowledge of the cause, if I may so express it, quite unknown to us, by a reflex mechanism, and may contribute to direct the harmony and regularity of these movements. Doubtless, in a healthy subject whose spinal-cord performs its functions normally, if these complex movements of prehension and locomotion, etc., which are repeated daily, have once been, so to speak, assimilated by the cord, they continue to be carried on almost exclusively by the spinal mechanism, automatically in some ways, without the conscious or unconscious intervention of the brain being necessary. But it is no longer thus when the cord carries on its functions abnormally, when the abnormal excitability of its gray ganglionic substance hinders it from fulfilling with regularity and precision its excito-motor functions. Then the movements become disordered; centres foreign to the intentional movement, excited by irradiation, add to the latter muscular movements which are foreign to the end in view; there is tremor, chorea, etc.

Under these conditions the intervention of the brain becomes useful; it moderates the excito-motor influence of the cord, it regulates movements that the cord, left to itself, no longer knows how to direct properly. It corrects, in a certain measure at least, the imperfection of the spinal mechanism; it corrects it so that it can appreciate what is going on in the muscular movements. When these ideas are wanting in it, when the sensorium is ignorant of the position of the limbs, their contraction, or relaxation, their flexion and extension, when the nerve-fibres by means of which the organs of movement keep it informed each second of their situation and needs, are broken, then the brain becomes powerless to help the disorders of motion, and the cord has full command. If the broken fibre be renewed, and the brain put into relation with the cutaneous and muscular periphery, it creates order there, and re-establishes, as far as possible, the muscular harmony which is subserved by the cord. Now, such seems to be the therapeutic influence of the magnet. Restoring the tactile and muscular senses, it allows the brain to correct the aberrations of the spinal excitability which are manifested by tremor, reflex trepidation, and chorea.

The magnet is able, at the same time, to moderate the muscular rigidity by means of a mechanism analogous to that by which it appears to modify the reflex trepidation and hemi-chorea. The encephalic ganglia also interfere to modify and correct this mode of exaggerated reflex spinal activity, which transforms the muscular tone into contracture. Warned by the centripetal muscular nerves of the degree of muscular contraction, the brain regulates this exaggerated contraction involuntarily, and puts it as far as is possible, back to its normal state, and re-establishes the physiological muscular tone.

Thus would be strictly explained, by the single and dynamic virtue of magneto-therapeutics, the esthesiogenic virtue (suggestive or otherwise) which restores the tactile, articular, and muscular sense, and the simultaneous efficacy of this therapeutic means in regard to these three phenomena, tremor, reflex trepidation, post-hemiplegic contractures, which are all spinal phenomena, bound up with a functional over-activity of the gray, excito-motor, reflex axis of the spinal cord.

But the contracture reappeared in our patient, although the restored sensibility was maintained. We must conclude, therefore, that the irritation ceaselessly transmitted by the pyramidal tract to the motor spinal centres, may be of such a nature that the influence of the encephalic centres, even aided by the information derived from the muscular sense, may be powerless to rule it.

Suggestion then has interfered efficaciously. By means of an inhibitory phenomenon of psychical origin, it has acted especially upon the contracture and reflex trepidation, phenomena which were simply dynamic in this case, and which were not rendered incurable by the condition of the organs.

I cannot insist too strongly upon this fact, which explains the efficacy of suggestion under many circumstances. *The functional trouble in diseases of the nervous centres often exceeds the field of the anatomical* lesion; this latter is reflected by shock or dynamic irritation upon the functions of neighboring zones. *And it is against this modified dynamic state, independently of a direct material alteration, that psycho-therapeutics may be all-powerful.* It remains inefficacious and restricted, or has only a transient use, when the functional trouble is directly kept up by the lesion. I have often tried suggestion against the slow contractures connected with descending degeneration, and distinct results are sometimes obtained, but they are ephemeral, while at other times there is no result. Suggestion does not restore a destroyed organ any more than the magnet does; it restores function as far as is compatible with the anatomical condition of the organ.

These considerations show what an enormous influence functional dynamic states play in the affection of the nervous centres; they show by what mechanism, in my opinion, suggestion acting through the mediation of the psychical organ to re-establish the disturbed dynamic condition may diminish a series of grave and obstinate perturbations, connected in reality with a simple functional modality, although a distant organic lesion may have determined them.

OBSERVATION II —*From September* 1, 1882, *to February* 15, 1884, *four severe cerebro-spinal, apoplectiform attacks, the first with paraplegia, most marked on the left side; the others with paralysis of the lower left limb, ulnar neuritis, pains in the loins, cephalalgia, etc.—Many slight attacks of isolated ulnar neuritis.—Efficacy of suggestion. —Total cure by a series of suggestions.*

P. (François), a workman fifty-two years old, came into the hospital September 3, 1882.

Constitution good, generally good health, no syphilitic, alcoholic, or rheumatic history. He says that when eleven years old he had epileptiform attacks daily for thirty-six days, in consequence of fright caused by the sight of a bear. Then they ceased, to reappear in 1856, when he was twenty-six years old. He had them three or four times a day for fourteen years. Since 1870, he has had none. He fell without pain or other sensation. He has never had headache.

During the past two or three years he has had pains in the loins at long intervals, which have lasted an hour or two, and have never prevented him from working.

On August 28, 1882, at five o'clock in the evening, the patient suddenly fell unconscious, and remained so for twelve hours. He was in the hospital at Pompey. He then experienced great stiffness with fatigue in his arms and legs, and a severe supra-orbital neuralgia. He left his bed on the 30th, and the hospital on September 1st. On the 3d, he came to Nancy on foot (12 kilometres), feeling very well.

Here he suddenly felt a sharp pain in his legs and again fell unconscious.

When taken into the hospital an hour afterwards he had regained consciousness.

4th.—Temperature normal; pulse slow and regular; arteries atheramatous; intelligence clear; heart regular. Complains of sharp pain in his lower limbs which he compares to the wound left by the bite of a dog, and further, of a burning sensation in the epigastric region. Sensation as of a blow from a hammer at the spinous process of the seventh dorsal vertebra; pressure causes sharp pain at the seventh, eighth, and ninth dorsal vertebræ, and at the corresponding intercostal spaces. There is a tow-like sensation in the hands. Severe supra-orbital neuralgia. Paraplegia exists. Patient bends his knees in bed, but cannot lift his legs. Anæsthesia with analgesia of the lower limb, as far as a horizontal line extending a finger's breadth above the pubes. No contracture, no reflex trepidation,—micturation painful; it takes from six to eleven minutes to pass 300 grams of urine; he passed water involuntarily for the first time during the night; no appetite; great thirst.

5th.—Cephalalgia persists; the dorsal and epigastric pain has disappeared; pressure at the level of the dorsal vertebræ and intercostal spaces still causes slight pain. Cutting and tearing pains in the legs, particularly in the knees, and spreading to the feet; pricking sensation upon pressure of the thighs.

Extension of the legs gives rise to the cutting pains in the knees; it is the same with the movements of the ankle. Pressure upon the muscles of the legs also causes sharp pain.

The analgesia extends nine centimetres above the condyles of the femurs; above that, there is diminished sensibility as far as the folds of the groin, where it again becomes normal. In the arms, sensibility to pain is much diminished; the tow-like feeling persists in the hands.

The paraplegia persists; the leg is flexed upon the thigh with more difficulty than yesterday.—During the night, from ten to three o'clock, the patient had tinnitis in his right ear, and violent neuralgia. This morning, hearing on the right side diminished; the ticking of a watch is perceived at a distance of six centimetres on this side and eighteen on the left (examination of the ear shows nothing abnormal); profuse perspiration (four cupping glasses applied. Bonjean's ergotine 1^{gm}, 20).

6th.—The lower right limb is better. The patient lifts the leg five centimetres. Sensibility has returned to the thigh and leg on this side, as far as three finger breadths above the malleoli. The left leg is still paralyzed; he cannot lift it. Analgesia exists as far as four centimetres above the condyles.

The right hand is better; the tow-like sensation has disappeared; only a feeling of stiffness remains. The left hand still feels like tow; further, the analgesia has increased in it, and is complete as far as three finger breadths above the wrist. With the dynamometer this hand gives 10, the other 60.

7th.—Complains of shooting pains from left elbow to fingers.—(*Application of magnet.*)

9th.—The application of a magnet to the left limb has been continued. —Motility and sensibility have returned to the right side. No change in the left.

11th.—Same condition, in spite of the application of magnets; profuse perspiration; insomnia.

12th.—Same condition. Persistent anæsthesia in the left hand, as far as 20 centimetres above the wrist. The dynamometer gives 13 for the left, and 67 for the right hand.

The situation remains the same until about the 20th of September.

The application of magnets, which has been discontinued since the 14th, is again begun.

Under the influence of a magnet applied to the sole of the foot, *sensibility reappears first in the thigh, then in the knee, and two days afterward it is present as far as the tuberosity of the tibia.*

24th.—Sensibility extends to the malleoli, the foot remaining insensible. Since six o'clock in the evening the patient has felt sharp pain in the sole of the foot, running along the internal plantar nerve to the ankle. Further, a contracture in flexion of the three last fingers on the left hand is noticed, and the thumb and index finger alone preserve their normal motility. The three contracted fingers are totally anæsthetic, the two others retain slight sensibility. It is the same with the palm and back of the hand; anæsthesia as far as the third metacarpal space; in the wrist the radial border alone is sensible, to a transverse extent of two centimetres. Finally, the entire ulnar area of the forearm is anæsthetic as far as ten centimetres above the wrist. In the arm sensibility is perfect. Pressure upon the ulnar nerve in the olecranon groove is very painful.—(Application of a blister at the level of the pisiform bone.)

25th.—Sensibility has reappeared in the sole of the foot, as far as the head of the metatarsus. Same condition in the upper limb.

26th.—Perfect sensibility in the entire foot.

On the evening of the 28th, he patient suddenly feels a sharp pain in the course of the ulnar nerve, from the elbow to the three last fingers. The pain is sharp and continuous, forcing him to cry out.

30th.—Under the influence of the magnet applied yesterday, the tactile sensibility of the fore-arm, which was abolished as far as ten centimetres above the wrist, reappears two and a half centimetres above. The condition of the hand remains the same.

October 1st.—Sensibility begins at two centimetres above the wrist. (Application of magnet continued.)

2d.—Sensibility recedes to the level of the two phalanges.

The patient is hypnotized. He falls into a profound sleep in a few seconds, without memory upon waking. I vigorously suggest the return of sensibility and motility to the fingers. *Upon waking, the contracture has disappeared;* the patient again moves his fingers and wrist perfectly; *sensibility has returned to the two last phalanges.* By the dynamometer the left hand gives 20, the right 60.

3d.—The result obtained continues. There is paresis of the lower left limb. Walking is slow and painful; the patient drags the lower limb, and cannot stand on the left foot.

New hypnotization. I suggest to the patient that he can walk very well.

When he wakes after ten minutes, the patient walks quickly, only dragging the leg slightly; he supports himself for three seconds on the left foot. He only complains of a certain heaviness in the limb. The dynamometer registers 30 for the left hand.

On the 4th, the left hand registers 32 to 34; the right hand 63. Same condition for the lower limb.

New hypnotic suggestion, after which the left hand gives 40, the right hand 70. *The heaviness in the leg is diminished to half; he supports himself for five seconds on this leg.*

5th.—The left hand gives 51, the right 70. Can raise the foot as high as twenty centimetres.—*After a new suggestion, the feeling of weight has entirely disappeared;* the patient walks about without dragging the limb, lifts the foot as high as forty-five centimetres, and supports himself for five seconds on this foot. The left hand gives 52.

6th.—The left hand gives 55, the right 64. He stands seven seconds on the left foot, and lifts the sole as high as fifty-eight centimetres. He has complained of involuntary crying for several days past. *New suggestion.*

7th.—He can still walk well; he can run, and stands twelve seconds on the leg; the involuntary crying has disappeared; his eyes were stuck fast together for one or two hours after he waked, and during the day the involuntary crying appeared at the least effort, at the act of bending over for example; this morning his eyes have not been so closed.

Patient, whom I have not hypnotized since October 7, continues to walk well; he runs without dragging his leg and without the least feeling of weight; his hand remains supple; on the 12th, the dynamometer gives 50 for the left, and 72 for the right hand. The involuntary crying has entirely disappeared.

The patient leaves the hospital and resumes his work on the 14th. After having kept on uninterruptedly until the 25th, he returns to the hospital on the 26th. For three or four days he has felt a cold sensation creeping from the left foot to the knee, which is calmed by heat; beside, there has been a sense of weight in the left hand. The evening before, all of a sudden, he felt shooting pains extending from the fingers to the left elbow, accompanied with cramp, and contracture in flexion of the hand, for ten minutes. At the same time, lightning pains spreading along the external surface of the thigh and of the left leg to the end of the foot, with a sense of weight in the limb without cramps, lasting five minutes. This attack, as sudden as a pistol shot, left him stupefied and speechless. He has been weeping for four or five days and his eyes are red.

This morning the symptoms disappeared spontaneously; the dynamometer registers 51 for the left hand. He feels nothing but a sense of weight in this hand. Is put into a profound sleep. After suggestion, this feeling of weight disappears and the dynamometer registers 61.

P—— goes back to his work and has no more trouble until the end of March, 1883.

On the 1st of April he comes to the hospital again. His hand has been growing weak for three or four days but he has had no pain.

The dynamometer registers 24 for this hand, 65 for the other. *After hypnotic suggestion the dynamometric pressure is 60 instead of 24*, and the patient is able to work again.

But he is again brought back to the hospital on the 5th. About ten o'clock on the 4th he suddenly felt sharp pains in his left leg from the knee to the malleoli, seven or eight times in succession during two or three seconds, and lasting over three quarters of an hour. In consequence, the leg became heavy and lost strength. The patient tried to continue his work, but had to give it up at half-past three and go home, dragging his leg; in the morning he took the train to come to Nancy. On the way from the station to the hospital he had another attack of cutting pains in the left leg and arm, and fell unconscious. He was lifted by a passer-by, and did not come to himself again until half an hour had passed. He was carried to the hospital, as he was unable to walk.

Since his fall he has complained of incessant and sharp pains in the knee, groin, and left ankle. The limb is completely paralyzed and anæsthetic as far up as the groin; the patient can only bend the first three toes slightly.—In the upper limb there is a contracture of the left hand. If closed it can only be forced open with difficulty, for it closes again like a spring. Sharp painful sensations running from hand to elbow. Pain in the epitrochlear groove, both spontaneous and on pressure. Analgesia of the last three fingers, and of the entire ulnar area. Pricking sensation in the fingers, which lasts until seven o'clock in the evening. Pain on pressure of the left buttock at the emergence of the sciatic. For two months the patient has had tinnitis and deafness of the right ear.

It is impossible to use suggestion in the morning on account of the violence of the pains. It is successful in the evening. *After hypnotic suggestion the patient can open his hand and stretch out his fingers* The sharp pains in the upper limb disappear in three quarters of an hour; in the lower limb in three hours. Little sleep during the night.

6th.—Patient opens the first three fingers three quarters of the way, the second phalanx remaining at right angles to the first. Pressure on the epitrochlear groove is still painful. Sensation has returned to the fingers. The dynamometer indicates 10 for the left hand and 64 for the right. The leg movements are almost nil.—*Hypnotic suggestion:* the hand opens more easily: 17 by the dynamometer.—Slight movements in the toes. Return of sensation to the external surface of the foot and leg.

At two o'clock in the afternoon the patient is seized with "girdle pains," like burning at the base of the thorax.—At six o'clock there is pain upon pressure in the 5th, 6th, and 7th intercostal spaces, over the four lower dorsal vertebræ. The sharp pains have not reappeared in the limbs. Sensibility is distinct in the entire foot and external surface of the leg.

Prolonged hypnotic suggestion with application of the hand to the painful and affected regions. *Upon awaking all the pains have disappeared the spontaneous ones as well as those caused by pressure.* The patient can open his hand more easily. Sensibility is perfect throughout the lower limb. He lifts his foot five centimetres easily and holds it up for three seconds.

7th.—Dream-troubled sleep during the night. The effect obtained is lasting. The restored sensibility continues. Patient moves his fingers and toes, opens his hand partially, presses the dynamometer up to 16, and bends his knee and lifts his leg a little. The tenderness of the epitrochlear groove persists, as well as the feeling of weight in the leg. *Hypnotic suggestion in the evening.*

8th.—The hands register 20 by the dynamometer. The patient opens and closes his hand more easily; lifts his foot higher, and holds it up for four seconds. Has constant buzzing in the left ear. During the morning has a sensation of vertigo on the left side of his head, and in his eye, which lasts until seven o'clock in the evening. No suggestion.

9th.—The left hand registers 25. The foot can be lifted ten centimetres and held up for four seconds. The pain in the epitrochlear groove persists.

10th.—Same condition. *New hypnotic suggestion in the evening, after which the hand presses the dynamometric needle up to 25, and the left foot is held as high as thirty centimetres for five seconds.* At nine o'clock in the evening there are new shooting pains along the ulnar tract, lasting several seconds, and succeeding each other every five minutes, with sense of constriction in the wrist.

11th.—The hand cannot be opened wide. Pain along the ulnar nerve. Sensation not abolished. *Hypnotic suggestion checks the pain.*

12th.—Patient can no longer extend the fingers entirely; dynamometer 17 to 20. Ulnar pain again present, but to a less degree. Condition of leg the same. At six o'clock in the evening, there is still pain upon pressure over the ulnar nerve. It disappears after hypnotization and the fingers are easily opened. Buzzing in the ear has disappeared.

At ten o'clock in the evening, the patient ate a little bread, being hungry; at eleven o'clock, after having taken some boullion, he was seized with a feeling of violent epigastric constriction, which lasted three hours; at one o'clock he became unconscious and remained so for about half an hour. Then, the constriction having ceased, he had a painful pricking sensation in his forehead, nose, and eyes.

18th.—Cephalalgia with pricking sensation; no pain along the nerve path. Hand gives 20 by the dynamometer. Very sharp pain at the seventh and eighth dorsal vertebra. *Hypnotic suggestion diminishes the sensation of pricking very much: spinal pains persist.* New suggestion during the evening causes the former trouble to disappear entirely, but has no effect upon the latter.

A moderate sub-cutaneous injection of morphine does not succeed in removing this excessive spinal pain, which makes the patient groan all night. Toward midnight cold sweat, with loss of consciousness, lasting half an hour.

14th.—Sensation of weight in fronto-parietal region, especially on the left side. Spinal pain persists in the sixth, seventh, and eighth dorsal spinous processes, and in the corresponding left intercostal spaces. "Girdle pain."

Hypnotic suggestion: pain in the head has disappeared: spinal hyperæs-

thesia persists. During the evening, injection of one centigramme of morphine *loco dolenti;* pain disappears: hypnotic suggestion.

15th.—Patient did not sleep, but had no spontaneous pains. In the morning the spinal hyperæsthesia and "girdle pain" still exist, but are much less severe. *Hypnotic suggestion. " Girdle pain," has vanished entirely, spinal hyperæsthesia has decreased.* For three hours during the night, sensation as of blows from a hammer, leaving the dorsal surface of the hand, and extending to the fingers.

17th.—Stiffness in the fingers, which cannot be stretched out completely. Sensibility persists; no pain in ulnar nerve. Dynamometer registers 15. Patient walks quite well, but the contact of the sole of the foot with the floor causes pricking sensations. (No suggestion for two days.)

19th.—Still opens hand with difficulty, and cannot extend fingers. Walks with difficulty, and complains of pain in heel. For several days micturition has been difficult and is accompanied with hypogastric pains which cease as soon as the urine begins to flow. The spinal hyperæsthesia has not reappeared.

21st.—Same symptoms. Micturition painful at first. Drags left leg and cannot hold fingers open. Dynamometer, 23 for left, 60 for right hand. *After hypnotic suggestion dynamometer registers 28 for left hand;* patient walks somewhat better.

23d.—Evening; continued stiffness of hand and complete extension of fingers impossible. Drags left leg and has pain in the groin, knee, and heel, while walking. After hypnotic suggestion, stiffness in the hand and pain in the knee and heel have notably decreased; pain in the groin persists.

24th.—Same condition. *New suggestion; upon waking, pain in the groin persists*, but diminishes spontaneously during the night.

12th.—Stiffness in the hand persists. The patient walks somewhat better, but drags leg with feeling of great weight in it, and cannot support himself standing on that leg alone. *After suggestion, sensation diminishes considerably but reappears rapidly.*

27th.—This morning, after suggestion of yesterday evening, leg is not as heavy, and patient is much less lame. Can stand for one second on the left foot alone. Pain in the groin has not reappeared. *Suggestion. Stiffness in fingers persists and only yields for a short time to suggestion.*

28th.—Leg is doing well, fingers remain straight. After prolonged hypnotic suggestion, patient can stretch them out completely; they are supple. Stiffness reappears about three o'clock in the morning.

29th.—In the morning, *hypnotic suggestion makes stiffness disappear again;* hand remains supple; retraction of fingers reappears at four o'clock in the morning.

30th.—Complains of sensation of hemp or crumpled paper in his hand when he closes it. Cannot pick up a pin with last three fingers. *Hypnotic suggestion. Stiffness disappears, as well as tow-like sensation in hand.* He picks up a pin with the three last fingers easily.

May 1st.—Stiffness in the hand has not reappeared. Dynamometer registers 30 and 25 for the left, and 68 for the right hand. Stands for two seconds on left leg. After suggestion, stands for three seconds on it. Dynamometer gives 36 for the left, and 70 for the right hand.

2d.—Patient goes out into the city and walks a considerable distance. In the evening, complains of slight weight in his leg and stiffness in the back of his hand. These symptoms disappear by suggestion, and the left hand gives 40 by the dynamometer.

3d.—Dynamometer registers 38. Patient lifts his foot five centimetres. *Last hypnotization: the leg is completely free from pain and moves as well as the other.* Dynamometric pressure with the left hand gives 63.

4th.—In the morning dynamometer gives 56 for the left, and 62 for the right hand. Patient walked about all day yesterday without feeling pain. Both ears hear equally well. He leaves May 5, cured.

July 1st, 1873.—Patient comes to the hospital again. Very well up to that time. Four days ago was troubled with left ulnar neuritis; can now only extend the three last fingers a little way. Dynamometer registers 24. Anæsthesia of ulnar area. Pain in left epitrochlear groove.

Hypnotic suggestion. All the symptoms disappear; sensibility has returned completely; the ulnar groove is no longer painful; patient opens and shuts hand at will. Dynamometer registers 46. Goes back to work.

Returns July 15th. Five days ago he had sudden sharp pain from elbow to fingers, which has kept up incessantly since. At the same time, the three fingers closed suddenly and the old ulnar pains returned. I make a *suggestion without hypnotizing him*, by touching his hand and assuring him that the sharp pain will disappear, that his hand can be opened again, and that sensibility will return. *Little by little the pain ceases; sensibility reappears first in the fore-arm, then in the hand; the fingers unbend gradually and completely.* In ten minutes everything is in good order again. Pain upon pressure in the epitrochlear groove remains. Dynamometer registers successively 28, 31, and 40.

After this result, I repeat the suggestion, *but this time in the hypnotic condition.* Upon waking the epitrochlear pain has disappeared. Only tenderness upon pressure remains. Dynamometer registers 60 and 67 for left, and 67 for right hand. Patient returns home cured.

Comes back to us again on the 25th of October, 1883, having been free from all trouble until just lately.

Fifteen days ago had conjunctivitis with involuntary weeping; was treated with blisters, which provoked œdema of the eyelids, with infra-orbital cephalalgia.

At two o'clock on the mornings of the 22d and 23d, shooting pains in the left shoulder accompanied with other symptoms of ulnar neuritis. The next day he comes to consultation; we try suggestion first in the waking condition;—no result; *the suggestion in the hypnotic condition which drives away the contracture, anæsthesia, and shooting pains in the ulnar area.*

Two hours afterward, however, the last three fingers of the hand were again contractured, and now the patient can only open them a third of the way.

25th.—In the morning, constriction with lightning pains around the base of the thorax, lasting from three to four seconds and persisting day and night.

26th.—We note: conjunctivitis cured; weeping continues, tenderness over the supra-orbital region; usual signs of ulnar neuritis very marked. Spinal pain; sensitiveness to pressure at the level of the sixth, seventh, and eighth dorsal vertebræ. Heaviness it the left leg. *Hypnotic suggestion: upon waking the symptoms of ulnar neuritis, olecranon pains, shooting pains, anæsthesia, and flexion of the fingers have disappeared; spinal pain persists.*

At eight o'clock in the evening, the patient is found unconscious, and he remains so for about six minutes. He had had lightning pains in his back during the day.

27th.—Ulnar neuritis has not reappeared. Spinal pain persists from the seventh to the tenth spinous process, and extends into the intercostal spaces.

Hypnotic suggestion, during which the patient complains of very sharp pains. Upon waking, they are slightly soothed, but reappear and are intense during the day. Injection of morphine at six o'clock in the evening.

28th.—The spinal pain has disappeared. *Suggestion.* Sense of weight in leg diminished. Olecranon groove slightly sensitive.

29th.—*Hypnotic suggestion. Heaviness in the leg and head disappears.* Patient does well during the day. Was waked suddenly in the night by the cries of another patient, and was seized with a burning sensation in the back and left side.

30th.—Dynamometer registers 34 for the right hand, and 13 for the left. Pain from the eighth to the tenth dorsal vertebræ. Pressure on this region when the patient is in the hypnotic state wakes him.

In the evening his pain is dissipated to a great extent by suggestion in the waking condition.

31st.—Doing well, except for heavy feeling in the head and pain in the ulnar groove. At five o'clock in the evening, *suggestion in the waking condition drives both troubles away.* But about eight o'clock shooting pains suddenly reappear, spreading from the elbow to the finger ends, and the hand again closes.

November 1st.—Tenderness over ulnar nerve persists; hand only opens three-quarters of the way; fingers anæsthetic. Dynamometer registers 19 for the left, and 60 for the right hand.

Suggestion in the waking condition dissipates the contracture and ulnar pain in a few minutes.

Suggestion in the hypnotic condition restores sensibility to the fingers. A third suggestion increases the muscular force of the hand.

Dynamometer registers 24, 26, and 27 successively.—About two o'clock in the afternoon the hand closes again, after two shooting pains.

2d.—Patient opens his hand four-fifths of the way with pain, but it closes again instantly. Pressure on ulnar nerve very painful. No anæsthesia. *Suggestion in the waking condition dissipates all these symptoms.* At ten o'clock two attacks of shooting pain in the elbow, and the hand again closes. Still complains of pain in the leg. *Another suggestion in the waking condition makes the contracture and pain disappear.*

A third suggestion in the hypnotic condition, drives away the pain in the leg. But at two o'clock the contracture in the hand reappears, as well as the heaviness in the leg. The head perspires during the night.

3d.—No pain. Only bends the hand three quarters of the way.

After suggestion in the waking condition, the hand can be opened completely and is again limber. Dynamometer registers 19 for the left, and 58 for the right hand; and, after a new hypnotic suggestion, 22 for the left hand.

At half-past one the stiffness has returned in the hand without any attack of pain. Tenderness over ulnar area. *Suggestion in the waking condition drives away the stiffness and pain.*

4th.—Slight tenderness still, upon pressure over the groove; the fingers cannot be completely extended. *Suggestion in the waking condition drives all the trouble away.*

5th.—Patient is doing well. Slight stiffness in the hand continues.

On the 6th, perfectly well; complains of nothing. The dynamometer registers 61 for the right, and 50 for the left hand. Patient leaves hospital November 7, and gets along nicely until February 19, 1884.

At three o'clock on the afternoon of this day, he suddenly felt shooting pain in the left foot. It began low down, but reached the knee by ten o'clock in the evening.

Attacks of pain succeeded each other every three minutes during the night. The next day, the 20th, he came to Nancy. On the way from the station to the hospital, he again fell in the street, and remained unconscious for an indefinite time. When he regained consciousness, pain still persisted in the lower limb. Moreover the ulnar neuritis was accompanied with very intense twitchings and pricking sensations in the ulnar area.

At the hospital, we note,—girdle pain in the three lower left intercostal spaces. Painful twitchings in the fore-arm, with clonic spasms provoked by the pain nearly every minute; the pain extends as far as the shoulder during these spasms. Paralysis and anæsthesia of the lower limb extending as far as the middle of the thigh. *Hypnotization fails* on account of the intensity of the pain. *Suggestion in the waking condition causes relaxation of the hand.*

February 21st.—Patient opens hand partly; phalanges remain bent, and fingers close again one after another, remaining from two to three centimetres distant from the palm of the hand. Very sharp pain on pressure over olecranon groove. Yesterday the patient could not lift his foot, to-day he lifts it as high as from six to seven centimetres; can hardly bend the three last toes; makes almost no knee or ankle movement. Sense of heaviness in the leg; the anæsthesia has disappeared. He cannot stand, and keeps the leg stiff. No contracture or exaggeration of the reflexes. (It has never existed). Spinal pain upon pressure of the fourth and sixth dorsal vertebræ, in the interscapular and left scapular region.

Suggestion in the waking condition, lasting two minutes, drives away the ulnar pain completely, and the stiffness in the hand almost completely; the patient keeps his fingers extended.

A second suggestion in the waking condition lasting five minutes, diminishes the paresis of the lower limb notably. The patient holds the leg up from the bed, bends the joints, gets up and walks, limping a little and dragging his leg slightly.

A third suggestion in the waking condition, lasting two minutes, makes the pains in the spine and loins disappear completely. The painful spasms have disappeared. This result holds during the day.

22d.—At one o'clock in the morning patient was waked by painful sensations in the ulnar area, and the three fingers were again flexed. To-day the fingers are at right angles to the metacarpus; no anæsthesia. The left leg is extended; he does not dare to lean on it. Slight pain upon pressure of the intercostal spaces. Hypnotic suggestion: the ulnar and intercostal pain disappears; the hand may be bent entirely, and is limber; the patient walks much better.

23d.—Slept well. When walking, complains of sensation of weight

HYPNOSIS AND SUGGESTION 241

from the internal malleolus to the middle of the leg. Dynamometer registers 17 for the left, and 68 for the right hand. Hypnotic suggestion. Sense of weight diminishes, but does not disappear. Left hand gives 25.

24th.—Same condition. *Suggestion in the waking condition makes the sensation of weight disappear.* Patient complains of nothing but a sensation of heaviness. Walks well, but still limps slightly.

25th.—Same condition;—left hand doing well, but the tow-like sensation remains; gives from 17 to 23 by the dynamometer. This sensation vanishes after hypnotic suggestion. The dynamometer registers 27. Heavy feeling in the leg has diminished.

26th.—Same condition. Dynamometer registers 25. *Hypnotization.* Dynamometer registers 50. Feeling of heaviness in the leg has diminished by half.

27th.—Dynamometer registers 43 for the left, and 56 for the right hand. After hypnotization the left hand registers 59, and patient says he feels hardly any heaviness in leg.

28th.—Continues to improve. Dynamometer registers 54 for the left hand; *after a new hypnotization* 57. Patient walks very well, goes out into the city, but at half-past two o'clock has the sensation of weight again.

29th.—Left hand registers 61. *Hypnotization makes the heavy feeling vanish.*

March 1st.—Very little heaviness. Cannot stand on left leg for more than a minute. When the foot touches the ground, patient again feels sensation of weight. *After hypnotization, this sensation disappears completely.*

Patient continues to do well. The dynamometric force of the left hand always exceeds 50. On the 4th, he walks five miles, not feeling any pain. Returns to his work on March 5, 1884.

Comes to consult me again on March 3, 1885. Says he has been well up to three months ago. Since then he has had continuous pain in the olecranon groove, which often wakes him at night. Can open and shut his fingers. If he makes an effort to lift an object or to press anything tightly, painful twitchings appear in the elbow and fingers. When the elbow is bent, the pain is only in the groove; if he stretches it out, the pain increases and appears in the last three fingers. Pressure on the groove causes sharp pain.

Thirty-six days ago he pricked himself with an iron filing in the last phalanx of the right middle finger, in consequence of which a diffuse inflammatory swelling appeared on the back of the hand, which was opened ten days after by the physician at the Pompey hospital. Suppuration kept up for fifteen days. Then the abscess closed. The back of the hand is still swollen and red; acute sensitiveness here and in the middle finger; pronation and supination are possible; wrist movements are painful; the extended phalanges cannot be bent without pain.

After hypnotic suggestion, the left ulnar pain has completely vanished. P—— can press hard with his hand, and can lift a log of wood without having the slightest pain in consequence of the effort.

The right hand is no longer painful; can bend the wrist and phalanges slightly, spontaneously, and without pain, as much as the swelling will allow.

Patient comes back on May 20th. Left hand has been doing well all the time. Right hand still sensitive and swollen; fingers stiff, and he cannot bend them. After hypnotic suggestion, pain disappears. The stiffness, due to the swelling, still persists.

He comes to see me again on April 9, 1886; there is only slight stiffness in the right hand, the result of the inflammatory swelling; the first phalanges are slightly flexed upon the metacarpus; but he has felt no symptom of ulnar neuritis, or of any other manifestation. I heard from him on May 13th. He was doing very well.

I have related this observation in detail because it so well shows how suggestion acts, how it struggles against serious functional troubles, and in spite of their obstinacy succeeds in incessantly repressing them, and finally in triumphing over them.

It also shows, as does the preceding observation, what part functional dynamism plays in cerebro-spinal affections. The first attack, leaving behind it a paraplegia with spinal, girdle, and lightning pains, seemed to point to an acute meningo-myelitis. The rapid disappearance of the symptoms through suggestion showed that it was nothing of the sort.

The total cure after each attack, the instantaneous disappearance of the ulnar neuritis through suggestion, evidently indicates that all these troubles were not due to a serious and diffuse lesion of the cerebro-spinal axis, as might have been supposed from the symptoms.

We think that it is a question of a localized lesion, situated perhaps, near the spinal origin of the left ulnar nerve. Might it not be a benign tumor lying latent and inoffensive, like certain cerebral tumors? From time to time this local lesion would become the seat of *dynamic irradiations* into the cerebro-spinal axis, and, according to the extent of these irradiations, they would give rise perhaps to ulnar neuritis alone, perhaps to lightning pains with paralysis and anæsthesia of the lower left limb, perhaps to paraplegia, perhaps to paralysis of the four limbs, and finally, perhaps, to encephalic troubles:—cephalalgia, involuntary weeping, facial twitchings, apoplectiform seizures. In the same way, a cerebral tumor which has been latent for a long time, may from time to time provoke apoplectiform or epileptiform attacks, with variable paralyses. When looked at from a distance, these phenomena, which are so frequent in nervous pathology, should force a certain reserve upon the topographical diagnosis of the lesion.

We have seen how suggestion may effectually interfere and drive away troubles which are not controlled by an irremediable material alteration of the corresponding organic elements. In these cases we also see how suggestion may contribute to rectify and assure diagnosis, by separating, so to speak, what is simply dynamic from what is organic.

OBSERVATION III —*Incomplete left hemiplegia dating back eight days.—Rapid improvement through suggestion.—Almost complete cure in three weeks.*

Louis C——, a house-painter sixty years old, enters the hospital on November 7, 1886. His constitution is good and he is generally very well. Six days ago he suddenly felt a *sensation of heaviness in his left leg;* he was able to get home. Two hours after he felt a *similar heaviness in his left arm, with pricking sensations* which have lasted ever since. He could still walk by supporting himself along the wall. When he tried to get up in the evening he could no longer support himself on his left leg.

November 8th.—We note: no fever; pulse regular; arteries hard and atheromatous. *Features are notably deviated to the right. Patient rises slowly, and cannot lift his left arm as high as he could. It is also more easily fatigued.* He can execute all movements with this arm. Dynamometer registers from 35 to 40 for both sides. Patient cannot stand. When lying down, can lift left leg, but cannot hold it up more than four or five seconds. Bends his toes with some hesitation. Cannot bend his heel. Reflexes seem a little more marked on the right side. Sensibility normal. Heart not hypertrophied; sounds clear; respiration normal; intelligence intact. Patient has been constipated for four days. Treatment: laxative injection, which takes effect.

9th.—*Patient is easily hypnotized and goes into profound sleep.* After waking can hold leg up for ten seconds and can move toes much better, but cannot yet bend heel.

11th.—Cannot hold leg up for more than four seconds.

16th.—*Suggestion.* Same condition.

17th.—Suggestion repeated. *After the séance, patient was able to stand alone and walk with slight support.*

19th.—*After suggestion, was able to stand alone and walk to the end of the room without being supported*, dragging his leg, however. Most difficult movement is the dorsal flexion of the foot. When lying down, can hold leg up indefinitely and lower it gradually.—Tendon reflexes slightly exaggerated.

20th.—This condition persists. Daily suggestion.

23d. Continues to do well. Walks alone. Tendon reflexes no longer exaggerated. Lifts foot very well.

Improvement continues. By December 2, patient can go down-stairs, and drags his leg but slightly. All movements can be made. *Dorsal flexion of foot is perfect.* No exaggeration of tendon reflexes.

Remains in the hospital until January. Condition remains the same. Walks well, still complains of heaviness in leg and arm, which prevents him from getting up on ladder and managing his brush as before.

OBSERVATION IV —*Cerebral disturbance.—Fracture of spine with recovery.—Sub-acute articular rheumatism.—Epileptic seizures of traumatic origin.—Gradual disappearance of the pains by suggestion.—Abortion of an epileptic seizure, and complete cure through suggestion.*

M. S——, a paste-board maker, forty years old, enters the clinic on December 21, 1882.

In January, 1881, he fell five metres, from a loft down to the pavement. He lay unconscious, with a wound on his head, and was taken to the St. Leon Hospital, where he remained unconscious for ten days. He could not stand for two months. Had pains in the loins and at the level of the lower dorsal vertebræ, extending forward; pains in the shoulders and right leg, which he could no longer bend. Vertigo, with a tendency to fall over on the left side, difficulty in moving head, and inability to bend body to pick up anything. Orbital pains up to about a month after the accident, cephalagia in the frontal and temporal regions; at the same time, deafness and buzzing in the ear, lasting about eight days. Sight became weak and dim, especially on the left side. Stammering, with a heaviness in the tongue, which rendered his speech almost unintelligible; a symptom, which, although diminishing day by day, did not disappear entirely for five months. Swallowing was almost impossible, at least for solid food; for four or five days nourishment had to be given through the sound, and the disphagia did not disappear completely until two months after the fall. No trouble with micturition, but constipation during a month's time. He went back to work after two months, but found that he was too weak on his legs to do much. Fifteen days after his departure, he had swelling and pain in his ankles and knee; then in his wrists, elbows, and shoulders. He went back to the hospital in April, remaining two months. It was sub-acute articular rheumatism. Seven or eight years before his fall, he had a poly-articular rheumatism, which lasted six months, and since then he has had frequent but slight relapses. At the end of two months, he went back home, but could only work a little. For the last six weeks he has again had articular pains in the elbows, wrists, and ankles; painful twitchings lasting from one to two hours, now in one, now in the other joint. The knees and ankles have been swollen for three weeks; the right elbow and wrist for fifteen days; nevertheless the patient has been able to walk all the time. For two months he has had no more cephalalgia, vertigo, or buzzing in his ears; he hears, sees, and sleeps well. We must add that last May, at the hospital, he had two epileptiform seizures two days in succession, and remained unconscious for five days.

In August he had another attack, and remained unconscious for six hours. He remembers that he had another attack at Champigneulles in October.

Present condition.—Temperament lymphatic; intelligence medium; works in a paste-board factory where he is always exposed to dampness. Thorax somewhat more convex on left than on the right side; spine slightly curved to the right, and projecting out behind to an extent of twenty centimetres, from the sixth or seventh dorsal to the middle of the lumbar vertebræ; this hump developed after his fall.

At the present time, patient complains of sharp pains in the loins and spine at the level of the projection, occurring both spontaneously and on pressure, and preventing him from standing erect when he walks. The right knee is sensitive to pressure; there is also sensitiveness in the back of the thigh and calf, extending to the tendon of Achilles; painful twitchings on sitting down and on walking. Both ankles swollen and sensitive to pressure, but can execute any movements. Supports himself four seconds on the left leg, and barely two seconds on the right; can bend the latter with difficulty; tendon reflexes normal. Upper limbs doing well, except for slight swelling of the right wrist. Movements in the right wrist are a little ataxic. He cannot touch the end of his nose with his finger without going through a series of oscillations. Sensibility to pain and to touch is diminished on the right side, especially in the lower limb, where only a few points of normal sensation remain at the root of the spine, at the internal side of the patella, and on the external surface of the tibio-tarsal articulation; several zones of very limited anæsthesia in the left leg. Hearing is notably diminished on the left side; patient hears the ticking of a watch at ninety centimetres on the right side; barely at two centimetres on the left. Other functions normal.

To sum up: *symptoms of cerebral disturbance, of medullary compression by fracture of the spine; articular symptoms from rheumatic diathesis.*

January, 1885.—Condition almost the same. Pains in the loins and right leg. Has complained of pain in the precordial region since seven o'clock this morning. Has had attacks of dizziness, which vanished spontaneously this morning.

The patient is hypnotized, and is very suggestible (somnambulism). *Upon waking, the precordial pain has disappeared, and the pain in the leg has greatly diminished.* These pains return during the night, but are much less intense.

5th.—New suggestion. Does well during the day.

6th.—Again complains of pains in the knee, the right calf, and right costal border. *They disappear almost completely by suggestion.*

7th.—At four o'clock in the afternoon the patient has an attack characterized by slight tremor, without convulsions, and without foaming at the mouth, closure of the eyelids, inferior strabismus, relaxation of the upper limbs, slight stiffness in lower limbs, dim sight (cannot count the number of his fingers); can shut his hand, but cannot press with it. Intelligence preserved. Painful sense of constriction of the epigastrium, which disappears at eleven o'clock in the evening. Sensation of shooting pains in the same region, which do not disappear until three in the morning.

8th.—The attack has disappeared. Only complains of pain in the right costal border, and pricking sensation in the knee. Presses well with both hands. Passes a good day.

At seven o'clock in the evening, pain in the precordial region (shooting pains) lasting two hours and a half; it is less to-day. Pain in the upper and internal part of the tibia, under the patella, lasting since four o'clock in the afternoon; disappears when the precordial pain appears. Pain in the lumbar region at the level of the spinal projection.

9th.—In the morning the precordial pain has vanished; the lumbar pain persists, as well as the pain at the right costal border and in the knee. Patient feels weak on his legs; cannot support himself at all on the right foot, and hardly on the left.

After hypnotization, the pains disappear and the patient walks well, but the lumbar pain reappears at the end of an hour.

10th.—Complains of pain in the internal part of the right knee, which came back in the night and kept him from sleeping. *It is relieved by suggestion,* but reappears during the day.

12th.—Slept well after suggestion. At two o'clock in the morning, shooting pains in the knee and calf waked him, and he complains this morning of dizzy feelings in his head. After suggestion, he feels no more pain during the day, but slight twitchings in his knee. The pains reappear in the knee and ankle.

I shall not follow the details of the history. This state of things continues nearly up to the beginning of March. The pains in the left lower limb, knee, calves, heel, and lumbar region, which are driven away, or notably diminished each time suggestion is tried, reappear after a few hours, or during the night.

The patient becomes more and more sensitive to suggestion however. He sleeps indefinitely, if he is ordered not to wake spontaneously. One day we let him sleep for fifteen consecutive hours. He realizes any hallucinations, either in the sleeping or waking condition; he can be made perfectly analgesic by a simple affirmation.

This susceptibility to suggestion being developed to this extent by the end of February, the pains more rarely return after suggestion, and disappear by simple affirmation, or touching of the limb, without hypnotization; the least inkling of a return of pain is immediately repressed; and in the early part of March, the patient passes eight days and more without pain either in the loins or knee; he walks well, can run, and helps with the work in the ward.

Between one and three o'clock during the afternoon of the 13th of April, he has a succession of severe epileptiform seizures.

At the same time on the 17th, in spite of daily suggestion, he again has seizures, preceded by prodromata in the morning.

On the morning of the 21st he has pain in his head, cephalalgia, dimness of sight, slight spasms in his limbs; these are the premonitory symptoms of a seizure. I hypnotize him at ten o'clock in the morning, and suggest that he shall sleep quietly until five o'clock in the evening. He wakes up at the hour indicated. During his sleep he has several sharp twitches in his arms and legs, and uncovers himself. It lasts only a second, but the seizure does not come.

He has had no more seizures or twitchings since. He remains in the hospital a year longer; he works about, complains only of slight pain in the loins from time to time, which is the result of effort, and is immediately abolished by suggestion. One day my *chef-de-clinique* pulled out five roots of his teeth, twisting them around in their sockets with the forceps. The operation lasted fully twenty minutes. I assured him beforehand that he would feel no pain and that he would laugh over it. He showed no suffering during the operation, and laughed as he spit out the blood. I add that in his normal condition he was not at all analgesic.

I have seen S—— again this winter (1885); he came to the hospital to be cured of a new pain in his legs; he has been able to continue his work, is very well, and has had no more epileptiform seizures.

We may ask if, in this case, the traumatic epilepsy would have become persistent without the help of suggestion. In cases such as this, where an old epilepsy is assimilated, so to speak, by the nervous system, cure is generally impossible.

I have tried hypnotic suggestion in several cases of long standing idiopathic epilepsy, and I have not succeeded in diminishing the number and frequency of the seizures in any very evident way. In two cases I thought I had obtained results momentarily; the seizures appeared to be less frequent; but in spite of the continuance of suggestion the result was not confirmed.

OBSERVATION V —*Hemiplegia with organic hemianæsthesia.—The magnet unsuccessful without suggestion.—Cure by the use of magnet with suggestion, without sleep.*

R——, a miner sixty-two years old, enters the hospital on July 5th. He has been troubled with slight left hemiplegia and hemianæsthesia for two days. The attack was preceded by prodromic symptoms. It is a case of embolism of the middle cerebral artery, with a focus of softening in the internal capsule or in its vicinity. The hemianæsthesia is complete in the upper limb; hemianalgesia in the trunk, face, and upper limb.

I will not relate this observation in detail, as it is not important for our object.

On July 11, the analgesia with anæsthesia, as well as the abolition of the muscular sense, remained complete in the upper limb. Sensation had partly returned in the lower limb; only slight movements could be made; slight movements were also possible in the fore-arm and hand.

A magnet is applied to the dorsal surface of the hand and wrist, and left on for three days, the 11th, 12th, and 13th of July.

The anæsthesia and paralysis remain the same.

On the following days, the patient has a supra-orbital neuralgia, which is treated with sulphate of quinine, but does not yield definitely until the end of the 20th day. The anæsthesia still persists. The motor-paralysis is diminished; the patient lifts the left arm to a right angle, and bends the elbow; he lifts his leg as high as twenty-five centimetres.

22d.—The magnet is again applied and left in place.

24th.—We note, that, in spite of the application of the magnet, the anæsthesia persists. We continue to apply the magnet, assuring the patient at the same time that it will cause the return of sensation; that he will again be conscious of his hand and of the position in which it is.

25th.—He says he has more feeling in his arm; when examined sensibility seems doubtful. Suggestion is repeated in the waking condition.

26th.—Tactile sensibility exists, but is dull; slight sensation upon the prick of a pin; the muscular sense has not returned. Suggestion is repeated, with the application of the magnet, but without sleep.

28th.—Tactile sensibility as well as sensibility to pain and the muscular sense (idea of the position of the limb), is present and very distinct, in the whole limb. Tactile sensibility has also returned much more distinctly in the lower limb and trunk.—The magnet is removed and this result continues.

This fact seems to prove that, in the present case, the magnet only acted by means of a suggestive influence. Nevertheless, I dare not draw a conclusion from one single case; repeated observation is necessary in order to bring out the truth as to the real efficacy of magnets.

OBSERVATION VI —*Diffuse rheumatic myelitis.—Decided benefit by repeated suggestion.—Condition stationary.*

A. (Michael), a laborer forty-six years old, comes into the hospital on Febuary 24, 1883.

He has been very well up to two months ago, when he experienced dull pain in his left fore-arm, and numbness, which still persists. At the least movement, if he wishes to take hold of anything for example, he is seized with a transient cramp, which extends the fingers and forces him to drop the object; he can hardly dress himself in consequence of these cramps.

For fifteen days past the right hand has also been affected, but to a much less extent. One day, about a month ago, while out walking, the patient suddenly felt a dull pain in both feet; he could no longer bend his legs, they had become rigid, and, when he tried to go on, he fell on the sidewalk. He picked himself up, took about a hundred steps, and fell again. After resting a few minutes, he was able to go on, but with great difficulty. On the following days he walked with great difficulty, and became greatly fatigued. The neighbors were often obliged to help him up the stairs to his room on the second floor.

Seven or eight years before, he had had pains in the loins and shoulders also, at times; since, he has been subject to rheumatic pain, but has always been able to do his work. He says he has been a little short of breath for two or three years, but can still do heavy work.

No syphilitic or alcoholic history.

February 25th, we note: strong constitution; pulse full, bounding, regular. Slight aortic insufficiency, without hypertrophy of the heart; slight diastolic murmur at the base. Respiration normal; no rales.

The patient gets out of the bed with difficulty, walks painfully and slowly, taking little steps, and with his legs far apart. He puts the soles of his feet flat down on the floor, bending his knees, but can hardly bend his ankles; he stops and turns quite easily; he stands up with his eyes closed, but loses his equilibrium quickly if he tries to walk. He can only stand for a second on one foot. He complains of a sensation of coolness in his lower limbs, but has neither sensations of numbness nor of pricking. If he squats on the floor he cannot get up again without pain. Lying in bed, he lifts his right leg ten centimetres with difficulty, but cannot keep it up; he can only bend his knees with difficulty. He lifts his left leg very well, but cannot keep it up any better than he can the other leg. The toe movements are good. Sensation is normal; the tendon reflexes seem diminished.

In the upper limbs, aside from the pricking sensation and cramps, which occur from time to time, sensibility and motility are very well preserved, and movements are dexterously made.

The dynamometer registers 25 for the left, and 30 for the right hand. There is no spinal pain and no cephalalgia.

Sight has been gradually growing dim for two or three years. At the present time vision seems to be only half as distinct as normally; there has been no diplopia. At times last summer he had a sensation of thoracic constriction.

Diagnosis: *diffuse sub-acute myelitis of the posterior columns.*

Treatment: one gramme iodide of potassium, *t. i. d.*

28th.—When lying down, the patient lifts his left leg better and holds it up for from five to seven seconds, but cannot hold up the right leg. He bends his knees better. Opens and shuts left hand with a certain hesitation; does better with right hand. Dynamometer registers 23 for the left, and 31 for the right hand. Patient says he has had transient diplopia at times during the last two days.

Evening; *hypnotization: 2d degree.—Suggestion.*

March 1st.—Iodic coryza; *walks better;* supports himself about a second on each foot; opens and shuts left hand more easily. *Dynamometer registers* 34 *for the left, and* 33 *for the right hand.*

This result is not sustained. On the 3d the left hand gives 32, the right 37. The patient still walks quite well.

6th.—The left hand gives 20, the right 19. He can hold his legs up, the left one for four seconds, the right for one second only; he cannot sit down on his bed without help; neither can he support himself on one foot.

8th.—*Since a new hypnotic suggestion given yesterday morning, the force in the upper limbs has increased. The left hand gives 34, the right the same. Walking is not any better, the patient cannot support himself on one foot.*—On March 9th both hands give 32.

Patient's condition improves slowly. Suggestion from time to time.

20th.—After a new hypnotization, the left hand gives 41, the right 47. The patient walks better, and stands for nearly two seconds on one or the other leg. When lying down he can hold both legs up from three to five seconds.

On the 2d C—— walks well, sometimes for a quarter of an hour at a time. His pace is regular. He drags the left leg slightly, and always complains of a certain weakness in it. He stands for three seconds on each foot. For the past four or five days he has gone up or down stairs easily. The dynamometer registers 45 for the left hand, and 48 for the right. Opens and shuts his hand easily, though he complains of slight stiffness. (Daily hypnotization,—sleep of 2d degree.)

3d.—Improvement continues. Patient walks, lifts his legs and bends both knees well; sits down on his bed without help, lies down by himself, but has to make use of his hands in order to lift his legs up on the bed.

Later hypnotization does not modify this condition to any noticeable degree. The improvement obtained is persistent.

August 2d.—C—— leaves the hospital. We do not see him for a month.

He walks well, but he says he still feels pain in the loins when he leans over or when he walks. When he straightens himself up, he has a sensation of weakness and cold in his lower limbs, extending to his feet. Left hand always feels somewhat cold, and when he carries anything, there is a sensation of stiffness in the hand and fore-arm. Muscular force preserved.

I have tried the suggestive method in different cases of incurable myelitis. In several ataxic cases, the lightning pains, gastric crises, and vesical tenesmus have disappeared momentarily. In one case, the walk was remarkably improved for a time; the patient, who could no longer stand up, improved so that he could walk without a cane. But these results are transient; the organic disease following its inexorable course, re-establishes the functional troubles.

In many patients troubled with spasmodic tabes, or insular sclerosis with spastic paralysis, I have been able to diminish for a time the exaggeration of the tendon reflexes and contracture by means of suggestion, but have never succeeded in arresting the evolution of the disease entirely. I do not consider cases of myelitis which are curable, or which disappear spontaneously, as in the preceding observation. But locomotor ataxia, insular sclerosis, muscular atrophy, affections which are progressive and incurable by nature, only receive from suggestion a more or less lasting diminution of certain functional dynamic troubles. As an example of a remarkable improvement obtained, I will cite the following observation.

OBSERVATION VII —*Symptoms of cerebro-spinal insular sclerosis.—Very remarkable amelioration and retardation of the disease for six months, after several hypnotic séances.*

D——, a laborer twenty-nine years old, is in the service of my colleague, Dr. Spillmann. I was asked to look at the case on October 9, 1884. The patient had been ill for three months. At this time he had begun to flex his legs. He had had violent pains in his limbs which he compared to lashes from a whip. The weakness increased, and tremor appeared in the hands. Three months ago he was obliged to give up work.

His constitution is good, he has had no previous disease and has never committed any excesses; he is of medium intelligence. Can give no other certain information about himself.

We note :—

1st, Very marked tremor in both upper limbs, resembling that of insular sclerosis, which is increased when the patient moves; for example, when he lifts a glass to his mouth he tips it over or seizes it with his mouth.

2d, Very marked rigidity in the lower limbs, with exaggeration of the tendon reflexes, the foot phenomena continuing indefinitely. The patient walks slowly and with difficulty, tottering; his limbs are rigid.

3d, He complains of vertigo. Certain difficulty in the articulation of words is noticed.

Sensibility normal. Evacuations occur normally.

October 9th. *I hypnotize him, and he goes into the second degree of sleep.* I suggest the disappearance of the tremor and rigidity.

Upon waking there is no tremor in the hand; the patient lifts a full glass to his mouth without spilling a drop; he walks better and faster; the exaggeration of the tendon reflexes still exists, but to a slighter degree.

10th.—The improvement persists. Patient walked better yesterday. Used his hand constantly without tremor; dynamometric force is from

28 to 32.—*New hypnotic suggestion.* Upon waking, he walks. His legs are still stiff, but to a less extent than before the suggestive treatment.

11th.—He says he has no more vertigo; no more tremor; walks very well but with slight stiffness still.—*Suggestion.*

13th.—Improvement continues; there is no longer any vertigo or tremor. Can lift a chair easily with one hand.

I put the patient into *somnambulism;*—amnesia upon waking. He feels stronger and *can lift the chair with his hand, holding it by one leg.* Tendon reflexes have diminished very decidedly.

14th.—The patient helps with the work in the ward.

19th.—Continues to do well. Says he had headache both yesterday and day before, and at times trouble with his sight. When looking at an object opposite to him, he sees it large and confused; this trouble is transient, however, only lasting about five minutes at a time. He walks well, says however that he still trembles a little on his legs; tendon reflexes are no longer exaggerated. Tremor in the hand at times. He spills the contents of a glass. The dynamometer registers 48 for the right, and 18 for the left hand.—Hypnotic suggestion.

23d.—Has done well since the 19th; has had no more headache or trouble with his sight; no more tremor; the exaggeration of the tendon reflexes is no longer noticeable; speech is still slow.

24th.—D—— is doing well. Certain stiffness in left leg still; cannot support himself on one foot. Still slight exaggeration of tendon reflexes. —*New hypnotic suggestion. Upon waking, can lift left leg nearly as high as right, and can support himself upon the left foot alone several seconds.*

Suggestion discontinued. Improvement persists. Patient well enough again to undertake a nurse's work. For more than six months I have seen him daily, trotting actively about, bringing the patients' meals from the kitchen into the ward. There is no more tremor, and he walks well.

But stiffness and tremor gradually reappear. He enters the service of one of my colleagues, and suggestion is no longer tried.

He has been in the department for chronic diseases (St. Julian Hospital) for several months. I saw him on the 5th of April. The symptoms of insular sclerosis were well marked; tremor of the hands, stiffness of the lower limbs, considerable exaggeration of the tendon reflexes, speech very slow, monotonous and scanning, etc.

OBSERVATION VIII —*Nervous troubles in the left brachial plexus, spreading at times to the thoracic and cardiac nerves; pricking sensations, numbness, contracture, constriction, and attacks of pain.—Suggestion causes these attacks to disappear momentarily, but does not prevent their return.*

B——, a shoemaker thirty-four years old, enters the hospital on May 11, 1883.

He had intermittent fever in Senegal, and, since his return in 1875, he has had an attack of fever each season.—Eighteen months ago he had pleurisy on the right side, which kept him confined to his bed for two months and a half, and left him weak for several months after. Since then he has been feeble, and his respiration is somewhat obstructed.

On December 25, he felt as if his whole left hand had become numb, and there were pricking sensations as if he had been lying on it; these pricking sensations kept up all day. At six o'clock in the evening they extended to the shoulder, then spread from above downwards along the arm-pit to the hip. Next morning his neck was stiff, and he felt as if a weight were in the left half of the back of his neck.

These pricking sensations lasted three days, accompained with complete insensibility of the whole upper left limb and paresis. After three days the prickings disappeared, and after five or six days sensibility was totally restored.

On the following days there was continuous, slight, tremor, persisting even when the patient was at rest. This lasted until March. Then attacks began, characterized by numbness in the hand, extending up the arm and down the left side of the thorax. The fore-arm was contractured in flexion, the hand in pronation. The fingers were bent with sharp pains. Sensation of constriction and suffocation in the precordial region. These cramps lasted about five minutes and were followed by a sense of weakness. Since March he has had five attacks in all; the last one took place twelve days ago. The arm did well in the interval, save for the sensations of numbness which came five or six times a day in some part of the upper limb, hand, fore-arm or arm, and lasted from five to six minutes each time. Since the end of April he has had tremor of the upper left limb, with twitching sensations, several times a day.

He is a married man, of industrious habits, and has no alcoholic or venereal history. Naturally his constitution is good. He is anæmic. Temperature normal. We note flatness with diminished respiratory murmur, and absence of vocal fienutus on the side which is not retracted. The pleuritic effusion seems to continue in a passive condition.

Heart sounds normal; no pain on pressure of the thorax or of the brachial plexus.—Appetite good, digestion normal.—*Diagnosis: lesion of an unknown nature in the path or roots of the brachial plexus, causing dynamic irradiations.*

May 13th.—Had several sensations of numbness yesterday, one in the shoulder, the other beginning in the left breast, spreading down the arm, and into the extremities of the fingers, coming as suddenly as a flash of lightning, lasting about five minutes, and followed by tremor.—*Hypnotization* (2d degree); *suggestion. The left hand gives* 38 *by the dynamometer before suggestion and* 41 *afterwards.*

Patient has no sensations of numbness on the 13th or 14th. He has not been free from them so long since the beginning of his illness.

But during the morning of the 15th, he has two attacks, like electric shocks, in the deltoid.—*Hypnotic suggestion in the evening.*

16th.—In the morning, sensation of pinching in the deltoid; twice during the day, sensations like electric shocks in the left shoulder.—*Hypnotic suggestion in the evening. Feels nothing more until the morning of the* 18*th.* Then numbness with contracture in the left hand, lasting five minutes. Numbness occupies the entire upper limb, and the hand, and lasts until six o'clock in the evening. *At this time hypnotic suggestion drives it away.*

19th.—At four o'clock in the morning rhythmical tremor and numbness without twitchings, preceded by a sensation as of an electric shock, spreading from the breast to the hand.—Later these phenomena disappear.—*Daily suggestion.*

The patient has no more pain until the morning of the 22d. Then he is again seized with cramps and pricking sensations spreading from the fingers to the elbow, lasting five minutes.

25th.—Pricking sensations followed by heat in the left arm, then tremor in the upper limb, lasting all day, and disappearing in the evening, after suggestion.

28th.—About two o'clock in the afternoon tremor of the left arm, preceded and followed by cutting pains, the pain lasting five minutes, the tremor half an hour. *Hypnotic suggestion at six o'clock in the evening.* About seven o'clock the patient is again seized with tremor, without pain. He sleeps part of the night.

At four o'clock on the morning of the 29th, tremor. At six o'clock, sensation of numbness in hand, which he cannot close. Sensation of constriction in the deltoid region; tremor appears especially when the arm is bent; sweats localized in the arm-pit accompany the severe pains. Compression of the brachial plexus during the attacks is not painful. *Suggestion makes all these symptoms disappear.*

30th.—In the morning slight constriction in the left arm-pit, with pricking sensations in the limb, *which are driven away by suggestion in the evening.*

On the 31st, at two o'clock in the afternoon, severe pain in the hand, spreading toward the shoulder, arm-pit, and left half of the hand. It lasts several minutes, with cramps when the arms are flexed. Then comes a fainting fit which lasts from five to six minutes, followed by a sensation of weakness. *Hypnotic suggestion in the evening.*—About seven o'clock shooting pains, with tremor of the hand.

June 1st.—In the morning, painful sensation of numbness in the deltoid and arm-pit, with local sweats.—*Suggestion at eleven o'clock: all symptoms disappear ;*—but at mid-day there is a sense of constriction in the wrist, in the hand, and about the arm and deltoid, *which does not disappear until six o'clock in the evening, after hypnotic suggestion.* The patient sleeps well.

On the morning of the 2d, new sensations of constriction with slight prickings in the wrist and hand. Pressure upon the olecranon causes pain, which spreads over the entire fore-arm.—*All symptoms disappear after suggestion at eleven o'clock ;* but at mid-day new sensation of constriction with stiffness in the wrist, until six o'clock in the evening. Since hypnotization, everything has vanished. Quiet sleep until four o'clock.

3d.—The same sensation upon waking at four o'clock. Patient can neither stretch nor bend the stiff elbow. *Suggestion in the waking condition makes the stiffness disappear in three and a half minutes.*

I will not follow this observation any farther. The nervous phenomena are always suppressed by suggestion either in the waking or in the hypnotic condition, and always re-appear. For example, on the 25th of June, the patient has sensations of numbness in the entire limb from shoulder to fingers. When he wishes to take hold of anything the limb is seized with slow oscillations, until it finds a place of support. After suggestion, the sensation of numbness and the tremor have entirely disappeared.

The patient leaves the hospital on the 26th, not cured.

The influence of suggestion on the nervous symptoms, referable principally to the region of the brachial plexus, is incontestable ; but its powerlessness to prevent the return of these symptoms might make one think that the functional trouble is kept up by some organic lesion which induces new attacks.

OBSERVATION IX —*Paresis of traumatic origin in the muscles of the hand.—Immediate restoration of movement by suggestion.*

C——, twenty years old, comes to consult me on January 8th, 1887. Three months ago *he was wounded in the hand at the level of the right pisiform*. The hand immediately closed; there was a certain degree of anæsthesia in the ulnar area, which has disappeared. Since this time C—— has not been able to use this hand; *he cannot stretch out his fingers, or open and shut hand spontaneously*. Dr. Guyon, thinking it a lesion of the ulnar nerve, sent him to my colleague, Dr. Weiss, who asked me to see the patient.

We hypnotize him, he goes into the third degree of sleep. I suggest that he can open and shut his hand, and extend his fingers, and I add manipulation to the suggestion. In ten minutes I awake him. *He can open and shut his hand, extend and flex his fingers.* He goes home the same evening, in spite of my wish to have him remain a few days in order to make sure of the cure. Has this immediate effect been maintained? In any case, in case of relapse, repeated suggestion will no doubt succeed in definitely restoring the function.

OBSERVATION X.—*Chronic lead poisoning.—Paralysis of the extensors of the hand dating back more than five months.—Anæsthesia of the back of the hand.—Cure of the anæsthesia by suggestion in the waking condition.—Complete amelioration of the paralysis of the extensors after the first séance, and gradually total cure.—Happy action of suggestion upon the neuralgia and vomiting.*

J——, a house-painter, thirty-nine years old, comes to the hospital for the second time on July 23d, 1886.

For twelve years he has had *attacks of lead colic.* For more than six months he has shown symptoms of a *general saturnine intoxication, with cachexia.* I do not wish to trace his history here, and will simply relate one episode bearing upon his case.

Since November or December, 1885, he has had obstinate neuralgia accompanied with delirium at night. Since April he has had amblyopia with hemorrhagic retinitis, generalized tremor, muscular pains in the limbs, hypertrophy of the left side of the heart, with a mitral murmur, connected with an interstitial nephritis with albuminuria.

Finally, since the end of March 1886, he has had *paralysis of the extensors of the right hand,* which has persisted. He has also had *analgesia with anæsthesia in the right fore-arm at different times.* These are the symptoms which are of interest to us.

August 7th.—Condition is the same. Patient can lift right wrist and put it in the line of the axis of the fore-arm, but cannot lift it higher; *the fingers are flexed at an obtuse angle upon the metacarpus,* and cannot be straightened. This condition has persisted since we saw the patient for the first time, since May, 1886. We noted on June 5, paralysis of the extensors of the hand; the extensor muscles of the little finger and of the thumb contract to faradic electricity; but the other fingers remain motionless on the application of electricity to the common extensor, which does not react.

The patient has *hyperæsthesia of both fore-arms.* Flexors and extensors are very painful to pressure. If the borders of the ulna and radius are pressed there is also pain, and the patient cries out. *Complete anæsthesia with analgesia, limited to the dorsal face of the hand, extending to the level of the wrist, also exists.* The palm of the hand and the fingers are sensible. The fore-arm is insensible. (Anæthesia with analgesia in the right fore-arm was noticed on July 23.) *Very marked tremor in both hands.* No pricking sensation or numbness in the limb.

The singular distribution of this anæsthesia over the entire back of the hand, the fingers and the fore-arm receiving the same innervation and remaining sensible, makes us think that this anæsthesia is not organic; that it is connected neither with an affection of the nerve centres, nor with a lesion of the peripheral nerves, but that it may be simply *dynamic*, unconsciously created perhaps, by the patient's imagination, and associated by it with the paralysis of the extensors. It is the dorsal surface of the hand and wrist that the patient imagines he cannot lift; it is there that imagination localizes the motor-paralysis; it is there also that it has been able to create a sensory paralysis. The patient can flex and extend the phalanges; there is no motor-paralysis there, and sensibility also is preserved.

Starting with this idea, I try to induce the return of sensation to the back of the hand *by means of suggestion in the waking condition.* I touch the patient's hand, saying that he can feel. At the same time I test sensation by means of a pin, and at the end of three minutes I note that *the sensation is restored;* the patient feels pain from the prick very distinctly in the upper part of the back of the hand; he feels less, but still clearly in the lower half. After this *I hypnotize the patient into profound sleep,* and make the suggestion of cure.

August 9th.—*The restored sensation is maintained.*

The patient thinks that he can extend and move his fingers better. Pain still exists in the fore-arm, in the muscles, and near the border of the ulna and radius. We also note pain in the extensor muscles of the left fore-arm and along the bone.—*Suggestion.*

10th.—The patient finds that since yesterday's suggestion *he can open his hand better, that the trembling has diminished notably, and that he can write his name,* which he could not do before.

Pressure upon the muscles or bones of the fore-arm no longer causes pain; there is only slight sensibility when the elbow is flexed. He straightens his wrist much better.—I put him into somnambulism; he goes into this condition by simple occlusion of the eyes; but each time he has a sudden shock at the end of ten seconds, and wakes up. I put him into somnambulism with his eyes open, and suggest complete cure of the upper limbs. Upon waking he can execute any movements. If the arm is held in pronation and horizontally, *he straightens his wrist completely*, which he could not do so well before; he cannot yet extend the fingers completely.

22d.—This result is maintained. There is restoration of sensibility; straightening of the wrist, complete disappearance of pains, and the thumb does well. *The fingers cannot yet be completely extended upon the metacarpus.*

I make a fourth suggestion.—The patient leaves the hospital.

He returns on November 7. For a week he has had convulsive attacks with amnesia lasting two hours. *He complains of frequent neuralgia in the frontal and occipital regions.* For a week he has also had attacks of vomiting, insomnia, agitation, buzzing in the ears, vertigo, etc.

But the improvement brought about by suggestion has lasted and even increased. *The patient bends and extends the wrists, and extends his fingers completely over the metacarpus.* The dynamometer registers 15 for the right hand, and 27 for the left. *Sensation is normal in the hand.*

Hypnotic suggestion also succeeded in a marked way in improving the patient's other symptoms. After three or four séances, we succeeded by suggestion *in maintaining the induced sleep for an indefinite time*, without shocks and spontaneous awakening. *The intense neuralgia and heaviness in the head were quickly calmed at each séance, and definitely cured in ten days. The vomiting also disappeared after two or three séances*, and the patient again slept at night. His intelligence, which was clouded by the neuralgia, and his memory, were reawakened, and the patient kept up well until the end of November. Then pulmonary gangrene slowly grafted itself upon the broncho-pneumonia, in the course of the interstitial nephritis, and was followed by death on the 24th of December.

This observation shows that even in chronic and incurable affections, suggestive therapeutics are not useless. Here is a case of saturnine paralysis of the extensors which yields to suggestion. Doubtless it should not be concluded from this fact that all saturnine paralyses are amenable to suggestion; we have tried it in other cases without any result. Where the radial nerve has undergone complete degeneration, suggestion can do nothing.

But the nerve may be partially affected, and certain fibres may be respected; or regeneration of the nerve may have occurred without its function being restored; dynamically, it remains compromised. Suggestion, acting in a dynamogenic manner, incites the nerve to arouse its muscular contraction.

Other functional troubles, such as cephalalgia, vertigo, insomnia, and the intellectual weakness resulting from them, were happily amended in our patient through suggestion.

II

Hysterical Affections

OBSERVATION XI —*Hystero-epilepsy in a young man.—Sensitivo-sensorial hemianæsthesia, remarkable restoration of the visual functions obtained by the use of magnetism, through hypnotic suggestion.—Has the magnet only a suggestive virtue?*

On February 28, 1883, Dr. Spillmann presented a patient suffering from hystero-epilepsy to the Society of Medicine. He was a young man, eighteen years of age, with seventeen brothers and sisters, none of whom had ever shown any symptom of nervous disease. The mother had a neuropathic taint.

As a child, the patient showed symptoms of somnambulism, getting up in the night and going to walk in the village. Three years ago L—— contracted syphilis and had syphilides on the scalp, skin, mucous membranes, etc. He entered the House of Refuge on November 4, 1882. He is below the average in intelligence, and can scarcely read or write. The penis is inflamed and large, and presents two deep ulcerations as large as a silver quarter, on the prepuce. Very pronounced congenital phimosis. From the orifice of the prepuce exudes purulent, yellowish, fetid matter. Mercurial treatment.

One month after admission L—— was seized, without any known cause, with an attack of unconsciousness, convulsions, and delirium followed by muscular relaxation and coma, and ushered in with grinding of the teeth and cries. The attacks recurred almost daily. Mercurial inunctions and iodide of potassium produced no effect. Examination of patient shows that the case is one of hystero-epilepsy. The attacks begin with a sensation like that of a ball, which, leaving the extremity of the penis, mounts into the left inguinal region and passes by the posterior surface of the trunk, following the crest of the ilium to the vertebral column, along which it rises as far as the sixth dorsal vertebra. Then comes a sensation of heat with vertigo, and the patient loses consciousness.

Patient presents a number of disorders of sensibility. There is complete anæsthesia, involving the skin and muscular system of the right side, and hyperæsthesia of the left side. The sensibility of the olfactory mucous membrane is dull on the right side. Smell is abolished on this side, and the sense of taste is diminished. Hearing is less acute than normal. The eyes were examined by M. Stœber on December 27. The left eye distinguishes four fingers held hardly a metre away, though the patient is unable to count them. The right eye perceives the hand distinctly three metres away. The left eye has no perception of form or of color.

Both visual fields are restricted. For the left eye the perimeter registers 30° externally, in the horizontal meridian, and 20° internally, in the horizontal meridian, and 40° above and below the fixing point in the vertical meridian. On the right side the limitation is less. Opthalmoscopic examination reveals left neuro-retinitis, cloudy papilla, and dilated veins.

Between the shoulder-blades, at the height of the fifth and sixth dorsal vertebræ, the patient presents a surface as big as two silver dollars, which is insensible to touch and to the prick of a pin. Moderate and prolonged pressure on this surface immediately brings on an attack. (Hysterogenic zones.)

January 22d.—Prepuce cut, and enormous accumulations of fetid sebaceous matter removed with thermo-cautery. From the time of this operation until the 28th of February, the day on which Dr. Spillmann presented the case to the Society of Medicine, L—— has had no spontaneous crises, and those which are induced by pressure on the hysterogenic zones are of short duration.

Patient hypnotized several times and easily put into somnambulism.

Dr. Charpentier examined the patient's eyes on the 27th of February. He found the acuteness of vision normal on the right side, and reduced to one third on the left. (Optometer of Badal.)

Field of vision normal on right side, restricted on left, and, after examination with Landolt's perimeter, reduced to 47° internally in horizontal meridian, and 40° externally, 35° above fixing point in vertical meridian, and 30° below (the field then had enlarged subsequent to the examination made by Dr. Stœber, on December 27).

Visual field for colors also restricted on the left side. Blue only perceived 10° externally, and 5° internally. Green recognized 12° externally, and 11° internally. Red 18° internally, and 15° externally.

Dr. Charpentier afterwards determined the degree of sensibility to colors, finding out by means of a special apparatus the least intensity a color might have in order to be recognized by the eye under examination.

The following are the results obtained :

Perception of yellow, normal on right side, $\frac{8}{100}$ on left.

Perception of green, normal on right, $\frac{5}{100}$ on left.
Perception of blue, normal on right, $\frac{4}{100}$ on left.
Sensibility to light reduced to $\frac{8}{100}$ on left side.

Examination with the opthalmoscope shows the presence of the neuro-retinitis already mentioned.

These different phenomena having been noted, Dr. Charpentier experimented with regard to the therapeutic influence of *application of the magnet*. He made the patient hold one end of a temporary magnet connected with a Planté element, and asked him to apply the projecting extremity of the bundle of soft iron wires near the external angle of the left palpebral fissure.

He left the patient under the influence of the magnetic action for fifteen minutes, at the end of which time he again examined the visual functions.

The acuteness of vision was normal on the right side. *On the left side it was equal to the right side*, that is, it was normal.

The field of vision was appreciably increased in size on the left side. It measured 55° internally, and 42° externally, 40° in the superior vertical meridian, 42° in the inferior vertical meridian. On the right side it had remained normal. (See chart of February 27.)

The visual field for colors was also increased. Blue was recognized at 20° externally and internally. Green, 21° internally, and 18° externally. Red 20° internally, and 21° externally. The most noticeable increase was for blue, for which color the visual field was almost tripled in extent.

Acuteness of vision for colors was normal on the right side. On the left it had become $\frac{32}{100}$ for red, $\frac{44}{100}$ for yellow, $\frac{25}{100}$ for green, and $\frac{21}{100}$ for blue. *The perception of the colors green and blue had thus become five times better than it was before the magnetic application, and the acuteness for red had quadrupled; while for yellow it had been increased two and a half times.*

To sum up:—*The interrupted magnetic application acted in a very remarkable manner on all the visual functions.*

These results were communicated to the Society of Medicine at Nancy.

The amblyopia which was diminished on February 21, after the application of the magnet, reappeared a few days later in consequence of a new excision of the growths on the fore-skin. On March 10 the acuteness of vision of the left eye was reduced to $\frac{1}{8}$. The acuteness for colors determined by Dr. Charpentier's method, was $\frac{7}{100}$ for red, $\frac{25}{100}$ for yellow $\frac{16}{100}$ for green, and $\frac{14}{100}$ for blue. The visual field was very much restricted, extending only from 12° to 15° in the various meridians.

Opthalmoscopic examination showed no change in the neuro-retiniits of the left eye. Right papilla slightly obscured, and the veins enlarged. The patient was submitted to the magnetic application for a quarter of an hour. At the end of this time the following changes were noted.

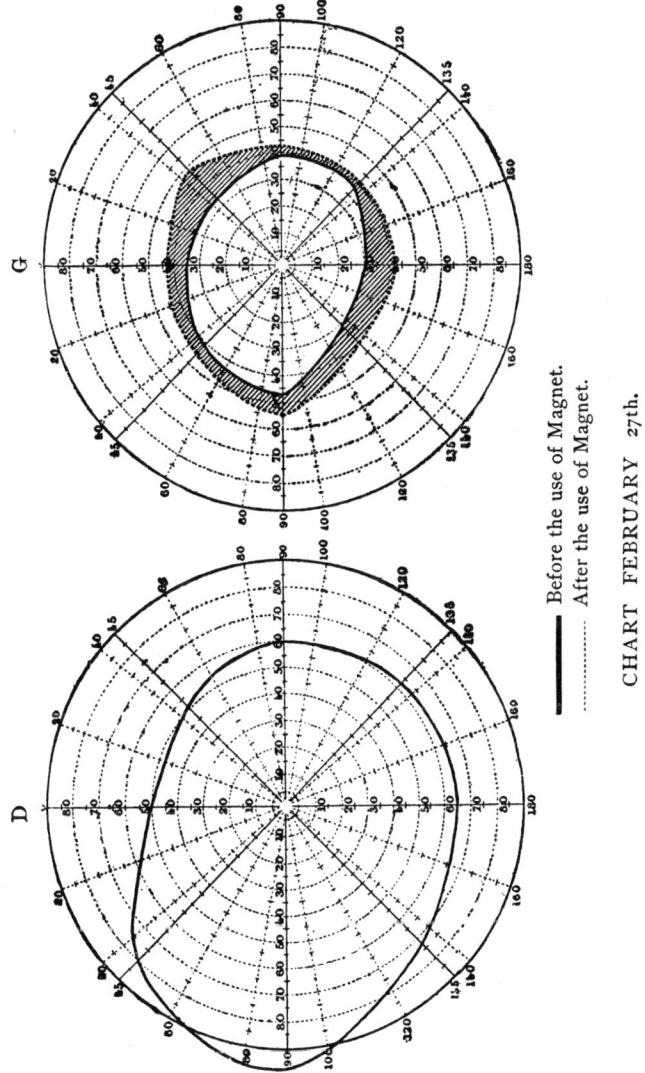

First, acuteness of vision had again become normal on the left side. Second, acuteness of vision for colors, normal for green, and varying from $\frac{36}{100}$ to $\frac{48}{100}$ for the three other primary colors. Thirdly, the visual field was increased in size to 38° internally and 32° externally in the horizontal meridian. The field was increased in all the meridians from 20° to 25°. Fourth, condition of fundus oculi same as before.

Dr. Bernheim, who was present, desired to see whether *hypnotic suggestion* would increase the benefit already obtained.

He hypnotized the patient and suggested that his field of vision would increase in all directions. *After waking, the visual field was found to extend 42° internally, and 40° externally in the horizontal meridian.* The visual field was extended on an average from 8° to 10° in each meridian. (See chart of March 10.)

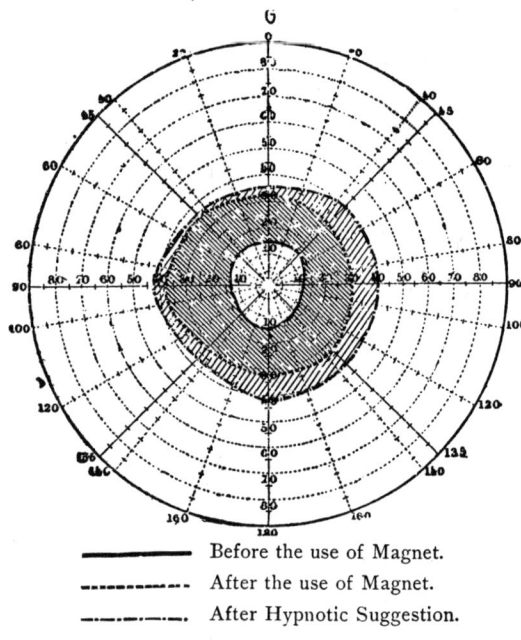

———————— Before the use of Magnet.
—————— After the use of Magnet.
—·—·—·— After Hypnotic Suggestion.

CHART OF MARCH 10th.

On the 12th of March, two days later, another examination was made. The improvement in the acuteness of vision and in the visual field still continued. The perception of colors was still feeble: red, $\frac{40}{100}$, yellow $\frac{18}{100}$, green $\frac{25}{100}$, blue $\frac{25}{100}$. Dr. Bernheim *hypnotized the patient* and suggested a further improvement during sleep.

On awaking, the acuteness of vision was normal, *and the visual field had increased from 2° to 10° in every direction. Color perception had become normal for green*, it had increased to $\frac{84}{100}$ for red, and to $\frac{88}{100}$ for yellow. For blue it was still very feeble. The application of the magnet was afterwards tried for thirty-three minutes, and it was noted, at the end of this time, that there was *a new enlargement of the visual field as well as a considerable improvement in the perception of colors*. The visual field had increased from 5° to 12° in every meridian (see chart of March 12); the perception for green and blue was normal, for yellow it had increased to $\frac{60}{100}$, and for red to $\frac{70}{100}$.

The patient returned three days later, on March 15. The improvement which had been obtained still existed, even in the perception of colors, which was at this time only slightly diminished for red and blue. Dr. Charpentier *hypnotized the patient*, and noticed when he waked up that *the visual field had increased still more in extent*, the increase being from 5° to 20° in the various meridians. The perception for colors had

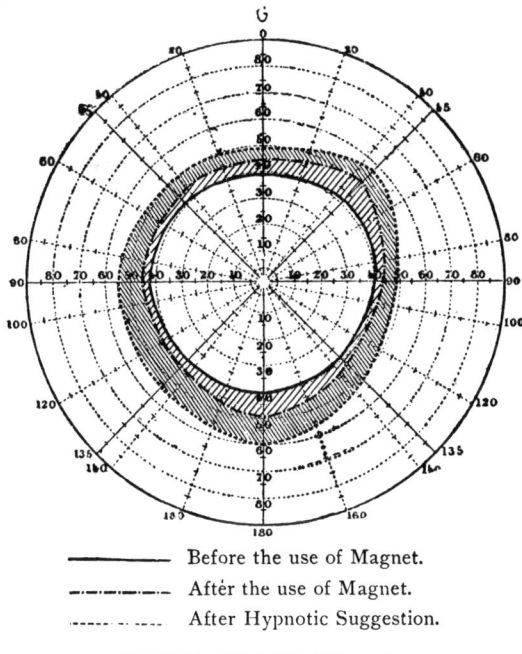

——————— Before the use of Magnet.
—·—·—·—·— After the use of Magnet.
·········· After Hypnotic Suggestion.

CHART OF MARCH 12th.

not been modified. The application of the magnet to the left temple for thirty minutes, produced *a new extension of the limits of the visual field*, the increase being 16° externally, and 6° internally in the horizontal meridian, so that the field had become almost normal, except in the external and inferior external regions. Color perception was normal. It is a curious fact that the right visual field, which had been considered normal since it extended to 95° externally and 60° internally, had shared in the improvement of the left eye. It measured 65° internally, and 110° externally in the horizontal meridian and 100° in the superior and inferior vertical meridians. These are extraordinarily wide limits. (See chart of March 15.)

Two days later, March 17, the patient still possessed this enormous visual field on the right side. On the left side the acuteness of vision and color perception were perfectly normal, excepting for red and blue. The visual field had not decreased since the last séance.

At this time it occurred to Drs. Bernheim and Charpentier to try the effect of *unconscious suggestion accompanied by the pretended application of the magnet*. The pole was applied as before to the left temple, but no current was passed through it. The magnet was left in place thirty-five minutes, and at the end of this time the visual field of the left eye had acquired the same extent as that of the right eye, an extent greater than that usually given as normal. It had increased $7°$ internally, and $25°$ externally in the horizontal meridian, and $20°$ in the superior and inferior vertical meridians. Color perception was normal (see chart of March 17).

Thus the pretended use of the magnet had acted upon the acuteness of perception of the visual apparatus with the same efficacy as the real magnet and hypnotic suggestion.

We see from this interesting experiment how closely suggestion is associated with many therapeutic methods, unknown to the patient and often to the physician himself. It is an element which we must take into consideration before pronouncing upon the value of certain therapeutic agents.

OBSERVATION XII —*Hysteria.—Varying sensitivo-sensorial anæsthesia.—Transient disappearance of the symptoms or transfer brought about by suggestion in the waking and sleeping conditions.—Unsuccessful use of suggestion for the permanent disappearance of the symptoms.*

L——, a servant, seventeen years of age, entered the hospital on March 27, 1883. On Good Friday she dislocated her shoulder, and the dislocation was reduced. The next day she had a nervous crisis, and since then she has been subject to such attacks.

She is fairly strong, and quite intelligent. She complains of pain in her left arm, in the anterior part of the thorax on the left side, in the back on the same side, and along the dorsal spinous processes. Anæsthesia of upper left limb.

28th.—*Hypnotic suggestion (somnambulism) restores sensibility of limb.* Passes a good night.

29th.—Shoulder still painful. *The anæsthesia which has returned to the limb is again removed by suggestion. The pain persists; it resists a second hypnotization.*

Evening.—Complete right sensitivo-sensorial hemianæsthesia, with loss of muscular sense. Pain in fore-arm and left hand. *Hypnotization causes the pain to disappear.* Anæsthesia persists. *A second hypnotization causes the hemianæsthesia to disappear.* Only the pain in the shoulder persists.

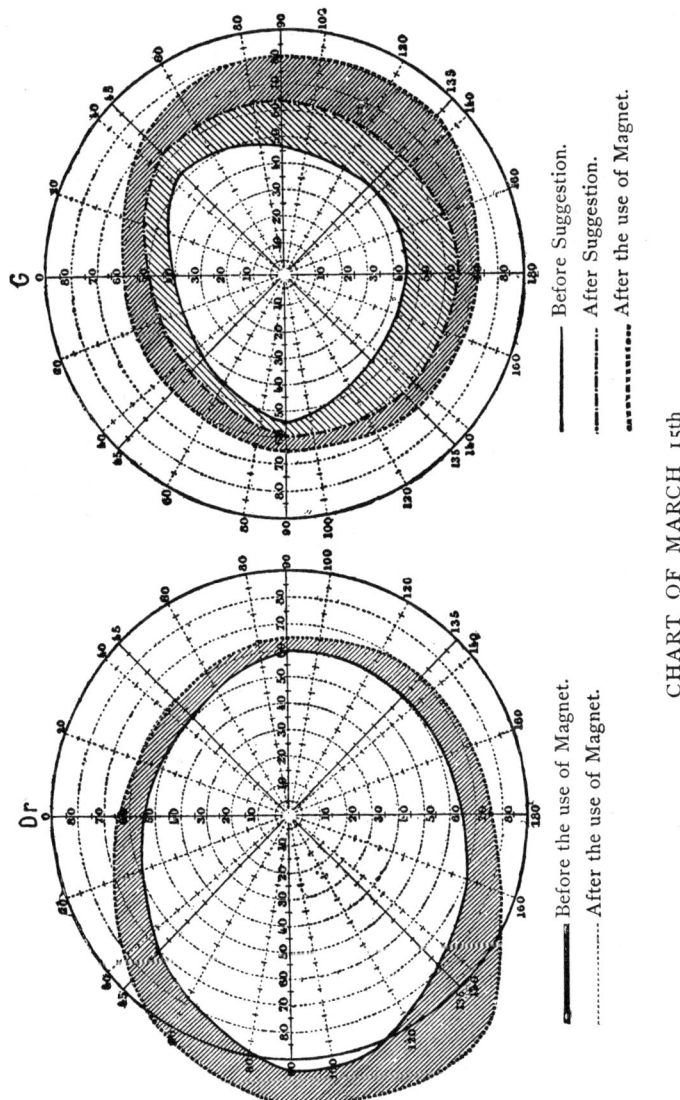

CHART OF MARCH 15th

30th.—Sensibility normal on right side, left hand and fore-arm anæsthetic. Acuteness of hearing diminished on same side. Loss of olfactory and gustatory sense. Diminution in sight (acuteness of vision reduced to one-third). Sensibility of lower limbs normal. Simple suggestion with application of diachylon plaster to left hand produces no change. *Hypnotic suggestion re-establishes sensibility on left side, but at the same time a transfer (not suggested) is observed to have taken place.* There is complete right sensitivo-sensorial hemianæsthesia. After another suggestion, the right side, with the exception of the fore-arm, becomes sensible.

At half-past five in the evening we note the following points. On the right side, anæsthesia of face, upper limb, thorax and back, to the level of the tenth dorsal vertebra; sensorial anæsthesia, and tenderness of the lower limbs and abdomen. On the left side, anæsthesia of face and upper limb. Shoulder and breast painful. Tenderness over abdomen and lower limbs. Left eye sees indistinctly; can read at distance of 30 centimetres (acuteness of vision $\frac{1}{5}$). Anæsthesia of senses of smell and taste.

Patient has had slight paroxysm, lasting eight minutes. Small bar of soft iron applied to hand and left fore-arm gives rise to no result, although applied for twenty-five minutes. A magnet is applied in its place, with suggestion (without sleep) at the end of the application. Patient complains of pain in fingers and hand. Sensibility restored in fore-arm, from middle third up. Face and special senses remain anæsthetic.

I then give *suggestion in waking condition* for return of sensibility to right side, holding the patient's right hand between both of my hands. Suddenly patient complains of sharp, cutting pain in arm. *Sensibility is restored* to right arm, down to wrist, hand remaining insensible. Thorax and neck are sensible, face continues anæsthetic. Left arm has again become anæsthetic. Anosmia persists. *Olfactory sensibility restored by touching right nostril and giving a suggestion at the same time.*

Finally, *I hypnotize patient and repeat the suggestion* for five minutes. Upon waking, *sensibility has come back in both sides*. Ticking of watch is heard at 0^m, 30 on right side, and at 0^m, 10 on left. Vision $\frac{3}{5}$ instead of $\frac{1}{5}$. Sense of smell present on both sides. Sense of taste alone requires a new hypnotization of one minute before it is restored. But the effect obtained is not lasting; the anæsthesia reappears.

Suggestion, either in waking or sleeping condition, readily restores sensibility, generally by transferring anæsthesia to other side. The experiments related above in regard to suggestion in waking condition have been frequently repeated in this case. I will not follow the case in detail. On April 14, *paralysis of extensors of left hand with anæsthesia of limb and contracture of arm disappeared rapidly through hypnotic suggestion.* But twenty minutes after waking, sudden cutting pains

HYPNOSIS AND SUGGESTION

began and the entire limb was contractured in extension. *This contracture also disappeared through hypnotic suggestion.*

But suggestion, although daily repeated, did not bring about lasting

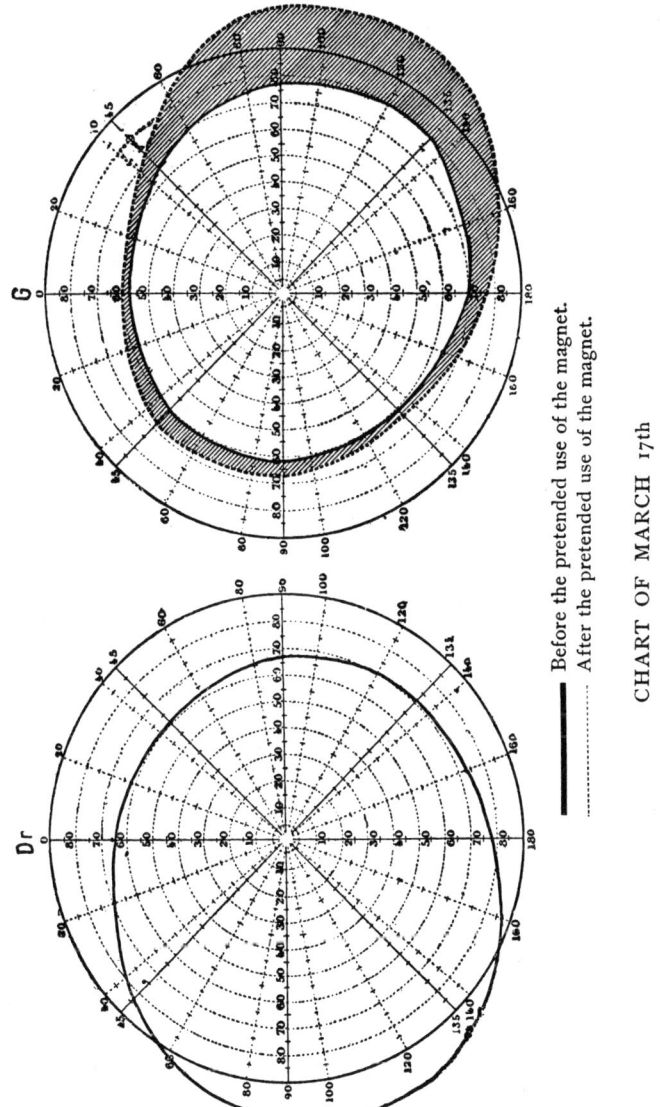

CHART OF MARCH 17th

—— Before the pretended use of the magnet.
······ After the pretended use of the magnet.

results. The anæsthesia generally reappeared as ordinary left hemianæsthesia; sometimes it was on the right side, sometimes throughout the body, and sometimes in three limbs. Hysterical attacks took place from time to time.

About the end of June the paroxysms and pains ceased; nothing remained but anæsthesia, varying in extent. The patient did well, but became intractable. She had frequent quarrels with her sister. We dismissed her on July 27.

Observation XIII —*Hemiplegia with left hemianæsthesia of hysterical character.— Restoration of sensibility by means of magnets, and rapid cure of the hemiplegia by suggestion and electricity.*

F——, forty-one years of age, married, enters the hospital on November 30, 1882.

Patient menstruated at seventeen years of age, and had her first child when she was nineteen and a half, at full term. Since then her periods have been irregular and recur too frequently.

Second child born at seven and a half months, no known cause for premature labor. During seventeen months following patient had three miscarriages, at the second, fifth, and sixth months respectively, the last one having occurred in 1870. Since then, there has been leucorrhœa and some metrorrhagia, and menstruation has occurred irregularly and at long intervals. Patient has never had any acute disease. About two months ago she passed seventeen days in the hospital in consequence of symptoms of spinal irritation and hysteriform pains. There were no hysterical paroxysms. From the time patient left hospital until November 23, she felt very well. On this day, without known or acknowledged cause, she was seized with an attack of syncope and nausea, glairy vomiting, and perspiration, and at the end of twenty minutes lost consciousness.

Patient remained in bed next day, suffering from pain in external part of shoulder and left arm. Sense of oppression, no globus. Condition same on the 24th. On the 25th, at four o'clock, she experienced a sensation of weight and pricking, spreading from left leg up to precordial region. Arms unaffected. At eleven o'clock patient complained of sense of fulness in epigastrium, involuntary weeping, and sense of constriction as high as left nipple. In addition, extremely sharp pain which patient compared to that of a knife-cut, then loss of consciousness for thirty minutes. On regaining consciousness her arm was the seat of twitching movements, accompanied with pains involving wrist, elbow, and shoulder. Pain in abdomen and pelvis. Violent palpitation for about fifteen minutes. Mobility and sensibility of arm preserved.

Examination on November 30, shows patient to be of nervous temperament, slightly pale, and anæmic. Pain in precordial region, pricking sensation in sole of left foot.

Hemiplegia with hemianæsthesia on the left side. Tactile sensibility in lower limb almost abolished. Moderately strong pressure gives rise only to slight sensation of contact. Complete analgesia of entire left side. On anterior surface of thorax sensibility is present four centimetres from median line above umbilicus. Below umbilicus, sensibility is present two centimetres left of median line. Same for neck and face. In upper limb all forms of sensibility are abolished, including muscular sense. Patient has no idea of the position of the arm and does not feel that she is lying on her left side. Arm is completely paralyzed and relaxed. When it is moved passively, the patient feels slight pain near external part of clavicle. Cornea and left conjunctiva insensible. Pituitary and buccal mucous membranes insensible as far as median line. Right ear hears watch 25 to 30 centimetres distant. Left ear, 3 to 4 centimetres distant. Smell abolished on left side. Acuteness of vision less on left side. Field of vision measured December 1, has undergone a concentric limitation, more marked on left side. The following are the dimensions on Landolt's perimeter:—

Left eye: superior meridian 15; left horizontal 20; inferior 30; right horizontal 20.

Right eye: superior meridian 40; left horizontal 35; inferior 50; right horizontal 55.

Color vision normal for both eyes.

Patient has eaten little during past four days. Heart and lungs normal.

November 30th.—A magnet is applied to left temple, negative pole applied to external angle of eye, positive pole to internal surface of arm.

December 1st.—During night, painful spot in breast disappears. Patient slept well. Motor and sensory paralyses stationary.

2d.—Same condition. Intense neuralgia yesterday evening.

3d.—Sight, hearing, and smell seem improved. Persistent pain in left shoulder. Patient complains of hunger, nausea, and salivation. Face anæsthetic except near opening of mouth and ear. Limbs continue anæsthetic, and motor paralysis persists.

The magnet has been applied to the temple for three days. The field of vision of left side has noticeably increased in size. The following are the measurements made this morning:

Left eye: superior meridian 40; left horizontal 55; inferior 55; right horizontal 45.

Right eye: superior meridian 40; left horizontal 50; inferior 55; right horizontal 52.

Thus the magnet has manifestly modified the sensorial anæsthesia. As to the *sensory anæsthesia, it has remained the same.* Hemiplegia remains complete, excepting the face.

I hypnotize the patient. She goes into somnambulism easily. Prolonged suggestion. *The suggestion of return of sensibility to the hand is the only one which is successful.* Finger movements are impossible.

At six o'clock in the evening, M. Ganzinotty, my *chef de clinique*, hypnotizes the patient by fixation. In less than a minute she is in profound sleep. At first she does not answer questions, but upon insistence she gives feeble answers. Series of suggestions made in order to provoke movements in the paralyzed arm. For quarter of an hour no result. Suddenly the patient lifts her arm, but it falls again immediately. Finally, *the fingers move, the hand is raised slowly as high as ten centimetres*, and brought toward the left side near the umbilicus. The patient complains of inability to do more. If we wish her to put her hand to her mouth, we can only make her do it by supporting her hand each time she makes the effort. Finger movements and the flexion of the fore-arm upon the arm remain possible. It is impossible to lift the arm, and the patient complains of pain in the external border of the biceps.

Upon waking, the patient is surprised to find herself in the hospital. Then memory returns, but she says she has neither heard nor said anything; she thinks she has awakened from a deep sleep.

In several minutes she moves her fingers and hand, and flexes the fore-arm upon the arm, which was an impossibility before hypnotization.

Complains of pain in shoulder and elbow, and of nausea accompanied by pain in precordial region.

M. Ganzinotty hypnotizes her a second time. *More extended and exact movements are obtained. Hand can be lifted as high as head*, but arm falls motionless if suggestion is discontinued. Some surprise upon waking. Painful sensations disappear. Heaviness in left shoulder and arm persist.

Upon waking, patient can perform all the movements which she has executed during sleep. In two consecutive hypnotic séances, partial restoration of the movements of the fingers, hand and fore-arm have been obtained.

Sensibility has not reappeared in the upper limb or elsewhere, excepting in the hand, in which it has been persistent since morning. The lower limb remains anæsthetic and paralyzed.

5th.—During the night, patient applies magnet to thigh and knee herself. In the morning, *sensibility has reappeared throughout the body.* Both eyes distinguish a watch at a distance of 25 centimetres. Very distinct gustatory and olfactory sensibility. Lifts hand and bends fore-arm; can also flex instep slightly but cannot lift foot. Pain in shoulder and left groin.

6th.—Yesterday, patient complained of burning sensation throughout body, especially low in back. Complains of nausea and bad taste in her mouth. Sensibility exists throughout, but is diminished in foot. Can bend all the phalanges, excepting the third; cannot close hand completely, can bend fore-arm, but cannot raise arm. When we lift it for her she feels pain in the humerus and in the acromio-clavicular articulation. Left toes can only be moved very slightly. Pain upon pressure of patella, tendon of triceps, fold of groin, and region of left ovary. Complains of palpitation. *Is hypnotized in the morning*, and told during sleep that she will be able to walk on the following Sunday. Upon waking, she can *lift her arm slightly*, the pain in the shoulder preventing her from lifting it higher.

In the evening, M. Ganzinotty held a séance lasting thirty-seven minutes. *Repeated suggestion* with reference to arm and shoulder. *No result.* Patient complains of nausea, and even makes efforts to vomit, which are dissipated by a single suggestion.

Suggestion is also ineffectual with regard to disappearance of pain in groin, thigh and knee. Finally, however, patient is able to flex and extend toes to a greater degree, and foot slightly.

After use of electricity, patient holds arm up for more than twenty seconds, deltoid contracts well, and pain has disappeared.

Patient is in vain assured that use of lower limbs has been equally restored, and that the pain in them has been cured. She makes useless efforts to move thighs and legs, and passive movements still cause pain. Movements of toes and foot, which were executed during sleep, are the only ones which persist.

7th.—Result gained still persists. Complains only of sensation of heaviness in upper limb, which she can move freely. Knee and groin still painful. She does not wish to be hypnotized, and says she is tired. In the evening, faradisation of nerves and muscles of lower limb for ten minutes. Patient cries out and moves. Afterwards she gets up and moves, supporting herself slightly. Complains of nausea and vertigo for two or three minutes after the séances. Vomits during the night.

8th.—Still complains of nausea and pain in epigastric region. Infra-orbital nerves painful. Electricity applied to legs and thighs, then hypnotization. *Pain in infra-orbital nerves disappears after suggestion.* Walks a little during the day with the help of a cane.

9th.—Is feeling well. Moves leg without pain. Complains of vertigo when sitting up. Has had no more nausea. Appetite begins to improve.

11th.—No more pain or nausea. Has been able to walk around the bed alone.

12th.—Can walk without a cane. Leaves on the 14th, cured. Complains of nothing but weakness in her legs. Says she has not control of her hands yet.

Returns on December 20th. Improvement continues. Both hands give 20 by the dynamometer. Complains only of not being able to control her hands.

In this case the hemianæsthesia yielded to suggestion, without transfer, and the use of the magnet and electricity were beneficial. Is this action due to a virtue inherent in the magnetic or electric agent, or is it but a psychical, suggestive action? It is difficult to answer.

OBSERVATION XIV —*Hysterical sensitivo-sensorial hemianæsthesia.—Sensibility restored after a single séance.—Increase in distinctness and range of vision.—Definite restoration.*

B——, seventeen years old, married, enters the hospital on March 18, 1883. On March 30, 1883, she was delivered of a child, at full term, which lived twenty days. The confinement was normal. Since September, she has complained of abdominal pains and leucorrhœa. For a week she has had pain in the left scapula and in the precordial region. Walking is painful. Digestion is bad, she has been constipated for a week, and has vomited several times. Her last period was on March 10th. Since the 12th, she has had frontal neuralgia, shooting pains about the temples, and rumbling sound in left ear.

Among the causes of this nervous condition must be mentioned frequent disagreement with her mother-in-law, in consequence of which she had to leave her husband's house.

19th.—We note: constitution delicate; temperament nervous; character irritable. Facial pain upon pressure on both sides. Pain upon pressure over the upper and lower left spinous fossæ. Acute sensibility of the abdomen to pressure, especially on left side, and below umbilicus.

Left sensitivo-sensorial hemianæsthesia; anæsthesia, analgesia, and abolition of muscular sense in upper and lower limbs. Tactile sensibility absent, but sensibility to pain exaggerated. Anæsthesia of the posterior part of the left side of the body up to the scapula, hyperalgesia above this point.

Ticking of watch not perceived on left side. Is heard on right side at a distance of 4 centimetres.

Senses of taste and smell wanting on left side; also nasal and lingual mucous membranes anæsthetic and analgesic.

19th.—Dr. Charpentier notes a concentric diminution of the field of vision for white light and colors, especially on left side.

HYPNOSIS AND SUGGESTION

For white light, the left eye registers the four following meridians on the perimeter: superior, 25; right, 30; inferior, 37; left, 28.

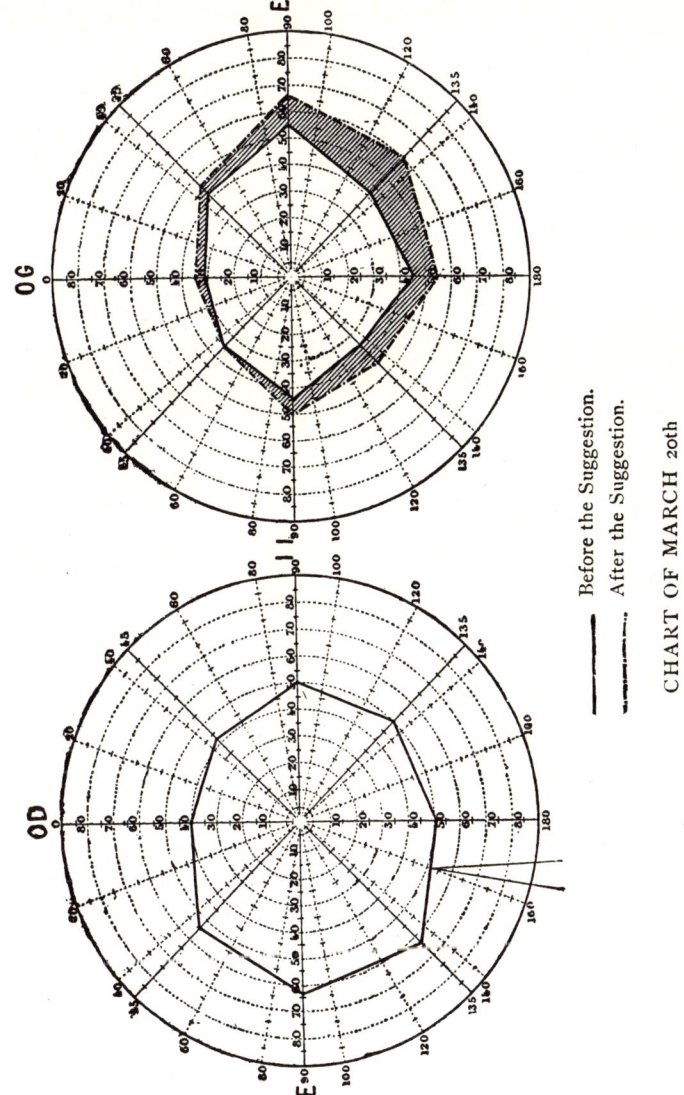

For blue the four meridians are: 18, 20, 16, 20.
For red: 25, 20, 23, 20.
For the right eye these four meridians are:
For white light: 45, 48, 55, 55.

For blue : 45, 45, 35, 45.
For red : 50, 65, 50, 50.
Acuteness of vision is 0.8 on the right side, and $\frac{1}{15}$ on the left.

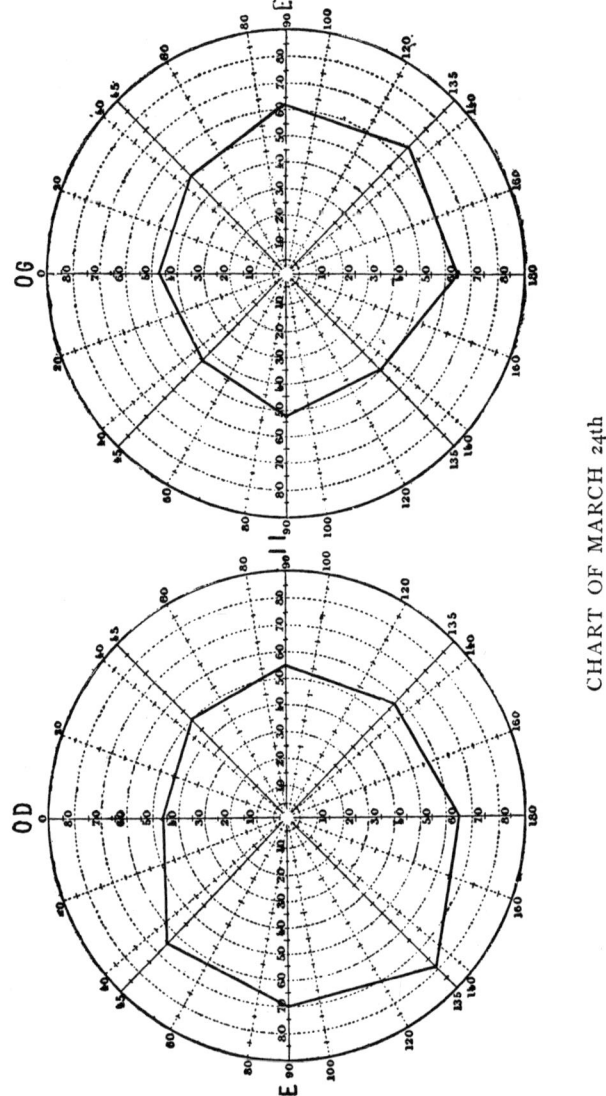

CHART OF MARCH 24th

20th.—Perimeter shows field of vision slightly increased on left side. The four meridians are : 30, 55, 45, 45. For the right they are : 40, 50, 50, 64.

For red the two horizontal right and left meridians are 50 and 35.

For blue, 50 and 40.

On the right side: for red, 40 and 60, and for blue, 45 and 60.

Acuteness of vision diminished on this day, being $\frac{1}{5}$ for both sides.

Color-perception. Left eye: Red and green (colored papers, 1 centimetre square) are distinguished at 45 centimetres; blue and yellow at about 60.—Right eye: Red and green are distinguished at 2^m, 50; blue and yellow at 2^m, 50. Normal distance of perception is about 25 centimetres.

Such is the condition of vision before suggestion.

The patient is hypnotized and goes into *somnambulism* easily. *Suggestion.* Immediately after waking, the distinctness of vision is 0.8 on the right side, and 0.6 on the left (instead of $\frac{1}{5}$ for both sides).

Color-perception, tested in the same way as before, is:

Left eye. Red and green distinguished at 3^m (instead of at 0.45); blue and yellow at 3^m, 30 (instead of at 0.60).

Right eye. Red and green are distinguished at 5^m, 30 (instead of at 2^m, 50); blue and yellow at 6^m, (instead of at 2^m, 50).

Field of vision has remained the same on right side. *It has increased on the left.* The four meridians are: 35, 65, 55, 50. (See chart of March 20.)

As for color-perception, there is only a slight enlargement of 5°.

The hemianæsthesia and pain in left spinous fossæ have disappeared. Ticking of watch perceived at 9 centimetres from left ear, and at 13 from right. *Odor of acetic acid noticed slightly* on left side. Abdominal pain is diminished.

Result continues. *New hypnotic suggestion* on evening of 21st. On the 22d, sensibility completely restored. Abdomen much less tender to pressure. Both ears hear at 18 centimetres. Odor of vinegar distinctly perceived.

24th.—After a new suggestion, field of vision is still much increased. The four meridians measure, 45, 63, 67, and 55 for the left eye; and 45, 55, 65, and 70 for the right. (See chart of March 24.)

Acuteness of vision is 1 for the right eye, and 0.8 for the left. Patient feels well, and leaves during the day.

In this case also, sensitivo-sensorial hemianæsthesia has yielded to suggestion, without transfer.

OBSERVATION XV —*Hysteriform crises with hysterical somnambulism.—Rapid cure by means of hypnotic suggestion.*

Mlle. X——, twenty-two years of age, in service at Malzéville, near Nancy, is brought to me by her mistress on April 19, 1886. The patient has had nervous attacks for three weeks, coming on regularly at about eight or nine o'clock in the evening, when she retired to her room. Sometimes she has violent convulsions lasting about an hour, then she falls asleep, and upon waking, remembers nothing that has happened. Sometimes she gets up and goes out into the street. Several people have to hold her down, to prevent her getting up.

The next day she is obliged to remain in bed, being worn out with fatigue. She has lost eleven pounds in three months. For the last three days she has eaten almost nothing.

For two years patient has shown signs of decline, and has been troubled with anorexia. Her mother is nervous and impressionable, but has never had hysteria. The girl herself has never had any sickness. She refused an offer of marriage from the valet of the house, and it is supposed that she has been annoyed by his attentions. She had an attack of hysteria the evening before she came to consult me.

She is an intelligent girl. Complains of nothing but loss of appetite. Digestion is good. No neuralgia, ovarialgia, or globus. Before the attack yesterday, she had a sensation of pressure upon the right side of the larynx, which embarrassed respiration. Her periods are regular and somewhat excessive. No leucorrhœa. Sensibility normal throughout body.

19th.—I put patient into *somnambulism* simply by closure of the eyelids. I suggest cure, disappearance of convulsions, and return of appetite; she will no longer get up at night, but will dream of sleeping quietly in her bed. Upon waking she remembers nothing.

20th.—When she left yesterday, *she felt hungry* and bought a roll on the way home. *No attack in the evening.* Ate her supper with a good appetite. I put her into somnambulism again. She tells me that she got up at ten o'clock last evening. I suggest vigorously that she will not get up any more.

21st.—Was very well yesterday. Did not get up during the night. Is now only troubled with *tremor in the arms*, which comes on about half-past eight in the evening. *Suggestion.*

Patient passed a restless night. After a quieting suggestion *she sleeps quietly.*

23d.—Patient seems to be cured. Is active and bright and has had *no more tremor.* Hypnotization for the last time. She is a good somnambulist and realizes the suggested hallucinations. She no longer gets up at night. Treatment is stopped, and the patient is to come back if the cure is not permanent.

OBSERVATION XVI —*Hysteria.—Anæsthesia.—Spinal pain.—First suggestion efficacious in restoring sensibility.—Increase of dynamometric force.— Total cure in three séances.*

E. M——, forty-two years of age, enters the hospital on November 4, 1884. She has had eleven children, seven of whom are living. Last confinement three years ago. Nursed eight of her children. She does not live with her husband on account of ill-treatment.

Pain between the shoulders and at the level of the xiphoid appendix for a month past. Also abdominal pain, with oppression, which kept her in bed for eight days. During the nights of November 1st and 2d, two weak turns with loss of consciousness. Patient cannot specify further. Loss of appetite. At eight o'clock on the evening of the 3d, violent epigastric oppression and loss of consciousness, lasting all night.

Had similar attacks at the age of 21 (hysterical). Has had them at different times since then, always as the result of emotion. Since she entered the hospital, she has only complained of prostration.

6th.—We note : Constitution delicate.—No fever. Pulse 68, regular and equal.—Intelligence clear. Heart and lungs normal.—Appetite poor. Can eat meat. Abdomen slightly distended. Constipated since day before yesterday. Abdomen tender, especially in infra-umbilical region. Abundant leucorrhœa for two years. Very acute sensibility from the 4th to the 6th dorsal spinal process.

Fingers of right hand sensible. Back of hand sensible to touch, but analgesic. Thorax, face, and lower limb on right side also analgesic, but their tactile sensibility is preserved. *On left side, general analgesia, without anæsthesia,* excepting the hand, which is sensible throughout. Muscular sense abolished. Sensibility of mucous membrane preserved.

Hypnotization. Sleep of third degree. *Suggestion. Upon waking, tactile sensibility has returned to fingers. Analgesia and spinal pain persist, but disappear almost entirely after a second hypnotic suggestion.*

7th.—Spinal and abdominal pain persist to a slight degree. They disappear entirely after a new suggestion.

8th.—Anæsthesia again present as far as middle of fore-arm, also analgesia and abolition of muscular sense. Same condition in right foot. Spinal pain has not reappeared. Slept better last night. Hypnotic suggestion. Upon waking, *tactile sensibility to pain, and muscular sense have reappeared throughout the body.*

9th.—Sensibility persists. Slept well. Appetite good.

10th.—Continues to do well. *Right hand gives 15 by dynamometer, and after hypnotic suggestion 31. Left hand gives 20 before, and 30 immediately after suggestion.*

11th.—Doing very well. *Right hand gives 36 before, and 38 after hyp-*

notization. *Left hand* 31 *before and after.* On the 14th, right hand gives 39, left 31. Patient continues to do well and asks for her discharge.

OBSERVATION XVII —*Hysteria.—Paraplegia (incomplete) with anæsthesia of the legs. —Restoration of sensibility in one séance, of power of motion in six.*

M. G——, a cigar manufacturer, twenty-one years of age, enters the clinic on October 18, 1884. Was married four years ago, but is divorced from her husband on account of ill-treatment. Typhoid fever followed by pleuro-pneumonia at twelve years of age.

Menstruation appeared at fifteen years of age, and has always been regular. No leucorrhœa. Has never been pregnant. Temperament neuropathic. Is subject to fits of passion. Frequent attacks of migraine and neuralgia. Seems slightly addicted to alcohol. Father died of consumption. Mother nervous, but not hysterical. Brother strong and healthy.

In 1879, an attack of hysteria, following a fit of anger. It lasted six hours, and was followed by general anæsthesia, and contracture of limbs and jaw lasting eight days. Was in hospital six weeks.

Another violent attack in 1881, which lasted two hours and was followed by paraplegia with anæsthesia.

On the morning of November 18, 1884, another attack without known cause. Had had neuralgia for two or three days previously. When she became conscious after the paroxysm, she had violent thirst, and her legs were rigid.

November 19th.—We note: Intelligence clear. Legs in extension. Bends feet and toes slightly; *cannot bend knees.* Can lift both legs as high as 8 centimetres only. *Anæsthesia with complete analgesia*, extending from patella to ends of toes in both legs. Reflexes feeble. Muscular sense in legs abolished. No neuralgia of ovaries.—Complains of pain in left fronto-parietal region.

Suggestion in waking condition useless. *Hypnotization. Deep sleep* with amnesia upon waking. Obeys suggestions during sleep, but does not realize post-hypnotic suggestions.

Upon waking, tactile sensibility and sensibility to pain have returned. Difficulty in bending knees at an obtuse angle still exists. Fronto-parietal pain has disappeared.

Pain comes back in afternoon, but disappears spontaneously in the evening. At one o'clock, pain in left shoulder and in supra-spinous fossa preventing patient from lifting arm above the horizontal. Cannot support herself on her legs.

10th.—Sensibility remains intact. Slept well. Pain in shoulder still exists. Can bend legs at a right angle.

Hypnotization. Rapid and profound sleep. Suggestion. Awakening slow.

After waking, pain in shoulder has completely disappeared. Can lift arm completely. Bends her legs at a right angle easily.

21st.—Condition the same. Bends legs at an acute angle, but with slight stiffness.

After suggestion, bends her legs more easily.

Second suggestion given, patient being seated in a chair. Movements are impressed upon the joints in order to aid the vocal suggestion in dissipating the rigidity. *Immediately after suggestion*, she walks well, but her legs are still somewhat stiff. *Three minutes afterward* pain and stiffness have vanished and she walks easily.

22d.—Walks well, but complains of weakness in bending her legs.—*Hypnotic suggestion.* Upon waking, feels stronger and more firm on her legs.

23d.—Weakness again in afternoon. Sensibility still intact.—*New suggestion.*

25th.—Patient feels perfectly well. No fatigue since yesterday.

26th.—Suggested a distaste for wine during sleep. No success. Has taken her portion of wine as usual. Continues to do well, and leaves the hospital on the 27th completely cured.

OBSERVATION XVIII.—*Symptoms of hysteria for two months.—Paroxysms.—Sensitivo-sensorial hemianæsthesia with dyschromatopsia.—Neuralgia and abdominal pain.—Cure of the hemianæsthesia from time of first suggestion.—Total cure in four or five days.*

Marie G——, a shoemaker, sixteen years of age, enters the hospital on July 29, 1887. Her trouble first appeared two years ago. She had syncopal attacks *preceded by dizziness, a desire to vomit, epigastric oppression and swelling and finally she lost consciousness*, without having convulsions and without crying out. She does not know how long these attacks lasted. She had four on the 25th, three on the 26th, one on the 27th, and none on the 28th. She often has a sensation of swelling without any paroxysm. Since the beginning of these attacks she has had *frontal, right temporal, and syncipital neuralgia* every morning. For the last two months *she has eaten little or nothing*, and sometimes she has had attacks of vomiting. Her digestion is, however, good. She menstruated exactly one month ago, and the last time three days ago, without pain. The evening of her entrance her temperature was 38.2°, pulse 112. The next day, temperature was 37.4° in the morning, and 37.8° in the evening. Then it became normal again.

July 29th, we note: temperament nervous. Constitution good.—

Has had no previous disease.—*Acute pain upon pressure of left side of abdomen*, not limited to region of ovaries.

Hemianæsthesia with complete right hemianalgesia limited to median line exactly. Muscular sense preserved. Olfactory, gustatory, auditory, and visual senses are intact. Dyschromatopsia is, however, noticed. Red is seen as black, blue as yellow, green as blue, and yellow as red. Same results after a second examination. *Dyschromatopsia is purely psychical.* I show her a ball of yellow wool; she calls it red. I put a prism before the dyschromatopsic eye; she sees two yellow balls. I take away the prism; she sees a single red ball. The prism has restored the ball to its true color by troubling the play of the diseased imagination. The experiment succeeds each time it is tried.

In order to show my colleague, Dr. de Smeth of Brussels, how easily the hemianæsthesia of hysterical patients may often be taken away, I hypnotize the patient. I suggest that sensibility will return throughout the body, and that she will distinguish colors correctly. I test the sensibility during sleep. I affirm that it will return. *In two minutes it is restored.* When I wake her, I state that it will persist, and that the *dyschromatopsia has disappeared.*

July 30th.—Restored sensibility and color-perception is permanent. Patient took bouillon and milk yesterday. Slept but little. Still complains of acute pain in right temporal region, and in left side of abdomen from the edge of the ribs to the pelvis. *I suggest the disappearance of the pain in the head. After waking, it has disappeared.*

July 31st.—Pain in head has not returned. Slept well. Abdominal pain persists. I suggest its disappearance.

August 1st.—Abdominal pain greatly diminished. Suggestion.

2d.—*No more abdominal pain.* Appetite good. Complains of toothache. Suggestion drives it away.

3d.—Still complains of toothache. Suggestion. Again the pain disappears.

4th.—Toothache returned in an hour. Patient wants to have tooth pulled. I hypnotize her and suggest that the pain has entirely vanished.

Pain does not return again. On August 6th, she complains of frontal headache. It is dissipated by suggestion, but reappears during the day.

7th.—After suggestion she is much better. Has no more trouble and goes home on August 14th, cured.

OBSERVATION XIX —*Symptoms of hysteria for five months, paroxysms of weeping, accompanied by convulsions.*—*Pains, lack of appetite, sadness.*—*Complete cure after two suggestions.*

Jeanne G——, twenty-seven years of age, married, enters the hospital on December 7, 1887, for the sixth time in two years. She has been here before on account of hysterical paroxysms, gastric trouble, jaundice, etc.

Two years ago she was in our service for six weeks, for anæmia, accompanied with neuropathic symptoms without paroxysms.

Her present trouble began on July 2d, with a paroxysm of weeping lasting ten minutes, brought on by the death of her daughter. Then she had symptoms like those of dysentery for two days, bloody stools with rectal tenesmus. She was weak and nervous, and lost all appetite. In August she had catarrhal jaundice, without colic. After her recovery, she went to work again. She has had sad domestic trouble.

I hypnotize her. She goes into somnambulism. I suggest that she shall be in good spirits. She laughs and sings, and when she wakes feels very well.

In the evening she complains of *dorsal and epigastric* pains, which prevent her sleeping.

December 9th.—Patient is anæmic and thin. Carotid murmur, no organic lesion. Heart and lungs normal. Sensibility normal throughout. *Sharp spinal pain upon pressure from the second to the seventh dorsal vertebra.* Sharp pain also at the *level of the 2d, 3d, and 4th intercostal spaces on left side. Epigastric pain.* Iliac fossæ not tender. Generalized sensation of cold. *Suggestion.*

10th.—Has done well since yesterday's suggestion. Slept well, has *good appetite and no pain.* Suggestion.

11th—.Continues to do well.

13th.—In consequence of some disagreement yesterday afternoon she had a crisis, about which she can give no information. Otherwise she has no more trouble, except slight weakness.

14th.—Feels stronger. Has good appetite, and does not complain of any more troubles. Remains in the service until January 1st. Since then I have seen her several times going to her work.

The manifestations of hysteria in this case yielded to suggestion rapidly.

Five or six times I have thus succeeded, by means of suggestion, in checking hysterical paroxysms at their height.

OBSERVATION XX —*Violent hysterical paroxysms dating back one year.*—*Complete cure from time of first suggestion.*

Mme. X——, twenty-six years of age, has always been well and strong, and has never had any nervous trouble. But in October, 1885, she was seized with an attack characterized by sleep which lasted ten minutes and from which it was impossible to wake her.

At the end of ten minutes she woke spontaneously. In about fifteen days she had a similar attack. They became gradually more frequent and were accompanied by nervous movements. It was noticed that she spoke in a low voice as if addressing some one, but giving both questions and answers herself. The development of these *hysterical paroxysms* coincided with great annoyance occasioned by a quarrel with an intimate friend. Between the attacks Mme. X—— showed signs of nervousness. Their occurrence bore no relation to her menstrual periods.

About July, 1886, these attacks assumed the character of *violent hysteria*. A sensation of general weight preceded them several hours, sometimes a day. Suddenly her feet became riveted to the floor, she had a sense of constriction in her wrists, and oppression in her throat, and immediately afterwards would fall asleep. This sleep generally lasted from ten to twelve minutes, and sometimes as long as an hour. Her jaws were set, but the limbs remained supple in this first phase. Soon convulsions involved the upper and then the lower limbs, being repeated at intervals of half a minute or a minute. Finally, the convulsions became general, degenerating into violent movements, with general rigidity. The body was extended in the arc of a circle. These violent convulsions lasted three or four minutes.

Finally the patient woke, worn out, and not remembering anything that had happened. One attack lasted for two hours. As a rule, the duration was from half an hour to an hour.

During the months of August and September the crises were more frequent, returning once every ten days. The last one took place on October 11th.

October 19th.—I find no psychical or organic trouble, no anæsthesia, ovarialgia, or globus.

I hypnotize her by suggestion. She goes into *profound sleep*. No muscular hyperexcitability. If lifted, the arms remain up. I suggest calmness and tranquillity of mind. I tell her she is sleeping naturally, that she is perfectly comfortable, has no preoccupation of mind, and will not have another crisis. I suggest that she will come to see me again on the 21st. After a quarter of an hour I wake her.

She comes to see me again on the 21st. She had not thought of it until one o'clock, when the idea suddenly entered her head that she would come to my consultation again. *New séance.*

23d.—Another séance. Has had no crises. Pain in the abdomen after walking. This pain has only been present since the beginning of her sickness. During her sleep I suggest the entire disappearance of all pain.

She comes on the 25th, 27th and 29th. Is *completely cured*. Can walk a long distance without pain. Has not had the least sign of a crisis.

The cure has been maintained since the first séance, that is, since October 19th.

In this case, definite cure took place after the first séance. This is not usual, as we have seen in other observations. It is often necessary to follow up the disease for several weeks, sometimes for months, in order to eradicate the symptoms and prevent the occurrence of relapses.

OBSERVATION XXI —*Hysteria, dating back fourteen months, convulsive crises, vomiting, sensitivo-sensorial hemianæsthesia, lameness caused by pain.—Cure of the anæsthesia and lameness in a few days.—Total cure in seven or eight weeks.*

Henriette W——, twenty-one years of age, enters the clinic on June 23, 1886. Her trouble began fourteen months ago, when she was in Paris, with *cramps in the stomach*. These cramps have occurred daily since, accompanied with a sensation of swelling in the epigastrium and in the left hypochondrium, with nausea, and bilious *vomiting*. They generally last from four to five o'clock in the evening, and are followed by headache, which lasts all night.

Two or three days after appearance of cramps patient was taken with *complete right hemiplegia*, anæsthesia and contracture of the leg. Electricity was used for six months. The hemiplegia gradually disappeared, but a *tongue paralysis*, with *aphonia*, and inability to swallow came on. This lasted three months.

In April, 1885, she had her *first attack of hysteria*, accompanied with violent convulsions, loss of consciousness, and sometimes with biting of the tongue. During a period of ten weeks, she had from three to six attacks a day. For eleven months, she has only had one a day as a rule. Sometimes two days pass without an attack.

Menstruation, which ceased with the beginning of the trouble, reappeared a month ago. Finally, the patient is constipated, and sometimes passes a week without having a movement.

Patient was under treatment at the Rothschild Hospital for fourteen months. A douche was given daily, and a sulphur bath every two days.

The stomach was washed out and food given through the sound for five or six months. She continued to vomit after the catheterization. She was hypnotized for some time without any result.

Condition stationary for last four months. Takes only milk and bouillon. Vomits after taking nourishment, and the vomiting is accompanied with pains in thorax and dyspnœa. Cramps every evening.

On admission we note : complete hemianæsthesia of right side, sensorial hemianæsthesia of left. Sight, hearing, taste, and smell abolished on this side. *Left amblyopia proved to be purely psychical* by means of prism and Stoeber's apparatus.

Complains of *continuous and intense sensation of constriction in right leg and foot.* Sole of foot very painful upon pressure. Patient limps badly on right leg, and only rests on the heel. Pain in right axillary border when standing. Constitution strong. No previous disease. Temperament lymphatic, with slight tendency to scrofula. Nervous heredity.

Two hysterical seizures on the 26th, one on the 27th, one on the 29th, and one on the 30th, intense and accompanied with opisthotonos and loss of consciousness. Headache, palpitation, pain upon pressure of lower part of right arm-pit, vomiting. Anæsthesia is modified spontaneously. Right thigh again sensible. Auditory anæsthesia changes to right side on July 1st. Two slight hysterical paroxysms on July 2d.

2d.—*Hypnotic suggestion.* Patient goes into *light* somnambulism. (5th degree.)

Left visual and auditory anæsthesia disappear *after suggestion.* Auditory anæsthesia reappears. Sensitive anæsthesia, headache, and vomiting persist. *Suggestion daily.*

4th.—Slight paroxysms. Has walked better since the 2d. Still limps slightly however.

5th.—Sensory and right auditory anæsthesia disappear after suggestion. Patient walks much better, and no longer complains of pain in legs. Vomiting persists. Slight attacks after waking from hypnosis.

6th.—Condition the same. Hearing almost equal on both sides. After hypnotization, patient has an uncomfortable sensation, catches her breath, and shows signs of an hysterical crisis, which is checked by means of suggestion.

7th.—Right side of face and right leg again anæsthetic. Walks well, limps but slightly. Sensibility returns after suggestion.

Slight hysterical attack on 8th and 9th. Vomiting diminished. Violent crises on 10th, 11th, 14th, 15th and 18th. Patient still walks well. Appetite good.

12th.—Only vomits her coffee in the morning. After the 20th no longer vomits anything.

More difficult to restore sleep. On the 17th and 18th she begins by sleeping for two hours during night. Sleeps the entire night on the 22d. Slight attack on 22d. Still digests without pain. No vomiting.

27th.—Crisis, accompanied with nausea. Sleeps from four to five hours during night. Period appears on the 31st, preceded by cramps in stomach. On August 1st, nausea, which yields to suggestion. On August 2d, cramps in stomach repressed by suggestion. On the 3d, slight crisis. On the 5th vomits again. On the 6th, cramps, which resist suggestion, and transient insomnia. Vomiting continues on the 7th and 8th, accompanied with pains in epigastrium and thorax, which resist suggestion. On the 9th, these pains disappear. Complains of neuralgia on the following days, and the vomiting diminishes.

Finally, on the 20th, slight attack, characterized by convulsive tremor. Still find *right hemianæsthesia and cephalalgia*. All disappears after suggestion.

No more crises after this. Patient vomits no longer, and walks without limping. Anæsthesia does not reappear. Complains only of slight gastric disturbance, the result of dilatation of the stomach.

On September 13th, she is taken with typhoid fever, contracted in the hospital. It develops regularly, without any nervous symptoms. Defervescence is reached on October 1st. Convalescence perfect. Patient leaves hospital on October 14, 1886. Had a relapse about November 13th, preceded by diarrhœa with anorexia, but without symptoms of hysteria. Since December 30th the patient has done well. Comes to consult me from time to time for troubles connected with a chronic stomach catarrh, the result of the hysteria. But the hysteria is definitely cured, or at least it is no longer manifested.

To sum up: The phenomena of anæsthesia yielded to suggestion in four or five days, the pain in sole of foot in three days. The other manifestations, vomiting, insomnia, hysterical crises, resisted for a longer period. Total cure by means of suggestion took place in from seven to eight weeks.

OBSERVATION XXII —*Hysteria dating back fourteen months.—Convulsive paroxysms, vomiting, pain, vertigo, and insomnia.—Cured in thirty-five days, by means of suggestion.*

R——, (Emilie), a servant-girl, twenty-one years of age, enters the hospital on December 7, 1886. Symptoms of hysteria appeared in July, 1885, when she was convalescing from typhoid fever. Since then she has had frequent attacks of vertigo, insomnia, headache, and digestive disturbances.

In December, 1885, she had her first attack of hysteria, which was accompanied with suffocation, strangulation, loss of consciousness, and convulsions. These attacks have been frequent since. The last one occurred two months ago.

She went to Prof. Kussmaul's clinic, in Strassbourg, in April, 1886, and remained until June. During this period she had hysterical paroxysms, and attacks of vomiting which could not be checked. For four weeks she could retain no nourishment. After that she was able to take milk, but no solid food. Faradism was tried for eight weeks. For four weeks the stomach was washed out and nourishment given through the sound. Patient continued to vomit food thus introduced. Hypnotism was tried five or six times without success. When she left Strasbourg, she had improved so far as only to vomit her evening meal.

Since June, only two paroxysms. Other symptoms still present. We note: continuous left dorsal, infra-clavicular and left supra-spinous pain. Insomnia almost constant since the typhoid fever. No ovarian neuralgia, or strangulation. Constitution strong. No previous disease. Nature impressionable.

7th.—Hypnotization. Patient does not concentrate her attention, says she cannot sleep, and laughs. I persist, and she soon goes into profound sleep, with loss of memory upon waking, but is not susceptible to hallucination. I suggest disappearance of pains, vomiting, and other symptoms. Upon waking, all have disappeared, but the sub-clavicular pain reappears during the evening. The first suggestions do not have any effect upon the insomnia, vomiting and anorexia. The pains reappear each time after an interval of several hours.

Pains gradually disappear. On the 9th, after a third séance, patient only complains of slight pain in dorsal region.

After fourth séance, sleeps an hour during night. Still vomits all food, excepting dried bread. Complains also of pain in stomach. Sometimes resists suggestion, and seems to have but little confidence.

During the nights of the 11th and 12th, patient taken with colic and diarrhœa. On the 14th, ate an egg, without vomiting afterwards. Slept pretty well on the 13th and 14th. Continues to menstruate without much pain.

16th.—Diarrhœa reappears, without colic. Has not vomited since the 14th, and is sleeping better.

From the 15th to the 28th, complains of palpitation. Had several attacks of vomiting. Insomnia reappears. After the 28th, these symptoms disappear. From time to time she has palpitation and headache.

Hypnotic séances discontinued from December 30th to January 7th. On January 2d and 3d, two hysterical paroxysms, in consequence of a quarrel. Also begins to vomit again.

Suggestion continued from January 7th. Since the 10th, patient has not vomited any more, has no more headache, sleeps well, and continues to improve.

Leaves hospital on the 12th. On the 21st, I saw her again. She had begun work again, and was feeling very well.

The duration of the suggestive treatment up to the time of complete cure was thirty-five days.

Patient came to see me again in May, having had severe pain in region of right hypochondrium for a week, which prevented her sleeping and eating. I took it away by suggestion in three minutes.

Since then she has been well and has kept on working.

OBSERVATION XXIII.—*Hysteria dating back seven or eight months;—convulsive attacks, vomiting, insomnia.—Cure after the first séance.—Relapse at the end of three weeks; crises, sensitivo-sensorial hemianæsthesia, pains.—Symptoms resist suggestion. —Cure in three weeks.*

Eliza S——, eighteen years of age, comes to consult me on December 22d, 1886, for crises of hysteria. Has had leucorrhœa since her eleventh year. Menstruated when fifteen. Was regular at first, but for the past year the periods have occurred every fifteen days, have been abundant, and have lasted from six to eight days. When she was eleven years old, she had attacks of vomiting, lasting nine months, which could not be checked. They disappeared spontaneously. Has cramps in the stomach, occurring as a rule twice a week. Mother died of some affection of the liver. Father is a hot-headed, impressionable man. Brother is very nervous.

Mother died on 17th of last May. When Eliza heard of her death, she had a nervous paroxysm, accompanied with weeping and loss of consciousness. Since then she has had one or two every week, and for the last four weeks they have been still more frequent. The attacks are preceded by sensation of foreign body in epigastrium rising into throat, with burning sensation, constriction in upper thoracic region and at the same time a tickling sensation in nose. Then in a few seconds, she falls unconscious, weeps, and has severe convulsions. When she becomes conscious again, she remembers nothing. The slightest vexation brings on the paroxysms. Since the 22d, patient has vomited everything, even water. Insomnia has been present since the first attack.

Constitution good. Temperament lymphatic. No organic trouble. Sensibility normal. No abdominal pain.

Hypnotization. Profound sleep. Has had no crises since first séance and has slept well. Vomiting ceased after special suggestion given on the 27th.

Patient comes to see me again on March 24th. Has had three relapses, brought about by vexation. Had no trouble in interval between attacks.

Attack came on yesterday evening without premonitory symptoms. *New hypnotic suggestion.*

Patient is well for three weeks. Then the attacks appear again.

She enters the hospital on May 17, 1887. We note: complete left sensitivo-sensorial hemianæsthesia. Almost complete left amblyopia. Colors, however, are perceived. A finger held before eye, recognized as a shadow. A pencil is not recognized. Amblyopia proved to be *purely psychical*.

Hypnotic suggestion on the 17th. Hemianæsthesia, excepting of ear and eye, for which I give no suggestion, disappears. Taste and smell restored on left side.

19th.—Condition the same. Sensibility restored, except to eye and ear. Patient complains of pain in synciput, at base of sternum. Hysterical crises on 17th, 18th, and 19th, in spite of daily suggestion. No crisis on 20th, on account of vigorous suggestion. Pains still exist. Restored sensibility is maintained. Left eye distinguishes nothing, not even color. Left ear hears at a distance of from 4 to 5 centimetres.

21st.—*Vision on left side restored by suggestion.*

Severe crises during nights of 22d and 23d.

Sensibility maintained. Vision good. Neuralgia has vanished. Suggestion.

24th.—Has had no crisis. Is feeling well. Sensibility is restored excepting to left ear, which does not perceive ticking of watch when held close to it. *After suggestion*, hears at distance of four centimetres.

25th.—No more pains or paroxysms. After suggestion, hears ticking of watch at distance of twelve centimetres.

On the 26th and 27th, crises during the night, for which no cause is found. Patient still feels well. Sensibility is maintained. Only complains of abdominal pain, which is acute upon pressure.

June 5th.—Complains of headache. Another violent crisis in the evening.

Has been doing well since, but complains of continuous abdominal pain.

8th.—Abdominal pain has partially disappeared in consequence of suggestion.

10th.—Complains of pain below left breast. I stop hypnotizing her, and pass by her bed saying simply, "You are doing well, you are cured." She has no more crises, no longer complains, remains in hospital about ten days longer, and then leaves in good health.

To sum up: A first series of hysterical manifestations dating back six or seven months, yielded at the first suggestion.

A second series, constituting a relapse, was more tenacious. The hemianæsthesia yielded readily after two or three suggestions. The paroxysms and pains resisted for three weeks.

In suggestive therapeutics it is important that suggestion should be varied and modified according to individuality. Its efficacy varies according to the subject and circumstances. As shown in some of the foregoing observations, the impression produced by the first suggestion is sometimes profound enough to overcome the symptoms. More frequently they reappear, to yield only after repeated suggestions.

In certain subjects it also happens that the suggestion wears away. Hysterical patients seem to delight in their nervous condition in spite of suffering, and do not allow themselves to be impressed by suggestion after a time. This more or less voluntary resistance is sometimes caused by a patient's surroundings. Other people laugh at them, make fun of "magnetism," say that it only affects simple-minded people, and can do no good.

The experienced physician takes exact account of the situation. He regains his control over the patient.

When it is found that nothing further can be gained from the use of suggestion, and that the patient continues to exhibit or complain of new symptoms daily, it is often well to leave it off, especially in cases of hysteria. In such cases it only helps to direct the patient's attention upon himself and indirectly invokes auto-suggestion.

OBSERVATION XXIV —*Hysteria dating back six weeks.—Convulsive paroxysms.— Left sensitivo-sensorial hemianæthesia.—Vomiting.—Pains.—Immediate effects of suggestion.—Reappearance of symptoms.—Cure in six or eight weeks.—Relapse in eight months.—Cure in three weeks by suggestion.*

G—— (Marie), sixteen years of age, enters the hospital on June 17th. Four years ago she was treated for nervous symptoms, especially abdominal pain.

For the last six weeks she has been subject to crises of hysteria. She complains of pain near the right axillary border, spreading toward the epigastrium and recurring frequently. Also frequent pain in right side.

Patient well-developed and moderately intelligent. Temperament lymphatic. Painful spot on forehead. Pain at emergence of supra and infra orbital nerves on left side. Acute sensibility on pressure over abdomen. Upon epigastric pressure, respiration becomes panting, face becomes congested, patient turns over on stomach, her eyes open wildly, in about twenty seconds the arms become rigid, and a paroxysm is imminent. If the pressure be stopped, the attack is checked.

Acute pain in lower part of left thigh extending below patella.

Complete left sensitivo-sensorial hemianæsthesia with hemianalgesia and abolition of the muscular sense.

Retinal vision exists. Purely psychical amblyopia.

Choreiform movements in hands for six weeks.

Other functions normal. We discover *dilatation of stomach*.

No treatment until July 2d. All symptoms still present. Hysterical paroxysm on 19th. Sharp epigastric pain, often preventing sleep. Paroxysms again on 25th, 26th, and 27th. Vomits all nourishment after 21st. Leaves hospital on 28th, but returns on July 1st, condition remaining the same. Daily paroxysms.

2d.—Slight paroxysm. *Light somnambulism* (5th degree). *Suggestion. Vision restored.* Other symptoms still persist.

4th.—Suggestion. Left eye reads letters 2 millimetres high at a distance of 9 centimetres. Same condition for right eye. Left ear hears at 5 centimetres, right at 7. Sensory anæsthesia disappeared yesterday, after suggestion, but is present again to-day. Epigastric sensibility diminished.

Slight paroxysm this morning. Neuralgia has disappeared. Patient sees distinctly with both eyes, and hears at a distance of from 4 to 5 centimetres on both sides. Suggestion. Return of sensibility.

Hears at 9 centimetres on right side, and 11 on left. Paroxysm on July 7th.

9th.—We note. Contracture in extension of lower left limb dating from preceding day. Similar contracture in hand disappeared this morning, spontaneously. We try to resolve contracture by suggestion. Patient resists, and only a partial result is obtained at first trial. After second hypnotization and vigorous suggestion, flexion, and relaxation of limb is obtained, simultaneously with disappearance of hemianæsthesia.

10th.—Severe paroxysm yesterday. Abdominal pains. To-day complains especially of headache, pain in sternum, and near right axillary border. Anæsthesia of upper left limb only.

By means of suggestion return of sensibility is obtained, first in hand, then in fore-arm, and finally in arm. Headaches and pains disappear after suggestion.

12th.—Two successive paroxysms yesterday after a visit from her mother. Hemianæsthesia has reappeared, excepting in trunk and back.

Contracture in extension of lower limb. Pain in head and epigastrium. After hypnotic suggestion, and passive motion of limbs, contracture disappears. Pains also disappear, and sensibility is restored.

Hysterical crisis on 14th. Two on 15th, and one on 17th. Restored sensibility maintained. Frequent epigastric pain.

No new paroxysms up to August 3d. Doing well. Hemianæsthesia definitely cured. Pain in head and thorax remains. It yields to suggestion, but reappears easily. Digestive disturbances connected with dilatation of stomach.

On July 29th and 30th, new contracture of leg, which yields to suggestion each time.

August 3d.—Severe convulsive paroxysm, lasting half an hour.

Since then, no more crises; and is doing well. Remains in hospital until the end of September, and complains of nothing but slight digestive disturbances. Occasional return of hemianæsthesia, which always yields to suggestion.

Goes out as servant and does her work well.

The cure, which is almost complete, has taken eight weeks.

Patient returns to hospital on April 28, 1887. Fifteen days ago she was seized with a convulsive hysterical paroxysm lasting an hour. Upon regaining consciousness she remembered nothing about it. Fatigue, buzzing in ears, and loss of sensibility of left side afterward. Deafness in left ear, and left eye sees less distinctly. Dull frontal pain, abdominal pain, and frequent cramps in stomach, without nausea or vomiting, have been present ever since. Complains also of sensation of heat in head, profuse perspiration, and frequent palpitation.

Menses, which had been absent for five months, reappeared profusely on the day of her entrance.

May 2d.—Acute pain upon pressure of epigastrium and of right side of abdomen. Frontal and syncipital neuralgia. Left sensitivo-sensorial hemianæsthesia, ear absolutely deaf, eye distinguishes color.

Hemianæsthesia instantly removed by suggestion. We purposely allow the olfactory and gustatory anæsthesias to remain. Paroxysm in the evening.

3d.—Doing well, sensibility maintained. Complains of pain only in lower part of abdomen on right side.

11th.—Doing well, no more crises. Cramps and headache have ceased. Sensory anæsthesia has reappeared. Eye and ear retain sensibility, gustatory and olfactory senses absent. *Suggestion. Hemianæsthesia disappears.*

21st.—Doing well. No paroxysms. Sensibility maintained. Digestion somewhat feeble. Pain low down in abdomen, which disappears after suggestion, to return in a few hours.

25th.—Pain disappears entirely. Patient remains ten days longer without manifesting any symptoms.

Thus, this relapse, or second series of hysterical symptoms yielded to suggestion in three weeks. There were no new crises after two days of suggestion.

OBSERVATION XXV —*Reappearance of hysteria eight months ago in consequence of a miscarriage, with pelvic peritonitis.—Sensitivo-sensorial hemianæsthesia, pain, globus, palpitation.—Transient effect of suggestion at first.—Complete cure in twelve days.*

Catherine V——, twenty-two years of age, enters the hospital on March 12, 1887, having been under Dr. Spillmann's treatment for four months.

Menses appeared at the age of eighteen. On this occasion she was seized with complete paraplegia, for which she was sent to Paris. Treatment of rubbing, electricity, and application of magnets for eight months. Paraplegia lasted a year and disappeared suddenly and spontaneously, but she continued to drag left leg.

Patient has complained of palpitation for two years. Coughs and expectorates a little, but has had no hæmoptysis.

Eight months ago, she had a miscarriage at six months and a half, in consequence of a fall. Abundant leucorrhœa, containing clots, with abdominal pain and vomiting for two months. Treated for pelvic peritonitis with blisters and actual cautery. Severe paroxysms of hysteria.

Peritonitis finally cured. Menses reappeared, but less abundantly, and always late.

Entered Dr. Spillmann's service for bronchitis and severe pain in left leg. Treatment, electricity and cold pack.

March 14th.—We note: Temperament lymphatic and nervous. Constitution debilitated. Temperature 37.2°. Pulse 120, and regular. Respiration 46—somewhat panting. No râles. Apex beat normal. Action of heart regular, but becomes tumultuous if patient walks. No murmur.

Slight tremor in fingers. Complains of pain in temples, often of sensation of suffocation. Slightest vexation causes globus hystericus.

Hemianæsthesia of left side of face, left upper limb, excepting hand, and of entire lower limb. Chest, back, and abdomen still sensible on left side. Acute pain in left supra-umbilical region. Left sensorial anæsthesia. Eyes cannot read and do not distinguish colors. Sense of vertigo and obnubilation. *Amblyopia and dyschromatopsia purely psychical.*

14th.—Patient put into somnambulism easily. Sensory hemianæsthesia is removed, but reappears next day. Is feeling better. Has no more palpitation when resting, and breathing has improved.

16th.—Same distribution of sensory and sensorial anæsthesia. Pain upon pressure of pit of epigastrium, in left supra-umbilical region, and above right groin. Continuation of suggestion.

17th.—Intense supra-orbital headache in the night. It is taken away and sensibility is restored by suggestion. Vision is also restored.

18th.—Is doing well. Anæsthesia and amblyopia have reappeared. Dyschromatopsia has definitely yielded. Colors are correctly perceived, excepting black, which is called gray. Suggestion.

19th.—Complains of nothing. Eats and sleeps well. Pain upon pressure very slight. Can read with left eye.

22d.—Restored sensibility has been maintained since yesterday. Reads more distinctly with left eye. Firm pressure upon abdomen no longer painful. Slight sensibility in back of right leg. Palpitation upon walking only.

23d.—Is doing well. Complete restoration of sensibility, excepting for the auditory, gustatory, and olfactory senses.

24th.—No feeling in right leg all night. This morning, complete right hemianæsthesia with hemianalgesia. Muscular sense still exists. Sensorial sensibility not modified.

25th.—Same condition. Sensibility restored by suggestion.

26th.—Restoration maintained excepting in right side of face. Left ear hears watch at three and a-half centimetres. Suggestion restored sensibility to face.

In evening, chill followed by pain in left side. Morning of 27th, temperature 39.8°. Evening, 40°. Pulse 128. Morning of 28th, temperature 38.4°. Pulse 124.

Cough and expectoration. Respiratory murmur diminished over lower three spaces on left side of chest. Pain in side disappears on 28th. In evening, temperature 39°. Pulse 128. Morning of 29th, temperature 28°. Pulse 108. Evening, temperature 38.8°. Pulse 116. Morning of 30th, temperature 37°. Defervesence of pneumonia.

Evenings of 30th and 31st, temperature rises to 38.6°, then becomes normal again both morning and evening. No nervous symptoms during this period. Restored sensibility is maintained.

April 2d.—Watch heard at four centimetres, on right side. Daily suggestion to improve hearing. On the 5th, hears at sixteen centimetres. On the 18th, at eighteen centimetres. Smell and taste also restored by suggestion.

Patient continues to feel very well. No more pain. Slight palpitation upon walking, still. Remains until May 14th, and goes home cured.

The almost total cure by suggestion was obtained in about twelve days.

OBSERVATION XXVI —*Hysteria since the age of twelve in a young man of twenty-one.* —*Transient cure by hypnotic suggestion, with isolation.*

On January 30, 1887, my colleague, Dr. Herrgott, asked me to look at a case of hysteria in a young man aged twenty-one, dating back to his twelfth year. He was strong and well-made, and there seemed to be no nervous history.

Trouble has been aggravated since the last of December. Continual discomfort, weeping, groaning, and sensation of constriction in throat. Severe paroxysms, beginning with intense constriction, almost strangulation. Oppression and suffocation becomes excessive, face is congested and swollen, general tremor without convulsions or contracture, sharp distressing cries. This condition lasts several hours. Afterward great fatigue, relieved by profound sleep.

During whole period of discomfort patient is powerless to work physically or intellectually, can neither read nor write, cannot fix attention on anything, and sometimes does not answer questions for several minutes. Takes him several minutes to rise from his seat. He cannot grasp an object. When walking, he sometimes has to stop for ten minutes being powerless to take a step further. Has no fear, and is not subject to hallucinations. Often irritable without cause. The more his family try to soothe him, the more nervous he becomes.

In this condition he is very impressionable. A sad story or a slight accident excites him, makes his heart palpitate, and gives rise to a sense of strangulation.

Functions normal. No trouble with sensibility, no pain, no globus. Digestion good. Cannot eat during severe crises on account of feeling of strangulation. Very intelligent. Understands his condition.

The following is the account of the progress of his trouble which he gave me after he was cured.

"My trouble began at Rocroy, when I was twelve years old, without any cause. I suffered from severe torment of mind, gloomy ideas, and slight fatigue, but I was not incapacitated for work.

"During the scholastic year 1878–1879 I worked at home. The mental distress was less frequent, but attending one lecture was enough to arouse it.

"In 1879–1880, I was at college in Reims. My trouble became very violent, and for the first time I had attacks of weeping, sometimes lasting two hours. Nevertheless I could study.

"In 1880–1881 the disease assumed an intermittent form, periods of calm alternating with periods of agitation, each of about three months' duration. I lost memory completely during the periods of agitation, so that study became impossible. I had beside a sensation of weight and dulness in my fingers. No crises as yet however.

"In July, when I was studying well, I had my first paroxysm, but it was not as severe as the following ones were.

"In June, 1883, I was well enough to continue my college course, but was refused a degree because of the interruptions forced upon me by my disease.

"In August the paroxysms became violent again. I was under hydropathic treatment at Benfeld. I improved, and the paroxysms ceased, but gave place to an inertia of body and mind which made it impossible for me to occupy or distract myself in any way.

"I improved after leaving the establishment, and kept up my studies until June.

"In January, 1885, I left college for good, and spent the whole spring in the country. In June I entered the army at Amiens, and for the first time had complete relief, and enjoyed bodily exercise. This lasted four months. I was away on sick-leave, then went to the military hospital, and finally in February, 1886, received my discharge and went home.

"I was very miserable all the spring, but became much better in the summer. Toward the end of December, however, I had continual discomfort, and violent paroxysms which kept on into January, 1887."

It was at this period that I was called in to see the patient.

Hypnotization. Patient goes into 2d degree easily. Feels calm and rested for ten minutes after suggestion. Daily suggestion, Improvement. Paroxysms cease. Suggestion has transient effect only. Patient is irritated by his surroundings, and is easily agitated.

He is removed to hospital and isolated, is free to walk about where he chooses, but forbidden to go home. Has had no paroxysms since admission. Heaviness in fingers, and general discomfort gradually disappears. Can occupy himself, but cannot yet take up his work again.

Well enough to go home in April. Comes to be hypnotized daily.

In May, discomfort, heaviness in fingers, and confusion of thought again. Suggestion instantly drives away these symptoms. Violent paroxysms about the middle of the month. He returns to the hospital for three months.

Daily hypnotization—3d degree. I let him sleep half an hour, suggesting calm and cure.

Three days after his entrance, all his troubles disappeared. He has not had the slightest return of any trouble. "During the entire month of June," he says, "I occupied myself as I pleased. Toward the end of July I could even do sustained intellectual work, which was impossible before, even at my best times."

At the present time,—Oct. 20th,—the patient is feeling better than he ever felt before.

Will the cure be lasting? With the aid of suggestion I hope and think it will.

OBSERVATION XXVII —*Hysterical aphonia dating back two months.—Rapid cure by hypnotic suggestion.*

Mme. C. L——, thirty years of age, has been hysterical for twelve years. She often has attacks of hysterical sleep, lasting from half an hour to two hours. Rarely convulsive attacks. Strangulation, globus, left ovarialgia and hemianæsthesia, are all, however, present. She is an intelligent woman, of lymphatic temperament. Various methods of treatment, bromide, hydrotherapy, etc., have been tried without great success.

She comes to see me about the last of June, 1887. Her voice is completely gone, but there is neither pain nor spasm. Left sensory hemianæsthesia. General health good. Attacks of hysterical sleep frequent.

I try to make her speak, in vain. Electricity is used without effect. I try to hypnotize her, but she is agitated and has spasms, and I give up the attempt fearing a paroxysm. The following day I hypnotize her into profound sleep, with loss of memory upon waking. Discomfort during sleep, sensation of epigastric and thoracic weight. She passes from hypnotic into hysterical sleep, and wakes spontaneously in about half an hour.

Hypnotization again on the third day. Somnambulism. I calm her by suggestion, and the crisis of the day before is not repeated. Hemianæsthesia disappears after suggestion, but aphonia is still present.

Hypnotization easy for the fourth time. I try to suggest cheerfulness. I make her hear music. She keeps time with gestures, and the anxious state of mind is driven away. Profiting by this experience I say, "You know you will be entirely cured in a few days. Your voice is coming back. You know on what day you will be cured and will speak. On what day?"—She replies, "In a week."—"Very well," I say, "it is understood then, next Thursday when you wake from the hypnosis you will be able to speak."—Upon waking she does not remember what has occurred.

Daily hypnotization. Perfect somnambulism. Post-hypnotic hallucinations are realized. At each séance I make her repeat that she will be able to speak next Thursday.

Thursday arrives. I try in vain to make her speak before the séance. She complains of laryngeal constriction. She thinks it is growing worse. Hypnotization. She says she will speak when she wakes.

Upon waking, sharp laryngeal pain. Fearing a paroxysm, I put her to sleep again, and suggest the disappearance of the pain, and that she will speak without any difficulty. Upon waking she says in a feeble voice, "I think I can speak again." I make her articulate her name in a loud voice. She tries, hardly daring to venture, as a person who has lain in bed a long time hardly ventures to walk upon first getting up. But her voice has returned clear and distinct, and the aphonia does not reappear.

I try the same method in order to cure her hysterical paroxysms. I hypnotize her daily, and suggest that she will soon be free from these attacks, making her fix upon a certain day. She tells me that after her return home, and after her menstrual period, the crises will disappear. I suggest that she will dream of this three successive nights, which she does.

The patient goes home. The paroxysms continue for about fifteen days, and then disappear almost entirely. This is what she writes in January, 1886: "I have been sick with pleurisy for two months. I have had paroxysms only very rarely, even when suffering most. For the last six weeks I have again lost my voice, and nothing seems to help me. It came on when I was convalescing, in consequence of throat-spasm which prevented swallowing. I have been treated with electricity for fifteen days, and if I am not benefited soon, will come to Nancy to see you, if you think it wise."

OBSERVATION XXVIII —*Aphonia in a nervous woman, dating back eight days.— Immediate cure by hypnotic suggestion.*

Mme. O——, who is fifty-five years old, is generally well. She says that every winter she has *hoarseness which lasts six weeks*. At the present time, January 23, 1887, she has had *severe hoarseness for eight days*, without any cough or expectoration; she has an enlarged gland over the right ear and pain on the right side of the neck. This has lasted from fifteen days to three weeks.

Mme. O—— has never had real nervous crises; but pretty often, every six weeks or at least every two months, she has what she calls *nervous spasms*, accompanied with pain in the chest, *the sensation of a foreign body rising into her throat, suffocation*, and uneasiness in her limbs, but never loss of consciousness. This lasts sometimes three or four hours. She has eight children who are all nervous. One daughter is subject to crises of hysteria; she is very easily hypnotized into deep sleep, and I have twice succeeded in hypnotizing her during a crisis and in dissipating the attack, without her remembering when she woke that I had been there.

One of her little boys has had nervous crises resembling syncope, which I have driven away by hypnotic suggestion. He was also susceptible of being put into deep sleep.

I therefore thought the mother was susceptible to suggestion, and that her *aphonia* was either of nervous origin, or at least aggravated and kept up by the nervous diathesis.

I hypnotize her; in a few seconds she is in *somnambulism*. I *suggest* the total disappearance of the aphonia; I make her talk in a loud voice. In a few minutes I wake her. To her great astonishment *her voice has come back*. She has remained cured of her aphonia.

III

Neuropathic Affections

Observation XXIX —*Hysteriform symptoms.—Sensation of emptiness in the head and buzzing in the ear.—Moral inertia.—Rapid and almost total disappearance of these symptoms by hypnotic suggestion.*

S. N——, a clerk in Paris, twenty-one years of age, came to consult me on April 12, 1886.

His trouble began, he said, on January 2. He was in Paris, feeling rather sad and weary at having left the place which he held three weeks since. At half-past nine in the evening he had a sensation of chilliness in his chest and in his head, over the left eye, which lasted five minutes. He had gone to bed, but he got up and spent the night in his arm-chair, shivering and trembling. The next day he kept his room, and purged himself; in five or six days his discomfort had nearly ceased. About the 8th of January, in the night, he had a violent paroxysm of convulsions, unconsciousness, delirium, and agitation. The doctor was with him five hours. The seizure lasted until six o'clock in the morning (hysterical seizure).

In a few days he was well again; but a new paroxysm occurred eight days after the preceding one, lasting from three to four hours. He returned to his family in Chatenois (Vosges); then consulted a physician in Nancy, who prescribed baths; the second bath brought on an attack of syncope which lasted a quarter of an hour. Since then he has had no more paroxysms, but about the beginning of February he was troubled with nervousness at night, which lasted for three weeks. It was impossible for him to remain in bed; he was obliged to get up every night, being unable to sleep. At this time he felt a sensation of weight in his head, succeeded by attacks which lasted a quarter of an hour, and recurred five or six times a day. This sensation of weight disappeared in about fifteen days, and gave place to a sensation of emptiness in the head, which has persisted. Since this time, too, he has complained of continual buzzing in his right ear. He has also had buzzing in his left ear, but it disappeared after a few days. Finally, during the last six weeks he has frequently had a sensation of constriction in his throat which has been very intense and almost continuous for fifteen days, preventing him from eating.

He is a young man of strong constitution, although of lymphatic temperament. He is naturally sad and morose. We have not discovered anything important in his family history. At my consultation on April 12 he complained of two principal phenomena : of a constant sensation of emptiness in the head, localized especially in both temporal regions, and of persistent buzzing in the right ear. For two months he has not read or written anything. He feels incapable of working, has no taste for anything, and does not care to walk. He sits with his head resting on his hands, and is always complaining. He fears that his mind may be deranged. This fixed idea has got possession of him. He is sad and demoralized. His appetite, however, is good, and he sleeps well.

I put him into somnambulism with singular ease, simply by stating that he is going to sleep. I suggest the disappearance of the sensation of emptiness in his head and the buzzing in his ear, and I tell him that he will be bright and gay. *Upon waking, his head feels better*, but the sensation of emptiness is still there to a slight degree. *The buzzing has ceased.*

13th.—The patient says that his head felt a little better yesterday evening, but the sensation of emptiness has returned. The buzzing, which ceased for several hours, has re-appeared, but is less intense. He says that his eyes are tired immediately, if he reads even a little. His acuteness of vision, however, is normal. *I put him into somnambulism three consecutive times*, and each time repeat the suggestion that all the morbid phenomena have disappeared. The first two times we saw him try to evoke these sensations in his head with his hands when he woke : "There, there, the emptiness is always there ; the buzzing is continual." It was only at the third suggestion that he admitted upon waking *that the buzzing had disappeared, and that his head was heavier, that is to say, less empty.*

14th.—Yesterday he had almost no buzzing in his ear, and the sensation of emptiness in his head was not so marked. In the evening he was quite bright for a few moments, admitting that he felt well. Since this morning he has again complained of the sensation of emptiness in his head and of slight buzzing, as well as of sore throat. Upon waking, after vigorous and repeated suggestion, he feels nothing more.

15th.—The buzzing in his ear which disappeared yesterday, only reappeared this morning at eight o'clock very slightly. The sense of emptiness in his head is much less. His parent, who is with him, told me that he was really better but that he hesitated in admitting it, and that he was always looking for something new. In a fresh trial, I suggest brightness and confidence. *Upon waking he confesses that he is doing well.*

16th.—The buzzing in his ear has not reappeared. He complains of a slight sense of emptiness in his head. He is brighter and walks about with more satisfaction than before. *Suggestion.*

17th.—The improvement has continued: *the buzzing in the ear has disappeared definitely; the sense of emptiness is very slight. He feels more confident, more sure of himself.*—His expression is more serene. The patient has gone back to Chatenois. He wrote me on April 21st that he was doing well, and that after Easter he would see if it was necessary to come to consult me. He has not come.

OBSERVATION XXX —*Nervous aphonia of one month's standing.*—*Cure by simple affirmation.*

M. B——, a servant girl sixteen years old, enters my clinic on March 3, 1885. She is small, delicate, and of lymphatic temperament. For twenty-five days she has had a cough, without expectoration. During the last ten days she has had pains in her side, and for fifteen days has had no appetite; she has been hoarse for a month; there has been complete aphonia during the past three weeks. She has had amenorrhœa for six months. We find in front, diminished pulmonary resonance about the fourth intercostal space on the right side, and subcrepitant rales near the anterior extremity of the third; behind, slightly diminished pulmonary resonance on the right side, extending from the infrascapular region to the base, slightly roughened expiration at both apices, with fine subcrepitant rales. No fever. *Diagnosis: pulmonary tuberculosis of gradual development.*

On the 7th the condition is the same; the aphonia persists and is complete. There is no cough and no expectoration, and as the patient has no dysphagia or laryngeal pain, spontaneous or provoked, or fever, and the tuberculosis is stationary, I ask myself if the aphonia may not be nervous. I tell my students that nervous aphonia sometimes yields instantly to electricity, which acts by means of its simple suggestive influence. I send for the battery. Before using it I wish to try *simple suggestion in the waking condition, affirmation.* I say to the patient, "I am going to give you back your voice;" and while I lay my hand upon the larynx and move it up and down I add, "Now you can speak aloud. Say *A.*" She says it in a low voice (aphonic). I insist, in a loud voice, "You can speak. Say *A, A.*" She says in a clear voice "*A*" then "*B.*" "Now say Marie." She says "Marie," and continues to speak very distinctly. It was indeed nervous aphonia, and *she was cured simply by affirmation.*

I then say to my students, "This patient being so easily influenced by simple affirmation, ought to be easy to hypnotize." In fact I simply close her eyes and say, "You are asleep." She is in profound sleep; her arms remain in suggestive catalepsy; suggestive anæsthesia is complete. She is susceptible to hallucinations during her sleep, but post-hypnotic suggestions do not succeed. The aphonia is definitely cured.

The insomnia of which she complained also disappeared by suggestion in two days. On the tenth the patient complains of neuralgia. *Induced sleep and suggestion in the morning.* The neuralgia gradually disappears in the afternoon.

The patient leaves the hospital on May 26th; she speaks well, sleeps well, and no longer complains of anything. The lack of appetite alone has resisted suggestion up to the present time.

OBSERVATION XXXI —*Epilepsy: tremor of the hands, insomnia, and repeated attacks of headache, cured by suggestion.—Increase of dynamometric force.*

Alphonse L—— is a weaver forty years old. He has epilepsy. He comes to the hospital on October 21, 1884. There is no direct hereditary history. Between the sixth and thirteenth year he had glandular abscesses in the sub-maxillary region. When he was eight years old he had his first attack, without any aura. Four years afterward, if his memory is correct, which is always doubtful in cases of epilepsy, he had the second, preceded by a burning sensation which went through his head, by a blow upon the head, epigastric weight, fear, and alternate flexion and extension of the thumb. He was pretty well, except for slight attacks, until he was twenty years old. Since then the attacks have been more frequent. Four years ago he broke his arm by falling. His wife says that he sometimes has three or four attacks a week. For the last twelve years he has gone two or more months without having an attack. For the last seventeen days he has had three attacks a day, after having passed eight days without one. The week preceding his admission to the hospital, he had three attacks. He often has besides three or four attacks during the day, with intervening coma. He has sometimes bitten his tongue, but has never urinated involuntarily. On the 18th, at eight o'clock in the evening he had an attack, and had two during the next day, the 19th, and one in the evening; the next day he felt too weak to go to work. Each attack is followed by tremor, which lasts for several days. Further, for the past two years he has had convulsive shocks nearly every night. Before or after the attacks, sometimes after an interval of eight days, he often has wanderings and transient hallucinations.

We find that his intelligence is somewhat dull, his temperament lymphatic, and his constitution delicate. There is slight tremor in both hands which has existed since the 18th. The right hand gives 22 by the dynamometer, the left 37.

23d.—Tremor still continues. He says that his upper limbs were rigid during the day.

24th.—Condition same. Neuralgia. Hypnotization; light somnambulism. *Suggestion. Upon waking the neuralgia has disappeared.* The next night the patient *sleeps well, which he has not done for eight days. The tremor has also disappeared.*

On the 26th, *a new suggestion;* the patient still feels better; the tremor, which was very decided before the first séance, has not reappeared; and the patient sleeps well.

On the 31st, *the right hand gives* 30 *by the dynamometer, and* 47 *after a hypnotic suggestion. The left hand gives* 27 *before and* 37 *afterward.*

On the 1st of November, *the right hand gives* 40 *before, and* 51 *afterward; the left still gives* 37.

On the 2d the patient is still doing well. He has had no paroxysms and no tremor. The right hand gives 37 before, and 43 afterward; the left hand 39 and 46. The patient stays until November 9th. He no longer complains of anything and asks for his discharge.

We have to do here simply with nervous troubles consecutive to epileptic seizures: neuralgia, tremor and muscular weakness, which hypnotic suggestion has benefitted.

OBSERVATION XXXII—*Nervous gastric trouble, epigastric pain, anæsthesia of the limbs.—Rapid disappearance of the anæsthesia by suggestion; transient amelioration of the gastric trouble.*

F. C—— is a single woman forty-nine years old. She has no children. She enters the hospital on April 29, 1884. She has been sick for three months. The trouble began with severe pains in the epigastrium and in the hypochondriac region. After eating she has a sensation of supra-umbilical and laryngeal constriction which lasts about an hour, as well as eructations and very frequent vomiting. Moreover when she has not eaten she also feels a burning epigastric sensation; she has no watery regurgitations. Habitual constipation; passage only once in three days. For three months she has had frequent nervous attacks, especially after a fit of anger. These attacks are accompanied with tingling in her fingers lasting about two minutes and followed by weeping. She has had vertigo for two years. She is neuropathic.

The vomiting ceased after her entrance to the hospital, but the other symptoms continued. We only find slight swelling with epigastric tenderness; the stomach is not dilated, the liver is not enlarged.

On the 7th of May we find beside this, *analgesia with anæsthesia of the trunk and upper limbs; the muscular sense is abolished.* In the lower limbs sensibility only exists in the sole of the foot.

The patient is hypnotized (profound sleep): suggestion. During the day *she digests what she eats well, and has the epigastric burning sensation but slightly. During the night she sleeps for six hours;* she says she has not slept as much for six months.

On the 8th we find that the *anæsthesia has disappeared;* the patient feels when we touch her, but the prick of a pin although felt is not painful; the muscular sense has also reappeared.

The restoration of sensibility is maintained.

The other gastric and psychical troubles are favorably influenced by repeated suggestions, but they generally reappear after a variable period.

OBSERVATION XXXIII —*Neuropathic pains suppressed by suggestion.—Distaste for meat resisting simple suggestion and only disappearing after fictitious change of personality.—Failure of moral suggestion.*

M——, seventeen years old, enters the hospital on March 25, 1884. For three weeks she has complained of pains in her limbs and of palpitation; for eight days of frontal neuralgia and vertigo; for fifteen days of a cough without expectoration.

Menstruation is irregular, slight, not painful.

She is a stout girl, has a strong constitution and has had no previous maladies. At the present time she complains of anorexia, of pain in her stomach, even when fasting, of regurgitation of glairy fluid, and of a sensation as of a foreign body in her throat after eating. No eructations, no nausea, no colic.

For two months she has had frequent palpitation. Nothing abnormal is found on examination of her heart. She coughs and expectorates a little. We find respiration normal upon examination of the thorax.

For eight days she has had frontal neuralgia, recurring twice a day and lasting five minutes each time. This pain does not prevent her from sleeping. She left her family two months ago in consequence of domestic trouble. She has frequent attacks of weeping.

She has never had hysterical paroxysms. The sensation of strangulation is only present after she has eaten. No ovarialgia. The right hand gives 26 by the dynamometer, the left hand 24.

Anæsthesia with analgesia and abolition of the muscular sense in the upper left limb; sensibility is present near the head of the humerus;

elsewhere it is perfect. For fifteen days there has been a sensation of tingling in the hand. The sense organs perform their functions normally. *Diagnosis: neuropathy.*

A piece of gold applied to the arm makes the sensibility reappear, without transfer, in three minutes; and since then this restored sensibility has been maintained.

On the 27th she complains of pains in her shoulders, and pressure evokes very great sensitiveness in the two supra-spinous fossæ and at the level of the second dorsal spinal process. *Hypnotic suggestion;* the patient goes into *somnambulism* easily. *Upon waking the pains disappear completely* and we can press upon the region which was hyperæsthetic without the patient showing the least reaction. The pain reappears in the afternoon and again *yields to hypnotic suggestion in the evening.*

It does not appear again until the 28th, at six o'clock in the evening, preventing the patient from sleeping.

Hypnotic suggestion makes it disappear; the patient has a good appetite. At eight o'clock in the evening the pain returns to the right shoulder. Further, she is taken with palpitation with tingling in her hands. She only sleeps an hour during the night.

On the morning of the 30th she vomits her coffee. We find that the right supra-spinous fossa is sensitive to pressure. At ten o'clock the patient complains of pain and tingling in her hands. *Hypnotic suggestion.* During her sleep I make the patient walk and work; I have found that active somnambulism, when it is possible to induce it, works a beneficial diverson, and often acts more efficaciously than passive somnambulism in suppressing nervous discomfort. *Upon waking she does not complain of anything.*

During the day she still has *tingling in her hands, which yields to hypnotic suggestion.*

After the first of April the patient no longer complains of any discomfort or nervous trouble.

Hypnotic suggestion rapidly suppresses any pain which appears.

In May we find a papular and eczematous syphilitic eruption. Treatment by mercurial applications. This eruption disappears.

We keep her in the hospital for some time, because she is an excellent somnambulist. During her sleep we make her work; she goes and comes, sweeps the ward, goes to the kitchen to get irons, and irons old linen according to the suggestions given, doing everything with her eyes shut. She will work thus for an hour without remembering anything about it when she wakes.

Sometimes, however, the suggestion has to be modified in order to take hold of her imagination. For some time she has had a dislike for meat and absolutely refuses to eat it. I have in vain given her decided suggestions every day that she likes meat and that she will gladly eat some. She promises me to eat some when she wakes. She does not eat any however. It is an unconquerable repugnance. One day after hypnotizing her, I tried the following subterfuge. " What is your name ? "—" M. M."—" But no, you are not M. M. You are Josephine D., her aunt ! You are her aunt ! " In an instant or two she says, "That is true, I am Josephine D." And now I say, " There is your niece, M. M. Give her a lecture ! She does not want to eat meat, thinking it is bad. Show her how we eat it. Tell her how good it is ! " And she puts herself in her aunt's place, gives her fictitious niece a little lecture and swallows willingly a large piece of beef which I had brought upstairs, asking for more to show her niece how good it is.

I again try, while she is in the hospital, to give her a suggestion for a moral end ; I make her promise that she will remain in the ward as a nurse, that she will be an honest girl, will have no more lovers, and that she will preserve her religious feelings, etc. She promises everything and during her stay at the hospital her queer, capricious, and gross character is transiently modified. She becomes docile and more reserved. But one fine day she leaves the hospital, and on the same day we met her in the city with unmistakable companions of her profession. She becomes more than ever a *puella publica*. She was susceptible to suggestion of every kind.

OBSERVATION XXXIV —*Neuropathy.—Pains in the epigastrium and lower limbs, which disappeared rapidly by suggestion.*

D. N——, a dressmaker, twenty-one years old, enters the hospital on January 8, 1885. On November 4, at the Maternity Hospital, she was delivered of a seven months child, which died fifteen days after birth. She was not taken sick until a month afterwards. Then pain came on above the right groin, which still persists and which she compares to uterine cramps. The pain is accompanied with fever and an excessive desire to make water. For fifteen days she vomited ; since then she has retained all her food. She has begun to lose color a little during the last fifteen days.

She is a girl of lymphatic temperament and quite pale in complexion. There is no fever. The abdomen is increased in size and somewhat distended. Cutaneous sensibility is normal and there is tympanitic resonance throughout; palpation shows nothing abnormal. She is troubled with habitual constipation; urine is normal. During the past two months she has had pains in her legs and thighs, especially on the posterior surface,—pains which often hinder her walking. Three weeks before her confinement she had pains in the loins and backs of the thighs, pains without cramps and without rigidity, which made it difficult for her to walk but did not prevent her sleeping.—*Neuropathy.*—On the 12th the patient had a passage, having been constipated for a week in spite of having taken four cathartic pills and Sedlitz water. The abdomen is a little less distended ; she complains of a burning sensation about the stomach ; twice during the night she had a sensation of suffocation. She bends her legs at an obtuse angle slowly and with difficulty. She complains of sharp pain upon pressure in both ankles, at the level of the calf, at the back of the thigh, in the distribution of the crural nerve on both sides, at the fourth dorsal spinous process, at the last dorsal vertebræ, at the sacrum, and at the point of emergence of the sciatics and of all the nerves of the face.—Insomnia.

On the 14th, hyperæsthesia is almost general. Complains especially of pain in the epigastrium and in the legs.—*Hypnotization at ten o'clock :* the patient goes into somnambulism. *Upon waking after the suggestion, epigastric pain has disappeared ;* it reappears at five o'clock in the evening. *The other pains have noticeably diminished.*

15th.—Is doing better; the nerves of the face are no longer painful; *the pain in the epigastrium again disappears by suggestion.*

16th.—Complains of no more pain except in the lower limbs, which prevents her from standing. Pressure upon the thighs and legs provokes very acute sensitiveness.

I *hypnotize* her and suggest the disappearance of the pains and the possibility of walking ; I affirm that she can walk. In fact, upon waking the *hyperæsthesia has almost completely disappeared and the patient can take a few steps*, dragging her feet over the floor.

During the days following, she continues to walk very well. The leucorrhœa has gradually disappeared. She remains in the hospital until February 28th. From time to time she complains of pains in her limbs; each time they are suppressed by suggestion.

OBSERVATION XXXV —*Neuro-arthritis.—Lumbar pain.—Insomnia.—Distaste for meat.—Rapid cure by suggestion.*

S. A——, a shoemaker, fourteen years old, enters the hospital on March 25, 1886. Sixteen months ago he was in the hospital six weeks for pains in his feet. At the present time he complains of pains in the loins, elbows, knees, and calves. Since day before yesterday he has hardly been able to walk. For the last five or six days he has been very hoarse, has had no appetite, has perspired profusely. Further, for the last two years he has hardly slept at night ; he is constantly changing his position and is very much agitated. His father died of alcoholic tuberculosis.

Present condition, March 26th.—Temperature 38° on the evening of the 25th; 37° on the morning of the 26th. Pulse regular. Constitution delicate; temperament lymphatico-nervous. Upon examination of the chest, we find that the apex beat is in the sixth intercostal space in the mammary line, the sounds are regular; expiration slightly bronchial in the interscapular region.

Sharp pain upon pressure of the last lumbar vertebræ; this pain was brought about by the effort necessitated by his work. Articular pains have disappeared since this morning; day before yesterday he had pains spreading from the knees to the ankle bones; the tendon-reflexes of the foot are slightly exaggerated.

Diagnosis: Nervousness.—Arthritis.—Spinal irritation.

The patient is *hypnotized;—profound sleep. Upon waking the lumbar pains have disappeared.*

27th.—The pains reappeared during the evening. The boy did not sleep during the night; he was constantly turning about. This morning, pretty abundant epistaxis. *New hypnotic suggestion.*

28th.—*The pain has disappeared.* He slept last night, but the sleep was broken.—Suggestion.

29th.—*Slept better;* was quiet all night.—Slight epistaxis.

30th.—Had pains in his loins last night for two hours; slept however; woke up five or six times. Slight epistaxis.—Eats a little.—Suggestion.

31st.—Waked up three or four times only: slept well: the patient in the next bed says that he is *much more quiet.*

He has had no more pain. He eats pretty well, but says he has no desire for beef.

April 1st.—Is doing well. Slept well. Still complains of slight pains in the loins.—Suggestion to make him eat beef.

2d.—Continues to do well; sleeps well. Ate beef with a good appetite. Has no more pain.—Leaves the hospital.

8th.—The patient, who is now selling papers in the street, came to the hospital one morning three days ago. He is doing well, sleeps at night, and continues to eat meat. He stands about all day, and still complains of slight fatigue in his knees; we take it away by suggestion.

OBSERVATION XXXVI —*Weakness with numbness in the right leg.—Neuropathy.—Rapid cure by suggestion.*

D——, fifty-three years old, enters the hospital on April 25, 1884. For several years she has complained of different dyspeptic and nervous troubles, only a few of which I have been able to relieve. For a year she has had weakness in the lower limbs, and walks in an unsteady way, without having vertigo. Since the month of December, she has been obliged to use a cane. For four years she has been subject to lightning pains in the lower left limb, which grow worse in bad weather. At the present time, the pain is either in the knee or in the anterior surface of the left thigh; tenderness over the external malleolus with sensation of numbness. She moves her right leg well; when lying in bed she also lifts her left leg well, but cannot keep the latter up and motionless. She has been able to stand upon this leg only for the last three weeks, she says. The patient takes little steps, and has a certain stiffness in her left leg, dragging it a little. This stiffness and numbness in the ankle, which is more marked on the left side, extends from the foot to the knee and sometimes as far as the groin.—She stands and walks with her eyes shut.—Sensibility is normal; the tendon reflexes are not increased.

26th.—*Hypnotic suggestion* (moderately profound sleep).—Immediately afterward the patient walks much better, more quickly, and drags her leg less. *The sensation of stiffness and numbness in the ankle has diminished, and disappears completely during the evening, in consequence of a new suggestion.*

28th.—The patient again has sensation of numbness in her ankle, and also complains of pain in her shoulder and right arm. *All these symptoms disappear by suggestion.* The patient stays about ten days longer in the hospital on account of a sore throat. During this time she continues to walk well and feels no pain, stiffness, or numbness.

OBSERVATION XXXVII —*Pains in the right leg, preventing walking for six weeks.— Improvement after one séance ; cure after four.*

B—— is a dressmaker, twenty-one years old. She enters the hospital on September 11, 1884.

She was married two years and a half ago, and has been a widow since January. In 1880 she was delivered of a seven months child, which lived. In March, 1882, she had another child. In June, 1882, her husband kicked her in the supra-pubic region when he was drunk, and since this time she has had pains in the abdomen with dysmenorrhœa; menstruation is painful. She sometimes goes three months without menstruating.

In December, 1883, she had a miscarriage at three months, preceded for eight days by metrorrhagia, with severe pains, which continued after the miscarriage; the leucorrhœa did not disappear definitely for about six weeks. She remained in bed fifteen days,—then menstruation became regular again, but the pains persisted with great intensity into March, so that often she was unable to walk. In March and April, 1884, she no longer felt any pain. The pains reappeared in May, especially in the right side; at the same time there were pains in the loins, the buttocks, and the right thigh, spreading to the bend of the groin and to the foot.

Since August the patient has neither been able to walk nor work, in consequence of pains in the right leg.

The patient has a neuropathic temperament; she complains of sensations of suffocation, of constriction in her throat, of tingling in her arms and hands, of an almost constant cephalalgia, and often of dental and frontal neuralgia. She has frequent fits of passion.

Examination of the organs shows nothing abnormal.

Diagnosis: metritis, neuropathy.

The patient is treated by hypnotic suggestion; profound sleep is obtained. The first séance on September 24th gives place to a *nervous crisis, which lasts but a short time; upon waking the pains persist. After the second séance, on the 25th, the patient is able to walk,* which she has not been able to do since August, and only complains of *slight pains.*

After the third séance, the patient *no longer complains of any pain* and walks very well. On October 6th, after twelve séances, she continues to do well, and complains of nothing but slight weakness.

11th.—She complains of slight pains in the right leg; they yield to suggestion.

She leaves the hospital on the 12th saying that she is cured.

OBSERVATION XXXVIII —*Rheumatic and nervous pains about the waist and in the lower right limb for twenty months.—Inability to walk.—Anorexia.—Rapid cure by suggestion in the waking condition.*

E. B——, forty-six years old, comes to the hospital on March 25, 1886. She is the mother of seven children, the youngest of which is three years old. She has nursed them all, and has always been well until August, 1884. At this period, she was seized with a sensation of cold in the right foot, upon which the heat of the stove had no effect. This sensation was accompanied by numbness and stiffness in the foot, which forced her to drag her leg. At the same time a pain in the lumbar region and in the waist was developed, which increased, especially in December, 1884, and prevented her from working from this time on. In February, 1885, another sharp pain appeared, spreading from the groin along the anterior surface of the thigh and the leg down to the foot, a shooting pain, which was present when she was quiet and grew worse when she walked.

In December, 1885, this condition was aggravated to such a point that she was almost unable to walk. She dragged herself about her room with difficulty, limping badly, and clinging to the furniture. It was impossible for her to go up or down stairs alone. When in bed she could not turn or sit up without crying out with the pains in the groin and the trunk, and especially in the loins. She could only lie down slowly and with great pain. She does not complain of any pain in the upper limbs, but is deprived of strength; she feels incapable of the least effort. Finally, she has had almost no appetite during the whole winter; she cannot eat either bread or meat; coffee and bouillon constitute all her nourishment. She menstruates every four months only, but without pain, or menorrhagia. She has never had any serious sickness nor any nervous manifestations.

She is a woman of ordinarily strong constitution, but deteriorated, and depressed, and of medium intelligence. I do not find any organic lesion. Pressure upon the lower thoracic region, especially at the level of the axillæ and of the back, causes sharp pain; it is the same with the right groin; the patient executes all movements well, the tendon reflexes are not exaggerated, sensibility is normal. She can stand well, but walks with pain, and limps, complaining especially of pain in the groin which restricts her movements. I think it is simply a question of rheumatic or nervous pains. For the last two years she has been living in a damp dwelling.

I hypnotize her on March 25th; she only reaches the *second degree of sleep*. I suggest the disappearance of the pains and the possibility of walking very well. When she wakes, in ten minutes, I make her get up and walk; I continue the suggestion in the waking condition. She walks around the room several times almost without pain and without limping. Her husband is surprised at the result. I tell her to come back on May 3d, being obliged to be away until this day.

She comes back on May 3d. The improvement has not lasted. She again complains of constant although less intense pain; she again limps, but not so badly.

I repeat the suggestion in the waking and in the sleeping condition; the pains diminish noticeably and she walks very well, almost without limping.

After May 5th I continue the suggestion daily. The sleep is not profound. After May 7th I content myself with making the suggestion in the waking condition. I affirm that she has no more pain, that she can walk without limping, that everything is in good order; I rub the painful places, the waist and the groins. Then I urge her decidedly to get up and walk, quickly, without pain, without limping; I make her walk around the room actively.

This *vigorous affirmation with coercion* succeeds better than passive suggestion.

Since May 6th the patient has walked very well without leaning on anything and without a cane. On May 6th she still complained of lassitude and of pain in the groin. On the 7th she walked nearly all the afternoon without fatigue ; she can lie down by herself, can turn about in her bed, and can sit down without any pain. Further, since the first séance, her appetite has returned. On May 9th she was able to walk about in the city for three hours without fatigue. She goes up and down stairs alone. On May 10th she walked well nearly all day. She also feels more strength in her arms and holds things better. There is now only tenderness in the lateral part of the lower ribs and in the groin.

When she has been seated for some time, and gets up to walk, she still feels pain in the groin, which causes a certain hesitation and limping, but, after she has taken about ten steps, she walks without pain and almost without limping.

Such is her condition on May 12th. I continue suggestion in order to correct this slight remaining trouble ; I make her remain seated for several minutes, and, after slight friction, accompanied with the affirmation that she is going to move about without any pain, I make her rise and walk. She begins to walk a little better each time, and I hope to dissipate this last vestige of her trouble, by continuing this suggestive coercion.

On May 13th, the cure is complete.

OBSERVATION XXXIX —*Neuropathy, insomnia, want of appetite, tremor, gloominess ; cure by suggestion in two séances.*

Mlle. X——, twenty-seven years old, generally enjoys good health. She is intelligent and has never been neuropathic, until, in August, 1885, she had two nervous crises, in consequence of some unpleasantness : the first lasted two hours, the second appeared four days after the first and was characterized like the first by severe convulsive movements with strangulation, without loss of consciousness, and lasted from nine o'clock in the morning to four o'clock in the afternoon.

The crises have not been repeated. Mlle. X—— was nervous for some time and impressionable. She had no appetite. Then a visit in the country restored her to her usual health.

Since November she has again felt a good deal of discomfort : complete loss of appetite, gloomy ideas, general demoralization, insomnia ; often she does not sleep until daybreak : if she sleeps she has nightmare, and for about ten days she has had vertigo, especially when in bed. Constant tremor agitates her limbs, to such an extent that she can hardly pour out a glass of water. This nervous condition has resisted all treatment : bromide, ether, and other antispasmodics.

Mlle. X——, who is very courageous, tries in vain to regain her self-control.

After long hesitation, she comes to consult me on February 15, with the idea of trying hypnotic suggestion in spite of her scepticism.

I hypnotize her easily; she goes into *profound sleep;* post-hypnotic hallucinations can be induced.

I suggest the disappearance of all the morbid symptoms, and sleep at night.

After two séances, on the 15th and 16th, *she no longer feels the slightest discomfort;* no more tremor; she sleeps until six o'clock in the morning without any disturbance, her appetite is better than ever, her melancholy has disappeared. The cure has continued up to the present day.

OBSERVATION XL —*Melancholy, insomnia, anorexia.*—*Rapid cure by hypnotic suggestion.*—(Observation communicated by Dr. Emile Lévy, of Nancy, formerly *chef de clinique.*)

Mlle. W——, twenty-four years old, living at Malzeville, near Nancy, is a fair girl, slightly delicate in constitution. I treated her several different times for a slight suppurative otitis accompanied with polypi, which I had to extract.

After two operations and local treatment, she left me, completely cured of her ear trouble. Under the influence of a general tonic treatment of wine of quinine and pills of the iodide of iron, she regained her usual color.

This young lady came to see me again in November, 1885, asking me to give her treatment to make her sleep. After being pressed with questions upon the cause of this insomnia, she confessed that for the last three weeks she had been worn out with ennui and sadness; weeping night and day, she had lost her appetite and her sleep: thoughts of suicide took possession of her at times. She did not know to just what to attribute this depression; some time before she had had annoyances and deceptions; she mentioned particularly the companionship of a cousin who visited her for several months during her pregnancy, and who was seized with gloomy ideas. I must also say that without showing any hysterical trouble herself, Mlle. W—— belongs to a family in which there have been nervous affections.

I proposed treatment by suggestion, which she accepted. I tried to hypnotize her. Although she only reached a light degree of sleep, I suggested by energetic affirmation that I was going to cure her. I repeated the same treatment for eight successive days. The third day she went into a deeper sleep, although she never reached somnambulism. The general condition improved more and more, sleep returned and with it appetite and gayety.

She kept on coming to see me at different times. After having driven away from her mind the melancholy and the thoughts of suicide, and having planted there bright and agreeable ideas, I also succeeded in re-establishing the mental equilibrium. A last idea, the most tenacious one, was mentioned to me by Mlle. W———. She could not understand why she was thus exposed to these gloomy ideas, and asked herself if any hereditary influence threatened the return of similar troubles. After several séances and not without a good deal of trouble, I succeeded in driving this uneasiness away. I suggested to Mlle. W———, who is very intelligent, that she should completely forget this transient sickness, and that she should imagine that she had never been ill. After three weeks of this treatment Mlle. W——— was completely cured, and the cure has been maintained up to the present day.

Dr. Lévy makes the following comments:
"The lypomaniacal condition which was developed in our patient, and which threatened to become very grave, has been so rapidly and so happily dissipated that I do not hesitate in affirming that no treatment could have obtained a like result. This happy effect was produced from the very beginning, and before the patient had gone into a deep sleep. Dr. Liébault has assured us that this effect is often observed in subjects who are hardly asleep.

"I attribute the authority and the influence which I obtained over this young person partly to the energetic affirmation of cure in the first séance. In fact I said to her: 'I am going to hypnotize you, and you will soon be completely cured.' The patient immediately said with a big sigh: 'Ah, Mon Dieu! if it were only true!' This impression also shows the profound emotional influence which my affirmation had exercised over the patient."

OBSERVATION XLI —*Insomnia contracted through habit.—Good effect, without complete success, of suggestion.*

G———, fifty-six years old, a dealer in flour, enters the hospital on October 26, 1884, for a chronic bronchitis with emphysema and chronic interstitial pneumonia, due to the breathing of the flour dust and of the silica to which he is exposed in grinding the flour. He is a man of medium constitution, lymphatic temperament, and in no way nervous. I shall not insist upon the details of his thoracic affection, which do not interest us. He has not been able to work for a month. As a miller, he was in the habit of rising at two o'clock in the morning, and since he has not been able to work, he continues to wake at this hour and cannot go to sleep again.

I try hypnotic suggestion in order to benefit this insomnia. A first trial on the 28th only produces drowsiness; a second trial immediately afterwards, puts him into *profound sleep*, without memory upon waking. I suggest to him not to wake during the night.

29th.—*In spite of the suggestion, he waked without being able to go to sleep again*, at two o'clock in the morning.—New suggestion.

30th.—Last night the patient woke at one o'clock and *went to sleep again between three and four*, but only slept an hour. This has never happened before. I continue the suggestion every day.

31st.—Slept from six o'clock to half-past eleven, and again from half-past eleven to four.

November 1st.—Awoke at midnight, went to sleep again an hour afterward, and slept until four o'clock in the morning. The dynamometric force measured for the right hand gives 45 twice, and 51 once. *After hypnotic suggestion, this force increases*, and we obtain when he wakes 56, 53, 52.

2d.—Awoke at midnight; went to sleep again to wake at two o'clock in the morning. *Daily suggestion continued*.

3d.—Did not wake at midnight, but at two o'clock. Went to sleep again in half an hour and slept until four o'clock.

4th.—Awoke at eleven, and after a fit of coughing went to sleep again and slept until five o'clock. Suggestion had made him sleep through the night up to five o'clock.

5th.—In spite of suggestion only slept from eleven o'clock until half-past one.

6th.—Woke at midnight and slept again until five o'clock.

8th.—Woke at midnight and slept again from half-past twelve until four o'clock.

9th.—Woke at midnight; slept again from one o'clock until four.

10th.—Woke at midnight, then went to sleep again from half-past twelve until four o'clock.

When he left the hospital he resumed his work, which he had given up on December 2d, and was able to work for three weeks; then, in consequence of cold, he was taken with a sense of suffocation and had to stop work again on December 20th.

He comes to the hospital again on February 3d with his habitual emphysema.

For three weeks he again wakes at midnight and cannot sleep again before four o'clock; he has feelings of suffocation, lasting two hours.

5th.—He slept in consequence of suggestion, from half-past seven o'clock until midnight; then did not go to sleep again until three o'clock in the morning, and slept until five.

6th.—He slept spontaneously from seven o'clock until two; then from half-past two until four. Suggestion.

On the 7th he slept from eight o'clock until two in the morning, then from four until five.

He leaves the hospital.

In spite of repeated suggestion the patient has not been able to sleep uninterruptedly until morning.

OBSERVATION XLII —*Cephalœa for three years.—Impressionability ; obnubilation. —Difficulty in studying ; weakness in the knees, perspiration caused by walking.— Noticeable improvement after a single suggestion.—Complete cure in three séances.*

Léon G——, eighteen years old, is a lymphatic, nervous, but intelligent young man. In 1879 or 1880, he had articular rheumatism in the lower limbs, which kept him in bed for three or four weeks. Then he had relapses, so that he remained for two months without doing anything. Three years ago I treated him for typhoid fever. Since then he has had *variable pain in the head*, sometimes occipital, sometimes frontal, and always more severe on the right side; this pain is continuous; it consists in a sensation of *heaviness*, with a sort of *buzzing in the head*.

From time to time, especially after confining work, as a rule every eight or fifteen days, this sensation degenerates into excessively acute pain, right supra-orbital neuralgia, which lasts an hour and an hour and a half.

For the last three years also his sight troubles him after half an hour or at most three quarters of an hour of work; he is obliged to stop. After from five to ten minutes he can work again; then he has to stop again, and so on. The pains in the head have increased, especially since July 1885, in consequence of his preparation for the baccalaureate degree. He is *excessively impressionable*, trembles when he recites a lesson, and feels himself blushing and perspiring when a professor questions him. Further, when he walks, *the right knee gives readily;* when he has walked a long time, or when it is cold weather, he feels a shooting pain in his knee and right shoulder; since March or April he has *perspired freely* when walking.

With these exceptions, G—— is very well, and has a good appetite and digestion.

The patient comes to consult me on October 5th. I put him into *somnambulism* easily, and *suggest* the disappearance of all these functional troubles. After this first séance *the pain in the head disappears* at two o'clock in the afternoon. It comes back again about half-past seven in the evening, but is less severe.

After the second séance, on October 6th, *he has no more pain in the head; he works the next day from nine o'clock until mid-day, without feeling anything, which he was not able to do before.*

On October 7th, the third séance. The patient can work all the evening and the next morning without pain. He says that for the last three years he has been unable to work as he has worked this evening, three consecutive hours. He has *not perspired* after quite a long walk.

8th.—Fourth séance : is doing well ; feels stronger on his legs.

9th.—Fifth séance : continues to do well ; his head is very calm ; *he sleeps very well; has no more tremor;* walked six kilometres very rapidly without perspiring.

G—— returns on the 12th. He has been very well up to yesterday evening at five o'clock.

At this moment, after working an hour, he felt *heaviness in his head* with rather a sharp pain on the right side of his forehead, which lasted half an hour and disappeared after rest. Otherwise he could have gone on; his head was clear; he has had no more tremor, or perspiration. Yesterday he was astonished at the facility with which he made a Greek translation ; he did it in two hours, while before he would have given from four to five hours to it without success. Sixth suggestion.

G—— comes to see me for the last time on the 14th. He has had no more pain and continues to work more easily. I have not seen him since.

OBSERVATION XLIII —*Vertigo, exhaustion, depression of psychical origin, rapidly suppressed by suggestion.*

H——, thirty-four years old, a commercial man, strong, and of a good constitution, has probably had from his infancy a murmur denoting aortic insufficiency, and a bounding pulse. In spite of the murmur, which I found in examining him about twelve years ago, H—— has always been very well, and has had neither dyspnœa nor palpitation. The heart is not hypertrophied. There is probably slight aortic insufficiency which is perfectly compensated, and not inconsistent with the normal action of the heart.

In 1880, he contracted syphilis, had secondary syphilides, and has since then continued to take iodide of potassium almost continuously.

In October, 1886, he had a severe nose-bleed. His physician doubtless attributed this bleeding to the aortic insufficiency, and fearing manifestations of cerebral congestion, put him under a light diet, with purgatives, for three days.

He became extremely weak. Fifteen days afterward, *he was taken with vertigo and obnubilation;* he was unsteady in his walk. Further, from time to time weakness took possession of him like a flash of lightning, his legs failed him and he felt as if he should faint. He has never had syncope, however. From this time, H—— has been depressed, restless, and troubled with gloomy ideas; his memory has grown weak. He has palpitation, and he believes that he is suffering from a grave affection of the heart.

He comes to consult me in December 1886, a month after the beginning of these troubles.

Upon examination I do not find anything abnormal, unless it is the aortic diastolic murmur already mentioned. Motility and sensibility are normal. Sleep is good.

I ask myself if these cerebral troubles, vertigo, titubation, and weakness of memory, are not connected with cerebral syphilis, and being in doubt, I prescribe treatment by mercurial inunctions.

After three applications of four grammes each of the mercurial ointment, there is no improvement; the patient is continually restless and nourishes the idea of heart trouble, his physician having told him that the symptoms in his head came from the heart. I then ask myself if these troubles are not of psychical origin, or at least aggravated by the psychical condition. H—— is impressionable: he listens to his heart, knowing that he has a murmur; he sometimes feels the arteries in his head beating more forcibly; some one has told him that the epistaxis was the result of congestion, referable to the heart. He fears cerebral congestion. An attack of vertigo, perhaps anæmic in character, having succeeded the epistaxis, his imagination has cherished the idea of the vertigo, has suggested the weakness and titubation in the legs, the obnubilation, the gloomy ideas, etc. I explain this idea to M. H——, and I propose *to hypnotize him.*

He reaches the third degree easily and, although he pretends not to sleep, he cannot modify the attitude impressed upon his limbs. I suggest the disappearance of all his troubles.

Since the first séance, there has been a marked improvement; after four or five séances, at the end of four or five days, H—— is feeling very well; he has *no more vertigo; no more titubation;* his ideas have become clear again, his head is lucid.

A month later, January, 1887, H—— comes back to see me. He again has vertigo, and a sense of precordial discomfort, and his head has been dull for several days. I learned that having met his physician he had had the unlucky idea of telling him that I had cured him by suggestion. His physician said : " Yes, but these troubles will necessarily come back again because they are connected with your heart trouble." Upon this his imagination is stimulated, and the troubles come back again.

I hypnotize him again, and suggest vigorously that his heart will perform its functions well, that his troubles are purely nervous, and due to his attention concentrated upon his heart. The proof is that all the symptoms disappear after suggestion.

Upon waking he again feels well, and after two séances is completely relieved.

He had no more trouble until July, 1887. Then, probably in consequence of business preoccupation, the vertigo takes hold of him again, with fear and uncomfortable feeling in the heart ; work again becomes painful to him. During July I hypnotize him two or three times at intervals of five or six days, with transient but not permanent result. Then I asked him to come eight consecutive days, and since the first séance, the cure has been permanent. H—— is again gay and self-confident ; he no longer complains of vertigo, and his head is clear. I persuade him to come every month in order that his nervous system may be *wound up*, so to speak.

OBSERVATION XLIV —*Anorexia, insubordination, and indolence in a child.—Rapid physical and moral improvement caused by suggestion.*

Henry H——, ten years of age, is brought to me by his mother (whom I have treated with suggestion) on December 20, 1887. This child is of strong constitution, his disposition is somewhat lymphatic, he frequently suffers with his throat in consequence of hypertrophy of the tonsils, and he has lost his appetite. He has never eaten any meat. Two years ago when he was in Alsace for two months his appetite was good and he ate meat ; but since his return he manifests the old repugnance for meat. Besides this, the child is frequently angry and naughty ; when his mother tries to correct him he strikes her, and throws everything around out of reach. He is always in a bad humor and disobedient. He only goes to school three or four times a week ; his absences average thirty a month. His mother brings him to me in order that I may correct his trouble by suggestion.

Like his mother the child is easily put *into deep sleep* at the first seance ; physical and moral improvement is noticed. He comes only once or twice a week. On January 20, 1887, after six séances I note : "the child looks better ; *he eats meat with appetite*, is very obedient, goes to school regularly, works well, and has made some progress."

I do not see him again until the 10th of February. He continues to do well, eats with a good appetite, goes to school gladly, and has not missed any more classes. Since his treatment he has gone up ten places in his class. Before he was always the last.

He comes back on February 17th, on the 25th, and on March 3d. The improvement which was so remarkable has lasted. He no longer complains of his throat, although the tonsils are still large ; he has had no more fits of passion since the suggestion.

On March 23d, his mother tells me that he is still eating well, and has not missed school. When he comes home from school he no longer plays before doing his duty. However, for the last eight days, he has been listless and bad tempered, and cries as soon as his brother speaks to him. *Suggestion.* When he wakes he is bright and good natured.

April 21st.—Patient comes back. He eats and works well, but during the last month he has had several fits of passion again, once every eight or fifteen days; these attacks are much less severe than before and cease almost immediately. When he came home from school a week ago, lunch not being ready, and his father not having returned, he did not wish to wait and was impertinent to his mother.—Suggestion.

May 3d.—The child has been obedient since the last séance, but this morning when his mother wished to wash him he got angry, cried and stamped his foot.—*Suggestion.*

I see him again on June 23d. He has had no more fits of anger, is very docile, and does his work well. His mother noticed that for the last fifteen days he has been easily excited, and has cried and sung without any motive.—*Suggestion.*

I go to see the child again on August 21st, to find out what has become of him. His mother tells me that the excitement was calmed after the last séance ; and that the child has been quiet and obedient since then. She finds that he has completely changed.

This fact of rapid moral improvement, of character-transformation, obtained by suggestion, shows that the application of hypnotism to pedagogy is not an illusion. Have we interfered with this child's liberty because we suppressed his bad instincts?

OBSERVATION XLV.—*Intermittent pseudo-paraplegia with convulsive tremor of the lower limbs, dating back nearly four years.—Cure by a single suggestion.*

On May 16, 1887, I received the following letter from Paris: "I wish to call upon your large experience for my wife who is in the most extraordinary condition of health. I wish to describe it in detail.

"I have submitted the case to Drs. Charcot, Jaccoud, Lancereaux, Tarnier, and many others; I have each time found myself in the presence of great astonishment and of more or less complicated medications, none of which have done the least good. My wife is twenty-six years old, and up to the age of twenty-two her health was perfect. She has had two healthy children. In the period between 1881 and 1884, Mme. S—— was deeply affected by several sorrowful occurrences: the death of her mother, then the death of a daughter, and her father's illness, which without her care would have been fatal.

"Finally, she had a very painful miscarriage (nearly four years ago), after which, just as she was about getting up, it was shown that she had been attacked by a *reflex paraplegia of the lower limbs.*

"This affection is so curious that it has been classed with the neuroses. It appears without any apparent cause for several weeks, then disappears in the same way, for two or three months, leaving my wife as well as before, and coming again suddenly, causing extreme weakness, and provoking yawning, accompanied with syncope, in one word upsetting her whole nervous system.

"After having tried together or separately, electricity, valerian, hydrotherapy, metallotherapy, and quinine, I have come to the conclusion to let nature work, which at least it can do as energetically and as efficaciously as all the remedies hitherto employed."

I see the young woman in Paris on May 29, 1887, the day of Pentecost. She has again been paralyzed for the last five or six weeks. She is of a good constitution, stout for her age, and of mixed temperament, has never had any nervous history before this trouble. No history of hysterical paroxysms. Menstruation is regular, and has no influence over the paralysis. Her uncle, who is her physician, has confirmed these facts. Her imagination does not seem to be exalted. "I sometimes ask myself," she says, " if my paralysis is not the effect of imagination, for there are times when I can walk well. Then again I make the utmost effort, I try, and I am obliged to state that in spite of all my best intentions I cannot."

Mme. S—— has no distubances of sensibility, no abdominal pains, and no neuralgia. She complains constantly of palpitation, and of a sensation of weakness and emptiness in the head, which she cannot define.

I note that when lying down the patient can execute all movements; flexion and extension of the thighs, legs, and toes, but when she lifts her leg it is seized with a fine irregular tremor. If she tries to stand up, her legs are immediately seized with tremor of wide range, the thighs flex upon the legs, the trunk upon the thighs, and in a few seconds the patient falls. She can neither stand nor take a single step. It is not a question of a real paralysis, but of an irregular tremor which prevents her from standing and is provoked by the slightest effort. The legs are otherwise lax. There is no exaggeration of the tendon-reflexes. When the hands are held out horizontally they also exhibit a slight and continuous tremor. The patient can press both my hands with hers, but with very little force.

The other functions are normal.

After having told her husband that I was going to try suggestion, but that I was doubtful of its success in one single séance, I assure the young woman that her trouble is purely nervous, and that I am going to cure it by suggestion. I hypnotize her by holding two fingers before her eyes and affirming the presence of sleep. She closes her eyes in two seconds; I tell her to keep them shut. Seeing that her respiration is becoming labored and anxious, I calm her by saying: "You are going to be very well, very calm, and perfectly at your ease; your respiration is as perfect as in natural sleep, etc." Her emotion disappears under the effect of this calming suggestion, and the respiration becomes regular again. I affirm her cure, and lift her arms saying, "See, your hands no longer tremble; your strength has come back; you will be able to press with great force." In fact I notice that the tremor has disappeared. Afterward I lift the legs, and affirm the disappearance of all tremor, "The patient will be able to rise, to stand up, to walk firmly and fearlessly, etc." I continue this energetic suggestion for a quarter of an hour, rubbing and manipulating her limbs. I notice that the patient is in the beginning of the second degree of sleep. The fore-arm alone is cataleptic, the entire arm falls.

When I wake Mme. S———, she asks if she has slept, because she heard everything and even spoke. I say to her: "Whether you have slept or not, you are cured. Give me you hand. Press mine strongly. You see that you no longer tremble." In fact she presses my hand with much more force and without tremor. Then I say: "Now get up and walk. Do not be afraid. You can do it." She hesitates, then she gets up, and to her great astonishment can stand. Then she walks, completely nonplussed, and wondering if it is really herself. She walks with a regular and firm step and goes around the room several times.

I see her the next day, and again the day after. The result has been maintained. The first night the patient did not sleep. She was agitated by the emotion of the cure. I suggest to her calmness and sleep and the second night she sleeps very well. Since the second séance Mme. S——— goes into the third degree of sleep. There are complete irresistible catalepsy, and automatic movements.

I saw Mme. S——— again in July at Nancy; she passed three days there. I hypnotized her three times, and each time she went into the third degree of sleep. The cure has been maintained since the first séance; she now walks several kilometres; her legs have grown stronger. The other nervous troubles, palpitation, vertigo, etc. have also disappeared.

IV

NEUROSES

OBSERVATION XLVI —*Choreic movements localized in one arm.—Cure in three séances.—Relapse at the end of a few months.—A new cure in three séances; each suggestion checks the movements.*

W——, sixteen years old, works in a factory. She comes to consult me on July 17, 1884, on account of her choreic movements.

One Sunday early in October last, after having been scolded, she went to Vespers; and there the choreic movements in her left arm appeared for two hours. The next day, Monday, at four o'clock in the evening the same movements appeared in both arms, and lasted half an hour.

Tuesday and Wednesday she had none, but they reappeared at six o'clock on Thursday in the arms and legs; and since then the chorea has continued, with more or less increase, for three months. In the shop where she works four other girls were taken with choreic movements by imitation.

For two months she went to M. Liébault, who treated her by hypnotic suggestion. A real improvement resulted: sometimes she remained two or three days without any movements, then they recurred. Moreover since January the chorea has not been general, but has affected the arms almost exclusively. The movements are identical with those presented by another young girl who lives in the same house and comes with the patient.

Last June she was almost free from these movements for a week, having them, however, in her arms and legs every evening. Since then these movements have never left her but have been more or less severe. For the past four weeks they have been in the arms exclusively. Sometimes the choreic movements are general. Fifteen days ago she had irregular movements of her eyes accompanied with vertigo.

July 17th.—She has movements in her hands only, which are sudden and spasmodic, lifting the hand and fore-arm as if by a strong electricity shock, but without pain. These movements are obstinately repeated every four or five seconds.

Her intelligence is clear. Sensibility is normal. The girl has never had any other nervous trouble. *Hypnotic suggestion on the 17th; profound sleep, without immediate result.*

19th.—A new séance; *the movements persist during the hypnotic sleep, but disappear when the patient wakes.* They do not reappear until the following night.

New suggestion on the 20th.

She comes back on the 22d and says that since the 20th she has only had five or six movements in all, and those during the past night. At the present time motion is normal.

24th.—Patient has returned to work, which she has not been able to do for four weeks. She says she has not felt so well since October. For the last few days she has complained only of pain in the wrist when she is tired, which sometimes lasts ten minutes and sometimes spreads up to the shoulder, especially in the evening.—Hypnotic suggestion.

26th.—She says she has had no more pain for two days. During the evening there is slight tremor of the right arm, but this soon disappears.

Patient continues to work and to do well up to September. At this time she again has spasmodic movements lasting for a week, and ceasing spontaneously. On the 30th she again comes to consultation. She has severe movements like those caused by electric shocks, in her arm and in the body, which are repeated twice in a second. They have existed for a week without interruption.

The patient is hypnotized; the movements become at first less frequent, then more intense, then in a few minutes they cease. The sleep is quite deep. Upon waking she only remembers a little of what I have said to her. She has two spasmodic movements then nothing more. I hypnotize her a second time: upon waking she feels very well. During the day she has not even a single spasm.

On the 31st when she started out she was exposed to cold and the movements began again. She came to see me. She had a movement nearly every second. *The movements were stopped in three minutes by suggestion in the waking condition.* Then I hypnotized her to make the suggestion more efficacious.

She does very well up to November 3d, when upon waking new movements appear, about one a minute. They again yield to hypnotic suggestion. The next day the girl comes for the last time to say that she is perfectly well and has had no more trouble.

OBSERVATION XLVII —*Choreic movements dating back fifteen days which appeared several months after a general chorea.—Cure in three séances.*

Caroline V——, eighteen years old, working in the same shop and living in the same house with Marie W——, was taken by imitation in November. She became involved in an altercation on Saturday. On Monday she had choreiform movements in the waist, and then in the arms, just as her friend had had. At times the chorea was general.

For five weeks she went to Dr. Liébault, and was completely cured. She began to work again and kept on until March 12th. On this day, a fright caused by a fire in a neighboring factory brought about the return of the chorea, which lasted six weeks.

At the end of six weeks she began to work again. Fifteen days ago she was again attacked, but more lightly, and, since this time she has had sudden and continual movements localized in her arms and shoulders. On July 17th, she came with Marie W——. The convulsive movements are like her friend's; they are repeated every two seconds. Moreover she is troubled with insomnia.—On the 17th, *hypnotic suggestion; profound sleep without immediate result.*

On the 19th, a second séance. At first the movements continued during the sleep; then, in from six to ten minutes they become more and more infrequent and finally disappear. *They do not reappear when the patient wakes.* During the day she has several movements, but they are much less extensive and frequent. Slept well during past two nights. We recommend that these two young girls should be separated, so that the reciprocal suggestive influence by imitation may be avoided.

21.—New suggestion. Since this, she has had no other attack.

23d.—Idem. She remains completely cured.

OBSERVATION XLVIII —*Choreic movements dating back eleven days.—Cure by suggestion in three séances.—Relapse at the end of six weeks.—Cure in several séances.*

Mlle. J——, teacher, thirty-two years old, comes to see me on February 17, 1887, for choreic movements in her right arm and leg. On February 4th, she was coarsely reprimanded it seems, by the inspector of the Academy. Deeply affected by this she experienced nausea during that day and the next. She could scarcely eat.—At the same time she had acute pricking sensations in both arms. During the night of the 5th she was as if wandering for about an hour, not knowing where she was. On February 6th, choreic movements appeared in the right arm and leg, and these increased during the following days and finally became continual. The patient hardly slept. The nausea has diminished since the 13th; she has been subject to it for years. Although very impressionable, patient has never had chorea or any other nervous affection before.

At the present time, February 17, there are *incessant movements of the leg*, now lateral, now of flexion of the foot. Similar movements begin in the right hand, and extend to the entire limb. She has from one to two movements a second; she writes with difficulty and her writing is irregular. At the same time she has a painful pricking sensation in her right arm. I hypnotize her; she goes into *somnambulism* easily. In three or four minutes the *movements cease in consequence of suggestion.*—Upon waking, they reappear, but are less frequent, being about one a minute. A second séance checks them completely. She then writes very easily and her writing is good and regular.

19th.—She says she was very comfortable yesterday; the *pricking sensation in her legs has ceased.* The movements ceased until this morning at nine o'clock; since that time she has had new movements, about eleven a minute. The patient remains quiet sometimes for a quarter or half an hour; then the movements begin again.—*New hypnotic suggestion during which the movements are checked;* they are absent when she wakes.

21st.—She says she had slight needle pains in her heel day before yesterday, lasting for an hour, without any spasmodic movements. Yesterday she had three movements during the day. This morning she feels no pain, and the leg feels only slightly heavy.

25th.—Is doing well. No more movements; says she is cured.

Mlle. J—— comes to see me again on April 8th. For the last ten days, in consequence of deep emotion, she has again had movements in the arm and leg lasting from half an hour to an hour, and appearing at six o'clock in the evening. For the last three days, she has had about ten movements during the day. For the last eight days, she has had shooting pains in her right shoulder, extending to the fingers and lasting from a quarter of an hour to an hour, being repeated five or six times a day. Nevertheless she sleeps very well at night, and was restless only one night last week.—*Suggestion.*

April 21st.—After the last séance she had no more trouble up to the 13th. *The pain in her shoulder had completely disappeared.* But on this day she was again taken with a nervous tremor which has appeared every evening since, and lasts from five minutes to half an hour. This morning, frightened by some one who suddenly entered the room where she was waiting, she developed a tremor which has since been constant.

Through suggestion this tremor disappears.

Mlle. J—— comes back five or six times to see me. She still has movements from time to time, which do not prevent her from attending her class. Each time she is freed from them by suggestion, and after three or four séances she is totally cured. I had news of her on October 20th; she had had not the slightest spasmodic movement.

OBSERVATION XLIX.—*Tremor in the left hand consecutive to chorea, and inability to write with this hand.—Cure in two hypnotic séances.*

Claudine D——, fifteen years old, was brought to me on July 21, 1884, by two of her friends, who work in the same shop and whom I had just cured of choreic movements by hypnotic suggestion in several séances.

Claudine D—— is generally well. She does not seem to be more than ordinarily nervous. In February, 1884, she was taken with chorea by imitation, being the fourth case in the shop. This chorea was general, involving the head, trunk and limbs. The patient bit her tongue. In six weeks, after having taken fifteen sulphur baths, she was completely cured.

Fifteen days ago she again developed general chorea. For the last eight days she has had only an incessant lateral rhythmical tremor, occupying the hand, the arm, and the left shoulder. The more she tries to stop this tremor the more it is exaggerated. Aside from this her health is perfect. She writes very well with her right hand.

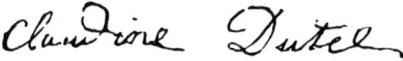

If she wishes to write her name with her left hand she only makes a confused mass of unrecognizable letters.

A line traced with this hand shows the tremor.

I hypnotize her, after having hypnotized her two friends in her presence; she only reaches the second degree of hypnotic sleep (that is to say relaxation, incomplete suggestive catalepsy, no automatic movements, perfect memory upon waking). I affirm that the tremor will disappear, that she will be able to use her left hand as well as her right. I rub the hand a little.

At first the tremor persists, and I do not expect to obtain an immediate result: but in several minutes it begins to diminish, more or less widely separated movements take its place, then it disappears. I make the patient write her name, and I make her trace a line during her sleep with her eyes shut and she succeeds very well.

I wake her in about twelve minutes. She writes her name very well with her left hand and also traces a line.

Another line traced in three minutes shows a slight tremor again.

The tremor has disappeared when the patient wakes; but she tells us the next day that it reappeared again as soon as she got into the street.

The next day, the 22d, Claudine comes again. The tremor again exists as distinctly as before. She cannot write with her left hand. This is the way she writes her name with her left hand and traces a line before the second séance.

I hypnotize her again in the presence of my students; I energetically suggest that the tremor will cease and that she will write very well.

In a few minutes the tremor again disappears, as it did the day before; and I make her write during her sleep, with her eyes closed. This is the writing with her left hand during the sleep, and a line also traced during the sleep:

We here see that the tremor has totally disappeared. I let her sleep a quarter of an hour, assuring her that the tremor will not come back, and that she may be sure of her hand.

Upon waking there is not the slightest tremor: she writes and traces a line clearly. This is the writing with her left hand, and a line traced after waking:

[handwritten signature: Claudine Dutel]

The cure has been maintained since the second séance. This is a specimen of her writing with her left hand on the 23d.

[handwritten signature: Claudine Dutel]

The patient has come back three times, at our request, to be hypnotized; the cure has been preserved.

OBSERVATION L.—*Trouble in writing consecutive to chorea.—Cure in a single séance of hypnotic suggestion.*

Henry Grosse, sixteen years old, of Hayange (Alsace-Lorraine), comes to consult me with his mother on June 5, 1884. The following is his history. When ten years old, he had an attack of chorea lasting four months. At twelve and a half, he had a second attack lasting three months. It was severe and general, involved his limbs, the trunk, the face, and the tongue, and was accompanied with difficulty of speech. Acute articular rheumatism preceded this attack by a month. When fourteen years old, he had another attack of poly-articular febrile rheumatism. It involved all the joints, including the articulations of the neck, which has been somewhat stiff ever since, and lasted six months. At the same time he suffered from dyspnœa, with palpitation.

Last February he had another attack of chorea lasting a month. The irregular movements were very wide in range, but limited to the upper limbs. Since March these movements have gradually diminished in intensity and have since disappeared. But the patient can no longer write. He has been obliged to discontinue his studies, and for that reason he has come to consult me. He has tried different kinds of treatment. In February he took bromide for three weeks, and then syrup of chloral, which diminished the movements. During March he took tartar emetic, afterwards arsenic for three weeks. During April and May the ether spray was used over the spine twice a day. The choreic movements ceased, but his hands remained awkward; he could neither write nor tie his cravat.

At the present time, June 5, he is a lymphatic boy, tall, timid, and quiet. He is intelligent, however. He sleeps and eats well; no choreic movement is noticed, there is hardly any twitching in his hand. Movements of rotation of his neck are slightly painful. Slight murmur at the apex of the heart, which performs its functions well and is not hypertrophied. I make him write with a pencil after having put him at his ease. This is a fac-simile of his writing.

I propose to his mother that I shall hypnotize him; she consents. The first trial does not succeed: he scowls, winks, and pretends that he cannot sleep. Then I hypnotize his mother, who gives up to it easily. Seeing her calmly asleep, he lets himself go easily, and in three minutes his body is relaxed. His limbs remain relaxed if I lift them. I then suggest verbally that he is cured, that his hand no longer trembles, and that he is doing very well. I repeat this suggestion several times. In ten minutes I wake him and make him write.

This is the result; it is not very brilliant.

HYPNOSIS AND SUGGESTION

I discover that the child had been in profound sleep or somnambulism, that is to say, he is without memory upon waking. Knowing that in this deep sleep immediate results are sometimes obtained, I propose to hypnotize him a second time, and in less than a minute I put him into somnambulism again. Then I repeat and emphasize the affirmation that he is going to write very well, and in order to make the suggestion more efficacious, I put a pencil into his hand, saying: "Here is a pencil; you hold it very well. Your hand is steady." I put a paper under the pencil and I make him write his name while he is asleep. He first writes his name Grosse.

I say: "You will write your Christian name better." He writes Henry.

I say: "Still better." He writes Hayange.

I say: "Still better penmanship." He writes Grosse.

Everything is written with his eyes shut. I tell him that upon waking he will write better. I make him say himself that he is and will remain cured, that his hand will guide the pen unhesitatingly. In about twelve minutes I wake him. He remembers nothing, and this is what he writes upon waking:

Grosse Henri à la Tenderie à Fves Hayange

Monsieur je vous remercie beaucoup je suis guéri Le 5 juin 1884

He writes a long letter to his father in the evening. I see him on June 6; the cure has been lasting. This is his writing before another hypnotization.

I hypnotize him for the last time, for the cure has endured. On July 9, I receive a letter from him in which he thanks me in his best writing, which is worthy of a professor of caligraphy.

OBSERVATION LI.—(Collected and related by M. Beaunis, *Gazette médicale de Paris*, 1884).—*Choreic movements in the hands.—Difficulty in writing.—Cure by hypnotic suggestion.*

Victorine L——, twelve and a half years old, of lymphatic temperament but strong constitution, is affected with right hemichorea, about which her mother gives me the following information:

First attack.—At the age of four years and a half, in consequence of fright, she was taken with very severe general chorea. The child could neither walk nor articulate words, and could hardly eat. Moreover, the disease was aggravated at certain times in the day; these crises or attacks lasted from ten to fifteen minutes and were repeated six or seven times a day. The duration of this first attack was three months. Cold water douches were the only treatment employed.

Between the ages of six and seven, patient had articular pains.

Second attack, at the age of seven years and a half.—This was as severe as the first and showed the same characteristics, but it only lasted six weeks. Same treatment.

Third attack, at the age of nine years and a half.—Only the right side was involved. Six to seven attacks during the day. Duration, six weeks. No treatment.

Fourth attack, at the age of eleven years and a half.—Same hemichoreic form. Same duration. Always from six to seven attacks per day. No treatment.

Fifth attack, patient twelve years and a half old.—The first attack took place on May 27, and was followed by six very severe attacks during the same day. On the 28th and 29th, the same number of very severe attacks. On the morning of the 30th she had two severe attacks. Her mother took her on this day to M. Liébault, who hypnotized her for the first time. She had two more attacks during the afternoon, but they were less severe.

On the 31st she was hypnotized. There was a single light attack, which was the last.

On June 9th, in consequence of fright, the choreic movements reappeared with less intensity, but the movements were very irregular, especially those of the hand and arm. Her mother brings her to be hypnotized.

I am with M. Liébault on this day. Prof. Bernheim had several days before given me a precise account of a case of chorea in which hypnotism had succeeded in one séance in arresting the irregular movements of the hand and in permitting the patient to write. I told M. Liébault about this and asked him to try the same experiment upon the little patient. He immediately consented.

I tell Victorine L—— to write her name. In spite of all her attempts, the intelligent and obedient child only succeeds in making a scrawl, in which L, the first letter of her name, is with difficulty distinguishable. The following is a fac-simile:

Then M. Liébault hypnotizes her, and tells her to write her name. This is what she writes, suddenly and without hesitation, her eyes being shut:

All the choreic movements disappeared during the sleep.

Upon waking, we make her write her name again, this time with her eyes open. The following fac-simile shows the result obtained:

On the following days the hypnotic séances are continued and the improvement is continued. At the end of several days the child had no more irregular movements, and could write, sew, and carry on all her manual occupations as before.

OBSERVATION LII —*Hemichorea, the result of fright.—Gradual cure by hypnotic suggestion in from six to seven weeks.*

C. K——, a child eight years old, was brought to me on February 23d. She had been bitten by a dog in the left cheek twenty-six days before. Two days afterwards she had choreic movements in the left arm and leg, and since then this hemichorea has persisted. She also complains of pain in the left cheek at the seat of the scar. The pain is acute upon pressure, and her mother cannot wash her at this spot. Her hand and entire limb present irregular movements of flexion and extension in the fingers, of adduction and abduction in the thumb, and of pronation and supination. She cannot write with this hand. She drags her leg and often falls. She passes restless nights.

She is very easily put into somnambulism by simple occlusion of the eyes. *The pain in the scar disappears at the first séance*, and her mother can wash her without causing the slightest pain.

After each séance the movements diminish in intensity. After four séances they remain distinctly less. Sleep after midnight is still disturbed. Before the séances she was not able to sleep at all. The little patient is now less depressed. She is still very much excited during the night of the 26th. She moves about in her sleep; her mother says that she is naughty and slaps her little brother. All these symptoms gradually disappear, but only disappear completely early in April. From this time on she is no longer restless and writes very well with her left hand.

After April 4, hypnotization is stopped. The child comes back on the 15th, and the improvement is maintained. I hypnotize her again several times, and a week later every trace of chorea has disappeared.

Thus localized troubles remaining after chorea, movements in a limb, tremor, trouble in moving or in writing, may yield rapidly to suggestion.

General chorea, taken in hand after its first appearance, seems to me more difficult to influence. I have tried in other cases beside the one I relate. Generally, it seems to me that the more general, intense and violent the chorea is, and when it involves the eyes and face and is accompanied with psychical troubles, the less suggestion takes hold of it. When the disease is in a less acute stage (*période d'agitation moindre*) hypnotization often succeeds very quickly in diminishing the intensity of the irregular movements; but it must be continued for weeks before it can arrest them completely.

OBSERVATION LIII —*General chorea dating back eight days.—Benefit after two seances.—Almost complete cure by suggestion, four or five weeks after its appearance.*

Jean A——, nine years old, was brought to me by his mother on December 9, 1886, for chorea.

When seven years old he had for the first time a violent chorea, which lasted three months. Eighteen months ago he was taken with articular rheumatism, which lasted fifteen days and was followed by intense general chorea, lasting three months. For the last fifteen days he has been waking at night with colic and diarrhœa.

Eight days ago he began to tremble in his right hand, and on the following days his other limbs were affected. During the night he has nightmare, and complains of pain. He is always hungry, and has eaten a great deal during this time. He has become disobedient; and moreover, is exacting and greedy.

He is a child of strong constitution. At the present time he answers questions well. He has incessant movements in both hands and legs, especially on the right side. He walks in quite an irregular way, dragging his right leg. He cannot write or do anything with his hands. He is troubled with irregular movements of flexion and extension, pronation and supination. We also notice movements of the face, especially of the orbicularis oris. His nights are very much disturbed. His general health is good. Heart and lungs normal.

I succeed in putting him into deep sleep easily; the movements continue during the sleep.

On the night of the 10th, the little patient fell out of bed without hurting himself.

On the night of the 11th, *after a second suggestion*, he was more quiet and the choreic movements were less intense. He does not write any better on the 12th. *Suggestion* on the 12th of December.

14th.—Yesterday the patient was very disobedient, wished to run away, and threatened to hang himself, and throw himself in the canal. He went into the street, took a walk alone, and then came back and began to laugh and cry. During the night he had a nightmare and cried for five minutes. The choreic movements are diminished. *Suggestion.*

16th.—Has done better since day before yesterday. Is more quiet.—*Suggestion.*

17th.—*The improvement continues.* Patient sleeps well, and the movements are less. Has fits of passion occasionally.—*Suggestion.*

18th.—Is doing well. Has not been in anger again.—*Suggestion.*

20th.—Is doing well. The choreic movements are less; *he writes better;* the letters are better formed. Sleeps well; woke during the night from fear.—*Suggestion.*

21st.—Had nightmare last night; cried for half an hour, then had colic, but no diarrhœa. We do not notice any more movements in the hand.—*Suggestion.*

Same condition on the days following.

24th.—Slept well last night without nightmare or fear. The patient is quiet in the daytime, his fits of passion are much less frequent.—*Suggestion.*

25th.—*Idem.* Nights quiet. Has still some movements, especially in the right leg and arm. Had some difficulty in speaking this morning. Nights quiet.—*Suggestion.*

27th.—Is doing well. Has had no more nightmares. Movements are less. Speaks well. His mother only complains that he still quarrels too readily with his sister.—*Suggestion.*

28th.—*Idem.*—Suggestion.

29th.—Is doing well. The movements are less. Sleeps well without waking, and without nightmare. Cannot yet write easily.—*Suggestion.*

30th and 31st.—Sleeps well, and is almost entirely well.—*Suggestion.*

Jan. 7th.—Although the suggestions have been stopped since the 31st, the benefit has continued. The child is quite calm, and is doing well. There are still some few movements; he had one nightmare on the night of the 3d.—*Suggestion.*

10th.—The child is doing well. His mother thinks he is almost completely cured. The attack has been much less severe and of much shorter duration than the previous ones.

12th.—He comes to see me for the last time; continues to do well. There is still slight movement at times in the frontal and facial muscles; almost none in the limbs.

To sum up, the affection seems to have been checked from the first séances; the choreic spasms diminished after two séances. The cerebral excitement diminished during the days following; the disease was almost completely checked in from four to five weeks. The two preceding attacks of chorea lasted three months.

OBSERVATION LIV —*Intense general chorea.—Improvement from the first séances of suggestion.—Almost complete cure after three or four weeks, eight weeks after the appearance of the disease.*

Jules G——, thirteen years old, working in a printing establishment, comes to the hospital on December 6, 1886, on account of chorea.

A year ago he underwent the amputation of a toe in consequence of a wound from a knife which fell upon his foot. A week before All Saints Day he contracted typhoid fever, which kept him in bed fifteen days. During convalescence, a month ago, *his character changed;* he became sullen, impertinent, and angry at the slightest cause. About the same time he had an hysteriform paroxysm with severe spasms, spasm of the ocular muscles and slight foaming at the mouth. There did not appear to be any loss of consciousness. The paroxysm lasted ten minutes. Fifteen days ago he had a second crisis; the next day a third.

The choreic movements commenced three or four weeks ago, after the first crisis; first the right hand, then the left hand, and then the left leg being involved. Fifteen days ago the left side was involved, and during the past few days there have been grimaces of the face. This affection came on without any apparent cause; there was no history of fright.

Present condition.—Constitution good; temperament lymphatic. The patient makes faces; his forehead wrinkles and is then smoothed out; his eyebrows separate and are then drawn close together, his eyes roll up, and his lips are drawn out every now and then. His tongue lies against the palate; he cannot protrude it from his mouth; his whole head is bent irregularly upon his neck. His arms are involved in curious movements, limited to the fingers or extending to the entire limb. For example, when a pen is put into his hand the child seizes it with difficulty, turns it around between his fingers, is obliged to use both hands in order to fix it properly, and when he tries to write, cannot. His pen does not touch the paper, the ring and index fingers are bent and the hand is raised; sometimes he suddenly lets go of the pen and moves his fingers as if they had been touched with a red hot iron. Similar phenomena are present in the legs. The child is told to get up out of bed; he makes a great many useless movements; his arms and legs are stuck out in all directions. He succeeds, however, in standing up quite easily, and his *walk is regular.* We notice that he draws his leg slowly forward, and that he *strikes the floor forcibly with his heel. He cannot stand on one leg;* if he tries it his arms and legs are projected aimlessly in all directions, the trunk bends from one side to the other, and the patient would fall if he were not supported.

The other functions are normal; digestion is good. Speech is *diffi-*

cult and jerky; the patient only pronounces a few syllables at a time or does not answer immediately, but waits for a moment of quiet. His intelligence is good; he is quite calm and much less passionate than when he was at home.

I *hypnotize* the child on December 7, by holding his eyes together for a few minutes. He is quiet during his sleep. His hands are still in motion; his face is tranquil. Before the suggestion I do not succeed in making him write a single letter. During sleep I make him write his name; it is only a scribble, in which, however, we can recognize his name. *Upon waking he writes very correctly;* but after this effort, his hands seem to be worn out and he can write no more. The night is passed quietly as is also the night following.—*Suggestion.*

9th.—The child is obedient; *he gets up and walks quite well;* he cannot eat alone; he has to be fed; he succeeds, however, in lifting a glass to his mouth. He cannot write; the pencil turns about in his hand; the fingers are moved in every direction; he cannot yet form a single letter. He picks up a pin without any difficulty. He cannot hold up his hands motionless. His arms bend, his hands come near together, etc. There is a tendency to movements of the lips, but the face is less disturbed. He gets up by making extensive movements with his arms, but walks well. His right leg is still sometimes suddenly projected in advance. The patient is doing well, and is less excited than when at home.—*Suggestion.*

10th.—Although he could not write yesterday, he succeeds in *writing his name very easily to-day.*—*Suggestion.*

11th.—*Idem.* Has been quiet. He sees himself that he is doing better. He still writes with great difficulty, and only succeeds in resting his three last fingers upon the paper after making many irregular movements.—*Daily suggestion.*

13th.—Holds his pencil much better and writes his name rapidly. Yesterday he was able *to go down-stairs and walk about in the court,* which he could not do before.—Since yesterday, also, the provoked sleep is deeper, and the restlessness which was at first exaggerated during his sleep, is immediately calmed. The arm remains in catalepsy, with almost no movement, and the fingers remain almost motionless. Upon waking, the patient writes his name but cannot write anything more.

14th.—Was more restless yesterday. This morning he makes faces. He cannot hold his arms up motionless. He writes Gross Ju, and stops after having written these letters, turning his pencil about in the hand without being able to write any further.

This condition continues during the days following. His nights are quiet; but there is no marked improvement. On the 18th, we notice choreic movements in his mouth and tongue.

24th.—He is more quiet and again succeeds in writing his name, though with difficulty. *On 28th, he succeeds in eating unaided; on the 29th, he writes faster and better*, and we still notice a slight movement in the lips preparatory to speech; but this is all in the face. He walks very well, and has very little movement in his hands. The movements are simply sudden and limited. The improvement continues, so much so that on January 10th he leaves the hospital almost completely cured.

He comes back to consultation on January 17th. He has only very slight choreic movements. He can eat alone. We still notice a slight difficulty in the articulation of words. His mother brings him back, because he has grown very passionate, exacting and naughty at home.—*Suggestion.*

19th.—Has been more calm; very slight movements. Still slight awkwardness in right hand.—*Suggestion.*

22d.—Is doing well; can press hard with his hands; *has no more fits of passion; speaks very well.*—*Suggestion.*

The patient has not come back.

To sum up, a very intense chorea of four weeks duration is promptly relieved after the first séances of suggestion, and is nearly completely cured after three or four weeks of suggestion, eight weeks after the appearance of the trouble.

OBSERVATION LV —*Writer's cramp, dating back three years.—Rapid improvement after the first séance.—Transient relapses.—Total cure after two months of suggestion.*

H. C——, forty-seven years of age, has been an accountant for twenty-five years. He comes to see me on November 18, 1885, for writer's cramp. He is a man of strong constitution, intelligent, not at all nervous, and has never had any disease. He says that about three years ago he experienced the first premonitions of his cramp, in flexion of his five fingers after he had written five or six lines. After resting for a certain time he could again write several lines, and then the cramp would again appear. These phenomena kept increasing; two years ago the cramp appeared after he had written three lines; a year ago he could only write half a line at the most, without having the cramp in flexion. He then fastened the pen to his index finger, and thanks to this expedient he could write pretty well for three or four months, but soon the other fingers began to bend so that they almost pressed into the flesh, he says. For two months, if he happened to be writing an address, the cramp would appear, and all five fingers would close when he got as far as Mons. The cramp disappeared when he laid aside his pen, and reappeared after he had written three or four letters, with such intensity that the pen would pierce the paper.

When the fixing of the pen to the index finger no longer succeeded, he tried another expedient; he held the pen applied against the extremity of the thumb, with the penholder held horizontally between the bent fingers, the extremity passing between the two last fingers. But soon the thumb, he says, pressed so strongly against the pen, that he had to stop. Two years ago he had to leave his place as accountant and go into an insurance office. For the last three months he has tried writing with his left hand.

On the 18th I hypnotize him. He goes into the third degree of sleep. I suggest the disappearance of the cramp, and upon waking, he writes two lines and a half before he is stopped by the flexion of the fingers.

On the 19th, sleep of the third degree is again induced. Upon waking he writes eight lines well without cramp.

On the 20th, I put him into somnambulism, without memory upon waking. He writes well when he wakes. At the ninth line only a slight flexion of the three last fingers appears, which is made to disappear by simple affirmation, but which reappears slightly on the following line. He also experiences a certain stiffness of the wrist.

21st.—He shows me a business letter that he had written the evening before. He has scarcely any cramp, but the stiffness in his wrist continues. Repetition of suggestion.

22d.—The stiffness has disappeared; he writes well. When he is writing there is still a slight tendency to flexion, but he straightens his fingers immediately. Moreover, before suggestion, he could not write a single letter with a short pencil, resting in the usual manner between the thumb and index finger. The flexion was immediate. As soon as the pen touched the paper, he had to hold it almost horizontally.—Since yesterday, he has been able to write with a short pencil.

23d.—This result is maintained; he has felt no more cramp or flexion in the fingers.—Daily suggestion.

24th.—He says that he is doing well. His wrist is still stiff. The fingers are more limber. I make him write during his sleep, by suggesting that his wrist is limber. Same condition on the following days. He always complains of stiffness in his wrist, which appears especially after he has been writing for a time.

As I am obliged to go away for two months on the 30th, I ask M. Liébault to continue the suggestions.

The following is what the patient has noted.

"30th.—I write after the séance: my wrist is always stiff. I can make no movement with it, which is very troublesome in writing. The fingers are doing well.

" December 1.—The wrist has moved a little, and it seems just now to be less stiff.

"2d.—After the séance and before leaving M. Liébault, I wrote every letter with a pencil, my wrist being more limber, but just now it has become stiff again and my thumb presses more strongly than the other fingers.

"5th.—By writing very slowly and continually thinking that my fingers must not press, I do better; but it is always the thumb which presses upon the pen. After having slept, the thumb presses less. I write better, especially when writing slowly. The wrist itself is less stiff.

"6th.—There is certainly improvement in the wrist; the thumb has only a slight tendency to press upon the pen."

On the 7th, H. C—— says he wrote three letters. He got through the first two well. The third was not so good, and he again wrote quite badly. The wrist moves a little; the thumb still presses upon the pen.

On the 16th, the thumb presses still more; however, the specimens of writing shown me each day by the patient indicate that he was writing well.

But the hypnotic sleep has been less profound for several days, which he atttibutes to the fact that M. Liébault hypnotizes him in a room full of people, where there is a great deal of noise, while with me he is hypnotized alone and in my office, where it is quiet. He does not go back to M. Liébault, and the treatment is discontinued until January 29, after my return to Nancy. The flexion of the thumb pressing upon the pen had increased, and hindered improvement.

29th.—This flexion is produced frequently, every two or three words. The other fingers are no longer bent, but the wrist is stiff.

After a new séance on the 29th, the thumb does not contract immediately, but at home the flexion is reproduced.

30th.—He writes four lines at home, and can get no further. Both the thumb and the index finger are flexed; the pen falls from his hand. He tries in vain to continue: the letters have no more form.

On February 1st, he writes quite well before the suggestion and very well after it.

2d.—He says that he writes very well at certain times, at other times the thumb and the index finger bend, and then he is forced to stop. When his fingers began to bend, on one occasion, he felt a pricking in his fore-arm. He also experiences this pricking when he is quiet and is not writing, especially in the evening.

I put him into somnambulism and I make him write in this condition with his eyes open: he writes very well; I suggest disappearance of the pricking.

3d.—He says he has no more pain or pricking; he writes well. But when he writes at home and not in my presence, the thumb and index finger bend, after a time; the painful prickling sensation has ceased.

4th.—He writes very well at my office. At home there is always slight flexion of the thumb, and his hand becomes heavy after a certain time.

5th.—He wrote a letter of a page and a half at home. The writing was good up to the end, but his hand felt tired.—He continues to write very well on the following days.

8th.—He still complains of flexion of the thumb and of stiffness in the wrist.—After each suggestion in my office, he writes very well without flexion and without stiffness. This is not the case when he writes at home.

11th.—He was able to write an hour without stopping. At the end of this time only the thumb began to bend; he rested his hand for twenty minutes and was able to begin again without having the flexion or stiffness.

I suggest that the more he writes the better he will write, that his hand will become limber by exercise and he will not get tired.

This condition continues on the following days and he improves gradually. On the 18th, he writes from an hour and a half to two hours. Only at the end of this time does the thumb begin to bend and his hand feel stiff.

19th.—His hand feels very light and he says he writes as if he had never had anything the matter with it.

20th.—While writing this morning his thumb bent two or three times, and the pen fell from his fingers; his writing, however, continues to be good.—I make him write fast, *currente calamo*, in the somnambulistic condition, with his eyes open.

20th.—In the afternoon it is impossible for him to write. He again has to fasten the pen to his index finger.

The next day passes without a new suggestion, and he does well, but cannot write long. After writing half an hour he has to stop. It is almost impossible for him to address his letters.

23d.—He works all the morning at his accounts; after a certain time, he feels twitchings in the back of his wrist which prevent his continuing. When he tries to go on, the pen falls from his hand; but he is able to begin again, and this morning he no longer feels any spasm.

25th.—He still says that he writes very well at my office, but that when he gets home his hand becomes stiff and he can no longer write with the same ease. I suggest that he shall write at home as he writes with me.

After the 27th, he no longer complains of any sensation of stiffness or of flexion. He writes a good deal on the 26th and 27th, and does it well. He writes letters and keeps accounts as he did before his cramp.

He comes to see me on March 2d, and the séances which were daily up to that time, are given up until the 8th. He writes every day during this interval and feels absolutely no premonition of cramp. "I write," says he, "as I please."

On the 8th a new séance. These séances are at longer intervals. He comes back on the 11th, 13th, 16th, 22d, 27th, and a complete cure has been maintained since the 27th of February. I still continue hypnotizing him twice a week for a month, in order to suppress any tendency to relapse. He has taken his position of accountant again, and writes all day just as he did before his trouble. The cure has been maintained.

We know how refractory **writer's cramp** often is to all medication. M. Wolff, a professor of caligraphy at Frankfort-on-the-Main, often succeeded empirically where physicians had failed.

Wolff's method is published by M. Romain Vigouroux in the *Progrès Médical* (1882, No. 3), in the following terms. It may be summed up under two heads: gymnastics and massage.

1st.—The gymnastic treatment is sometimes active, sometimes passive. Two or three times a day the patient should execute a series of movements of the upper limbs, successively, in all directions. These movements are generally sudden, the hands being now open, now closed. The number of movements in each series, and consequently the duration of the séances, is augmented progressively and. varies according to the case.

The passive movements consist in the more or less forced stretching, we might almost say elongation, of the muscles which are specially affected. This is the most delicate part of the treatment, because, according to M. Wolff, it is dangerous to exceed a certain degree. In addition, the patient repeats this manœuvre upon himself three or four times each day.

Writing exercises begin as soon as the spasmodic condition is notably diminished, that is to say after the first days.

2d.—Massage and friction are also very carefully practised by M. Wolff every day. He insists upon the importance of what we shall call the tapping of the muscles.

The duration of that part of the treatment which is carried on under M. Wolff's immediate direction is about fifteen days. A course of treatment which after four or five séances has produced no improvement, ought, according to him, to be abandoned.

We might ask if suggestion has not its share to claim in the cures obtained. The patients come to a specialist who is reputed to cure the disease with which they are affected; the specialist affirms the cure. The manipulation practised for half an hour, the massage and friction, the passive movements repeated three or four hundred times a day, all these things concentrate the attention upon the idea of cure, and incite the brain to put in action the inhibition necessary for the control of the spasm.

When we see ignorant bone-setters and quacks succeed in curing certain sprains and pains, rapidly, by methods which have nothing reasonable in them and sometimes nothing rational, is it not here too that the patient himself, to a certain degree realizes or facilitates his cure by auto-suggestion?

OBSERVATION LVI.—*Tetany of the upper limbs.—Attacks of somnambulism and nightmare.—Tetany cured in two séances, the somnambulism in one.*

A——, twenty years old, a shoemaker, comes to consult me on January 28, 1886, on account of tetany of the upper limbs. He has morbid antecedents. His mother says that between the second and seventeenth months of his life he had convulsions more than two hundred times. Since his infancy he has had double *talipes varus equinus*. His constitution is delicate, his disposition lymphatic, but he has had no serious illnesses. For the last four winters he has had cramps in the hands from six to ten times during the winter. Once only the legs were affected at the same time.

At the present time, he complains of cramps in his hands and of a pain spreading from his shoulder into his fingers, which have been present since four o'clock yesterday. The three last fingers on both hands are bent. They can be extended with pain, but the flexion is immediately reproduced. The index finger and the thumb remain extended. He can perform all other movements well. He can bend his elbows, and lift his arms to his head. The arm and fore-arm are painful upon pressure, especially in the region of the biceps. When this muscle is pressed flexion of the fore-arm results.

I put him into *somnambulism* by quiet and prolonged suggestion, and I suggest the disappearance of the pains and contracture, moving the joints of his fingers meanwhile. These movements continue to be painful during the hypnosis, and the extension of the fingers is not lasting.

Upon waking, after twenty minutes, *the cramp and pains had diminished notably*, but had not disappeared.

Four hours later the cramp disappeared in the upper limbs, but was replaced by a cramp in the right leg and heel, which persisted three hours. Since then he has had no more trouble, until four o'clock on the evening of February 8th. At this time he was taken with pains in the neck and shoulders without any apparent cause. At four o'clock on the afternoon of the 10th, flexion of both hands made its appearance, and has lasted ever since. He has had to be fed. He has slept well at night.

On February 11th his mother brings him to see me. The fingers are flexed into the palm of the hand. They can be stretched out, but complete extension is very painful, and the flexion is instantaneously reproduced. There is pain without rigidity in the neck and shoulders.

His mother tells us that for more than four or five years he has had dreams and nightmares, and that he gets up and goes to her bed weeping.

I hypnotize him, and he goes into profound sleep, but memory is preserved upon waking. I suggest the disappearance of the pain and rigidity. During the hypnosis the *contracture disappears;* he extends his fingers spontaneously and executes every movement. When he wakes the relaxation is maintained; he only complains of pain on the right side of his neck.

I hypnotize him a second time, and he goes into deep sleep, with amnesia upon waking. I suggest the disappearance of the pain, at the same time affirming that he will sleep quietly in his bed, will have no more bad dreams, will not think of getting up, and will only think of keeping warm in his bed.—*Upon waking the pain has disappeared.*

On February 14th his mother comes to bring me news of him. The upper limbs are doing very well; the cramp has not reappeared. Moreover, he has slept quietly for four nights. He had never passed two nights before without talking in his dreams.

He comes back to see me on March 23d; at three o'clock in the morning he was taken with cramp in his feet and hands. He had had no such attacks for six weeks. His mother says that he has never passed a winter in which he has been so free from them. During this time too, he has dreamed two or three times a night, talking aloud, but he has not got up.

The last three fingers on both hands are bent. They can be extended, but the flexion is quickly reproduced. The two other fingers are in extension: the patient cannot open his hands spontaneously Moreover, he walks unsteadily, and complains of sharp pain in the gastrocnemii.

Hypnotization: profound sleep for half an hour, passive movements of flexion and extension of the fingers. Upon waking he can open and shut his hands; but the fingers still have a tendency to bend inward;

the movements of adduction and abduction of the thumb are always difficult. He walks better, but still complains of pain in the calves of his legs.

After a new hypnotization, immediately after the first one (less profound sleep), *the pains in the calves disappear.*

The patient has not come back.

OBSERVATION LVII —*Attacks of nocturnal somnambulism.—Temporary cure by means of hypnotic suggestion.*

H——, a grocer's boy, fifteen years old, comes to see me in November, 1885. He has been at Nancy three months, and has had attacks of spontaneous somnambulism every night without exception. He gets up, goes about, often knocks over or breaks objects, and it is the greatest trouble to get him to go back to bed again. In the morning he remembers nothing about it. Before coming to Nancy he had similar attacks, but they were much less frequent, about two or three times a week, he thinks.

I hypnotize him; he goes into profound sleep. I suggest that he will remain quietly in his bed, and that he will only think of keeping warm when he is asleep. I suggest to him to come to me at the end of four days. He comes, in fact, to tell me that he is cured; that he has not gotten up for four nights.

The cure lasted three weeks, so the patient says. He went a few months later to be hypnotized by M. Liébault. After four new séances from the 16th to the 31st of February, 1886, the somnambulism had ceased. The patient discontinued the treatment from carelessness. The attacks reappeared after a certain time. I have no doubt that repeated suggestion would have brought about a perfect cure.

OBSERVATION LVIII —*Nocturnal incontinence of urine cured by suggestion in a single séance.*

M——, thirteen years old, a lymphatic, delicate child, is at Nancy at a boarding school. This boy, who is more than ordinarily intelligent, wets his bed two or three times during the week. He has not been able to break himself of this habit since his infancy.

The child comes to see me on October 16. He wet his bed four times during the ten days preceding this.

I hypnotize him on October 16; he only goes into the second degree; suggestive catalepsy, memory upon waking. I suggest that he will not wet his bed again; that he cannot make water when lying down, but only when standing in the vertical position.

He comes again to see me on the 17th, the 18th, and the 23d of October; since the time of the first suggestion he has not wet his bed.

OBSERVATION LIX —*Nocturnal incontinence of urine since infancy, relieved by a single suggestion.*

S——, seventeen years old, is a tall, well-behaved, though rather stupid boy, who comes to consult me for incontinence of urine, which he has had since infancy. In summer he wets his bed three or four times a week ; in winter every night. During the day he never passes water involuntarily. He says he makes water about six times during the day. He usually wakes but once during the night. No treatment has been tried.

He comes on December 28. *I hypnotize him easily into profound sleep ;* I suggest that he shall wake each time he wants to make water, and that he shall not wet his bed.

He comes regularly until the 31st. *He has not wet his bed since the first suggestion ;* he has waked four times during the night. The second and third night he waked three times. He comes again on January 7 and on the 10th. He has not wet his bed again, and does not wake up more than twice during the night.

He has not come back again and I do not know whether the result obtained has been permanent or not.

OBSERVATION LX —*Aphonia consecutive to pneumonia, cured by an energetic affirmation.—Nocturnal incontinence of urine in process of cure by suggestion.*

G. C——, fifteen years old, living with her parents, enters the hospital in my service on April 13, 1886, with a pneumonia involving the entire lower lobe of the right lung, six days advanced. Defervescence takes place on the morning of the 9th day, the 16th day of the month.

On the third day of the pneumonia she developed sore throat with hoarseness and absolute aphonia, which has lasted ever since. As this aphonia has remained the same in spite of defervescence, and in the absence of laryngeal pain, I think that the slight laryngitis which accompanied the pneumonia does not account for such a complete extinction of the voice, and believe that nervous inhibition has some share in its causation.

I try hypnotic suggestion on the 17th, 18th and 19th of April, without therapeutic result. G. C—— goes into somnambulism easily, but does not carry out hypnotic hallucinations, or post-hypnotic suggestions.

On the 21st, after a hypnotization without result, I try suggestion in the waking condition. It is useless at first; the little patient laughs easily and receives my assertions lightly, without allowing herself to be impressed. I pretend to be angry, and command her to speak in a loud voice, to say a, b; I state that she can do it and that I wish her to do it; she tries, and distinctly articulates a, b, and then her name. The aphonia disappears when she makes an effort. During the day the voice becomes perfect. She still articulates distinctly on the next day, and after the evening of the 23d she can talk as well as she could the day before.

This is not all. This young girl has had an infirmity since her infancy; incontinence of urine. During the night she passes water freely in bed; she has to be waked three times in order to prevent it. During the day she cannot go more than an hour and a half without making water. In consequence of this infirmity she has not been sent to school; she does not know how to read or write. Two years ago she spent two months in the hospital in order to be relieved of this trouble. She was treated with compresses of cold water applied over the hypogastric region, but without result.

About the 20th the patient passed water freely in bed every night. After the 21st I try the hypnotic suggestion that she will not wet her bed, that she cannot do it, that she can go a long time without feeling the need of making water.

Since then she has been able to go three hours during the day without urinating. On the night of the 22d she does not wet her bed, but on the 23d she again does it.

On the 24th she goes all day without urinating, and since this time has only urinated twice a day.

Continuation of suggestion.—During the night she wets her bed a little, although she gets up three times.

I am away from Nancy for several days. The suggestion is discontinued. The incontinence of urine is cured in regard to the daytime. During the night she still wets her bed a little, but very little. She is waked once every night.

Therapeutic suggestion is begun again on May 6.

She does not wet her bed during the night. She was waked once during the night.

May 8th.—Has not wet her bed. Was waked once. I order her not to be waked; I suggest that she shall wake spontaneously.

9th.—She did not wake last night and did not wet her bed.

10th.—She wet her bed again; she attributes this to fright; the patient in the next bed died during the night.—*Daily suggestion.*

11th.—Wet her bed very slightly.

12th.—The patient was chloroformed yesterday in the opthalmological department (she has a *pannus* due to *entropion*); she went to sleep in the afternoon and wet her bed a little; during the night, *idem.*

13th, and 14th.—She has not wet her bed. Only wakes once during the night; I suggest that she shall wake twice.

15th.—She wet her bed very slightly. She only waked once.

16th and 17th.—She has not wet her bed again. She waked twice during the night to make water. I repeat this last suggestion emphatically, and insist upon it that she shall not forget it when she wakes. During the day she does not make water more than twice voluntarily. On June 1st the cure may be considered as established. For ten days the patient, whom I have ceased to hypnotize, has not forgotten herself once.

M. Liébault has treated a large number of children with this trouble, generally successfully. Usually from one to three séances are sufficient to insure a cure. Sometimes there is a relapse after a certain number of days; but a new suggestion re-establishes the cure.

The following are the results which M. Liébault has given me: "In seventy-seven cases of incontinence of urine, I have had twenty-three rapid and certain cures in cases from which I have heard later on, and the cures have been permanent. Twenty-three rapid cures after treatment, without hearing from them again; ten slow, certain cures, news of them again; nine improvements; eight not benefited. Four subjects were hypnotized once and have not returned since; I have not had any news of them."

V

Dynamic Pareses and Paralyses

Observation LXI —*Sense of weight and muscular weakness of the left upper limb.—Marked improvement after one séance.*

J——, eighteen years old, a locksmith, comes to see me on February 25, 1885. Ten or twelve years ago he felt a heaviness in his left hand, which has persisted ever since and prevents his using this hand. He can shut it, but with a good deal of difficulty. He opens it slowly; he flexes the arm and fore-arm with a certain stiffness; his fingers feel as if they were made of rubber; he can only take hold of a sheet of paper with difficulty; there is no pain elsewhere, either spontaneous or on pressure; tactile sensibility is preserved; in the region of the deltoid there is a sensation of weight and swelling. There is trouble with the left knee; upon walking the movement of flexion is sudden and impresses a gait upon the foot which resembles ataxia.

The left hand registers fifteen or sixteen by the dynamometer; the right hand thirty-seven.

The patient is hypnotized and goes into profound sleep. *After suggestion and waking, the dynamometer registers 22 for the left hand, and 32 for the right; he takes hold of a sheet of paper with his left hand very well.*

The patient is submitted to a second hypnotization immediately after the first, with a new suggestion. *Upon waking, the left hand registers 26 by the dynamometer, the right 31.* He only feels slight stiffness in his hand; he walks somewhat better.

He has not come to see me again.

OBSERVATION LXII —*Dynamic psychical paraplegia dating back two months.—Notable improvement after one séance.—Complete cure after three séances.*

L——, sixty-seven years old, enters the hospital on April 12, 1884, for pneumonia of the inferior right lobe nine days advanced, defervescence having already taken place. The temperature continues to rise occasionally in the evening to 38° C., until the 24th of April. The cough and expectoration have disappeared, the appetite is good, and all the functions seem normal. Constitution is slightly debilitated by age and privation; but the disease terminated some time ago and the convalescent still remains in bed.

On May 8 I ask her why she does not get up; she then says that she cannot stand. Two months ago, she says (a month before her pneumonia), walking became difficult. She dragged herself about painfully, and, since her pneumonia, she cannot stand. Her sensibility is perfect, the tendon reflexes are normal, and the muscles are not atrophied. Lying in bed she can perform any movements. I make her get up; she cannot stand without leaning against her bed, her legs soon bend and she falls. She says she had epileptic seizures during the active period of her life, quite frequently. She has not had any more during the past two years.

I do not find any sign of myelitis, and I think it is a case of *dynamic weakness*, which the patient's impressionability has transformed into *psychical paralysis.*

I hypnotize her on May 8, and she goes into *profound sleep;* I suggest that she can walk. Upon waking, she stands without support for three seconds, showing a marked tendency to fall backward.

On the 9th, after the second séance, she stands better and takes a few steps, very much astonished at being able to do it.

On the 10th, after the third séance, she walks slowly, without falling, and without showing any tendency to fall back. When she stands, she spreads her legs apart in order to make sure of a firm basis.

On the 11th she walks about all day without support, which she has not been able to do for more than two months.

I still hypnotize her from time to time; she continues to walk very well; on the 24th she goes up and down-stairs alone.

She remains cured.

OBSERVATION LXIII —"*Growing pains*" *and muscular weakness in the lower limbs.—Marked improvement after the first séance.—Complete cure in five séances.*

S——, fifteen and a half years old, a boy of strong constitution, without any previous illness, has complained for the last six months of weakness in his legs, which has been accompanied with pain in the back of the thigh for the last three weeks. He notices it in walking and especially in going upstairs. When he walks upon sloping ground he makes false steps every minute; his foot turns inward. He cannot run. He walks as sailors do, swaying about.

He comes to see me on May 30, 1885. I do not find any lesion, or any functional trouble other than the pain in the back of the thighs and the difficulty in walking; the muscular force is normal. I think that it is a question of a dynamic muscular trouble connected perhaps with growth. The boy says he has grown a head during the past six months.

I hypnotize him; he goes into the sleep of the third degree, memory being preserved upon waking. He has almost no more pain when he walks, and holds himself much better.

31st.—He continues to do better; he only made two or three false steps going down the hill. He is able to walk from an hour and a half to five hours without being fatigued, while before he got tired after walking for a quarter of an hour; he still has pain in going upstairs. Second séance.

June 3d.—Third séance. 4th.—Fourth séance. Still complains of pain when he bends his thigh and when he gets up.

9th.—Says he walked yesterday for three hours without fatigue or pain; two months ago could not have walked a quarter of the distance. Suggestion continued.

11th.—Says he no longer feels any pain; no pain in going upstairs; since the first suggestion he has walked without swaying about.

13th.—Last séance. He runs, jumps, and no longer makes any false steps. He feels no more trouble.

I continue to see the young man frequently; the cure has persisted up to this day.

VI

Gastro-intestinal Affections

Observation LXIV —*Chronic alcoholism.—Gastritis.—Insomnia ; weakness in the legs. Rapid improvement by means of suggestion.*

T——, a laborer, fifty-two years old, enters the hospital on February 9, 1884. He has alcoholic habits contracted in Africa, where he passed ten years; he boasts of being able to drink a litre of absinthe in three hours.

A month and a half ago he developed pain in the right axilla, accompanied with cough and expectoration. This pain has disappeared during the last four or five days. At times for the past three weeks he has complained that the passage of food is obstructed at a point near the lower end of the sternum. There is no vomiting and no regurgitation. After having eaten he feels an epigastric swelling, which lasts about two hours. There are often acid eructations, which last half an hour, and at times there are cramps in the stomach. His movements are regular. His sight has been troubled for fifteen days. He has nightmare, sleeps very little, and his sleep is disturbed.

Two years ago he says that he had left sciatica lasting one year, which obliged him to walk with a stick. *He was cured in from eight to fifteen days by hypnotic suggestion, by Dr. Liébault.*

He is a man of strong constitution; we do not find any cardiac or pulmonary trouble. The epigastric region is sensitive; the stomach does not seem dilated, the liver is not increased in size. There is slight tremor of the hands, accompanied with analgesia (without anæsthesia) limited to the upper limbs. He complains especially of epigastric pains, of acid eructations, nightmares, and weakness in his legs.

(Diagnosis; *chronic alcoholism; alcoholic gastritis.*)

10th.—He is hypnotized: profound sleep: suggestion. The next day he says he ate and digested better. The analgesia persists, he still has nightmare.—Suggestion.

12th.—Says he felt well during the day yesterday but did not sleep during the night. He again complains of frontal cephalalgia and of twinges of pain in the epigastrium, which disappear by suggestion. He leaves the hospital on this day, but comes back three times to be hypnotized before the 16th.

16th.—He says that for the first time in three months he has slept quietly, "like a French peer." He has no more acidity or epigastric pain. He feels stronger, looked for work yesterday and engaged himself as a grave-digger. He promises that he will drink no more brandy;

nevertheless, although we have suggested a distaste for alcohol, he does not feel it.

He comes the following year on January 31, 1885. He says he has been well until fifteen days ago. He complains of having had attacks of intermittent fever during this time. Twenty-two years ago he had frequent attacks of fever in Africa, where he was a soldier, and since his return he has had three or four attacks every spring, which disappear after the use of sulphate of quinine. Since this fever, he has experienced weakness in his limbs, loss of appetite, dislike for food, and also a ringing sound in his head and left ear.

On Februrary 2, we find him anæmic, his constitution is deteriorated, his temperature normal. Respiratory sounds normal except for some sibilant sounds on inspiration.

Heart normal; slight mitral systolic murmur. He says that he was well and digested his food well up to fifteen days ago.

If we can believe him, he has not relapsed into his alcoholic excesses since last year, and is content with a dram in the morning.

From some cause, however, he has again had eructations after eating, and lack of appetite for the last fifteen days. He does not vomit and his movements are regular. Finally, during the same period, he has again had insomnia and nightmare.

The fever has not reappeared since his admission to the hospital.

He is hypnotized on the evening of the 2d and sleeps very well during the night without dreaming, waking three or four times. He complains of a burning sensation in the chest. Suggestion.

4th.—Appetite and digestion better. Burning sensation in the chest and ringing sound in the head and left ear persist. Suggestion continued.

5th.—Is doing better. He slept, but only until one o'clock this morning. The burning sensation in the chest has greatly diminished in consequence of suggestion. The ringing sound persists. He has no more eructations.—He demands his dismissal.

OBSERVATION LXV —*Chronic gastritis.—Dilatation of the stomach.—Marked improvement and cessation of the vomiting in consequence of suggestion, without complete cure.*

H——, twenty-three years old, enters the hospital on January 20, 1885, from the blind asylum. He lost his sight when he was fourteen years old. At this time he also had a gastritis which lasted two months; he vomited all nourishment.

At the present time he has been sick for four years. The trouble began with obstinate constipation, which lasted from eight to ten days. Diarrhœa followed the use of a purgative and lasted three months, accompanied with colic and slight tenesmus.

After the diarrhœa had existed a month, attacks of vomiting came on which still recur at intervals of from ten days to six weeks. During this time there has been a sense of weight in the stomach. He has often been stopped in his work. Since December 6, there has been no intermission. Years ago he was treated by washing out the stomach.

We note: delicate constitution, lymphatic temperament, emaciation; no fever. Appetite ordinarily irregular, sometimes very good. At the present time no appetite, no loathing of food. Complains of a sensation of pain in the stomach which lasts from five to six hours after eating. Vomiting at times immediately, at times one or two hours after eating. Sometimes at the evening meal he vomits what he has eaten in the morning.

He often has eructations which last the entire day. They are frequently acid, with pyrosis, even when he has not eaten. They appear especially after the attacks of vomiting. At times he is troubled with hiccough. The vomiting is always alimentary. Frequent pains in the pit of the stomach, sensation of pain and hunger after vomiting. Cramps in the morning until he has eaten. Tendency to constipation for the last three months; only has a movement every four days; at times colic without diarrhœa. Urine scanty.—Sometimes complains of palpitation and of severe neuralgia. At the present time, the left facial nerve is sensitive to pressure. Insomnia provoked by pains. Stomach sounds are heard as low as two inches above the umbilicus; the region is not sensitive. In the chest, respiration is slightly bronchial at the right apex. The patient has coughed and expectorated slightly for six weeks. Diagnosis; chronic gastritis. Dilatation of the stomach. Incipient tuberculosis. Treatment: washed chalk and calcined magnesia, half a teaspoonful before each meal. Eight drops of hydrochloric acid after each meal.

This treatment, in addition to that of washing out the stomach, remains inefficacious. Patient continues to vomit everything he takes.

28th.—Hypnotization and energetic suggestion in the morning. He only goes into the first degree of sleep: drowsiness without catalepsy. Before being hypnotized he vomited his bouillon.

29th.—We note that the patient has not vomited since the suggestion. He has not gone for so long a time without vomiting since the 6th of December.

He slept better last night.—Suggestion.

30th.—Hardly vomited at all yesterday.—Milk diet. Sleeps better.

On the following days he hardly vomits at all. On February 6, he eats rare meat without vomiting. He sleeps quite well, but sometimes has nightmares still. On the 7th, he vomits a watery fluid. On the 10th, he still complains of bad digestion, but does not vomit. Induced sleep does not exceed the first degree.—Asked for his dismissal.

OBSERVATION LXVI —*Gastric troubles.*—*Burning sensation near the stomach.*—*Insomnia.*—*Cure in four séances.*

Widow C——, forty-seven years old, enters the hospital on March 30, 1886. She is the mother of thirteen children, five of whom are living; the last child was born twelve years ago; her husband died of tuberculosis.

She has been sick for a week. When she went to bed in the evening she felt dizzy, as if sparks of fire were dancing before her eyes. Nausea, cold sweats, tendency to syncope. She lay in bed and shivered all night; sensation of cold persisted the next day, accompanied with extreme weakness of the legs. The cough which she has had for some time became more severe. For three or four nights, she has felt twinges of pain in the temples every now and then.

Digestion has been imperfect for twelve years. Appetite usually good, has grown poor in the last three weeks. Epigastric weight, acid eructations, glairy regurgitations. Movement every two or three days. Menstruation normal.

16th.—*Present condition :* weak constitution; temperament lymphatic. Pulse regular. No fever. Upon examination of the chest, we find the inspiration rough at the right apex, and expiration slightly bronchial at the left apex. Dilatation of the stomach : sounds as low as the umbilicus. For the last four or five days has complained of a burning sensation, which she localizes along the sternum. She had a painful spot in the anterior part of the right axilla, which only lasted ten minutes. Had pain in temples three or four different times during the night, lasting half an hour each time. Continually has eructations. Vomited once yesterday evening. Had cramps in stomach all yesterday afternoon. Has not slept an instant since her admission (13th of March).

In the evening I try suggestion; I only obtain simple drowsiness. I suggest the disappearance of the existing troubles, and leave her, telling her to continue sleeping.

17th.—Says she slept from six o'clock to half-past seven yesterday evening. Her head is clearer. The other troubles persist.

New suggestion : patient goes into *somnambulism.* Upon waking, the burning sensation in the sternum has diminished greatly. I put her to sleep again and suggest that she shall sleep an hour.

18th.—Slept two hours last night. Condition the same as yesterday; *the burning sensation in the sternum still exists.* She vomited once. Interscapular pains. Suggestion, and sleep lasting an hour.

19th.—*Slept four hours last night. The pains have greatly diminished. There is less sensation of burning.* Has not vomited. No more dorsal pains, and no shooting pains in temples. Only complains of slight tenderness over right temple. Scarcely any eructations.

New suggestion : She sleeps an hour and a half.

20th.—Slept the whole night. Complains of no more pain in the sternum or elsewhere. Eats with a good appetite this morning. Feels perfectly well and asks for her dismissal.

OBSERVATION LXVII —*Parenchymatous metritis.—Gastro-intestinal catarrh.—Neuropathic pains.—Temporary amelioration by means of suggestion.*

A——, 31 years old, enters the clinic on April 25, 1885. She is married, and is the mother of four children, all of whom she nursed. She has been ailing since her last confinement. She got up on the third day, and developed a metrorrhagia, which kept her in bed three weeks, without abdominal pain. Since this time she has had leucorrhœa. The menses are irregular and scanty, recurring once every two months as a rule. In December last, she had an abcess at the edge of the anus which lasted for some time, and an inguinal adenitis on the left side, which suppurated.

Five or six weeks before this abscess appeared, she says she had a sensation of abdominal enlargement. After using a purgative, she had diarrhœa for a month, followed by constipation, which has lasted up to the present time.

For the last two or three months, there has been bloody leucorrhœa without fetor, with occasional discharge of fibrinous shreds, and abdominal pains, which she says prevent her from sleeping, and severe colic when she has a movement. For six months her appetite has been poor. A desire to vomit after each meal has been present. She has lost thirty-six pounds in six months.

On April 28, while I was talking to the patient, she developed an attack of weeping and tremor.

Temperament lymphatico-nervous. No fever. Pyrosis lasting from two to three hours and frequently repeated. Frequent colic; she often has bloody movements accompanied with tenesmus and borborigmi. Abdomen is flat and soft, no pain upon pressure except over the epigastrium; stomach sounds as low as the umbilicus. To the touch, the neck of the uterus is low, the os is patent and projects forward, the posterior lip is indurated and thickened, and there is slight retroversion. She has never had convulsive paroxysms, but has experienced a sensation as of a lump rising from the epigastrium into the throat. Pain upon pressure of the right renal region and at the inferior border of the ribs. She sometimes has vertigo. *Diagnosis: parenchymatous metritis.—Chronic gastro-intestinal catarrh.—Neuropathy.*

April 28th.—Patient is *hypnotized;* she goes into profound sleep or somnambulism.—*Suggestion.*

29th.—Says she *slept better* last night, but still complains of pains in the hypogastrium and about the sacrum. *Suggestion.*

30th.—She complains less of pain, has no more in the sacral region, but always in the epigastrium. Pressure is also painful over the hypogastrium. Has had no movement since the 27th. Leucorrhœa. Insomnia.—*Suggestion.*

May 2d.—A small abscess is found in the left buttock, which is opened during hypnotic sleep, and the patient remembers nothing about it upon waking. The constipation has not yielded to suggestion. Rectal injections.

3d.—Is doing better. Slept all last night. Appetite poor.

5th.—Abscess is doing well. Passed a good night. Yesterday evening, *pain in right side of the abdomen, which disappeared after suggestion.* This morning, acute tenderness over hypogastric region as far as the umbilicus. It diminishes in consequence of suggestion.

7th.—Since yesterday evening, the patient has had painful spots about the left breast, which have prevented her from sleeping. Still complains of pain about the xiphoid appendix when she has eaten. Has no more nausea, and no more leucorrhœa. Tenderness upon pressure of the left interscapular region. *Suggestion is continued, but irregularly.*

10th.—She still complains of supra-umbilical pains after having eaten.—*Suggestion.* In the evening she eats without much appetite but without pain.

13th.—Again complains of a painful sensation in the epigastrium. Did not sleep during the night.—*Suggestion.*

14th.—Yesterday she ate a little at mid-day after suggestion. Ate better in the evening and slept pretty well at night. Appetite is still poor.—*Suggestion.*

15th.—Is doing well; *has eaten her food without pain.*

16th.—She continues to do well. Asks for her dismissal.

VII

Various Painful Affections

OBSERVATION LXVIII —*Epigastralgia relieved by a single suggestion.*

M——, forty years old, a railway employee, comes to consult me on May 28, 1884. His constitution is strong, but he is very nervous. He came to me two months ago for an epigastric pain, which disappeared after hypnotic suggestion.

Two days ago this pain reappeared. It no longer exists spontaneously, but when he is on night duty he is suddenly taken with sharp pain and epigastric oppression, lasting from quarter to half an hour. Then it disappears, giving place to a renal pain which lasts the same length of time. It recurs twice in the course of twenty-four hours. Appetite is fair and digestion good. Pressure over epigastric region determines very sharp pains.

He goes *into profound sleep upon suggestion,* without memory upon waking. *When he wakes he no longer feels any pain.*

Several months later he comes back with the same pain. *It again yields entirely to one hypnotic suggestion.*

OBSERVATION LXIX —*Slight catarrhal nephritis.—Epigastric and umbilical pains which rapidly yield to suggestion.*

G——, fourteen years old, a shoemaker's apprentice, comes to the clinic on June 12, 1883.

At eleven o'clock on June 9, he had a chill followed by fever and sweating. The next day he felt weak, complained of temporal neuralgia on the right side, which still persists, of lack of appetite, and of abdominal pains.—Two years ago the boy had an attack of chorea, and last year typhoid fever.

He is delicate, and of lymphatic temperament. Temperature normal, pulse regular, respiration clear, tongue dry, and slightly coated. He has no appetite, eructations without nausea, no movement for four days. Complains of a pain in the epigastrium and in the right renal region. Says he has xanthopsia. Urine is bloody, contains traces of albumen, and white and red blood cells. Sp. gr. 1012. (Hemoglobinuria? Slight catarrhal nephritis?)

14th.—*Hypnotic suggestion;* he goes into *somnambulism.* The renal and epigastric pains disappear, but return in half an hour.

15th.—Feels sharp pain from the xiphoid appendix as far as the umbilicus and about the borders of the ribs; the pain disappears instantly upon hypnotic suggestion.

19th.—Urine is still bloody, and cloudy. Sp. gr. 1014, with traces of albumen. Pains have not reappeared.

In the evening he again complains of pain at the borders of the ribs on both sides. It disappears immediately after hypnotic suggestion.

He continues to do well, still feels slight lassitude, but no more pain; the urine has become normal.

On July 8 he comes again, complaining of a pain in the region of the umbilicus which has existed since day before yesterday, especially during micturition. He also complains of palpitation; we find a slight systolic murmur at the base of the heart. Suggestion makes the umbilical pain disappear. It does not reappear, and the patient returns feeling very well, on July 14.

OBSERVATION LXX —*Severe interscapular pain cured in one hypnotic séance.*

J——, twenty-seven years old, married, constitution delicate, temperament nervous, comes to consult me on March 6, 1886. Since ten o'clock yesterday morning he has had pain in the left interscapular region, with a sensation as of an iron bar when he wishes to bend over. When resting he feels no pain, but if he wishes even to lift a package of shoes (he is employed in a shoe-factory), he has to let it fall on account of the pain. Yesterday evening it was so severe that he had to be taken home. He slept well during the night, but this morning he could not bend over, or put on his boots.

He had pneumonia last year, which lasted two months. He is not subject to neuralgia and has no other nervous affection.

Pressure over the interscapular region and about the angle of the scapula causes very severe pain.

I propose to hypnotize him by closing his eyes. He gives himself up to it with a bad grace. He is very impressionable, and fears that I wish to perform an operation upon him. I reassure him and continue *suggestion* holding his eyes closed. His nervous anxiety is with difficulty dissipated. His hands tremble. However, he goes into *profound sleep*; there is relaxation without catalepsy, and no memory upon waking. I energetically suggest calmness of mind; I affirm that the pain has disappeared.

Having let him sleep alone for about six minutes, he has several nervous spasms and calls out: "I am falling!" and then awakens as if coming out of a nightmare. He remembers having dreamed that he was falling into a ditch.—*The pain has almost completely disappeared;* he is surprised at being able to bend over, feels his back to find the spot and does not find anything. He lifts a chair easily, which he could not do before.

I hypnotize him a second time. He gives himself up easily. His sleep is more quiet; there are slight nervous movements in his hands.—I suggest the complete disappearance of the pain. Upon waking, he remembers having heard talking but does not know what I said. He remembers, however, having heard me say that military music was playing! But this suggestion did not succeed; he did not hear the music.

He only complains of a certain general dulness. There is not the slightest pain; he can bend over and lift an object from the ground, and make muscular efforts without any pain. He does not trust his own feelings, he tries to find the painful spot but does not succeed. He does not understand it; his astonishment has something comical about it.

OBSERVATION LXXI —*Tubercular diathesis.—Restoration of sleep and disappearance of the thoracic pains by suggestion.*

B——, sixteen years old, a shoemaker's apprentice, enters the hospital on February 15, 1885.

Six months ago he had a painful spot in the left axilla which yielded to blistering in about six days. At the same time he had oppression, without cough or expectoration. He has always been able to work. For the last six days, there has been palpitation and cough without expectoration; appetite medium for about three weeks. During the last three nights he has had night sweats. His parents died of tuberculosis.

He is of lymphatic temperament, but good constitution. No fever, pulse 80, and regular. Digestive functions normal, thorax well formed. The heart beats normally. Slight systolic murmur at the base and over the carotids. Respiratory sounds normal; we only find roughened expiration, with slight bronchial respiration at the right apex.

(Diagnosis: *tubercular diathesis.*)

The evening of his entrance, *hypnotic suggestion; somnambulism.*

He sleeps well during the night; did not sleep at all the preceding night. Has slept very little for two months.

17th.—Patient slept very well again last night, after suggestion. He no longer complains of oppression.

18th.—He complains of pain in the right shoulder, which disappears immediately after hypnotic suggestion.

The thoracic pain does not reappear. He remains in the hospital until the 24th, complaining of nothing more than slight palpitation of the heart.

OBSERVATION LXXII —*Hypogastric and suprainguinal pains on the left side, connected with a former pelvic-peritonitis.— They disappear in several séances.*

B——, twenty-one years old, a seamstress, enters the service on January 24, 1885. A year ago she was confined. The placenta had to be extracted; part of it remained. A week after she had fever, which lasted fifteen days, accompanied with pains in the left side of the abdomen. She nursed the child for a week, and then had an abscess of the breast.

After a month she took a place again; her periods came back normally until April. In May, without apparent cause, she had leucorrhœa for about three months, without pain. She came to the hospital, and, was treated with injections of ergotine. The leucorrhœa was stopped and she left in June feeling very well.

In July, she developed pains in the left flank, in the inferior region of the left axilla, and in the back. *These pains disappeared after blistering and hypnotization.*

She left about the end of July, cured. The periods came again normally and were not excessive.

For the last nine days, she has again had pain above the groin and in the hypogastrium. The patient has been in bed for a week. The pains occur especially in the evening and morning, lasting about an hour.—Insomnia for a week.

On January 27, we note: temperament lymphatic, constitution delicate. Pulse regular, 96. No fever.—Abdomen tympanitic and soft. Pain upon deep pressure above the left crural arch and in the hypogastrium; at times spontaneous.—The patient has eaten little for a week, but does not complain of dislike for food or other digestive trouble. Movements normal since she has been at the hospital; two months before, constipation with colic.—Hypogastric pain in urinating.—To the touch, the os is large and patent. Slightly sensitive on the left side. Marked antiflexion of the uterus. Cul-de-sac free.—Abundant non-odorus leucorrhœa for three months.—Pains in the loins co-existing with abdominal pains.—no evidences of hysteria. Respiration normal. *Diagnosis: Antiflexion of the uterus; old pelvic-peritonitis.*

On the night of the 26th, the patient *slept a little* in consequence of hypnotic suggestion.

27th.—In the morning, *hypnotization:* patient goes into profound sleep: the disappearance of the abdominal pain is suggested. *Upon waking, the pain upon pressure has completely disappeared. It reappears in an hour.*

28th.—Pain upon pressure of the hypogastrium and above the left groin. She complains moreover of a pain in the right ear, and pressure at the emergence of the facial nerve causes very acute pain.—Hypnotization at ten o'clock in the morning: profound sleep with automatism, suggestive anæsthesia, and amnesia upon waking. I suggest the disappearance of the pains. Upon waking, the pains have disappeared. Pressure of the hypogastrium and of the facial nerve does not provoke them.

29th.—Abdominal pain returned about three o'clock to-day. The facial pain has not returned. Patient slept a little last night. At eight o'clock this morning, more severe pain lasting a quarter of an hour. At the present time, ten o'clock, it only exists upon pressure.—*Suggestion : disappearance of the pain.*

30th.—The pain did not reappear during the day yesterday. This morning slight pain for ten minutes.—Continuation of suggestion.

31st.—She had no more pain yesterday. This morning it came back and was very severe from five to six o'clock.—Continuation of suggestion without any other treatment.

February 3d. Patient has no more pains: the leucorrhœa still persists. She sleeps well at night.

OBSERVATION LXXIII —*Neuralgic intercostal pain dating back fifteen days, relieved by suggestion.*

Eugenie G———, 17 years old, left the hospital on June 22d, after having been there five weeks for erythema nodosum of the legs. She comes to consultation on September 14, 1883, for a neuralgic intercostal pain in the seventh space on the left side, sometimes too, but rarely, on the right, dating back fifteen days, and manifesting itself especially when she coughs, preventing her from sleeping. Pressure upon the intercostal space is painful. She is hypnotized and goes into the second degree of sleep. *Upon waking she feels no more pain either spontaneous or upon pressure. The patient has not come back.*

OBSERVATION LXXIV —*Obstinate thoracic pains consecutive to pneumonia.—Transient disappearance after suggestion.—They do not disappear definitely until after ten days of suggestion.*

L———, of Saverne, thirty-three years old, enters the hospital on September 20, 1883, for a pneumonia with bronchitis. He has been convalescent for fifteen days (October 7), and walks about in the ward. There remains a shooting pain extending from the left border of the ribs to the level of the umbilicus on one side, and to the clavicle on the other, following the mammary line. The pain is constant and very sharp, obliging him to catch his breath three or four times before continuing to breathe. Last night, after having been out the day before and getting tired, he was waked at midnight by an increase of the pain, which lasted all night.

Patient is *hypnotized October 7 ; light sleep ; suggestion.* Upon waking *the pain has manifestly diminished.* A sore spot remains limited to the border of the ribs.

8th.—Was waked last night at one o'clock. The pain had increased and respiration has been embarrassed since this time. To-day the pain extends from the umbilical line to the sixth space.

New hypnotic séance.—a first trial only produces drowsiness without result; a second brings about profound sleep. Upon waking, the pain has greatly diminished: it extends from the umbilical region to the ninth space; respiration is accomplished without effort.

9th.—The pain returned yesterday at three o'clock. Two painful spots in the umbilical and infra-mammary region. *Third séance: total disappearance of the pains.*

10th.—The pain reappeared at half-past twelve; the patient could not sleep after ten o'clock in the evening. (Two blisters were applied.)

11th.—Pain in the eighth intercostal space, in front of the mammary line, very intense, tearing, with sensation of weight over the sternum.—It has disappeared below the costal border.—It appeared yesterday evening at ten o'clock and prevented the patient from sleeping.—Upon auscultation, there are always slight rales at the right base. When he is made to sit down, the patient complains of vertigo due to his pulmonary trouble. Cephalalgia.

After hypnotic suggestion, the painful spot persists upon pressure; but the weight over the sternum is less.—A second séance immediately after the first, makes the painful spot disappear as well as the cephalalgia.

At half-past one this spot returns, but the pain is less severe and unaccompanied with the sensation of weight over the sternum. Hypnotic suggestion at half-past four, makes it disappear completely.

12th.—Passed a good night, no pain. Patient has slept well for the first time. Since yesterday evening there has been a sensation of weight over the sternum, and slight burning. Slightly painful spot at the border of the axilla.—Hypnotic suggestion. Upon waking, the painful spot has disappeared, as well as the sensation of burning. There only remains a slight sensation of weight over the sternum.

He leaves on the 12th, and returns to the hospital on the 14th. The painful spot has not disappeared. Slept well on the night of the 12th. Since yesterday morning, he has again experienced a sense of weight over the sternum and a sensation of burning about the middle of the sternum. There has been a desire to vomit, accompanied with bitter regurgitations this morning.—*After hypnotic suggestion he no longer feels any trouble.*

15th.—Painful spot returned at half-past eleven in the morning but the pain was less intense. He slept during the night, and this morning took an emetic; he vomited twice and had one movement.—At the present time, the burning sensation exists along the whole length of the sternum.—After hypnotic suggestion the patient feels better, but the burning sensation still exists. He stills complains of having a slight sense of thoracic constriction.

16th.—The burning sensation has disappeared since yesterday morn-

ing. Patient only complains of a slight feeling of thoracic constriction.
—*Suggestion.*

17th.—He no longer has the burning sensation; when he breathes he still feels pressure at the inferior part of the sternum and nipple. Yesterday, stabbing pain from five to six o'clock in the evening. The feeling of thoracic constriction reappeared at half-past two.—Suggestion, after which he feels slightly relieved. When he breathes he still feels two painful points external to the nipple.

18th.—He feels no more pain or burning sensation; nothing but a sense of pressure which disappears by suggestion.

19th.—*He is completely relieved.*—*Suggestion.*

20th.—He continues to do well, and only feels slight pressure. Asks for his dismissal.

22d.—He comes back to show himself; is doing well and has scarcely any more trouble.

OBSERVATION LXXV —*Painful contusion of the deltoid.*—*Inability to raise the arm.*— *Almost complete cure in two séances.*

S——, sixty-three years old, a workman at Nancy, while carrying a beam on September 3, at nine o'clock in the morning, fell and struck his left shoulder against a wall.

On September 4, I find a simple contusion. The patient cannot lift his arm or hold it out from the body without using the other hand; the pain exists at the antero-internal part of the deltoid. *I hypnotize him :* he goes into the second degree of sleep; I suggest the disappearance of the pain and the possibility of raising his arm. Upon waking, he raises it to 45° without using the other hand, and as far as his head with the use of the other hand. *Pain has much diminished.*

September 5th.—Second séance, third degree. After the séance, he can lift his arm as far as his head and hold it vertically in the air. Before the séance, if his arm was lifted, he could not lower it gradually; it fell suddenly. At the present time, he can hold it up. There is only slight pain in the deltoid.

OBSERVATION LXXVI —*Muscular pain in the side, dating back a month, relieved in two hypnotic séances.*

M——, twenty-nine years old, a stone-layer, in good health, has complained for a month past of pain between the costal border and the anterior superior iliac spine on the right side. When in repose, he only feels a certain pricking. The pain appears when he lifts his arm up; when he has worked all day he feels the pain until midnight. At the present time, he cannot lift his arm or make the slightest effort without sharp pain. *I hypnotize him; he goes into deep sleep;* remembers upon waking that he heard me talking, but does not know what I said. *Upon waking he no longer complains of any pain,* and can lift a chair with his arm extended without any pain.

He comes back to see me on October 9. The pain, which disappeared for two hours, reappeared at six o'clock in the evening. At the present time, pressure determines a pain above the spine of the ilium; effort induces intermittent shooting pains. At the left border of the ribs he also has painful spots at times. *After a new hypnotic suggestion, the pain completely disappears.* The patient has not come back, and has resumed his work.

OBSERVATION LXXVII —*Painful spot in the side, almost cured by suggestion.*

M——, a guard at the Agincourt station, comes to consult me on October 4, 1884. A week ago, in consequence of a fall, he had a contusion of the right side. However, he continued to work. I find a painful spot upon pressure, near the right costal border in the axillary line. It is especially noticeable when he moves about and when he works, and when he gets up after having lain down.

After sleep (third degree) and suggestion, the painful spot *has almost completely disappeared.*

OBSERVATION LXXVIII —*Pain in the epitrochlear muscles, dating back two months.— Cure in two séances.*

T——, twenty years old, a workman in the founderies at Pompey, comes to consult me on March 8, 1885. For two months he has had pain in the epitrochlear muscles, in the lower third of the arm near the internal border of the biceps, and in the epitrochlear group of muscles. Pressure over this region gives rise to acute pain. Last month patient had to stop work for sixteen days; he has worked steadily this month.

I hypnotize him, and he goes into somnambulism. Upon waking there is *no more spontaneous pain.* He can grasp powerfully and without pain.

He comes back on the 14th. Has had no more pain; from time to time he has painful pricking sensations near the epitrochlea, lasting usually from one to two hours. Pressure only determines pain at the epitrochlea. The arm is no longer sensitive; the epitrochlear muscles are only slightly so when squeezed. *Second suggestion. Upon waking, he feels no more pain.*

Returns on the 23d.—Has been able to work without having any pain; he still has the pricking sensation when he moves his limb quickly. *Third suggestion. Complete cure.*

OBSERVATION LXXIX —*Pains in the shoulder and in the right upper limb, with tremor and weakness after effort.—Cured by suggestion in two séances.*

V——, a paper glazier, comes to consult me on February 11, 1887. Six months ago, while lifting a heavy box, he experienced a sharp pain in the right arm and fore-arm. In two days and a-half he was again able to work; but this pain has persisted until to-day, in spite of the repeated application of the cautery. He can lift the arm, and flex and extend the fore-arm. But certain movements of the latter, pronation, and supination, are accompanied with tremor. Upon pressure we find tenderness near the posterior half of the deltoid, triceps, and olecranon, and in the inferior half of the external border of the radius. There are no tingling sensations.

By the dynamometer, the right hand gives 23; the left hand 30. *I hypnotize him easily*, he goes into the third degree. Suggestions repeated for half an hour, and passive motion of the arm. Upon waking, the right hand gives 52 (average of six trials), the left hand 45. No longer complains of pain in the deltoid. Slight tenderness at the postero-external border of the olecranon. The tremor has disappeared, movements are easier and more rapid.

After the second suggestion, the pain has almost completely vanished; it still exists to a slight extent upon pressure. The right hand registers 56.

February 12th.—The patient worked better yesterday, and felt more strength in his arm. He slept all last night without pain, while on other nights he often had pain in his arm. We still find slight pain in the deltoid and in the elbow. The dynamometer registers 56 on the right side. After suggestion, there is no more tenderness of the deltoid, and only slight tenderness in the elbow.

13th.—Continues to do well. Complains of no more spontaneous pain. Pressure still determines slight pain in the elbow.—Suggestion.

The patient has not come back.

VIII

RHEUMATIC TROUBLES

OBSERVATION LXXX —*Rheumatic paralysis of the fore-arm and right hand.—Sensation totally restored in one séance.—Total cure in four séances.*

G——, forty-nine years old, a laborer, was in a café on June 21, 1884, at six o'clock in the evening, when he suddenly felt that he could not lift his right hand. The fingers and the lower third of the fore-arm were anæsthetic and felt dull and heavy. Seven years ago, he had articular rheumatism localized in the upper limbs: the pain and swelling lasted four days, then disappeared; but the arms were paralyzed for six weeks. G—— has neither a syphilitic nor an alcoholic history; he works in a damp atmosphere. *Diagnosis: rheumatic paralysis.*

He came to the dispensary for four days, and electricity was used without result.

He then went to consult my former *chef de clinique*, Dr. Emile Levy, who found complete paralysis with anæsthesia of the limb. The patient could not make the slightest movement.

Dr. Levy hypnotized him (profound sleep). Upon waking, *sensibility was restored*, and the patient could again lift his hand.

After the second séance, the movements were still more pronounced.

Dr. Levy sent the patient to my clinic on June 30. We find the right hand slightly swollen. The middle, fourth, and little fingers are bent into the palm of the hand at an angle of 120°. The patient can grasp well with the hand. He straightens the wrist, but with some difficulty. No anæsthesia.

After two hypnotic séances, the patient opens his hand easily, and straightens his wrist perfectly. The cure is complete.

OBSERVATION LXXXI —*Former scapulo-humeral rheumatic arthritis.—Marked improvement from the first hypnotic séance.—Subsequent condition stationary in spite of the continuation of suggestion.*

C——, thirty-four years old, enters the hospital on May 2, 1885. She is married, and is the mother of two children. For four or five years she has had pains in the right arm and shoulder, with weakness of this limb, which has increased progressively. Since then she has not been able to lift her arm.

About the same time she experienced pain in the left arm, which she was nevertheless able to use until December, 1884. Since then she has not been able to lift it.

Finally, for the last four weeks, she has complained of pain in the left knee when she walks. Menstruation is regular,—no leucorrhœa. Patient digests well except for slight occasional acidity. She perspires a good deal, and sometimes has an excessive desire to make water. She lived in a damp house until two years ago.

On the 4th, we find: constitution somewhat delicate, temperament lymphatic, no fever, heart and lungs normal.

Right upper limb: the patient executes all movements with the forearm. Some movements both forward and backward can be made with the arm, but the patient cannot hold it out from the body. Movements may be passively impressed upon it and it may be held out horizontally. The scapula tends to follow it. There is severe pain limited to the right acromio-clavicular articulation and extending slightly below it. The biceps is not painful to pressure.

Left upper limb : the same condition as to motility. Sharp pain upon pressure below the acromio-clavicular articulation. The latter is slightly tender to pressure. Pressure upon the head of the humerus is painful. The movements of the left knee are free. The knee is not tender to pressure. The fingers are not painful, and the joints are not deformed, but are abnormally mobile. *Diagnosis : rheumatic arthritis of the scapulo-humeral and acromio clavicular articulations.*

The patient is *hypnotized :* she goes into deep sleep, almost without memory upon waking. After suggestion given for the right arm, the patient can lift the right hand to her head by bending her head sideways, and the pain in the shoulder has diminished.

On the evening of the 4th, *suggestion and profound sleep.* I impress movements upon the arm to aid the suggestion, and affirm that the pain will disappear and that the patient will be able to execute every movement without pain. I continue the suggestion energetically for twenty minutes.

Upon waking, *the pains have almost entirely disappeared* on the right side; that of the left humerus still persists. The patient can reach out for something held above her bed spontaneously, and she can make slight movements of abduction. The arms are easily lifted into the horizontal position, but the patient cannot keep them there and lets them fall.

On the 7th, she again complains of severe pain in the acromio-clavacular articulation on the right side, and at the head of the humerus on the left. She can hold both arms out at a right angle from her body.

9th.—After the suggestion given yesterday, she has no more *spontaneous shooting pains.* The pain upon pressure in the right side has diminished. She lifts her arm at a right angle.—*Suggestion.*

11th.—Suggestion ; the acromio-clavicular pain on the right side and the pain in the humerus on the left side have almost disappeared ; but the patient still complains of a sense of weight in both arms which prevents her from sleeping. She holds both arms out at an angle of 45° from the body. Same condition on the days following.

On the 12th (she has not been hypnotized), there is again pain in the arm and left fore-arm. During the night there has been a pricking sensation in the left hand.

She is hypnotized on the 13th. She sleeps better on the following night but on the 14th she still complains of pain in the left arm, and the entire humerus is tender to pressure. She holds out her left arm well, but cannot keep it out.—Suggestion.

15th.—The pain in the left humerus disappeared after the suggestion of yesterday. The patient can again hold out the left arm at an angle of 45° for a few minutes. During the night, she had shooting pains in the sheath of the left triceps.—Suggestion in the evening. She has no more pain during the night.

19th.—The patient has not been hypnotized for three days. The pain has returned, especially in the left shoulder and arm. She sleeps little at night. *Energetic and prolonged suggestion* accompanied by passive motion of the joints of the shoulder. We succeed in making her hold her arm out almost vertically during this sleep. I allow the patient to sleep and permit her to awake spontaneously.

20th.—Patient still has slight pain on the left side. She lifts both arms well, but does not succeed in holding them out horizontally. She slept quite well during the night. In the evening, *prolonged suggestion* accompanied with passive movement of the arms. The arms are held *almost vertically up*.

21st.—She has no more pain and can hold her arms out horizontally. This condition is maintained until the 26th. *Daily suggestion.*

26th.—She has scarcely any more pain at the level of the shoulders, but when she wishes to lift her left arm she complains of a painful sensation in the fore-arm. Nevertheless she can lift this arm as high as 90°. She can extend the right arm almost horizontally.—Appetite is good.

During the night the pains again appear in the shoulders. The patient has not slept. The next day she does not eat and seems to be exhausted. For several days she has yielded to hypnotization with bad grace. She wishes to go back to her own village in the Vosges.

28th.—The patient is continually complaining. The right arm is doing well. It is somewhat painful. She can extend it easily to a right angle; but she complains continually, in spite of suggestion, of pains in the shoulder and left arm. She eats nothing; her disposition has become sour. We learn that her husband came to see her and that he did not wish her to be hypnotized any more. She herself says that she prefers to keep her arms as they are and does not wish to continue this treatment. We think that she has been submitted to some counter-suggestive influence which perhaps has neutralized the efficacy of the treatment. She leaves the hospital on the 29th.

OBSERVATION LXXXII —*Muscular rheumatism with cramps in the limbs.—Rapid cure by suggestion.*

C——, a gardener, seventy-two years old, enters the hospital on November 6, 1883. For four weeks he has complained of pains throughout the body, especially in the limbs, which take hold of him two or three times a day and last three quarters of an hour. Two or three times a day he also has cramps in the back of the thigh, causing flexion of the knees, lasting several minutes. He is often exposed to rain, and was wet through four weeks ago. Since this time he has had a cough; there is an opaque mucous sputum. Slight dyspnœa when he walks. His appetite has always been good.

Patient is a well-preserved man of strong constitution. The thorax is slightly convex and resonant. Respiration is broncho-vesicular in front. Expiration normal. Breathing is broncho-vesicular over the left apex posteriorly, and slightly bronchial over the supra-spinous region. A few sub-crepitant rales at the left base. Heart sounds normal. (*Slight senile emphysema, bronchitis, senile induration of the apices.*) The joints of the fingers are slightly deformed (*arthritis deformans*) and creak slightly when moved. By pressing the muscles of the buttock and the left thigh, pain and contractures are caused, (*muscular rheumatism*). When left without treatment for several days his condition remains the same; cramps every day; on the 7th three attacks of cramps in the legs and wrists; on the 8th four attacks of cramps in both arms.

On the 11th we note : the patient complains of pains in the tendon of Achilles and at the inner surface of the thighs. He often has cramps which appear simultaneously or alternately in all the limbs, accompanied with a pricking sensation, the fingers and knees being contractured in semi-flexion.

After the 12th, the patient is *hypnotized every day* (profound sleep) with suggestion. *Since the first séance he has had no more cramps;* the diffuse pains decrease; they do not exist when the patient is quiet, but reappear when he walks.

After the 21st he does well and has no more pain on walking.

OBSERVATION LXXXIII —*Rheumatic ileo-lumbar neuralgia.—Rapid improvement in one séance. Perfect cure in eighteen days.*

T——, fifty-five years old, enters the hospital on November 27, 1884. She is a widow and the mother of twelve children, all of whom have died as their father did, of phthisis.

Several days ago this woman, who is usually very well, was suddenly interrupted in her work by a pain in the right side, spreading toward the anterior spine of the ilium. She had to go home, where she had a rigor. The pain was so intense that she could not get to her bed. This lumbar pain has persisted ever since, accompanied with painful irradiations, sometimes in both legs. Otherwise she is very well and has a good appetite.

29th.—We note: constitution good; no fever; patellar bursa on the left side. Excessively sharp pain at the level of the lumbar vertebræ, below the lower border of the ribs on the right side, and at the emergence of the right sciatic nerve. The pain is less intense on the left side. These pains often spread to the lower part of the abdomen and to the limbs on the right side. (*Rheumatic ileo-lumbar neuralgia.*)

Hypnotization.—The patient goes into *somnambulism;* during sleep she has an active spontaneous dream; she speaks of scrubbing the floor. I drive away this dream and affirm the disappearance of the pains. Upon waking she is very drowsy and goes to sleep again spontaneously, sleeping until three o'clock in the afternoon (from eleven in the morning).

30th.—She is much better, and slept well during the night. The lumbar region is only slightly painful. The sacral region is still painful to pressure in the median line: she has had no more painful irradiations. The patient can turn over in bed, which she could not do before.

December 1st.—She has again had very sharp pain upon pressure of the sacrum, but the pain remains limited to this region. The loins, the lower border of the ribs, and the origin of the sciatic are no longer painful. No more irradiations. *Suggestion nearly every day. The sacrococcygial pain is persistent.*

3d.—The pain grows less; the patient has been able to walk a little. On the 9th she has continual pain when she gets up and when she walks. After the 18th only does she get along well. Having felt no pain and the last trace of sensitiveness having disappeared on the 20th the patient asks for her dismissal.

This woman has never had any nervous history but is an excellent somnambulist. I say during sleep, "You are perfectly cured. Get up. You are to clean Mme. X——'s house." She rises with her eyes shut, dresses herself, looks for a chair, gets upon the window-seat, and opens and begins to wash the window. Then, obedient to suggestion, she makes her bed or brushes the floor of the ward with a brush which is handed to her. She works for several hours. When suddenly waked she does not remember anything and thinks she has been sleeping quietly in her bed or in a chair.

OBSERVATION LXXXIV —*Arthralgia consecutive to an arthritis.*—*Immediate cure by suggestion.*

D——, twenty-one years old, comes to consult me on April 2d, 1884. Three months ago, after having wheeled a wheelbarrow, he developed a swelling of the left heel, and was unable to bend the joint. Six weeks ago a physician applied a starched bandage, keeping it on three weeks and two days. The bandage was taken off fifteen days ago, and there was no improvement.

D—— limps and bends his knee when he walks. He cannot bend the left heel, which is painful to pressure. The swelling has disappeared.

On the 2d *I hypnotize him :* profound sleep ; memory perfect upon waking. Suggestion and passive movement of the joint during sleep.

Upon waking he bends the tibio-tarsial articulation very well and spontaneously without pain. He walks well, only complaining of sensitiveness about the internal malleolus.

He has not come back. I have learned, through a fellow-workman, that the cure has been maintained.

OBSERVATION LXXXV —*Pleurodynia helped by suggestion.*

P——, an employee on the chemin de fer de l'Est at Varangeville, eighteen years old, has complained for four days of a sharp pain under the right breast (*pleurodynia*).

On May 18, 1885, at my clinic, I hypnotize him into profound sleep. Upon waking the pain *has almost completely disappeared*, to the patient's astonishment.

P—— returns on May 6, 1886. For the last six days he has complained of a painful spot in the left lumbar region, which prevents him from working. Although the pain has decreased since the 2d, the patient can only bend to grasp an object with difficulty. I put him into *somnambulism and when he wakes the pain has disappeared;* he can bend over very easily.

OBSERVATION LXXXVI —*Apyretic articular rheumatism.*— *Temporary cessation of the pains by suggestion.*—*Gradual cure.*

D——, eighteen years old, a waiter, enters the hospital on April 13th, 1883. He has just been in M. Parisot's service for seven weeks on account of sub-acute articular rheumatism, of which he has had two successive attacks. He left after being in the hospital two weeks, but had a relapse in two days and returned to the same ward.

Having no pain he left on the 11th, but **the next day he had pain again, and returned to our ward on the 13th.**

In the evening he has intense pain, both spontaneous and upon pressure in the *insteps* and in the *calves*; he limps, and walks with some difficulty.

I hypnotize him: he goes into the third degree. Suggestion. *Upon waking, he complains of no more pain* and walks well and without limping.

The next day, the 14th, he says he has had no more spontaneous pains and he walks without limping. Pressure of the tibio-tarsal articulations, however, still causes pain.

In the afternoon he complains of sharp pain in the groin extending into the crural plexus. Tenderness in the calf.

I hypnotize him at six o'clock in the evening; *the pains disappear instantly, not to return.*

16th.—In the evening he again complains of severe pain at the level of the malleoli and walks with difficulty, limping. The pains are relieved by hypnotic suggestion; he can walk and run for the time being.

17th.—Since this evening he has had pain in the right supra-spinous fossa, near the anterior border of the trapezius, near the inferior part of the biceps on both sides, and in both insteps. Nevertheless the patient walks without much pain. In the evening hypnotic suggestion: *all the pains disappear.*

18th.—In the morning he only complains of sensitiveness about the trapezius, which disappears by suggestion.

20th.—The patient again feels pain in the instep; he can only stand three seconds on the left foot. This pain is again relieved by suggestion on the 21st.

This pain, which is each time completely removed by suggestion reappears obstinately. We find it again on the evening of the 23d; it is driven away by suggestion, but reappears in several hours, especially behind the external malleolus, and is again helped by suggestion on the 24th.

This continues about eighteen days, when the cure becomes permanent.

OBSERVATION LXXXVII —*Chronic articular rheumatism localized in the wrists and insteps dating back three years.—Rapid cure in six séances.*

R——, thirty years old, enters the hospital on December 13, 1883. He has just come from the hospital where chronic diseases are treated and where he has been since the 13th of September. He has been troubled with articular rheumatism for three years. Disease began with pain in the knees, without noticeable swelling, which did not prevent him from continuing his work. After about three weeks this pain disappeared and was replaced by another pain in the insteps below the malleoli which lasted two months. Then a pain in the middle of the arm, and afterwards in both wrists, developed, which made motion difficult for two or three years, although the swelling was not noticeable. The right wrist was swollen last July for three days; the left wrist was swollen for two days a month ago. Finally, the feet were swollen and painful, the left one for two years, the right for a month and a half. The rheumatic pains have developed without fever or reaction; at the time when they began the patient was sleeping in a freshly plastered room. At Fronard he was able to work until the 25th of June in spite of these arthropathies; since this time the pains have been too sharp and movement too difficult for him to continue his work.

Present condition: constitution good, temperament lymphatic. General health good. Pain in the articulation of the right wrist. The movements of adduction and abduction are impossible: when made by passive motion they are very limited and cause sharp pain in the articulations concerned. The carpal and carpo-metacarpal articulations of the back of the hand are noticeably swollen and painful. The interossei muscles and those of the thumb (thenar eminence) are notably atrophied. The phalanges are free.

Same condition of the left hand; pain especially in the cubito and radio-carpal articulations. In both hands then, the movements of the wrist are the ones which are almost totally destroyed.

The right foot is swollen at the level of the joint of the instep. It is especially painful around and at the level of the external malleolus.

The left foot is more swollen at the level of the instep; the pain exists especially about and in front of the external malleolus. The movements of adduction and abduction are possible, but painful. Pressure and walking cause pain in the malleolus. The patient abducts the left leg and cannot stand upon it alone.

14th.—*Hypnotic suggestion.* Profound sleep. After the séance the patient *stands a short time upon the left leg unaided,* which he could not do before. He passes the day well. He still has some pain during the night.

16th.—Exactly the same condition is found as when patient was admitted; same condition of the wrist and insteps. The patient continually abducts the left leg in walking; he cannot stand upon the sole of the foot without leaning upon something.

Second séance. *Hypnotic suggestion. Sleep is profound with absence of memory upon waking;* he stands two or three seconds upon the left leg without leaning upon anything with his hand. During the day he felt great relief from pain in comparison with other days. During the night he had no pain. The right hand is still painful about the head of the ulna. He thinks that the wrist movements are easier.

17th.—The wrists are still painful. Flexion and extension of the wrists are easy. Abduction is very limited and adduction impossible. The left foot is still sensitive. After sleep and suggestion, these pains disappear almost entirely. During sleep, movements of adduction and abduction are impressed upon the hands easily and painlessly, which was impossible before. Upon waking, these same movements are possible, and the patient stands four seconds upon the left foot. Passed a good night. Night-sweat.

18th.—Movements of adduction and abduction continue easy for the left hand; they were impossible a month and a half ago. They are also easy for the right hand: he performs the movement of abduction without any pain, which he has not been able to do, he says, for three years. The pain has almost disappeared.—Pressure upon the insteps and malleoli does not determine any pain. The patient walks very well, without spreading his legs apart, and without pain. The left foot, which once turned out easily, no longer does so. He says that for two years he has not walked as he does now. He stands at first four seconds, then seven seconds upon this foot, which has been an impossibility for two years.

19th, and 20th.—This condition *is further improved by hypnotic suggestion.* On the 20th, he stands upon the left foot for twenty seconds; he goes out into the town and takes quite a long walk without having any stiffness or pain.

We were truly surprised at this great change; the patient was very much astonished at being able to walk so well.

21st.—We learn through the nurse, that the patient told the other patients in the ward that he did not sleep. I questioned him, and he says that he slept. He remembers absolutely nothing, but refuses to be hypnotized again. He says he has been cured too quickly, and it is not natural, and that his trouble will return. This was at the beginning of our hypnotic experiments, when they were regarded with doubt by some people who were not very well informed about the subject. We did not doubt that a *counter-suggestive influence* had been exercised over the patient, who became afraid and left the hospital cured and not very grateful.

OBSERVATION LXXXVIII —*Muscular, articular and nervous rheumatism. Improvement at each suggestion.—Return of the pains.—Gradual cure in twelve days.*

J——, a railroad employee about fifty years old, of strong constitution, comes to consult me on October 11, 1884. Last week he had rheumatic pains in his limbs, which obliged him to take a five days leave of absence. He took up work again on March 9, and had to leave again on the 11th.

I go to see him at home; he complains of severe pain in the lumbar region on the left side, which prevents his getting up.

I hypnotize him; *profound sleep*. Memory confused upon waking. *The pain is less.*—During the night, sharp pains. He is very restless.

12th.—There is sharp pain at the acromio-clavicular articulation on the left side, in the scaleni and in the lumbar region. He cannot sit down without pain.—Hypnotization at five o'clock in the evening; profound sleep and suggestion. Upon waking the pain is less, having disappeared in the shoulder and scaleni. The patient can use a handkerchief with his left hand without sitting down, which the pain in his shoulder would not allow him to do before suggestion.

He continues to sleep badly. The pains return, less intense in the loins but severe in the neck and arms.

13th.—At four o'clock temperature $38\frac{6}{10}°$; pain in the metacarpo-phalangeal articulation of the right index finger, and in the right sterno-mastoideus, which is very sensitive. Pain in the loins continues, but is very slight.

After suggestion, pains greatly diminished; upon pressure there is only slight sensitiveness in the sterno-mastoideus. The metacarpo-phalangeal pain has almost disappeared.

October 18th.—The improvement continued until yesterday. Since then patient has again had pains along the course of the sciatics, at the sciatic foramena, in the nates, along the back of the left thigh, and along the postero-external surface of the leg. These parts are very painful upon pressure. Further, there is tenderness of the right sterno-mastoideus. The lumbar region is free from pain. The axillary temperature is $38\frac{6}{10}°$. Hypnotism and suggestion. Pain much less upon waking. After a second hypnotic suggestion, consecutive to the first, and accompanied with rubbing of the painful parts, the pains have almost entirely disappeared.

19th.—Slept well during the night. Pains have reappeared but are slight. He lifts his leg easily. In the neck also the sensitiveness is less. The back of the thigh is still sensitive to pressure. Temperature 38°. After two consecutive séances the pain *has almost entirely disappeared*.

Since then, the patient has continued to do very well. His wife comes to tell me on the 23d that he has no more trouble, only slight lumbar fatigue.

He comes to see me on the 29th. The cure has been maintained. He complains only of slight pain in the left knee, which disappears at the last hypnotic suggestion.

OBSERVATION LXXXIX —*Poly-articular rheumatism cured by antipyrine.—Persistence of the acromio-clavicular and xiphoid pains.—Definitive cure by suggestion in two séances.*

M. C——, a cooper, thirty-three years old, enters the hospital on March 16, 1886. He has been troubled with sub-acute articular rheumatism for a week past.

He is a very strongly constituted man, addicted to alcohol. Upon admission his temperature is $38\frac{2}{10}°$, the pulse 112. Pains exist in the acromio-clavicular joints, in the knees, in the insteps, about the left malleoli, and at the level of the last lumbar and sacral spinous processes. The patient takes six grammes of antipyrine on the 16th, and eight grammes on the 17th. The articulations have been rapidly improved since the first days of the medicine; the acromio-clavicular pain still persists.

21st.—The temperature, which has been normal since the morning of the 19th, has risen to 38°. We still find pain upon pressure of the acromio-clavicular joints, and of the head of the left humerus. The articular movements are free. Further, since night there has been a painful spot near the xiphoid appendix, which woke the patient at three o'clock in the morning and prevented his sleeping again, and another similar point at the level of the lower border of the ribs in the axillary line on each side. Pressure of these regions causes sharp pain.

I hypnotize the patient: he falls into profound sleep rapidly, without memory upon waking. I suggest the disappearance of the pains. In five minutes I wake him; the xiphoid pain, which existed spontaneously and upon pressure, has *totally disappeared*, as well as the pain in the acromio-clavicular joints and at the head of the left humerus.

22d.—The xiphoid pain has not returned; the acromio-clavicular pains reappeared in the night, more sharply on the left side. New hypnotic suggestion; upon waking there is *no more pain*, either spontaneous or upon pressure.

23d.—The pains have not come back. The patient walks, but with a good deal of difficulty; the articulations are somewhat stiff he says. After hypnotic suggestion, he walks more rapidly and more easily.

24th.—He walks for half an hour, and feels no more pain of any kind.

The cure is maintained; M. C—— leaves the hospital on the 26th.

OBSERVATION XC —*Lumbo-crural muscular pain with obstinate sacro-sciatic neuralgia, dating back six months.—Notable improvement after several hypnotic séances; almost complete cure after five weeks of repeated suggestion.*

H. C——, a plasterer, thirty-two years old, enters the hospital on January 30, 1886. For two months he has complained of sciatica, characterized by pains spreading from the buttock to the left foot. At the commencement the pain was limited to the posterior spine of the ilium. He was able to walk until December, but a constant pain in the loins prevented him from bending over. For the last eight days he has not been able to get up or to stand; the pain prevented him from sleeping. Seven weeks ago he entered the hospital in another ward, and was there a month, during which time he was ineffectually treated by a blister and the application of the cautery.

On January 31 we note: Very strong constitution, without morbid or alcoholic history. Pain upon pressure at the level of the lumbar spinous processes and from the sacrum to the coccyx. This pain also exists at the transverse processes, at the level of the iliac crest, at the level of the sacro-iliac articulation, and of the trochanter, and at the inferior border of the gluteus. Sharp pain is also caused by pressure of the postero-internal muscles of the thigh, at the popliteal space, at the head of the fibula, and at the anterior surface of the thigh in the triangle of scarpa. Finally, the patient complains of a pricking sensation in the heel when he gets up. Moreover, he cannot stand on account of the pain. He can bend his foot, knee, and thigh without pain.

He takes six grammes of antipyrine on February 1; a gramme of sulphate of quinine on the 3d, 4th, and 5th, and five grammes of salicylate of soda daily from the 6th to the 10th, without any noticeable result. He sleeps better, however. When he is resting the pains are no longer present, but reappear on the least movement. He lies upon the right side, with the thigh and knee bent, unable to stretch out the limb.

From the 11th until the 15th the patient is *hypnotized*. Although he is in the third degree, with suggestive catalepsy and rotatory automatism, he thinks he does not sleep, because he remembers everything upon waking. The pain, however, has markedly diminished from the time of the second séance; the muscles of the thigh and of the ham-string are no longer painful, but the entire buttock is still very sensitive, and he cannot lie upon his back or stretch out the limb.

On the evening of the 15th I put him into *profound sleep*, without memory upon waking. Since then he has been convinced that he sleeps. After suggestion, he is very much astonished at being able to stretch out his limb and to lie upon his back. But the pain upon pressure is still present in the sacro-iliac articulation, and extends to the sacrum. The next day he drags himself about painfully, limping, and using a cane. When he walks he complains of pain at the level of the lower border of the ribs on the left side. This pain disappears instantly by suggestion.

Continuation of induced somnambulism. The sacro-gluteal pain diminishes each time, but returns after a variable period, when he moves about or walks.

19th.—In the evening I suggest during sleep that he will be able to walk without a cane. After waking he walks about the ward well without a cane, and only complaining of slight pain in the sacrum. At six o'clock he has a chill; sweats during the night.

Next day, temperature normal. Patient is doing well. He walks, and lies upon his back. Continuation of suggestion.

23d.—He only complains of slight tenderness over the coccyx and general weakness in the limb.

28th.—Complains of pain when he rests his foot upon the ground, and of pain in the lumbar region. They disappear by suggestion, and he walks quite well during the day.

March 4th.—The tempero-maxillary articulation, which has been sensitive to pressure since yesterday, is instantly relieved by hypnotic suggestion.

The patient walks well, but still complains of tenderness at the back of the thigh.

5th.—Walks quite well but feels some lumbar pain, which prevents him from standing straight. After suggestion, he stands straighter and walks better.

6th.—Complains of tenderness above the lower border of the ribs on the left side, at a point eight centimetres external to the spine, near the external iliac fossa, a little in front of the posterior spine of the ilium, and over the ischium. These painful spots are helped by suggestion.

7th.—He continually complains of a painful feeling at the sacrum, and of some stiffness when he walks. When he walks about a little he feels tired and has pain in the loins. Hypnotic suggestion. I make him walk quickly during his sleep, and by *prolonged suggestion I destroy the pain.* He walks without limping, and when he wakes no longer feels any pain.

8th.—He again complains of a sensation of stiffness in the sacro-lumbar region, which prevents him from standing erect. New suggestion. He is forced to walk during his sleep. He walks well during the day and also on the next day, complaining of nothing but a certain difficulty in standing erect. On March 12 he complains of tenderness in the buttock, which extends upward as far as the angle of the scapula, especially when he is walking. This tendency diminishes after suggestion.

But this slight tenderness is very obstinate; it is constantly manifested when he has walked for some time. On the 14th and 15th I use faradism for the sensitive region during sleep. He complains of sharp pain but does not remember anything upon waking. Sensation of stiffness in the buttock is less.

Since then he complains of nothing but slight tenderness in the buttock when he is walking; this tenderness diminishes daily. On the 17th he stands erect when he is walking. He leaves on the 18th, only complaining of this slight trouble which is very persistent.

OBSERVATION XCI —*Apyretic articular rheumatism.—Temporary improvement after each suggestion; gradual cure.—Augmentation of the dynamometric force by suggestion.*

W——, sixteen years old, a mason, has been sick for forty-five days. Since the beginning of his trouble he has had pain in the right heel and at the posterior internal part of the foot, near the internal tuberosity of the os calcis. He has pain when he walks upon his heel. In the same foot there is pain with swelling and inflammation at the metatarso-phalangeal articulation of the great right toe. Same condition of right foot. Twenty-five days ago, the left wrist was swollen and remained so for eight days; the patient could lift nothing, and after one or two hours of work was obliged to stop. There is still slight swelling in the wrist and pain in the carpus, especially near the head of the second metacarpal bone.

Patient enters the hospital on October 25, 1883, and I *hypnotize* him. He only reaches a light sleep: drowsiness with the beginning of suggestive catalepsy. This first séance *does not bring about any change.*

Second séance on the 26th.—He says that *the pain is less*, and he walks better during the day.

27th.—Pains have returned. They are perhaps somewhat less severe at the articulation of the great toe and heel of the right foot, and are certainly less upon pressure of the wrist and carpus.

Third séance, immediate improvement of the pains. This improvement exists from eleven o'clock in the morning until four o'clock; then the pains return. He went out during the day.

28th.—The wrist is doing better; the patient bends it more easily, but he cannot stand without pain. A new hypnotization (simple drowsiness) with suggestion, diminishes the pain slightly; he walks better. During the night he again feels very badly.

29th.—The left hand presses the dynamometer to 31; after hypnotic suggestion to 40. He says he has less pain than before, but the pain has not completely disappeared.

Suggestion each time produces a marked diminution in the articular pains; the patient walks better each time, but the result obtained is not perfectly maintained.

31st.—The left hand gives 45 by the dynamometer before suggestion and 52 afterward.

November 1st.—The pains become less every day, although we make the patient walk about in order to exclude the curative influence of rest; he walks better. There is hardly any pain in either heel, but he still complains of pain in the metatarso-phalangeal articulations. There is only slight tenderness in the hand. Suggestion is continued.

2d.—He is doing well; complains of no more pain, either spontaneous or upon pressure. The hand registers 50 on the dynamometer before, and 55 after suggestion.

4th.—He says he has more pain in the tuberosity of the os calcis, but complains of no more pain in the metatarso-phalangeal articulation or in the hand. New suggestion; the pain in the os calcis is less. The patient, decidedly improved, leaves the hospital.

OBSERVATION XCII —*Rheumatic pains in the acromio-clavicular articulations dating back three or four months.—Total cure in two séances; light sleep.*

Emile L———, a glazier, sixty-one years old, comes to consult me on November 31 for rheumatic pains of three or four months standing. He has never had acute articular rheumatism, but, nine years ago, he had an attack of sciatica lasting three years.

At the present time the pains exist in both shoulders, but especially on the right side. Their seat is at the level of the acromio-clavicular articulations. Another painful spot exists above the anterior superior spine of the ilium, on the left side. It is particularly noticeable when the patient bends. He has beside slight pains in both knees.

The patient is *hypnotized* on the 31st; first degree, *light sleep*. Upon waking, the pains in the knees *have disappeared;* those in the shoulders *are much less sharp*. The patient dresses himself for the first time in three weeks; the left shoulder is almost completely free from pain.

He comes back on November 3d. New hypnotization, light sleep. Upon waking he no longer feels any pain in his shoulders, but continually a painful sensation about the left anterior spine of the ilium. *Immediately after a second hypnotization* (sleep of the second degree), *all the pains have disappeared*, and all movements are unrestricted.

OBSERVATION XCIII —*Rheumatic muscular pains, first in the left arm, then in the right leg.—Cure each time in a single séance.*

Marie X———, ten years old, comes to see me on February 20, 1886. She is usually very well and has had no previous illnesses. For four or five days she has complained of pain in her right arm. The arm is sensitive to pressure; the child cannot lift it to her head. I *hypnotize* her by occlusion of the eyelids; I suggest the disappearance of the pain, and rub her arm. Upon waking, the child remembers nothing. The pain *has almost entirely disappeared*, and she can lift her arm to her head easily. During the day, all painful sensations disappear and do not return.

On April 14, the child comes back. Since four o'clock yesterday she has had pain in the right leg and thigh. Pressure is painful over the anterior surface of both limbs. She drags her leg when she walks. The knee and heel are almost rigid.

I put her into *somnambulism* again, and suggest the disappearance of the pain. Upon waking, she has almost no pain, but still drags her leg, although not as much as before.

I hypnotize her a second time, and repeat the suggestion. I make her walk during her sleep. Upon waking *she walks very well* and only drags the leg very slightly. She does not complain of any more pain. Her father tells me the next day that she came skipping home, and that she is completely cured.

OBSERVATION XCIV —*Gonorrhœal rheumatism dating back more than three months.—Pains in the soles of the feet, cured in a few séances of suggestion.—Very persistent malleolar and lumbo-dorsal pains.—Almost complete cure in five séances.*

D——, thirty-seven years old, a commercial traveller, comes to the clinic March 19, 1887. Last September he contracted gonorrhœa, the acute duration of which was three weeks. He had two previous attacks of gonorrhœa, one eighteen and one eleven years ago.

In December, he developed severe pains in his ankles and insteps without inflammation, without fever. The swelling increased, especially when he walked. He continued to walk, but with great difficulty, and with the use of a stick. For fourteen days he has not been able to walk; pain no longer exists when he is quiet, but only when he stands. For two months also he has had severe pains in the loins, which are continuous and prevent his sleeping.

He also had an acute conjunctivitis which lasted eight days. At first there was pain at the level of the left clavicle. Early in January pains in the tempero-maxillary articulations lasting fifteen days. Has had no previous illness.

He is a man of strong constitution, well made, and of a mixed temperament. His feet are flat. Upon examination on March 21 we do not find either swelling or pain on the dorsal surfaces of the feet; there is marked swelling below both internal malleoli, especially on the right side. He can flex and extend the feet, but a movement of dorsal flexion is painful. He localizes these pains below the internal malleoli. Upon pressure the pain is very severe, at the level of both malleoli, more so on the right than on the left side. It is also very severe in the soles of the feet, near the plantar aponeurosis. The heels are not tender. The patient walks with difficulty and only presses upon the heel. He avoids flexing his feet.—Further, there is spontaneous pain, and tenderness upon pressure on each side of the vertebral column from the angle of the scapula to the sacrum.—Other functions normal.

March 21st.—D—— is very easily put into *deep somnambulism* with amnesia upon waking. *Suggestion.*—In spite of the suggestion he did not sleep last night on account of dorsal pain. Pressure upon this region always provokes pain. On the 22d there was less pain than on the 21st. Hypnotic suggestion is repeated almost every day.

22d.—I make him walk during his sleep; when I have neutralized the pain by a vigorous and prolonged suggestion accompanied with rubbing, he walks well; then he leans the sole of his foot on the ground, which he could not do before, and straightens himself, while before he was bent over by the dorsal pain.—Upon waking he does well, but after a time the pains reappear.

24th.—He complains less of pain in the back and in the soles of the feet. But he did not sleep during the night and was very restless.

25th.—Did not sleep last night. Dorsal pain less.

26th.—Soles of the feet much less sensitive. The pains persist about the internal malleoli. Complains of a painful spot near the lower border of the ribs on the right side. He does not sleep at night.—During the hypnosis the patient walks without pain. But the result is not maintained. If he wants to walk one or two hours afterward the pain reappears. On the 28th of March, however, the soles of the feet are but slightly sensitive. The malleolar pain is more tenacious and persistent. The dorsal pain is localized in the lumbar region and is decreasing.

29th.—The feet are doing well. The pain in the malleoli is much less sharp. The patient walked much better yesterday than on the preceding days; but he is always complaining of pain in the loins.—After suggestion in the morning he walks very well; in the afternoon the pains reappear.

30th.—The patient is bent over, cannot stand up straight, and complains of sharper pains in the back. They exist to-day especially at the level of the lower border of the ribs on both sides. Plantar pain has disappeared; and we only find slight sensitiveness at the internal right malleolus.—After hypnotic suggestion the patient can stand up and walk without pain. The pain comes back three hours later.

From the 30th of March until the 3d of April the patient no longer complains of any pain except that in the loins. The feet are doing well. On April 3d he stands bent almost double on account of this lumbar pain. After suggestion and rubbing for ten minutes, he no longer feels the pain and walks erect. He can walk for two hours then fatigue brings back the pain, but it is less intense than before in the right foot.

The renal pain diminishes on the following days but does not disappear. Suggestion always suspends it for two or three hours, but does not suppress it.

Suggestion is discontinued through the Easter vacation. For four days we give him salicylate of soda, dose from four to five grammes, which diminishes the pain for the time being. Suggestion is begun again about the 19th. The lumbar pains no longer have their previous intensity; the patient walks better. There is still a slight swelling with sensitiveness at the level of the internal right malleolus which is brought on by prolonged walking.

After the 22d of March the improvement makes rapid progress: the patient holds himself erect and only complains of a painful feeling in the loins. The feet are nearly free from pain. On May 6 he feels hardly any pain and is well enough to take up his work again.

The gonorrhœal plantar pain yielded rapidly to several séances of suggestion; the malleolar pains resisted for a longer time. The lumbar pains were excessively persistent, recurring obstinately after suggestion had driven them away. It took five weeks to distinctly improve the trouble.

OBSERVATION XCV —*Articular rheumatism dating back ten days helped by the use of antipyrine.—Persistence of acromio-clavicular pain on the left side and of pain at the xiphoid appendix.—Cure in two days by suggestion.*

M——, thirty-three years old, a cooper, enters the hospital on March 16, 1886. For ten days he has had articular rheumatism. Pain in the acromio-clavicular articulations, pain and swelling in both knees, tenderness and swelling at the level of the left malleolus. Very sharp pain upon pressure at the level of the sacrum and the lumbar spinous processes. Alcoholic history.

Antipyrine is administered for three days; on the 20th, all the articulations are nearly free from pain. The temperature, which rose to 38° in the evening, has become normal again.

21st.—We still note tenderness in the acromio-clavicular articulations and at the head of the left humerus. This pain is very persistent, has existed since the beginning of his trouble, and has resisted antipyrine. Moreover during the night he complained of a painful spot at the xiphoid appendix, which prevented his sleeping. Pressure at this level and about the lower border of the ribs on both sides is very painful.

I hypnotize the patient, and he goes into *profound sleep*, without memory upon waking. After suggestion, the pains, both spontaneous and upon pressure, *completely disappear*.

22d.—The xiphoid pain has not reappeared. The acromio-clavicular pains reappeared during the night, especially on the left side where they extended to the head of the humerus and to the spine of the scapula. After suggestion in deep sleep the patient feels no more pain.

23d.—Pains have not reappeared since yesterday. After suggestion, the patient, who had a certain stiffness in the joints of the lower limbs, and who walked with pain, walks much better. He still walks well on the 24th, goes a mile and a half on foot, and no longer complains of tenderness of the acromio-clavicular articulations. Pressure does not evoke the pain. M—— leaves the hospital on the 26th, completely cured.

OBSERVATION XCVI —*Rheumatic articular pains dating back three months.—Cure by suggestion in two days.*

Jeanne M——, seventeen years old, comes to the hospital on August 3, 1877.

Last May she developed sub-acute articular rheumatism, without fever. The articulations of the fingers, feet, and knees were affected. She walked with pain until July 1st, when she was obliged to take to her bed and was treated with antipyrine and antifebrine. Feeling better she tried to get up on the 14th but could not stay up until evening. She could not walk. She also has trouble in respiration. For the last eight days the pains have increased in the knees and feet and the young patient is brought to the hospital in a carriage, helped by two people, and not able to stand. Last March she had a nervous paroxsym in consequence of some vexation.

She is a girl of strong constitution, but of lymphatic temperament, delicate and quite pale and thin. Her temperature is normal. In the evening it rises to 38°, the pulse rate being 108. Since the morning of the 5th it has remained normal. I find sharp pain at the external part of both wrists, without swelling. All the articulations of the first phalanges are very much swollen. Pressure determines very severe pain at the level of the joints of the index and middle fingers. The left knee is slightly swollen; sharp pain upon pressure in both patellar tendons. Pain back of and below the external right malleolus and at the level of the articulations of the first with the second phalanges of the last three right toes. Tenderness to pressure of the dorsal spinous processes.

Heart sounds normal. Respiration normal. Digestion good. Leucorrhœa. Last menstrual period on July 15th. Insomnia.

The patient is put into *deep sleep* easily; when she wakes she does not remember that she has been asleep.

On August 6, after two séances, she feels much better. Her appetite has come back; she did not eat anything for a month. She has slept well for two nights, and feels no more pain in her legs, which she can move without the slightest discomfort, and no more pain at the level of the wrist. The finger joints are still swollen and there is still tenderness at the level of the articulations of the first with the second phalanges of the fourth, middle and index fingers of the right hand. After suggestion the pains disappear.

8th.—Has had no more pain. Moves the hand, flexes and extends the fingers without pain. Appetite good. Patient still complains of heaviness in her legs; she is still sad and cries easily. I hypnotize her. I suggest that she shall feel strength in her legs and that she shall be bright and gay. She awakes laughing.

9th.—Has no more pain. Got up yesterday; had slight nausea; no longer complains of sad feelings.

10th.—Continues to do very well; appetite good; was up all yesterday afternoon. No more leucorrhœa.

The patient remains in the hospital until the 20th of August. She gets up every day, moves her arms and legs without the slightest discomfort, and leaves entirely cured.

OBSERVATION XCVII —*Dorsal and metacarpo-phalangeal pain of the middle finger, of rheumatic origin.—Cure in two days by suggestion.*

R——, nine years old, comes to the hospital on November 16, 1885. Three years ago he had acute articular rheumatism, which lasted some time and prevented his walking. At the present time, he has again been sick with rheumatism for three months. The affection began with pain in the hip which prevented his walking. Then the knees and the ankles were successively involved. Eight days ago, the patient, who seemed cured, got up and walked about, but took cold and had pains in the back and knees again. He has coughed slightly for some time. He has had palpitation for three months without oppression.

He is a boy of lymphatic temperament and of delicate but not deteriorated constitution. On the evening of the 16th his temperature was $38\frac{6}{10}°$; on the morning of the 17th, $37\frac{5}{10}°$; in the evening, $37\frac{8}{10}°$; after the

18th it was normal. We find a slight presystolic and systolic murmur at the apex of the heart, and dry disseminated rales. The left hand is slightly swollen still and pressure causes sharp pain in the metacarpo-phalangeal articulation of the middle finger. The other joints are free from pain. But the child complains of sharp pain in the dorsal region, both spontaneous and on pressure.

This pain is *immediately driven away by hypnotic suggestion* (profound sleep) on the evening of the 16th. The next morning *I drive away the metacarpo-phalangeal pain.* The child leaves the hospital on the 20th cured; the pains have not reappeared.

OBSERVATION XCVIII —*Rheumatic pains in the loins, right thigh, and along the course of the sciatic for fifteen days.—Cure by suggestion in ten days.*

W——, a machinist, thirty-five years old, enters the hospital on March 31, 1887. For fifteen days he has complained of shooting pain in the loins, lower half of the back, and posterior surface of the thigh. This pain appeared suddenly at ten o'clock in the evening. He could not sleep, and was unable to work the next day, March 8th. He has been in bed since then. The pain is continuous, and accompanied with exacerbations of shooting pains which last five or ten minutes. He sleeps badly and is waked by the pain, which has extended from the nates to the fold of the groin. For eight days the patient has complained of tingling in his fingers, hand and right arm, and in the lower limb on the same side. These tinglings appear two or three times a day and last five or six minutes; they are accompanied by a sense of weight. Patient had dysentery a year ago, and was treated in the hospital for a month.

Present condition.—March 29th. Strong constitution. No fever. The digestive, circulatory, and respiratory functions are normal. All movements of the limbs are normally executed; the muscular force is preserved; there is no exaggeration of the tendon reflexes. Sensibility is normal. Pain exists, spontaneous and on pressure, in the postero-external surface of the right thigh and throughout the buttock. We also discover tenderness in the vertebral column from the tenth dorsal vertebræ to the coccyx and throughout the extent of the vertebral groove on the right side. No girdle pain.

Diagnosis: spinal or neuro-muscular rheumatism.

March 23d.—The patient is easily put into *deep sleep.* *Suggestion.*

Upon waking, the painful sensation upon pressure persists.

24th.—He says that the pain is less intense; he only experienced a sense of weight for ten minutes at two o'clock this morning. We find that the tenderness still exists in the thigh and in the vertebral groove on the right side. *Suggestion.*

25th.—Has had no more tingling or sense of weight in the limbs. Has had less shooting pain; still suffers when he walks. *Suggestion*.

26th.—*Idem*.

28th.—Is doing better. The dorsal pains and those in the thigh are less intense. Was able to walk somewhat better. The sense of weight has disappeared. *Suggestion*.

29th.—Was able to walk yesterday afternoon without much pain. Daily suggestion.

30th.—Continues to do well. The pain in the loins and nates has diminished.

31st.—Only complains of slight pain in the loins.

April 4th.—The pain has almost completely disappeared. The patient has been able to walk easily. I suggested that the slight persistent pain in the loins should be replaced by an itching sensation, which he feels.

8th.—The improvement continues; there is only a slight sensation about the loins.

W—— walks well, but still limps a little. He leaves on the 12th almost totally cured.

IX

NEURALGIAS

OBSERVATION XCIX —*Sciatica, dating back seven weeks.—Injections of chloride of methyl without complete result.—Cure by suggestion in six days.*

L——, a shoemaker forty-four years old, enters the clinic on May 15, 1885. For seven weeks he has complained of sciatic pain along the posterior surface of the thigh and especially in the calf on the left side, pain which increases when he is seated. The pains are continuous; they are pricking sensations which spread from above downward; they increase when he is in bed, and are often accompanied by a sense of numbness in the leg, as if it were dead. L—— has grown very thin since his trouble began. Moreover, he has coughed and expectorated for seven years. He has had dyspnœa for three or four years whenever he made any effort.—He is a debilitated thin man of lymphatic disposition. There are signs of pulmonary emphysema with bronchitis.

We discover pain upon pressure over the sciatic foramen, in the popliteal space, of the head of the fibula, at the middle of the calf, and back of the external malleolus.—No treatment has been tried. We try injections of chloride of methyl on the 17th, 18th, and 19th; the patient says that the spontaneous pains have diminished without having disappeared; the pain upon pressure exists and is quite as severe.

20th.—The spontaneous pain being intense, although less, I try *hypnotic suggestion* (third degree). During the day, the *pains are not so severe;* at eight o'clock in the evening they again increase and the patient cannot sleep.

21st.—*New suggestion* at ten o'clock in the morning; the pains are less severe until midnight; he wakes and the pains reappear. Daily continuation of suggestion.

26th.—*Pressure causes scarcely any pain;* the patient complains at times of pain in the left leg. On the whole he is doing much better, and would sleep well at night if he were not waked by fits of coughing.

The improvement continues; on the 27th we suspend suggestion for two days. No more pains upon pressure, or of spontaneous occurrence. On the 29th he only complains of tingling in the heel. The cure is maintained; on June 14th L—— leaves the hospital.

OBSERVATION C —*Sciatic pain dating back three days, cured by a single suggestion.*

S——, a type-setter, twenty-two years old, enters the hospital on March 17, 1887. On the evening of the 14th he was suddenly taken with pain in the knee which he describes as being below the patella, spreading back along the thigh to the buttock and along the calf to the tendon of Achilles. He was still able to walk, but it gave him severe pain and he could not bend his leg. This pain has been almost continuous with exacerbations of shooting pains. Last night he was taken with it twice. The first time, the attack lasted half an hour, the second time, one hour. During the day the paroxysms of pain seize him five or six different times. In the interval, the spontaneous pain is slight. It is accompanied by a sense of weight. Last year, S—— had a similar attack of sciatica which lasted from the first of January to the end of May. He was not able to walk during a whole month. He has had no previous illness.

S. has a good constitution, but is somewhat delicate. His disposition is lymphatic.

On March 18, I find that he bends the thigh and leg with difficulty. Upon pressure there is sharp pain below the lower border of the left ribs, very sharp at the level of the upper border of the gluteus, at the sciatic foramen, and all along the course of the sciatic to the popliteal space. No pain in the head of the fibula or in the leg. The other functions are normal.

I put him into *somnambulism* very easily. He is very susceptible to suggestion, and to *hallucinations* in the waking as well as in the sleeping condition.—*After suggestion, the pain has completely disappeared;* the patient can bend his leg and thigh. He has no more pain upon pressure of the sciatic or below the border of the ribs.

This result is maintained the next day. The patient passed a very good night. After a new suggestion, I make him run in the ward. The cure remains complete; he leaves on March 23d.

OBSERVATION CI —*Sciatica dating back fifteen days.—Inefficacy of the chloride of methyl and of the sulphate of quinine.—Cure by suggestion in fifteen days.*

C——, a workman sixty-three years old, enters the clinic on November 22, for a left-sided sciatica dating back fifteen days, and developing into a shooting pain starting from the nates and extending to the toes and accompanied with a sense of weight. At the beginning, the pain was intermittent and lasted from six o'clock in the morning until eleven in the evening. For three days the pain has been continuous; walking has become difficult. C—— can only walk with a stick and is obliged to stop every two or three steps.

He is a man of good constitution, and of mixed temperament. The joints of some of the fingers are slightly swollen and present traces of rheumatoid arthritis. Pressure at the level of the left sciatic causes very sharp pain throughout the limb. On the 23d the patient is given an injection of chloride of methyl over the course of the nerve. The pain is quieted for two hours and then comes back with increased severity.

The next day, the 24th, we find that the painful spots at the nates, popliteal space, and malleoli still exist. New injections of chloride of methyl.

25th.—The pains are less; but the patient can neither sit nor stand. Rubefaction by blisters in the places marked by the injections.

The pains having become as severe as they were before the 26th, I try *hypnotization with suggestion* (second degree). The *pain is less* during the day, but is intense again in the evening. It spreads to the inguinal region.

The suggestion is not repeated. The condition remains the same. On December 3, the patient takes twenty-five centigrammes of antifebrine; he perspires profusely, and the pain diminishes for the time. On December 5 he takes one gramme of sulphate of quinine at four o'clock in the afternoon. The intense pain reappears at ten o'clock.

On December 6 he takes 1.5 grammes of sulphate of quinine between four and five o'clock in the afternoon. He has attacks of vertigo, and buzzing in his ears. The pain reappears at eleven o'clock, though less severe. It continues less severe the next day, but does not disappear.

8th.—He takes two grammes of quinine at the same hour; vertigo and buzzing in the ears. He perspires all night and has no pain.

The next day, the 9th, he does not complain of spontaneous pains in the morning; but the points which are painful upon pressure persist at the sciatic foramen, in the popliteal space, and at the head of the fibula. But at mid-day the spontaneous pains again appear, are very severe, and last through the next day.

Thus the injections of chloride of methyl and the sulphate of quinine have been of no avail.

11th.—I try hypnotic suggestion again. No pain during the day and very little during the night.

12th.—New suggestion. Slight shooting pains during the day. Sleeps during the night, waking several times, but without pain. *Walked better during the day* than he has walked since he came to the hospital.

13th.—We still find the painful spots, but they are *less severe* at the level of the sciatic foramen, at the head of the fibula and over the malleoli. *Suggestion.* The pain reappears in the evening, but is slight. Patient sleeps all night.

14th.—Same condition.

15th.—Continues to improve. Slept three or four hours during the night. Daily suggestion.

16th.—*Hardly any pain when lying down;* it is present but less intense when the patient walks. Upon pressure, also, it is less.

17th.—Continues to improve. Slept pretty well. Persistence of the painful spots.

20th.—Patient walked better yesterday. Slept better. Still complains of a sense of weight and of tingling in the foot.

21st.—Is doing well. He still walks with difficulty, using a cane, and feels the heavy sensation in the foot and knee. *After hypnotic suggestion, he walks much better and without using a cane.* The pain in the nates and at the trochanter upon pressure, has disappeared. There is still tenderness in the malleolus and over the back of the thigh.

On the following days, the patient walks about with his cane; there remain only slightly painful sensations provoked by walking. The patient remains in the hospital until January 5 without complaining, and leaves entirely cured.

OBSERVATION CII —*Sciatica dating back three months.—Suppression of the pains at each suggestion.—Cure in from three to four weeks.*

P——, forty-eight years old, married, enters the hospital on June 21, 1887, for sciatica. She has had no other illness, but seven years ago had an attack of sciatica less painful than the present one, and which only lasted two months.

Present trouble began on March 20, with pain behind the right external malleolus; this pain disappeared after about a quarter of an hour of walking. This continued for three weeks, then suddenly the pain spread from below upward to the nates. The affection has thus been confined to the sciatic for three months. This pain became constant, with exacerbations in the popliteal space lasting two or three hours. For three months she has walked with great difficulty and with a cane, bending over. Six weeks ago she had attacks for eight days, which appeared every evening at nine o'clock and were accompanied by a sense of rolling in the epigastrium, spreading up to the throat, with distress, depression, and a feeling of suffocation. These sensations appeared every day and night and lasted from quarter to half an hour. At the beginning of her sickness, she had severe pain in the top of her head. Ever since there has been a feeling of frontal constriction with weight and a desire to vomit. Bowels regular. Seven blisters and the cautery have been applied *loco dolenti*.

Mme. P—— is of somewhat delicate constitution, and of lymphatico-nervous temperament. We find *pain upon pressure at the ischium, at the trochanter, near the sciatic foramen and at the posterior surface of the thigh*. No malleolar pains. She can hardly stand, even with a cane. *Tenderness over the epigastrium*. No abdominal pains. Menstruation normal. The patient is sad, demoralized, anxious, and cries easily. No anæsthesia.

I hypnotize her from the time she enters the hospital, on June 21st. She reaches the third degree, and I tell her that she will walk without pain. After a vigorous suggestion, I wake her; she thinks she has not slept. I command her to walk, and to the great astonishment of all the other patients in the ward, she walks from one end of the ward to the other without a cane, and without complaining of pain. This result however is not lasting. In the evening the pains reappear.

The next day, the 22d, after a new suggestion, the pains again disappear; she walks, complaining of nothing but the painful spot in the nates. Pains, which disappear at ten o'clock, reappear at eleven and last until eleven in the evening. A better night is passed; she sleeps a little. During the day she has suffocating sensations lasting half an hour. Her moral condition is, however, much improved.

23d.—The menses appeared this morning. New suppression of the pains by suggestion; they again appear, in about an hour, in the back of the thigh, where they continue throughout the day.

Sleeps quite well during the night.

25th.—No suggestion yesterday. Very sharp pain until five o'clock in the evening. Patient goes to sleep; the pain returns at seven o'clock; she sleeps, nevertheless, during a part of the night. In the morning the pain is not severe. She still complains of depression with a sensation of rolling in the epigastrium. Suggestion.

Condition the same on the 26th and 27th. After suggestion, the pain disappears, but reappears in the evening. She has slept badly during the past two nights.

28th.—She takes two doses (0.50 grammes) of antipyrine. She does not perspire and has no pain during the day; but at midnight severe pains come on lasting an hour. Then she goes to sleep again.

29th.—In the morning she has shooting pains in the leg; after suggestion she walks better.

30th.—She has scarcely any more pain. On the 1st of July less severe pain comes on at seven o'clock in the evening and lasts three quarters of an hour. She no longer complains of rolling in the epigastrium and is no longer sad, but gay, and amuses herself with the jokes of the other patients. Suggestion continued.

On July 3 she walks about all day without experiencing any pain. From ten to eleven o'clock in the evening, there is a paroxysm of pain.

After the 4th she has *no more pain in the leg*. It is *only when she rests upon the foot* that she feels a shooting pain in the buttock.

5th.—Patient walks about a good deal and only complains of not being able to rest easily upon her foot, on account of the pain in the buttock which results. She was restless during the night. Suggestion.

6th.—She walks better. Passed a quiet night. She continues to do well; has no more shooting pains. Her appetite is good and she is bright. The tenderness of the nates when she walks, still persists for some time, but tends to diminish. She goes home on July 22, almost completely cured. I learn later that the cure is completed and has been permanent.

Thus there was temporary cessation of the pain after the first suggestion. But the pain reappeared with persistence; the general nervous condition is rapidly improved in a few séances. From three to four weeks are needed, however, to obtain an almost complete cure.

OBSERVATION CIII —*Neuralgia of the trigeminus lasting a year, with tic douloureux for four weeks. Rapid improvement, and almost complete cure by suggestion in ten days.*

C——, a workman sixty years old, enters the hospital on July 27, 1885, for a facial *tic douloureux*.

The affection began a year ago with painful sensations in the right side of the nose, coming on several times a day and lasting from several minutes to two hours. During the last four weeks these pains have spread to the eye, forehead, and all over the face on the same side. The disease takes the form of paroxysms, beginning in the morning, generally about five o'clock, and usually lasting from half an hour to an hour. These paroxysms very often recur both by day and at night. In the intervals between these attacks C—— only feels a burning sensation in his nose and jaw. During the paroxysms the pains are exaggerated and spread over the whole side, being accompanied with convulsive movements of the face.

C—— has a good constitution and is well preserved. He denies any previous disease. We find tenderness on pressure throughout the supra-orbital to the parietal region, in the upper and lower eyelids, and pain in front of the ear and at the emergence of the trigeminus. The entire cheek is tender, but to a less degree. During the attacks, the pains are excessive; there is spasm of the face with rigidity of the jaw. This spasm has existed for four weeks; during this time only have the pains spread to the jaw. Before they only involved the forehead and eye. For four weeks he has only been able to eat liquid food. After a first trial of hypnotization on the 28th, which was doubtful, but in consequence of which the patient felt better and said he slept during the night, I *hypnotize* him on the 30th. I close his eyes, suggesting quiet and cure, etc. I invite him to continue to sleep for half an hour. He continues to sleep, as if spontaneously, for half an hour.

30th.—*Upon waking the pain had completely disappeared.* It reappeared half an hour afterward; in the afternoon it was less intense. The night was good. C—— says that he has not slept as well for four or five weeks. He can again eat solid food by moistening it, but cannot chew it. The right side of the face is still sensitive to pressure. No suggestion.

31st.—Had a great deal of pain yesterday; did not sleep last night.—*Suggestion.*

August 2d.—The patient has been treated with suggestion for two days; each time he has been allowed to sleep for an hour. He is much better and only has slight pain *localized in the nose and right eye,* as at the beginning of his affection. The pains are not accompanied with spasm. There are burning sensations which occur every three or four minutes. He has no more pain in the jaw, and has been able to eat a crust of bread, which he could not do four weeks ago. He slept last night from eight o'clock to one o'clock, and after lying awake for an hour slept again until morning.—*Suggestion.*

3d.—Has had pain in the forehead and nose, at the upper external part of the right ala of the nose. At the points of emergence of the supra and infra orbital nerves, there is slight tenderness on pressure. There is scarcely any pain in the jaw. Nevertheless pain has prevented his sleeping.—*Suggestion.*

4th.—Was very well yesterday and had almost no pain. Slept during the night.—No suggestion to-day.

5th.—Was well yesterday; only experienced slight pricking sensation in the nose. At midnight was awakened by lightning pains in the jaw which lasted a quarter of an hour. Had these pains again at about three o'clock. This morning we find tenderness of the nose and forehead. Pressure is somewhat painful. The patient can eat.—No suggestion.

6th.—Continues to improve; sleeps and eats well; only complains of slight dull pain in the nose.—*Suggestion.*

7th.—Has felt slight pain extending from the nose to the internal part of the right side of the forehead as far as the synciput. No symptoms referable to the jaw. Sleep was broken by shooting pains recurring every three or four minutes and unaccompanied by spasm. The patient thinks he is well enough to begin work again and asks for his dismissal. I make him promise to come to the hospital every day.

9th.—He comes again and says he has been well. Yesterday, from mid-day until evening, he had slightly painful pricking sensations in his nose and forehead. He slept all night; this morning he again complains of nasal and frontal pricking sensations. Upon pressure we only find tenderness of the right ala of the nose.

C—— has not come back since. A patient who met him in the street a year later told me that he had been well ever since and had had no more pain.

X

Menstrual Troubles

Observation CIV —*Retardation of the menstrual period.—Suggestion for the appearance of the menses on a fixed day.*

Mlle. C——, a teacher, twenty-five years of age, is a neuropathic patient of Dr. Liébault's.

She comes to consult me on November 17th, for retardation of the menses. Her last period began on October 7th. The menses have not reappeared, and for several days she has complained of a sensation of constriction about the waist, with swelling. She eats more than usual and her digestion is very good. She says that she is not pregnant.

I put her into *somnambulism* easily; *I suggest that her period will begin on the* 30*th*. She herself repeats in her sleep that she will be ill on the 30th. I suggest that she will come to tell me about it.

On the 30th, she comes to tell me that the *menses appeared* in the morning without any pain; the day before she had premonitory symptoms: pain in the loins, headache, irritability.

I suggest the next period for *the 28th of December;* she is to come and tell me about it.

On December 28, she comes to tell me that *the menses appeared* in the morning, that is, according to the suggestion I had made.

OBSERVATION CV.—*Profuse menstruation every eleven or fifteen days.—Interval increased by suggestion to twenty-eight or twenty-nine days.*

Mme. H——, thirty-five years old, and the mother of three children, the youngest of whom is nine and a half, is a woman of strong constitution, slightly obese, and of medium intelligence. She comes to consult me on September 20, 1886. She says that for the last sixteen years she has had a cold every year accompanied with hoarseness and lasting nine months. Four years ago I treated her for one of these colds with electricity and cold water compresses upon the neck; she was cured in fifteen days. At the present time she has had hoarseness for nine months, and oppression, particularly at night. She has coughed for the last three months. Her sleep is disturbed. She often has painful spots at various parts of the body

At the age of sixteen she had *paroxysms of the " Grande Hysterie,"* with agitation and loss of consciousness. These paroxysms were induced by the least contradiction, emotion, or fright. She had them at least every eight or fifteen days They have diminished in frequency during the past five years. She has had two this year. The last one, occurring five months ago, provoked by trouble with her children, lasted half an hour, with cries, strangulation, and suffocation.

Before her first confinement Mme. H—— menstruated every *twenty-one days.* For the last two years the menses have appeared *every fifteen days* at the longest, sometimes every eleven or thirteen days. The last period extended from the 11th to the 15th day. Menstruation is very abundant, and sometimes accompanied with sharp cramp. Two or three days before each period, she trembles, is irritable and nervous, and cannot get on with her children. These symptoms disappear with the appearance of the menses.—The respiratory and digestive functions are normal.

The patient is *easily put into somnambulism* on the 20th. She improves after the first séance; the painful spots disappear after the second; the oppression and hoarseness diminish on the 24th. After the fourth séance, the hoarseness has totally disappeared; no more restlessness at night and no more oppression. *I suggest at each séance that her next period will come on October 9, without pain, and will last three days.*

27th.—Fifth séance; the patient says she feels *premonitory symptoms*. Since the 22d (eleven days after the preceding period), she has had twinges in the back and a sensation of weight in the stomach, as is usual at the approach of her period. In the morning (sixteen days after the preceding period), she had headache, which is now passing away. Her voice is clear; she does not cough and has no more oppression. I suggest that all these premonitory symptoms will disappear and that she will menstruate on the 9th.

29th.—Has been well since the last séance. Yesterday evening from four to five o'clock she had *cramps*, as at the approach of her period. She passed a good night. No loss of blood. Her voice is clear; she says that at one time, when she talked a little to her children or when she walked, her voice would disappear entirely.

October 1st.—Had slight leucorrhœa yesterday. *Pains* this morning for ten minutes, as at the approach of her period. Otherwise is doing well.

3d.—Yesterday evening slight hoarseness and cough. Did not sleep well; woke up at two o'clock. No uterine pain. Yesterday morning and this morning she had *neuralgia* which disappeared in the afternoon, together with *nausea and a desire to vomit*, which lasted an hour. At the present time she still complains of vertigo and nausea. She says that she usually has these symptoms when she is pregnant. Suggestion that she will sleep the whole night and that these symptoms will disappear.

5th.—Has been very well since the last séance; day before yesterday slept until five o'clock, last night until six. Her voice is still excellent. Slight leucorrhœa since yesterday. Infra-orbital left neuralgia since nine or ten o'clock this morning. I hypnotize her. *No more pain after the first séance;* complains simply of heat about the eye and on the cheek. After the second séance this heat has also disappeared.

7th.—Complains of no more pain; sleeps well at night. For the last few nights she has only gone to sleep after an hour of slight restlessness. But she continues to sleep well. Yesterday morning when she got up she was again hoarse, and coughed until she vomited. She attributes this to the fact of having eaten nuts the day before. She felt her throat sore immediately afterward; and nuts usually produce this hoarse feeling in her.

This morning she had slight pain on respiration, from the larynx to the middle of the sternum; it lasted two hours.

Has no more leucorrhœa; did not usually have it when she menstruated every eighteen days.

Said that at one time she had headache, especially when she was hoarse; has none now.

Menses appear on the night of the 7th of October, at the end of twenty-six days, instead of on the 8th as had been suggested. She says in her sleep that if it came a day earlier it would be on account of fatigue due to over exertion. The interval between two periods had never been more than twenty-one days, and during the last two years not more than fifteen days. Further, she has no pain; hardly any even in the loins. Usually she has severe pain in the abdomen and loins the day before; they are less on the first day, but again increase on the second day and last two or three days; this time she has none. She has also been less nervous than usual. On the 8th and 9th, however, she is slightly irritated by her children.

Menstruation lasted three days and was moderately profuse as had been suggested, while as a rule it lasted five or six days, never less then five days.

I see Mme. H—— again on October 18; she has been well since. Last week she had slight irritation in her throat which brought on cough at night for three days.

I suggest the next period for the night of the 4th of November, and that the menses shall appear, as a rule, every four weeks, every twenty-eight days.

Is doing well. In damp foggy weather her voice is at times husky, but that is all.

30th.—In consequence of having been angry and cried on the 26th, she is again hoarse and has a sensation of constriction in her throat. Since then, she has had pain in the larynx, and cough with expectoration in the morning. No premonitory sign of menstruation. Suggestion at each séance.

November 7th.—*Menses appeared on October 31 during the night, at the end of twenty-four days.* The period lasted three days, and the patient was not nervous as she usually is. Since the last séance she has had neither hoarseness nor sore throat. *Suggestion of the period for November 28.*

20th.—Is doing very well.

27th.—Menstruation began *on the evening of the 25th*, about four or five o'clock (*at the end of twenty-five days*), with neither pain nor colic. She felt it as she was scrubbing the floor. She thinks that if it had not been for this work it would have been retarded until the 28th.

December 9th.—Is doing very well. Complains this morning of *malaise*, with pain near the heart, and expectoration, as at the approach of her period. It should come on the 23d.

16th.—Has had no more pain in the heart nor expectoration since the last suggestion.

23d.—*Menstruation appeared on the 20th, the 26th day, without pain.*

It lasted hardly three days and was slight. Day before yesterday, in the evening, she caught cold and was hoarse yesterday. Further, yesterday morning at ten o'clock, she had neuralgia, and vertigo, vomited once and had to lie down until three o'clock; then all trouble disappeared.

January 10th, 1887.—The patient has been very well; has had no more discomfort. Her period began *on the 15th, the 26th day* (as had been suggested) without pain or hoarseness. It lasted three days.— *I suggest it again for February 10th.*

February 10th.—*Menstruation appeared on the 8th instead of the 10th*, on the 24th day instead of the 26th, without pain. Mme. H—— caught cold and since the 5th has been hoarse, has coughed, and complained of pain in her back and left side.

After suggestion the hoarseness and other symptoms disappear.

15th.—She again takes cold; has been hoarse all day.

The next day the hoarseness disappeared.

On the 20th she is taken with paroxsyms of coughing which last an hour. Since then she has continued to cough without being hoarse.

25th.—I suggest the disappearance of the cough, and the *next period for March 6th.*

March 3d.—The cold disappeared after the first séance. On February 26th she had an attack of migraine, with malaise, want of appetite, expectoration, and a bad taste in her mouth. She has been well again for two days. At the present time she feels a headache coming on, which I drive away by suggestion.

23d.—Since the last visit, March 3d, she has been perfectly well, without the least discomfort, cough or hoarseness. *Menstruation began on the 7th, instead of on the 6th,* that is to say on the 27th day; was moderately abundant and lasted three days without any hoarseness.

April 21st.—The patient menstruated on April 5, *that is on the 29th day.* She expected it on the 4th. She has been very well up to eight days ago. Since then she says she has not slept or eaten anything; eating suffocates her. She has a sensation of heat about the head. I drive away the discomfort by suggestion.

May 12th.—The patient comes to see me for a cold dating back eight days. She menstruated on May 3d, the *29th day.* The period lasted three days. Is doing well.

I do not see her until June 23d. She says she has been very well since the last séance: the cold disappeared. *She always menstruates exactly on the 28th or 29th day.*

I went to see her again on August 21st. The cure had lasted; she had no more hoarseness. *Her periods continued to appear regularly, on the 28th or 29th day, or a day or two before or after.*

To sum up. A woman who menstruated profusely for five or six days, every eleven or fifteen days, and who never had an interval of more than twenty-one days between two periods, under the influence of hypnotic suggestion comes to menstruate successively on the 26th, 24th, 25th, 26th, 26th, 24th, 27th, 29th, and 29th days and since then regularly two days either before or after the 28th or 29th day.

At first the period did not begin exactly on the day suggested.

On the first occasion, at the time when menstruation would have appeared without suggestion, Mme. H—— felt premonitory symptoms : twinges in the back, sensation of weight in the stomach, then uterine cramps ; then, at about the 26th day she experienced pain over her heart, nausea and vertigo. These were the usual symptoms of her being pregnant. The suggestion acted as an inhibition until the 26th day. Further, menstruation was slight and only lasted three days instead of five or six.

The following periods came without premonitory symptoms and without pain ; the patient's organism succeeded in regulating the menstrual interval to 28 or 29 days under the influence of suggestion.

Let us glance at these observations arranged in the following order :

A —Organic diseases of the nervous system : 10

1. Cerebral hemorrhage, hemiplegia, hemianæsthesia with tremor and contracture. *Cure.*
2. Cerebro-spinal disease : apoplectiform attacks, paralyses, ulnar neuritis. *Cure.*
3. Partial left hemiplegia. *Cure.*
4. Traumatic epilepsy with traumatic rheumatism. *Cure.*
5. Sensory organic hemianæsthesia. *Cure.*
6. Diffuse rheumatic myelitis. *Improvement.*
7. Cerebro-spinal insular sclerosis. *Marked improvement for six months.*
8. Nervous troubles (organic cause ?) in the brachial plexus. Temporary suppression of the symptoms. *No Cure.*
9. Paresis, of traumatic origin, of the muscles of the hand. *Cure.*
10. Paresis of the extensors of the hand and saturnine anæsthesia. *Cure.*

B —*Hysterical diseases :* 17

11. Hystero-epilepsy in a man, sensitivo-sensorial hemianæsthesia. *Cure.*
12. Hysteria, sensitivo-sensorial anæsthesia. Transient suppression of the symptoms. *No Cure.*
13. Hemiplegia with left sensitivo-sensorial hemianæsthesia. *Cure.*
14. Hysterical sensitivo-sensorial hemianæsthesia. *Cure.*
15. Hysteriform paroxysms with hysterical somnambulism. *Cure.*
16. Anæsthesia. Hysterical spinal pain. *Cure.*
17. Paralysis with hysterical anæsthesia. *Cure.*
18. Convulsive hysteria with hemianæsthesia. *Cure.*
19. Hysteria: paroxysms of convulsive weeping. *Cure.*
20. Convulsive hysteria. *Cure.*
21. Convulsive hysteria with hemianæsthesia. *Cure.*
22. Convulsive hysteria. *Cure.*
23. Convulsive hysteria with hemianæsthesia. *Cure.*
24. Convulsive hysteria with hemianæsthesia. *Cure.*
25. Hysteria with hemianæsthesia. *Cure.*
26. Hysteria in the male: weeping and convulsive paroxysms. *Cure* (at least temporary).
27. Hysterical aphonia. *Cure.*

C —*Neuropathic affections :* 18

28. Nervous aphonia. *Cure.*
29. Moral inertia with subjective sensations in the head. *Cure.*
30. Nervous aphonia. *Cure.*
31. Post-epileptic tremor, cephalalgia, and insomnia. *Cure.*
32. Nervous gastric troubles. Anæsthesia. *Improvement.*
33. Neuropathic pains. *Cure.*
34. Epigastric pains. *Cure.*
35. Neuropathic lumbar pains. Insomnia. *Cure.*
36. Paresis with sense of weight in the right leg. *Cure.*
37. Pains in the right leg. *Cure.*
38. Girdle-pain and pain in right groin, with difficulty in walking, for twenty months. *Cure.*
39. Insomnia, loss of appetite, mental depression, tremor. *Cure.*
40. Gloomy ideas. Insomnia, loss of appetite. *Cure.*
41. Insomnia through habit. *Partial cure.*
42. Cephalalgia, intellectual obnubilation. *Cure.*
43. Vertigo. moral depression connected with cardiac disease. *Cure.*
44. Laziness, disobedience, and loss of appetite in a child. *Cure.*
45. Pseudo-paraplegia with tremor. *Cure.*

D—*Various neuroses:* 15

46. Choreic movements consecutive to chorea. *Cure.*
47. Id. id. id.
48. Choreic movements from moral emotion. *Cure.*
49. Post-choreic tremor in the hand. *Cure.*
50. Post choreic trouble in writing. *Cure.*
51. Choreic movements in the hands. *Cure.*
52. Hemi-chorea. Rapid improvement. *Gradual cure.*
53. General chorea. *Gradual cure.*
54. Id. id.
55. Obstinate writer's cramp. Rapid improvement. *Gradual cure.*
56. Attacks of tetany, nocturnal somnambulism. *Cure.*
57. Nocturnal somnambulism. *Temporary cure.*
58. Nocturnal incontinence of urine. *Cure.*
59. Id. id. id.
60. Nocturnal incontinence of urine. Aphonia consecutive to pneumonia. *Cure.*

E—*Dynamic pareses and paralyses:* 3

61. Sense of weight with paresis of the left arm. *Cure.*
62. Dynamic psychical paraplegia. *Cure.*
63. Pains and paresis of the lower limbs. *Cure.*

F—*Gastro-intestinal affections:* 4

64. Alcoholic gastritis with insomnia and weakness of the legs. *Improvement.*
65. Chronic gastritis. Dilatation of the stomach and vomiting. *Improvement.*
66. Gastric troubles. Burning sensation over sternum. Insomnia. *Cure.*
67. Gastro-intestinal catarrh. Metritis. Neuropathy. *Improvement.*

G—*Various painful affections:* 12

68. Epigastric pain. *Cure.*
69. Umbilical and epigastric pain. *Cure.*
70. Interscapular pain. *Cure.*
71. Thoracic pain. Insomnia (Tubercular diathesis). *Cure.*
72. Hypogastric and supra-inguinal pains on the left side connected with an old pelvic-peritonitis. *Cure.*
73. Intercostal pain. *Cure.*
74. Thoracic pain. *Gradual cure.*
75. Painful contusion of the deltoid. *Cure.*

76. Muscular pain in the flank. *Cure.*
77. Painful spot in the side. *Cure.*
78. Pains in the epitrochlear muscles. *Cure.*
79. Pain in the shoulder and upper right limb from effort. *Cure.*

H—*Rheumatic affections:* 19

80. Rheumatic paralysis of the right fore-arm. *Cure.*
81. Rheumatic scapulo-humeral arthritis. *Improvement without cure.*
82. Muscular rheumatism with cramp. *Cure.*
83. Ilio-lumbar rheumatic neuralgia. *Cure.*
84. Arthralgia consecutive to an arthritis. *Cure.*
85. Pleurodynia and lumbar pain helped by suggestion. *Cure.*
86. Apyretic articular rheumatism. *Gradual cure.*
87. Chronic articular rheumatism (wrists and insteps). *Cure.*
88. Muscular articular and nervous rheumatism. *Gradual cure.*
89. Acromio-clavicular and xiphoid rheumatic pains. *Cure.*
90. Muscular lumbo-crural rheumatism, with sacro-sciatic neuralgia. *Rapid improvement. Almost total cure.*
91. Apyretic articular rheumatism. *Gradual cure.*
92. Acromio-clavicular rheumatic pains. *Cure.*
93. Muscular rheumatism in the arm and right leg. *Cure.*
94. Gonorrheal rheumatism. *Gradual cure.*
95. Acromio-clavicular and xiphoid articular rheumatism. *Cure.*
96. Rheumatic articular pains. *Cure.*
97. Dorsal and metacarpo-phalangeal rheumatic pains. *Cure.*
98. Rheumatic, dorso-lumbar, and sciatic pains. *Cure.*

I—*Neuralgias:* 5

99. Rebellious sciatica. *Cure.*
100. Recent sciatica helped by one suggestion. *Cure.*
101. Rebellious sciatica. *Cure.*
102. Rebellious sciatica. *Gradual cure.*
103. Neuralgia of the trigeminus with facial *tic douloureux. Almost complete cure.*

J—*Menstrual troubles:* 2

104. Menstrual retardation. Suggestion of the periods for a fixed day.
105. Profuse menstruation every eleven or fifteen days. Interval lengthened by suggestion to twenty-eight or twenty-nine days.

CHAPTER II

Suggestive therapeutics acts upon function.—Rôle of functional dynamism in disease.—Dangers of hypnotism.—Spontaneous sleep.—Exaggerated hypnotic suggestibility.—Suggestion corrects these inconveniences.—Can hypnotism injure the cerebral faculties?—Abuse of induced hallucinations.—Susceptibility to hallucination in the waking condition.—Medical advice.

BY relating these numerous observations I have tried to show how vast is the field of suggestive psycho-therapeutics. It is not only in hysteria, in neuroses and in purely functional nervous maladies that suggestive therapeutics finds an application. We have seen the results which it can bring about in organic affections of the nervous system, in chronic articular rheumatism, and in gastric troubles, etc. I have tried to explain (see Obs. I. and II.) by what mechanism suggestion may act efficaciously in cases of this kind. It may seem puerile, at first sight, to call upon the imagination to cure or improve functional troubles connected with cerebral hemorrhage or degeneration, with rheumatic arthritis or chronic myelitis. Many physicians will shrug their shoulders and raise their hands to heaven, to protest against such assertions. May they reflect and verify, before protesting. They will be forced to bow before the evidence of facts.

I do not pretend that suggestion acts directly upon the diseased organ to suppress vascular congestion, resolve inflammatory exudation, and restore the destroyed or degenerated elements of the parenchyma. What drug in the materia medica is capable of creating such a direct curative activity? Diseases are cured, when they can be cured, by their natural biological evolution. Our ordinary therapeutic methods consist in putting the organism in a condition such that the *restitutio ad integrum* may take place; we suppress the pain, we modify function, we let the organ rest, we calm the fever, we retard the pulse, we induce sleep, we encourage secretion and excretion, and, acting thus, we permit nature the healer, or, to speak in modern language, we permit the activity of the forces and the properties inherent in the biological elements to accomplish their work. The therapeutic agents which we use are only functional medicament. **Suggestion**, also, is a powerful functional medicament.

Every organ and every function is under the control of the nervous centres. Each element of the organism has, so to speak, its centre of action bordering upon the brain. Sensibility, movement, nutrition, secretion, excretion and calorification are governed, or at least influenced, by this central organism, which presides over the complex mechanism of animal physiology. This central organism may interfere efficaciously in order to re-establish the working of the disturbed organs and functions as far as possible.

I say as far as possible. Let us take a case in which we suppose a cerebral hemorrhage to have destroyed the entire internal capsule; a descending degeneration occurs in the pyramidal tract, and a spastic hemiplegia is the result. Here the motor organ, the *sine quâ non* which controls the movements of one-half of the body, is destroyed. No organic substitution is possible. No medication can restore what has been destroyed. Suggestion cannot, any more than other therapeutic means, re-establish a function, the organ indispensable to the control of which no longer exists.

But let us suppose that the hemorrhage has left unharmed a number of fibres sufficient for the transmission of the centrifugal influence of the will to the motor cells. These fibres are only functionally affected, stunned by the shock to the neighboring fibres, affected potentially. Being powerless to arise spontaneously from their torpor, suggestion may act dynamically upon them; the psychical activity aroused and concentrated upon these fibres gives them a new stimulus, which revives their dulled modality. By this dynamogenic excitation the cerebral influx succeeds in forcing its way to the motor cells, and the interrupted conductivity being re-established, function is restored.

Now we have seen how important a rôle dynamism plays in the functions of the nervous system. We know that organic hemianæsthesias obstinately persisting for years (for four years in one of my cases) have been rapidly cured by various methods of treatment, electricity, metallotherapy, magnetotherapy, suggestion. We know that dynamic paralyses and contractures, hysterical and psychical, after having persisted for years, defying all therapeutic methods, sometimes yield as if by enchantment to a violent moral disturbance. There is nothing exceptional in the living organism: each act induced is susceptible of being reproduced, because this act implies the activity of a physiological mechanism inherent in the organism.

A consideration which should never be lost sight of in regard to therapeutics is this: a functional trouble may survive the cause or the organic lesion which gave it birth; this trouble is no longer kept up by the lesion, but is retained, if I may so express it, by the nervous system. The latter has a great tendency for preserving certain modalities which have been impressed upon it. A child who has been susceptible to convulsions, repeats these convulsions under the slightest influence.—Spasms, nervous movements, hysterical paroxysms, nervous cough, vomiting, diarrhœa, etc., are acts which the nervous centres execute spontaneously, if by frequent repetition these acts are, so to speak, assimilated by these centres. Certain pains last when the lesion which is the cause of them, no longer exists. For example, every surgeon has seen a limb after a contusion remain dynamically affected: the patient continues to suffer and the limb is motionless: nevertheless the contusion seems to be cured. Electricity, hydrotherapy, massage, moral influence, and suggestion often interfere efficaciously to drive away the troubles which remain.

It is willingly conceded that psychical influence may have a certain efficacy in the domain of nervous pathology: but it is more difficult to conceive that, outside of this domain, it may exercise some influence. Here says one, is a chronic rheumatic arthritis. The articulation is diseased, the articular and peri-articular tissues are extensively altered. Do you pretend to suggest the resolution of the lesion, that the synovial membrane will regain its normal structure, that the destroyed cartilage will be re-formed?

I do not pretend this. I have found from experience that suggestive therapeutics is sometimes incontestably efficacious in diseases of this kind. Blinded by prejudice, many will see and will deny the evidence of facts, because they are saturated with the idea of the infallibility of their own judgment, because they close their eyes systematically to truths which do not adapt themselves to their preconceived ideas!

Doubtless suggestion can do nothing for a dislocated joint, for an osseous or fibrous anchylosis, for an old articular fungosity. But such is not the case with all chronic rheumatic arthropathies. Here is a man whose joints remain swollen and painful; but the lesion is not incompatible with the joints performing their functions; it is susceptible of resolution; the cartilages and synovial membranes have not yet undergone an irremediable alteration; it is the immobility of the articulation which may partly help to keep up the lesion; it creates retraction of the articular and peri-articular cellulo-fibrous tissue; it perhaps robs the synovial membrane of its oiling quality; it makes the cartilaginous surfaces uneven; it maintains a passive stasis of blood in the capillaries. Surgeons treat arthritis by prolonged rest. The suggestion which calms the pain, gives the patient back the power of impressing upon the joint the movements which are necessary for its well-being, which thus restores to the fibro-serous tissues their suppleness, to the synovial membrane its oiliness, and to the capillary circulation its activity, may act efficaciously to improve and cure the arthropathy.

M. Delbœuf has shown by ingenious experiments, that a sore produced by burning, for example, causes less inflammatory reaction, and cicatrizes more quickly, if the part has been made insensible beforehand by suggestion. "Pain," says this eminent psychologist, "makes the patient think of his trouble; and thinking of it, he exaggerates it. Hypnotism, which distracts his attention, acts in a contrary way upon the pain; it diminishes it by making us think no more of it." (*De l'origine des effets curatifs de l'hypnotisme. Bulletin de l'Académie royale de Belgique*, 1877.)

Suggestion takes hold of one of the elements of the disease, and the suppression of this morbid element may react favorably upon the whole pathological apparatus, in which all elements are reciprocally dependent one upon the other. And what else do our usual therapeutic agents do? Opium, quinine, the salicylates, rubbing, revulsion, blisters, massage, electricity, what else do they do but take hold of the disease by one of its elements? Have we many medicines which possess the property of modifying the material lesion directly? It is the functional respiration which brings about the organic respiration, when it is possible to bring it about.

I have said enough to indicate the ground I take in the explanation of the results of suggestive psycho-therapeutics. I was not acquainted with this therapeutic method when, in 1875, I wrote the article *Réaction*, in the *Dictionnaire encyclopédique*:

"Often the moral control, that is to say, the putting into

activity of the psychical functions, has salutary effects. To console a patient, to sustain his courage, to drive away from his mind the great anxiety which consumes him, is often to react efficaciously upon the disease. By the quiet persuasive voice of the physician the patient is restored as by a salutary balm, feels his confidence arise and his discomfort disappear. Doubtless the psychical alterations which occur once, persist despite of all moral influence. But the numerous functional troubles, precordial anxiety, nervous palpitations, shortness of breath, and gloomy ideas, may be improved by a new modality impressed upon the nervous centres. Thus is explained, or rather conceived, the immense influence which a physician of tact may exercise over a patient by this moral medicine, a true neurosthenic reaction, which is not the least powerful among therapeutic agents."

One word more before terminating this book, upon the *dangers of hypnotism.*

Is hypnotism in itself dangerous to those submitted to it? From experience, I do not hesitate in stating that, when it is well-managed, it does not produce the slightest harm. It does not interfere with the functions of organic life; we have seen that respiration and circulation are not influenced in subjects whose minds are at rest. If, in the first séances, some subjects manifest nervous phenomena, such as muscular twitchings, shortness of breath, discomfort, acceleration of the pulse; and if some hysterical subjects have convulsive paroxysms during the operation, these symptoms, auto-suggestive so to speak, and due to moral emotion, to a sentiment of fear, always disappear in the following séances, thanks to a quieting suggestion which brings back confidence. When the habit has been formed, the subjects go to sleep peacefully and naturally and awake in the same way, without the slightest discomfort, if the operator has been careful to suggest no discomfort upon waking.

In my already long practice I have never seen any harm produced by sleep induced according to our method, for the suggestion is always present as a corrective to any disagreeable symptoms which may arise.

There is a danger which it is important to recognize and which I am going to mention. After having been hypnotized a certain number of times, some subjects preserve a disposition to go to sleep spontaneously. Some have been hardly awakened when they fall to sleep again of themselves in the same hypnotic sleep.

Others fall asleep thus during the day. This tendency to auto-hypnotization may be repressed by suggestion. It is sufficient to state to the subject during sleep that when once awakened he will be completely awake, and will not be able to go to sleep again spontaneously during the day.

Others are too easily susceptible to hypnotization when they have often been put into somnambulism. The first comer may sometimes put them into this condition by surprise, simply closing their eyes. Such a susceptibility to hypnotism is a real danger. Delivered over to the mercy of any one, deprived of psychical and moral resistance, certain somnambulists thus become weak and are moulded by the will of the suggestionists.

Those moralists who are careful of human dignity, and who are pre-occupied with the thought of such great possibilities of danger, are in the right. They are right to condemn a practice which may rob man of his free-will without the possibility of resistance on his part; they would be a thousand times right, if the remedy were not side by side with the evil. When we foresee such a tendency in our cases of somnambulism, we take care to say during sleep (and it is a good rule to follow): " Nobody will be able to hypnotize you in order to relieve you, unless it be your physician." And the subject, obedient to the command, is refractory to any foreign suggestion. One day I tried to hypnotize an excellent somnambulist whom I had already hypnotized several times; I could not succeed. I called M. Liébault to aid me; he hypnotized her in a few seconds. I then asked her why I had not succeeded. She told me that, several months before, M. Beaunis had suggested during sleep that M. Liébault and himself were the only ones who could hypnotize her. This idea, written in her mind, and of which she was not conscious in the waking condition, had forewarned her against me. Thus the danger of a too great susceptibility to suggestion may be forestalled by suggestion itself.

A graver apprehension and one which forces itself naturally upon our attention, is the following: Some one will say, do you not fear that hypnotism may finally do grave harm to the mental faculties, even when it is used prudently, and solely for a therapeutic end, without provoking hallucinations? The mind dulled, the intelligence demoralized, and the mental activity diminished, the subject falls into a condition of intellectual torpor and remains in it.

Experience alone can answer. I have hypnotized very intelligent people daily, and sometimes twice a day for months and even years, and I have never found the slightest harm done to the faculties of understanding. Cerebral initiative was quite as active, and it sometimes became more active; for the functional troubles from which the patients suffer, such as pain, restlessness, nervous disturbance and insomnia, react in a harmful way upon the psychical activity. To suppress these troubles by suggestion, is to put the mind into a condition of rest, is to drive away the impressions which undermine its functional liberty, is to protect the functional integrity of the organ which is the generator of thought. Hypnotic sleep in itself is beneficial and is free from harm, as is natural sleep.

But another order of dangers may result from provoked hallucinations, and here I should speak as I think. Doubtless inoffensive hallucinations provoked at long intervals, whether hypnotic or post-hypnotic, trouble the mind momentarily, in the same way as do dreams, but the equilibrium is quickly reëstablished as soon as the hallucinatory dream has disappeared.

Is it the same if these hallucinations are frequently suggested to the imagination? In the long run may not some trouble remain in the mind? Is it not to be feared that a more or less marked derangement of the intellectual faculties may survive? I should not like to state that certain delicate brains, predisposed to mental alienation, could not receive serious harm from inopportune and awkward experiments of this kind, knowing that all emotion, all violent disturbance can make an insanity bud out, the diathetic germ of which, often hereditary, is inherent in the organism. I simply should say that in the many experiments which I have performed, I have never known any psychical trouble to result. In one case of which I have spoken, M. G., a very intelligent woman, affected with loco motor ataxia, I allowed myself to perform some experiments toward this end, watching over her psychical condition carefully, and ready to check the experiments at the slightest sign of restlessness which might be manifested. At different times, and on consecutive days I submitted her to complex, repeated, hypnotic, and post-hypnotic hallucinations to be carried out after a short and after a long interval; and of all that nothing has remained. During the three years that she has been in the service, in spite of the many suggestions, her intelligence has remained as quick as it was, and her initiative has not been harmed. I hasten to add that this fact should not serve as encouragement; a like experiment is dangerous; experiments of provoked hallucination should only be performed prudently and with reserve.

Another real danger is this: After many hypnotizations, after many hallucinations provoked during sleep, certain subjects become susceptible to suggestion and hallucination in the waking condition.

Their minds realize with extreme facility every conception insinuated; every idea becomes an act, every image evoked becomes a reality; they no longer distinguish between the real world and the imaginary world suggested. The majority it is true, are only thus susceptible to hallucination through the one person who is accustomed to hypnotize them.

But among these subjects, especially if the physician has not taken the precaution to attribute a monopoly of the ability to give suggestion to himself, some may be susceptible to hallucination and suggestion at the hands of any one who knows how to force it upon them.

And if this extreme susceptibility to hallucination is once produced, if this nervous disease is once created, it is not always easy to cure or to improve it by a new suggestive interference. But it is not necessary to subject the human mind to influences of this sort. Doubtless some experiments of hallucinations induced from time to time are inoffensive, if they are performed with reserve; repeated frequently upon the same subject they may become dangerous.

Must we proscribe a thing which may be efficacious, because the abuse of it is injurious? No one proscribes wine, alcohol, opium, quinine, because the immoderate or intemperate use of these substances may bring about accidents. Doubtless suggestion used by dishonest or awkward men is a dangerous practice. Law can and should intervene to repress its abuse.

Suggestion is only beneficial when used prudently and intelligently for a therapeutic end. It is the physician's part to separate the useful from the harmful effect, and to apply it to the relief of his patients. In cases where I believe that suggestive therapeutics has some chance of success, I should deem myself reprehensible as a physician did I not propose it to my patient, and did I not urge him to decide to submit himself to it.

The following are the rules to which I believe I ought to bind myself, and to which all physicians should bind themselves before using hypnotism, in order to protect their conscience and professional honor:

"1st. Never hypnotize any subject without his formal consent, or the consent of those in authority over him.

"2d. Never induce sleep except in the presence of a third person in authority, who can guarantee the good faith of the hypnotizer and the subject. Thus any trouble may be avoided, in the event of an accusation, or any suspicion of an attempt which is not for the relief of the subject." (Beaunis.)

3d. Never give to the hypnotized subject, without his consent, any other suggestions than those necessary for his cure. The physician has no rights but those conferred upon him by the patient. He should limit himself to the therapeutic suggestion: any other experiment is forbidden him, without the formal consent of the patient, even if it be in the interest of science. The physician should not profit by his authority over the patient in order to provoke this consent, if he thinks that the experiment which he wishes to perform may have the slightest harmful effect.

It is the application of suggestion to therapeutics which as a physician and clinical professor, I have felt it my duty to study in a special way.

Resting upon numerous facts, I have a right to affirm that suggestive therapeutics exists, without wishing to say that this therapeutic means is always applicable, or always efficacious. But it is frequently both applicable and efficacious.

It was not for any idle end, nor simply to gratify a vain scientific curiosity, that more than six years ago, with many obstacles in my way, I began this study, and have followed it out rigorously in spite of derision.

PREFACE TO THE REVISED EDITION

THE singular facility with which the immense majority of subjects of any age, of both sexes, and of all temperaments may be hypnotized always astonishes the gentlemen who honor us by coming to our clinic to verify the statements contained in this book. They imagine the hypnotic state to be the exclusive lot of rare neuropathic cases, and they now see *all or nearly all* the patients in a ward fall under the dominion of suggestion in succession. "How have we been able to let a truth so easy of demonstration pass us by for centuries," they ask, "without discovering it?"

Some of the subjects whom we hypnotize fall into a deep sleep with loss of memory upon waking: we call such cases somnambulists. According to M. Liébault one fifth or one sixth of all subjects are somnambulists. In our hospital service, where the physician has greater authority over the patients, and where imitation and the force of example, perhaps, form a veritable suggestive atmosphere, the proportion of somnambulists is much larger, and we sometimes succeed in putting half if not a larger proportion of our subjects into this condition.

Although the other patients remember everything that has happened upon waking, and sometimes imagine that they have not been asleep, they have been influenced in varying degrees. Suggestive catalepsy, induced contracture, automatic movements, the suppression of pain, etc., decisively prove the existence of the influence.

The patients in deep sleep with loss of memory upon waking lie quietly like natural sleepers, if left alone. There is nothing by which to differentiate this induced sleep from natural sleep. The phenomena of sensibility, motility, ideation, imagination, illusions, and hallucinations, do not appear spontaneously, but are brought about by means of suggestion. The same phenomena may be induced in these subjects when we put ourselves into relationship with them in their natural sleep; the same passive attitude of the limbs known as catalepsy, the same automatic movements, the same illusions, the same active or passive hallucinations. Hallucinations are only suggested dreams; dreams are only spontaneous hallucinations. Whether spontaneous or suggested, these hallucinations remain passive; that is, the subject is motionless as in the normal dream. They do not become active; that is, the subject does not move, does not walk, and only plays an animated part in the hallucination induced, when roused from his torpid condition by suggestion. In like manner the dreams of spontaneous sleep become active in some cases and constitute natural somnambulism. The fact will bear repetition that all manifestations realized in the hypnotic condition may be realized in natural sleep in the same subject.

No: hypnotic sleep is not a pathological sleep. The hypnotic condition is not a neurosis, analogous to hysteria. No doubt, manifestations of hysteria may be created in hypnotized subjects; a real hypnotic neurosis may be developed which will be repeated each time sleep is induced. But these manifestations are not due to the hypnosis,—they are due to the operator's suggestion, or sometimes to the auto-suggestion of a particularly impossible subject whose imagination, impregnated with the ruling idea of magnetism, creates these functional disorders which can always be restrained by a quieting suggestion. The pretended physical phenomena of the hypnosis are only psychical phenomena. Catalepsy, transfer, contracture, etc., are the effects of suggestion. To prove that the very great majority of subjects are susceptible to suggestion is to eliminate the idea of a neurosis. At least it is not an admission that the neurosis is universal, that the word hysteria is a synonym for any nervous impressionability whatever. For, as we all have nervous tissues, and as it is a property of such tissues to be impressionable, we should all be hysterical.

The sleep itself is the effect of a suggestion. I have said that no one could be hypnotized against his will. M. Ochorowitz has opposed this proposition energetically. Perhaps he has not quite grasped my idea. It is certain that any one who does not want to be hypnotized, and who knows that he need not be influenced if he does not wish to be, successfully resists every trial. It is also true that certain subjects cannot resist because their will-power is weakened by fear, or by the *idea* of a superior power which influences them in spite of themselves. *No one can be hyp-*

notized unless he has the idea that he is going to be. Looked at in this light my proposition cannot be attacked. The idea makes the hypnosis; it is a psychical and not a physical or fluid influence which brings about this condition. It is a singular thing that psychologists like M. Janet and M. Binet have failed to recognize the purely psychical nature of these manifestations. M. Delboeuf has not been deceived in the matter.

The experiments lately made by M. Bourru and M. Burot, of Rochefort, have been cited in opposition to the doctrine of suggestion. I have reference to the action of drugs at a distance. Certain subjects in the hypnotic or waking condition are supposed to have a singular aptitude for being influenced by a substance contained in a bottle placed by their side, and of whose contents they are ignorant, the effect being as if the substance had been injected.

I confess that this experiment has never been successful in my best cases of somnambulism, and I will frankly state my opinion regarding it, though perhaps I may be wrong. I was present at an experiment of this kind and in it, at least, I was convinced that suggestion was the explanation of the phenomenon. *One should first be aware of the fact that in all degrees of hypnosis the subject hears and understands everything even though he may appear inert and passive.* Sometimes the senses are particularly sharp in this state of special concentration, as if all the nervous activity were accumulated in the organ of which the attention is solicited. These subjects think that it is their duty to try to carry into effect the operator's thought, and they therefore use all this sensorial hyper-acuteness, all this concentrated attention, in trying to guess what is wanted of them. Knowing that they are expected to feel the effect of a substance held in a bottle, they suggest to themselves vague phenomena such as discomfort, anxiety, agitation and nausea, which correspond to the effects of most poisons; as alcohol, opium, emetics, valerian, etc. If there is any one among the assistants who knows what the substance in question is, and who, astonished by these primary manifestations on the subject's part, betrays his sentiments by word, the subject hears each word, though spoken in a low voice, and seizes upon the suggested aid held out to him. If no one speaks, he tries to find some indication to set him on the right track, in the faces of those present, in the gestures, in the slightest sign of approbation or disapprobation, and in odors; he gropes his way, and sometimes he guesses rightly. If there is no sign, if none of the assistants and not even the operator knows what the bottle contains, the subject returns to his passive state after making a few manifestations which are not very sharply defined, and the experiment has failed.

I hasten to add that good reliable observers state that they have succeeded under conditions such that suggestion could not enter into the result. I suspend judgment here. The facts which I have not been able to produce in my subjects, have been produced by others in their subjects. To deny them without fuller information would be acting in an unscientific spirit.

Facts relative to thought-transmission, or mental suggestion are also appealed to. Highly enlightened men have observed facts which appear conclusive.

Dr. Gilbert of Havre, M. Pierre Janet, MM. Myers of London, Dr. Perronnet of Lyons, and M. Ochorowitz, have published a large number of observations. I have tried to produce phenomena of thought-transmission in hundreds of cases, but without success. I have found nothing definite, and here also I remain in doubt. If, on the one hand, the action of drugs at a distance, and on the other, thought-transmission exist, they are phenomena of another order, which have still to be studied. They have nothing in common with the phenomena of suggestion. In this book I only consider verbal suggestion and its application to therapeutics.

Susceptibility to suggestion exists in the waking condition, but it is then either neutralized or restrained by the faculties of reason, attention and judgment. In spontaneous or in induced sleep these faculties are dull and weakened; imagination rules supreme; impressions are accepted without verification, and the brain transforms them into actions, sensations, movements and images. The psychical state thus modified and the new state of consciousness induced, render the brain more docile, more easily moulded, more susceptible on the one hand, and on the other more apt to react upon the functions and organs by inhibition or dynamogeny. It is this susceptibility increased by suggestion which we employ in the most efficacious way for a therapeutic end.

Such are the principal ideas which the reader will find developed in this book.

This edition is not simply a reproduction of the old one. It contains a new classification of the different degrees of hypnotism, a classification which at the same time seems to me to be a new conception, and I might almost say a vivid demonstration of the psychical nature of the phenomena.

It contains beside a more complete study of a phenomenon of the highest importance from the social and judicial point of view, namely the phenomenon of retroactive hallucinations, which I was the first to mention and which was observed by M. Liégeois, at the same time.

It contains also a large number of new observations on suggestive therapeutics.

The Nancy School placed the study of hypnotism upon its true basis, suggestion, and thus created this most useful and most fruitful application, an application which is the cause of this book's existence. To M. Liébault belongs the honor of first introducing this application; an honor which cannot be denied him. We have been the first to follow him in this path. I have no hesitation in saying that the preceding edition of this work was a real revelation to many physicians who desired to experiment in their turn.

The evidence of facts will finally force itself upon the most skeptical minds, and suggestive therapeutics, accepted and practised by all physicians, will be one of the fairest conquests of contemporary medicine.

H. BERNHEIM

November, 1887

AUTHOR'S INTRODUCTION
TO THE REVISED EDITION

THE first part of this book was published in 1884. I have revised it, added new facts and considerations, and answered criticisms sent me. The second part is entirely new and its object is suggestive therapeutics.

I have entitled this book Suggestion. The word magnetism, born of an erroneous interpretation of the phenomena, has no longer any cause for existence. Suggestion rules the greater part of hypnotic manifestations, and in my opinion the phenomena which are called physical are only psychical. The hypnotized subject grasps the operator's thought. His brain excites and carries it out by means of an exalted suggestion, which is produced by the special concentration of mind in the hypnotic condition. Suggestion is the key to Braidism.

This doctrine has led us to follow M. Liébault in his method of suggestive therapeutics. I owe the knowledge of the method I use to induce sleep and to obtain certain incontestable therapeutic effects to M. Liébault, Doctor of Medicine at Nancy.

For more than twenty-five years our colleague has braved the ridicule and discredit which attaches to the practice of what is called animal magnetism, carried on his researches and devoted himself to the treatment of disease through sleep. The idea of suggestion put forth by Faria was more successfully applied by Braid. M. Liébault has perfected the method and brought it to its most simple expression. He has shown like Braid, that the very great majority of subjects are susceptible of being influenced, and that many obtain beneficial results by means of the psychical condition thus induced. The first researches of the Nancy physician are recorded in the volume entitled: *Du Sommeil et des états analogues considérés surtout an point de vue de l'action du moral sur le physique.* Paris, 1886.

M. Liébault's assertions met only with incredulity. His practices appeared so stamped with oddity, not to say naïveté, that the physicians rejected them without fuller examination. M. Liébault lived in solitude outside of the medical world, giving himself up entirely to his patients (almost all of them from the poorer classes) and to his convictions.

Five years ago, M. Dumont, chief of the physical works of the faculty of medicine, having followed M. Liébault's consultations, was convinced of the reality of the phenomena observed. He experimented successfully in the Mareville Asylum, and had the satisfaction of making a contracture of the right leg, dating back three years, in a case of hystero-epilepsy, and attacks of hystero-epilepsy recurring five or six times a day, disappear.

At my request he presented to the Society of Medicine at Nancy on May 10, 1882, four subjects, in whom he produced a certain number of experiments which greatly astounded the members of the society. Since this time I have experimented myself, with great scepticism in the beginning I must confess. After some hesitation I have not delayed in stating results which are certain and striking, and which force the duty of speaking upon me.

In the first part of this book I shall state first the method employed in inducing hypnotism and the different manifestations which may be determined in hypnotized subjects.

I shall then give a short historical sketch of the question. I shall examine into the theoretical views put forth upon this subject, and I shall state my personal opinions upon the psychological mechanism of the phenomena.

Finally I shall examine the applications of the doctrine of suggestion to psychology, to legal medicine, and to sociology, in a general way.

In the second part I shall make a special study of suggestive therapeutics and I shall relate my personal observations.

H. BERNHEIM

June, 1886

INDEX

A

Abbot Faria, lectures of, 109
Affectation, 128
Affirmation, analgesia by, 83
Alexander Bertrand's theory, 110
Amaurosis, psychical, 46
Amnesia, visual, 50
Anæsthesia, spontaneous and suggestive, 22
Anæsthesia, suggestive, 14
Andry and Thouret's report, 193
Analgesia by affirmation, 83
Animal magnetism a phenomenon of suggestion, 28
Answer to criticisms, 87
Apparatus of Stoeber, 47
Applications of doctrine of suggestion, 159
Author's classification, 11
Author's criticism of Binet and Féré's experiment's, 94
Author's experiments, 96
Author's theory of hypnotism, 125
Auto-hypnotisation, 413
Auto-suggestion, 102
Auto-suggestion, unconscious, 214
Automatic movements, 25
Automatic movements by imitation, 26
Automatic obedience, 29
Automatic rotation, 7

B

Balassa's observations, 119
Beard's trancoidal states, 119
Beaunis' table, 20
Berger's theory, 121
Bernheim's classification, 11
Bernheim's explanation of variation in pulse and respiration, 74
Bernheim's reply to Paul Janet, 182
Binet and Féré, criticism on, 45
Binet and Féré's criticism, 45
Binet and Féré's transfer experiments, 91
Blisters, suggestive, 75
Bloody stigmata from suggestion, 76
Bourru and Burot's observations, 76
Braid's discovery, 111
Braidism and Braidic suggestion, 111
Braid's observations, 73
Braid's theory, 114
Braid's views, 28
Burcq's theory, 195

C

Case illustrating suggestive action of magnet, 92
Cases of catalepsy, 24
Cases of suggestion at long intervals, 51, 52
Castellan, story of, 160
Catalepsy, cases of, 24
Catalepsy in typhoid fever, 24
Catalepsy, suggestive, 6
Cataleptic stage, 87
Cataplexia, 119
Cerebral docility, 133
Chambard's classification, 142
Characteristics of first degree, 5
Characteristics of second degree, 6
Characteristics of third degree, 7
Characteristics of fourth degree, 7
Characteristics of fifth degree, 8
Characteristics of sixth degree, 8
Charcot's researches, 120
Charcot's stages, 87
Charpignon's theory, 115
Children, susceptibility of, 2
Chloroform, hypnosis by, 4
Circulation and respiration in hypnotism, 73
Classification of author, 11
Classification of Chambard, 142
Classification of Liébault, 5
Communication of Richet, 85
Contracture, suggestive, 7
Correspondence, hypnosis by, 4
Credulity, 131
Criticism by Binet and Féré, 45
Criticism on Binet and Féré, 45
Crossed sensibility, 80
Cures at Lourdes, 200
Czermak's observations, 118

D

Dangers of hypnotism 412.
Dangers of induced hallucinations, 414
Deafness, psychical, 50
Deep somnambulism, 8
Definition of hypnotism, 15
Degrees of susceptibility, 3
Delboeuf's experiments, 411
Discovery of Braid, 111
Distinction of true and false evidence, 177
Doctrine of Grimes, 113
Doctrine of suggestion, applications of, 159
Donato's method, 16

Dr. Dod's lectures, 113
Dr. Philip's essay, 115
Dreams, spontaneous, 67
Dynamic pareses and paralyses, 353

E

Effects of prisms, 103
Effect of suggestion on functions of organic life, 74
Effect of verbal suggestion, 6
Electro-biology, 113
Espinas' views, 122
Essay of Dr. Philips, 115
Examples of suggestion in waking state, 81
Experimentation, precautions to be observed in, 104
Experiments of Delboeuf, 411
Experiments of Forel, 76
Experiments of Ganzinotty, 47
Experiments of Kircher, 118
Experiments of Liégeois, 163
Experiments of Richet, 119
Explanation of Suggestion à longue échéance, 144

F

Fascination, 16
First category, 9
First degree, characteristics of, 5
Fourth degree, characteristics of, 7
Fifth degree, characteristics of, 8
Fluid theory, 28
Forel's experiments, 76
Formula for inducing hypnosis, 2
Functions of organic life, effect of suggestion on, 74

G

Ganzinotty's experiments, 47
Gastro-intestinal affections, 356
General Noizet's theory, 110
Gestures, influence of, 2
Grimes' doctrine, 113

H

Hack Tuke's observations on pulse and respiration, 74
Hallucinations, negative, 43
Hallucinations, post-hypnotic, 40
Hallucinations, suggested, 30
Hansen's travels, 120
Heidenhein's results, 74
Heidenhein's theory, 121
Hemorrhage, suggestive, 76
Historical sketch, 105
Hypotaxic condition, 114
Hypnosis by chloroform, 4
Hypnosis by correspondence, 4
Hypnosis by telephone, 4
Hypnosis, rapidity of, 1
Hypnosis, susceptibility to, 5

Hypnotic neurosis, 89
Hypnotic sleep, phenomena of, 21
Hypnotising, manner of, 1
Hypnotising, precautions to be observed in, 416
Hypnotism as an anæsthetic, 22
Hypnotism. author's theory of, 125
Hypnotism, circulation and respiration in, 73
Hypnotism, dangers of, 412
Hypnotism, definition of, 15
Hypnotism in surgery, 116
Hypnotism, recent literature of, 123
Husson's report, 107
Hysterical affections, 262

I

Illusions of personality, 59
Illusions, suggested, 30
Illustrations of somnambulistic types, 53
Imaginary indications, 100
Imagination as a therapeutic agent, 192
Individuality in somnambulism, 60
Induced hallucinations, dangers of, 414
Induced sleep, reflections on, 72
Inflammation, suggestive, 75
Influence of gestures, 2
Influence of passes, 2
Influence of suggestion on vaso-motor system, 75
Instinctive imbecility, 179

K

Kircher's experiments, 118

L

Lasègue's researches, 116
Latent memories, 144
Le grand Hypnotisme, 89
Lectures of Abbot Faria, 109
Lethargic stage, 87
Lids, simple closure of, 3
Liébault's classification, 5
Liébault's method, 206
Liébault's table, 19
Liébault's theory, 117
Liébault's treatise, 117
Liégeois' experiments, 163
Light somnambulism, 8
Limitation of visual field, 84
Louise Lateau, 76
Luys' theory, 125

M

Magnet, therapeutic virtue of, 226
Magnetism in America, 113
Magneto-therapeutics, 193
Manner of hypnotising, 1
Manner of waking, 17
Maury's observations, 130
Mechanism of suggestion, 138
Menstrual disturbances, 399
Mesmer and mesmerism, 106

Method of Donato, 16
Method of forestalling bad effects, 413
Method of Liébault, 206
Mind-blindness, 49
Mosso's plethysmograph, 74

N

Negative hallucinations, 43
Neuralgias, 392
Neuropathic affections, 300
Neuroses, 324
Neurosis, hypnotic, 89

O

Observations of Balassa, 119
Observations of Bourru and Burot, 76
Observations of Braid, 73
Observations of Czermak, 118
Observations of Maury, 130
Observations of Preyer, 119
Observations of Tambourini and Seppili, 74
Organic affections of the nervous system, 218

P

Paralysis by suggestion, 27
Passes, influence of, 2
Phenomena of hypnotic sleep, 21
Phenomena of transfer, 79
Plethysmograph of Mosso, 74
Post-hypnotic acts, 31
Post-hypnotic hallucinations, 40
Post-hypnotic suggestions, 31
Precautions to be observed in experimentation, 104
Precautions to be observed in hypnotising, 416
Preyer's observations, 119
Prisms, effects of, 103
Prosper Despine's theory, 122
Psychical amaurosis, 46
Psychical deafness, 50

R

Rapidity of hypnosis, 1
Rationale of suggestive therapeutics, 408
Recent literature of hypnotism, 123
Reflections on induced sleep, 72
Reflex acts, 126
Report of Andry and Thouret, 193
Report of Husson, 107
Researches of Charcot, 120
Researches of Lasègue, 116
Resistance to post-hypnotic suggestions, 36
Results of Heidenhein, 74
Rheumatic affections, 370
Richet's communication, 85
Richet's experiments, 119
Rumpf's theory, 121

S

Schneider's theory, 121
Second category, 9
Second degree, characteristics of, 6

Sensitivo-sensorial suggestion, 38
Simple closure of lids, 3
Sixth degree, characteristics of, 8
Sleep by suggestion, 2
Sleep, natural and suggested, 15
Somnambulism, 8
Somnambulism, individuality in, 60
Somnambulism, types of, 53
Somnambulistic stage, 89
Spinal automatism, 126
Spontaneous and suggested anæsthesia, 22
Spontaneous dreams, 67
Stages of Charcot, 87
Stoeber's apparatus, 47
Story of Castellan, 160
Suggested and natural sleep, 15
Suggested hallucinations, 30
Suggested illusions, 30
Suggestion à longue échéance, 37
Suggestion à longue échéance, cases of, 51, 52
Suggestion a longue échéance, explanation of, 144
Suggestion by imitation, 16
Suggestion in lead paralysis, 260
Suggestion in the waking state, 78
Suggestion, mechanism of, 138
Suggestion, post-hypnotic, 31
Suggestion, sensitivo-sensorial, 38
Suggestion, therapeutic, 202
Suggestive anæsthesia, 14
Suggestive blisters, 75
Suggestive catalepsy, 6
Suggestive contracture, 7
Suggestive education, 3
Suggestive hemorrhage, 76
Suggestive inflammation, 75
Suggestive therapeutics, rationale of, 408
Susceptibility, degrees of, 3
Susceptibility of children, 2
Susceptibility to hypnosis, 5
Surgery, hypnotism in, 116
Synopsis of cases, 404

T

Table of Beaunis, 20
Table of Liébault, 19
Tambourini and Seppili, observations of, 74
Telephone, hypnosis by, 4
The Tisza-Eslar affair, 167
Therapeutic suggestion, 202
Therapeutic virtue of the magnet, 226
Theory of Alexander Bertrand, 110
Theory of Berger, 121
Theory of Braid, 114
Theory of Burcq, 195
Theory of Charpignon, 115
Theory of Heidenhein, 121
Theory of Liébault, 117
Theory of Luys, 123
Theory of General Noizet, 110
Theory of Prosper Despine, 122
Theory of Rumpf, 121

Theory of Schneider, 121
Third degree, characteristics of, 7
Trancoidal states of Beard, 119
Transfer experiments of Binet and Féré, 91
Transfer, phenomena of, 79
Transitional grades, 8
Treatise of Liébault, 117
Types of somnambulism, 53

U

Unclassified painful affections, 361
Unconscious auto-suggestion, 214
Unconscious cerebration, 158

V

Variations in pulse and respiration, Bernheim's explanation of, 74
Verbal suggestion, effect of, 6
Views of Beard, 28
Views of Espinas, 122
Visual field, limitation of, 84
Visual amnesia, 50

W

Waking, manner of, 17
Wolff's method in writer's cramp, 347
Writer's cramp, Wolff's method in, 347

Library of the Mystic Arts
A LIBRARY OF ANCIENT AND MODERN CLASSICS

APOCRYPHA, The. Intro. by Morton Enslin, Professor of Biblical Languages and Literature, St. Lawrence University. Size 7¼" x 11", xv + 239pp., bound in white and gold, 3-color slipcase. 62-12335. $15.00   REL
"A good book, like a virtuous woman, can be valued for a number of qualities. This makes its initial appeal through the beauty of its binding and printing. Only after one has admired these qualities does he read the familiar passages and move back to the excellent Introduction.
"In 1924 the Nonesuch edition of the Apocrypha appeared, limited to 1325 copies. This new edition is an almost exact facsimile of that very beautiful work, bound in a most attractive cover with stamped gilt design, and boxed. Most marked of its changes from the original, and one that enhances the value of the work considerably, is an Introduction by the editor of this Journal, Dr. Morton S. Enslin, who in brief, concise paragraphs provides excellent prefaces to the work as a whole and to each of the books individually. He places the Apocrypha in its proper context in biblical literature, indicates the inappropriateness of the name when applied to the books as a whole, and shows how it was that Luther split off these writings and placed them 'in the limbo between the Old Testament and the New.' The individual introductions serve to provide the backgrounds, probable datings, and general contents of each of the fourteen pieces. This is a valuable work for both the biblical scholar and the lover of fine books."—*J. Calvin Keene,* JOURNAL OF BIBLICAL LITERATURE

BIRREN, Faber. Color: A Survey in Words and Pictures: From Ancient Mysticism to Modern Science. index. 250 illus. 7⅝" x 10½", slipcased, 224pp. 62-18889. $15.00   PSYCH
In this marvelous encyclopedia of color facts and fancies, Faber Birren, leading consultant in America on the subject, offers a kaleidoscope of information for both the users of color in industry and science and the many who are intrigued by color artistically and psychologically. His contributions to the development of color application in government and industry have influenced us all. Here he offers the results of a lifetime devoted to his studies.
Illustrating his survey with more than two hundred and fifty illustrations in color, Mr. Birren conducts the reader on a leisurely stroll through primitive, ancient, medieval, and modern color conceptions, explaining color's mystic function, its many religious uses, the significance of gem stones, the relation of color to marriage and fertility.
A stimulating section on heraldry precedes an examination of color symbolism today. Color in medicine, from ancient cures to modern diagnoses, is dwelt upon at length, and medieval theories of alchemy are discussed.
The author includes an amusing account of the feud between Goethe and Sir Isaac Newton on color theory, and continues on to a consideration of modern spectroscopy and the wonders of human vision. The human aura is scrutinized, and the language of color, with charming and sometimes unexpected word derivations, dealt with extensively.
The relation of color to music, perhaps less well-known, is the subject of an unusual chapter, giving the history of color scales and color organs. In art, Renaissance artists, Impressionism, and Modern Painting are detailed with excellent illustrations.

CHANG, Garma C. C. Teachings of Tibetan Yoga. Introduction by John C. Wilson. 128pp. 62-22082. $5.00
                                                                                                                                    YOGA
The author-translator who gave us the translation of *The Hundred Thousand Songs of Milarepa* now provides an introduction to the spiritual, mental, and physical exercises of his religion. Tibetan Yoga, or Tantrism, is summarized by the author in the following words: "The divinity of Buddahood is omnipresent, but the quickest way to realize this truth is to discover it within one's body-mind complex. By spiritual exercises and the application of Tantric techniques one can soon realize that his body, mind, and the 'objective world' are all manifestations of the divine Buddahood."

DINGWALL, Eric J. Some Human Oddities: Studies in the Queer, the Uncanny and the Fanatical. ill. bibliog. 198pp. 62-14948 $6.00　　　　　　　　　　　　　　　　　　　　　　　　PSYCH

DINGWALL, Eric J. Very Peculiar People: Portrait Studies in the Queer, the Abnormal and the Uncanny. ill. index. bibliog. 224pp. 62-14949. $6.00　　　　　　　　　　　　　　　　　　　PSYCH

"These reissues of two fascinating books, originally written in 1946 and 1951 respectively, will be welcomed by all the lovers of true tales of the weird, strange and abnormal. Here are stories, scholarly written and scientifically analyzed, of visionary mystics like Emanuel Swedenborg, masochistic saints like St. Mary Magdalene de Pazzi, flying friars like Joseph of Copertino, mediums *extraordinaires* like D. D. Home and Eusapia Palladino, pornographers de luxe like Hadrian Beverland, transvestites like James Allen, and many others."—M.D. PUBLICATIONS

"Dr. Dingwall recounts some real-life stories that rival fiction for strangeness. He views and interprets the lives of these queer folk through the eyes of a psychic researcher—one of great note, indeed, and one with a sound academic background. The author has combined his talents as historian, psychologist and psychic researcher to produce a work for the scholarly with a taste for the macabre."—MEDICAL JOURNAL OF AUSTRALIA

FLOURNOY, Theodore. From India to the Planet Mars; Intro. and final chapter by.C. T. K. Chari. xxxvi+469 pages. 63-16228. $10.00　　　　　　　　　　　　　　　　　　　　　　PSYCH

The passing years have served to confirm the eulogistic estimates of those best fitted to judge this work of the author, who was professor of psychology at the University of Geneva and died in 1921. F. W. H. Myers' *Human Personality* called Flournoy's book, "a model of fairness throughout." William McDougall's *Outline of Abnormal Psychology*, summed up the merits of the book: "Among the many cases of the trance-medium type, one stands out preeminent by reason of the richness and variety of the phenomena presented, of the thoroughness and competence with which it was studied, and of the success attending the endeavor to throw the light of science upon its complexities; I mean the case of Hélène Smith most admirably studied and reported by Th. Flournoy." William James praised it in equally high terms. Recent research into extra-sensory perception and the problems of survival and reincarnation has given a new and decisive importance to this classic. Flournoy's gift for narrative is unquestionable. One learns from him that a popular treatment is consistent with scientific carefulness.

The medium he studied became famous especially for two of her most convincing and most bizarre "incarnations." In the one she re-lived the life of a queen in 15th century India. In the other she was allegedly transported to Mars and described and drew pictures of its flora, fauna and intelligent beings, and wrote in the "Martian language."

Flournoy's critical studies of this medium demolished most of the claims made for her. But what he left standing is amazing enough. Some of what he left is now taken away by the new studies contributed to this volume by Professor Chari, a professor of philosophy and an eminent parapsychologist in India. Even he, however, must testify to the extraordinary verisimilitude of the medium's "memories" of 15th century India.

FOX, Oliver. Astral Projection: A Record of Out-of-the-Body Experiences. xiii + 160 pages. 62-19195. $5.00　　　　　　　　　　　　　　　　　　　　　　　　　　　　　　　　　　　　OCCULT

The noted psychic researcher, Dr. Hereward Carrington, reports in one of his works: "The only detailed, scientific and first-hand account of a series of conscious and voluntarily controlled astral projections which I have ever come across is that by Mr. Oliver Fox, published in the *Occult Review* for 1920." The articles were expanded into a book. This is its first publication in the United States.

The literature of psychic research includes many instances in which a person has an out-of-the-body experience. Sometimes it arises out of a very serious accident. Sometimes it comes in the course of a profound illness. At other times it results from the shock of tragic information or a harrowing experience. A considerable amount of material on out-of-the-body experiences is found in other books published by us: F. W. H. Myers' *Human Personality and its Survival of Bodily Death*, Mrs. Sidgwick's *Phantasms of the Living*, G. N. M. Tyrell's *Science & Psychical Phenomena & Apparitions*.

FRAXI, Pisanus (pseudonym of **ASHBEE, Henry Spencer**). 3 vols. Each indexed. v. 1. Index Liborum Phohibitorum. intro. by G. Legman. 51+lxxvi+543pp. v. 2. Centuria Liborum Absconditorum. lx+587pp. v. 3. Catena Liborum Tacendorum. lvii+591pp. All bound in buckram and boxed. 63-13985 $35.00 per set BIBLIOG
"The random bibliographical articles of which the present volumes are composed, sampling and describing at length the more difficult but elusive masterpieces of erotic literature in various languages" is the most important work of its kind in English. A 50-page introduction by G. Legman, whose name will be familiar to many librarians as a great bibliographer in his own right, makes clear the importance of this work, originally privately published a volume at a time (1877, 1879, 1885), of which this edition is a facsimile. "Henry Spencer Ashbee—to quote 'Pisanus Fraxi' by his real name—set out to do only a very limited thing, but in a thorough and profound way. He proposed simply to describe, and copiously to quote, some of the many hundreds of erotic books in various languages that had passed through his hands, and through the hands of some of his friends, during a long and assiduous career as a collector. His striking success, as opposed to the abysmal failure of most of his imitators, rises clearly from the limitations within which he was satisfied to work, without any megalomaniacal vaunting and flaunting of his interests and his evident erudition. Ashbee remains the principal guide-book and source work for the future moral historian of England and the 18th century, and has a great deal to tell any similar historian of England and the rest of Europe as well as America, to nearly the end of the 19th century as well."—*G. Legman*

GRILLOT DE GIVRY, Emile. Picture Museum of Sorcery, Magic and Alchemy. Introduction by Cynthia Magriel. 376 ills. index. 395pp. slipcased. 63-11177. $17.50 OCCULT
By common consent of students of these subjects, the best and most representative illustrations ever gathered in one volume are here. The text, excellently translated from the French, is equal to the illustrations. For the author is one of the great savants in this difficult and complex area of scholarship. Grillot De Givry (1874-1929), after a lifetime largely devoted to translating from Latin into French most of the famous hermetic texts, including Paracelsus, Savanarola, John Dee, Khunrath, Basilius Valentinus, gave the last years of his life to collecting this iconography of occultism.

HARRISON, Jane Ellen. Epilegomena to the Study of Greek Religion [and] Themis: a Study of the Social Origins of Greek Religion. 152 ills. index. lvi + 600 pp. 62-16379. $10.00 REL
"Jane Harrison (1850-1928) symbolizes the meeting between the more traditional classical studies and the disciplines of cultural anthropology and psychoanalytical psychology. She was a contemporary of Sir James Frazer, Sigmund Freud, and C. G. Jung and one of the first classical scholars to identify and discuss the *primitive* bases of the Greek religious tradition. It is largely under her influence that Olympian gods have come to be recognized as relatively late and predominantly literary figures, whereas she maintained the idea that it was the Mysteries, Dionysian and Orphic, that were the core of Greek religion. It is not surprising that the academic world has met her message with scepticism and hostility. In recent years, her books have become scarce on the market. The most recent reprint of "Themis" (1912) was in 1927, and the "Epilogemena" here reviewed is the reproduction of the one edition ever printed at Cambridge, England, in 1921. While she had numerous critics among her academic peers, she has also won the support and admiration of such great scholars as F. M. Cornford and Gilbert Murray, who contribute two long chapters to "Themis." The preface to the present edition, by John C. Wilson, and the "Jane Harrison Memorial Lecture," by Gilbert Murray, with which it concludes, are very helpful for an evaluation of her contribution to classical studies for the less well informed readers. Without taking sides on strictly scholarly issues, which are always open to revision and re-evaluation, one can claim the quality of greatness for Jane Harrison's writings and rejoice at their being made available to the reading public."—LIBRARY JOURNAL
"A book that changed my life—there are times when I think it is the most revolutionary book of the 20th century—has just been reissued, marking the 50th anniversary of its publication. It is *Themis*...Jane Harrison is truly what Edith Hamilton is popularly taken to be, the great lady who found Greece marble and left it living flesh."—*Stanley Edgar Hyman*
THE NEW LEADER

JAMES, William. The Varieties of Religious Experience; A Study in Human Nature; Enlarged Edition with Appendices and Introduction by Joseph Ratner. bibliog. index. 672pp. 63-14505. $10.00   REL

William James (1842-1910) began as a chemist and a physician. The physical side of medicine very soon ceased to interest him and he devoted his life to psychology and philosophy. Very early, too, he understood how shallow and unthinking was the attitude toward science of his colleagues at Harvard Medical School. He introduced Freud to his first American audience at a time when the medical profession anathematised psychoanalysis. He was the first to recognize the epochmaking importance of the discovery of the subliminal parts of the mind by F. W. H. Myers. He spent years studying the mediumship of Mrs. Piper and was the first American to become President of the Society for Psychical Research. He outraged the medical profession by becoming the principal spokesman in a successful fight to prevent requiring medical licenses of mental healers in Massachusetts. Finally, himself free of Christian belief or any other sectarian belief, he yet considered the cental task of his life to defend the legitimacy of religious belief. This is the great theme of this most fascinating and readable book.

James felt himself peculiarly fitted to explain mystics to non-mystics and vice versa and it is this successful role that makes this book a supreme triumph. The present edition of *Varieties* is notable for two things. James always meant to revise and expand it but never did. What Professor Joseph Ratner does now is to provide, in ten Appendices, about 100 pages of William James' other writings which bear on the central theme of *Varieties* and so, in effect, tell us the story of James' ideas on religion up to his death. Second, Professor Ratner provides a long Introduction which serves as a guide to those who may be perplexed by the various misleading interpretations of James foisted upon him during the 60 years since he wrote *Varieties*.

JUNOD, Henri A. The Life of a South African Tribe; 2 vols. intro. by Keith Irvine, Research Officer of the Ghana Mission. 150 ills. photos. index & glossary. 1230 pp. 62-18890. Slipcased. $20.00   AFRICA

"This is the first American edition of a classic anthropological study of an African tribe written by a Swiss missionary and first published in Europe as long ago as 1912 (this is the 1927 revised edition text.) Henri Junod came to what is now Mozambique in 1889, and lived for many years in the interior among the Bathonga people. On his return to Europe he wrote this monumental monograph, surprisingly enough in English when his own language was French. He died in 1934. Junod was inspired by a chance remark of the famed British historian, Lord Bryce, who regretted that no Roman has taken the trouble to investigate fully the ways of the Celtic people. Junod determined to perform this task for the Bathongas, who were still living in what might be described as their primeval state. The book examines in great detail their daily lives as individuals and as members of the tribe, their religion, culture, and social life. It is a massive and masterly performance, all the more valuable now since it represents a way of life that has virtually vanished. Half the Bathonga men now work in the South African mines, and civilization has profoundly affected their traditional customs. The two volumes are illustrated with photographs, maps and diagrams, and come boxed."—*John Barkham*, SATURDAY REVIEW SYNDICATE.

"The finest monograph on any African tribe."
—AFRICA, Journal of Anthropology.